A GUARANTEED ANNUAL INCOME
Evidence from a Social Experiment

This is a volume of

Quantitative Studies in Social Relations

Consulting Editor: Peter H. Rossi, University of Massachusetts, Amherst, Massachusetts

A GUARANTEED ANNUAL INCOME
Evidence from a Social Experiment

Edited by

Philip K. Robins
Robert G. Spiegelman
Samuel Weiner
SRI INTERNATIONAL
MENLO PARK, CALIFORNIA

Joseph G. Bell
SEATTLE INCOME MAINTENANCE EXPERIMENT
STATE OF WASHINGTON
DEPARTMENT OF SOCIAL AND HEALTH SERVICES
OLYMPIA, WASHINGTON

ACADEMIC PRESS

A Subsidiary of Harcourt Brace Jovanovich, Publishers

New York London Toronto Sydney San Francisco

ACADEMIC PRESS, INC.
111 Fifth Avenue, New York, New York 10003

United Kingdom Edition published by
ACADEMIC PRESS, INC. (LONDON) LTD.
24/28 Oval Road, London NW1   7DX

HC
110
.I5
G8
1980

Library of Congress Cataloging in Publication Data
Main entry under title:

A Guaranteed annual income.

(Quantitative studies in social relations)
    Includes bibliographies.
    1.   Guaranteed annual income — United States —
Case studies — Addresses, essays, lectures.   2.   Income maintenance programs — United States — Case
studies — Addresses, essays, lectures.   3.   Guaranteed annual income — Washington (State — Seattle —
Addresses, essays, lectures.   4.   Income maintenance
programs — Washington (State) — Seattle — Addresses,
essays, lectures.   5.   Guaranteed annual income —
Colorado — Denver — Addresses, essays, lectures.

6.   Income maintenance programs — Colorado — Denver
— Addresses, essays, lectures.   I. Robins,
Philip K.
HC110.I5G8   362.5'82   80-23150
ISBN 0-12-589880-0

To the memory of David N. Kershaw,
whose death has deprived the social science research community of one
of its most inspiring leaders

Contents

CHAPTER 8   Labor Supply and Childcare Arrangements
            of Single Mothers

C. Eric Munson, Philip K. Robins, Gary Stieger

PART III EXPERIMENTAL EFFECTS ON FAMILY BEHAVIOR

CHAPTER 9   Marital Dissolution and Remarriage

*Lyle P. Groeneveld, Nancy Brandon Tuma,
Michael T. Hannan*

CHAPTER 10   Income and Psychological Distress

Peggy Thoits, Michael T. Hannan

APPENDIX   Data Collection and Processing

Virgil Davis, Arlene Waksberg

Contributors

Numbers in parentheses indicate the pages on which the authors' contributions begin.

MARCY E. AVRIN (291), National Bureau of Economic Research, Stanford, California 94305

DAVID BETSON (101), Institute for Research on Poverty, University of Wisconsin — Madison, Wisconsin 53706

VIRGIL DAVIS (307), SRI International, Menlo Park, California 94025

DAVID GREENBERG (101), SRI International, Menlo Park, California 94025

LYLE P. GROENEVELD (163), SRI International, Menlo Park, California 94025

ARDEN R. HALL (263), SRI International, Menlo Park, California 94025

HARLAN I. HALSEY (33), SRI International, Menlo Park, California 94025

MICHAEL T. HANNAN (163, 183), Department of Sociology, Stanford University, Stanford, California 94305

TERRY R. JOHNSON (223, 281), SRI International, Menlo Park, California 94025

RICHARD KASTEN (101), United States Department of Health and Human Services/ASPE, Office of Income Security Policy/Analysis, Washington, D.C. 20201

MICHAEL C. KEELEY (3, 207, 241), SRI International, Menlo Park, California 94025

C. ERIC MUNSON (143), SRI International, Menlo Park, California 94025

JOHN H. PENCAVEL (223), Department of Economics, Stanford University, Stanford, California 94305

RANDALL J. POZDENA (281), Federal Reserve Bank of San Francisco, San Francisco, California 94120

PHILIP K. ROBINS (59, 85, 125, 143), SRI International, Menlo Park, California 94025

ROBERT G. SPIEGELMAN (3), SRI International, Menlo Park, California 94025

GARY STIEGER (143), SRI International, Menlo Park, California 94025

PEGGY THOITS (183), Department of Sociology, Princeton University, Princeton, New Jersey 08540

NANCY BRANDON TUMA (163), Department of Sociology, Stanford University, Stanford, California 94305

ARLENE WAKSBERG (307), SRI International, Menlo Park, California 94025

RICHARD W. WEST (3, 73, 85), SRI International, Menlo Park, California 94025

Foreword

Dissatisfaction with the welfare system has been expressed for nearly as long as welfare has been provided. During the last two decades, public outcry against welfare has become especially intense. Recipients, program administrators, and taxpayers alike have joined in the chorus for welfare reform. While there has been little consensus among its critics as to what in fact constitutes "reform" of the welfare system, there have been almost constant attempts to respond to this criticism. These have included a considerable amount of tinkering with the system, as well as several attempts at a major system overhaul. Basically, however, while program participation has grown and aid to the aged and disabled has been federalized, the structure of welfare has not been appreciably altered in the past 20 years.

A radical departure that, in principle, would consolidate existing programs was suggested by Nobel laureate Milton Friedman in 1962. Friedman's negative income tax (NIT) would extend the conventional income tax system to low-income families, who would receive cash rebates in place of other types of transfer payments. Such a system would provide a basic level of support to families without other sources of income and would reduce these benefits as income increased.

The idea of an NIT was the conceptual basis for several large-scale experiments undertaken during the late 1960s and the early 1970s. The experiments differed from current welfare reform proposals: They did not provide jobs, and there were no work requirements attached to the receipt of benefits. The main purpose of the experiments was to test the effects of a pure cash transfer system on the social and economic behavior of participating families. The first experiment was conducted in New Jersey and Pennsylvania from 1968 to 1972. Subsequent experiments took place in Gary, Indiana, from 1970 to 1974 and in rural areas of Iowa and North Carolina from 1969 to 1973. In 1970, the largest of the experiments began in Seattle and Denver. The Seattle/Denver Income-Maintenance Experiments, which came to be known as SIME/DIME, cost about $70 million and involved 4800 families, a scale larger than all the other experiments combined.

Major social programs in the United States have routinely been introduced or substantially modified with little knowledge of their expected consequences for the beneficiary population or the larger economy. When the income-maintenance experiments were launched, they represented a novel attempt to produce statistically reliable estimates of the expected impacts of substantial modifications in the United States transfer system in areas that economic theory and conventional wisdom suggested should be of major policy concern.

The two main areas of interest to policymakers in the income-maintenance experiments were the effects of an NIT program on work effort and marital stability. Because of its size and scope, SIME/DIME is the only experiment to date to provide definitive evidence on these issues. These findings are ably presented in this volume.

In addition to being provided with estimates of the effects of an NIT program on various aspects of individual behavior, the readers of this volume are also presented with a vivid account of the issues involved in undertaking a social experiment. Social experimentation is very costly. Before investing additional money in such studies, it is important to look closely at the results and ask whether comparable findings could be obtained with a less costly research design. In my view, there is no alternative research design that could provide the insights and guides to policy that have come from the income-maintenance experiments.

JODIE T. ALLEN
DEPUTY ASSISTANT SECRETARY OF LABOR
FOR POLICY, EVALUATION AND RESEARCH
UNITED STATES DEPARTMENT OF LABOR
WASHINGTON, D.C.
November 15, 1979

Preface

The last decade has witnessed a marked growth in both the sophistication and the complexity of the discussion of welfare reform alternatives in this country. Substantial progress toward social equity has unquestionably been made through restructuring and expanding individual programs, but the easy solutions sought during the years of the War on Poverty have not been found. Poverty in the United States cannot be addressed by quick-fix remedies; problems reach too deeply into the fabric of social, economic, and political life to be handled by strategies based on intuition and opinion alone. While basic value choices remain the same, the scope of the consequences of changes in welfare policies is now generally seen as being broader than was commonly understood a decade ago. This awareness has underscored the need for hard information on matters of controversy in social welfare.

Over the past decade, the federal government has invested heavily in obtaining such information. A major element of its strategy has been the funding of a series of experiments designed to test various welfare program alternatives. Four separate, large-scale studies have been conducted since 1968, each providing information on the effects of administering a program of income-maintenance benefits based on a negative income tax (NIT), in different settings and to various types of households. The first and most well-known project was the New Jersey Graduated Work Incentive Experiment, which ran from 1968 to 1972 and studied primarily two-parent families in urban areas in New Jersey and Pennsylvania. The Rural Income-Maintenance Experiment, administered in counties in Iowa and North Carolina between 1969 and 1973, included both white and black two-parent families, and some female-headed families. The Gary, Indiana, Experiment was begun in 1970 and covered a sample of black urban families, focusing particularly on those with female heads of household.

The Seattle/Denver Income-Maintenance Experiments (SIME/DIME) were the last in the series, running from 1970 to 1976. They were the largest and most expensive of the experiments, and the most comprehensive in nearly every respect. Compared to the earlier studies, more families—black, white, and Chicano—were enrolled; families were chosen to represent a greater range of income and age levels; single individuals were eligible; more generous financial treatments were offered, along with training, education, and childcare options; and families and individuals were followed for longer periods of time. Administration was also complex, combining the efforts of the United States Department of Health, Education and Welfare (HEW); the states of Washington and Colorado; two major research institutions—SRI International (formerly Stanford Research Institute) and Mathematica Policy Research, Inc. (MPR); and community colleges in Seattle and Denver. In the course of the project, each of these organizations became involved with many other agencies, including federal, state, and local governments, community organizations, and independent groups.

In all, SIME/DIME was a social research enterprise of massive dimensions. It presently offers a wealth of information on welfare issues, on the effects of income maintenance on work and family behavior, and on questions of program administration and finance.

This book brings together the first accounting of evidence on the impact of the experiment on participating individuals and families. It is based on a selection of papers delivered to policymakers, program administrators, and researchers at a conference held at Orcas Island, Washington, in May 1978. The conference, sponsored by HEW and the State of Washington, represented the first effort to disseminate to a wide audience the findings emerging from early analyses. It was hoped that the presentation of early findings would initiate the long process of translating experimental outcomes into implications for policy and program development. The success of the conference and the encouraging response of those who attended provided the motivation to make these papers available to a broader public.

The focus of this collection is on several of the enduring issues in the debate over welfare reform alternatives, and which led to the undertaking of the income-maintenance experiments to test the effects of alternative NIT plans. How do income guarantees affect work and family behavior? Are program recipients better off than they would be under conventional welfare plans? What would be the social and financial costs of a national NIT program? These questions were addressed in SIME/DIME with data and methods of analysis at a level that significantly extends the findings of the earlier experiments.

The topics covered span the economic, social, and psychological effects of providing income guarantees and related benefits to individuals and families. The treatment of the subject matter is intended for a diverse audience, but also one that has a serious interest in understanding the meaning and the derivation of the experimental results. The reporting of research pays careful attention to both theory and method, to allow a critical examination of the findings as well as to ground the results within the overall experimental framework. This background is essential to a balanced interpretation of the outcomes. On the basis of the evidence, for example, it might be said that an NIT program leads some people to reduce their efforts to work for a living; others to find more satisfying jobs; some to divorce or separate; and others to have more children, to move to warmer climates, or to obtain better housing. Yet, to say only this would miss much of the point of the purpose of the experiments and the information they have to offer. SIME/DIME were designed to test the effects of a *range* of welfare policy options provided to individuals and families in varied circumstances. These options consisted of different guaranteed support levels in conjunction with different subsidies and counseling programs for education and training. In some cases, there was no straightforward or unequivocal pattern of response to the experimental NIT plans. This result was in itself valuable because, in designing real-world programs, it is important to know the range of responses to be expected from different persons under different plans. The greatest value of the research presented here is in showing this variation of response with respect to program options.

Several broad lessons of significance to audiences concerned with policy and programs are suggested by this book and other discussions of the research findings. Perhaps the clearest theme of the evidence from SIME/DIME, as well as from the earlier experiments, is that program design is necessarily a process of making trade-offs among competing objectives. Participants with higher benefit levels tended to work less, yet they experienced fewer marital separations and divorces than did those receiving less generous payments. At the same time, higher benefit levels led to greater overall program costs. Work behavior and family stability impacts may thus run counter to the concerns of program costs and adequacy. The experimental results show empirically where these trade-offs occurred over the range of participants and benefit plans. The research may facilitate the process of setting priorities by more clearly laying out the choices to be made and their likely impacts.

The SIME/DIME results also demonstrate the sheer complexity of the response to the 11 NIT plans among families and population groups. On most questions examined, families with children differed from those without; male wage earners differed from female wage earners; blacks, whites, and Chicanos all tended to behave differently, and even individual family members sometimes responded differently from one another. Moreover, responses varied across the scales of income and benefit levels, for example, according to whether a recipient had income above or below the breakeven level or whether he or she was participating in a low- or high-benefit plan. While this variation may not be surprising to those who continue to believe in the infinite variety of human behavior, it does underscore the principles that no program will affect everyone who participates in it in the same way, and that to establish policies on the basis of an "average" will surely disadvantage many.

The experimental results address many issues, some of which had been given limited attention in earlier research. The significance of "nonpecuniary" effects is suggested by the set of findings on the differential effects of Aid to Families with Dependent Children (AFDC) and NIT payments on marital dissolution. One interpretation of these results suggests that the stigma associated with receiving welfare benefits through the AFDC program causes a married recipient to discount the value of support payments in determining financial prospects when seeking independence from a marriage. Thus, the same income may be treated differently depending on its source, on the way in which it is obtained, or on how it is perceived by others. There is evidence that an NIT reduces the welfare stigma, and, hence, some measure of the reluctance to seek a divorce in cases where finances are a consideration. The questions this raises for determining program participation levels and costs are critical, and ones which are at present not well understood.

As is noted throughout the book, there are limits on the power of these results to predict the effects of an NIT implemented on a nationwide basis. Some of the influences due to the experimental setting itself have been studied, while others have not been fully assessed. A number of factors—including the distinctive characteristics of the sites of Seattle and Denver, the methods used to draw the sample, possible problems of self-selection and Hawthorne effects, and the unknown length of time necessary for participants to adjust to the program—suggest that caution be applied in generalizing these results. In addition, it should be emphasized that the findings reported here are preliminary, and in many cases they do not account for the complete set of observations or all the time periods studied. Care has been taken to descirbe and evaluate each of these limitations. A comprehensive examination of the complete results must await the project's final report.

At least two applications of SIME/DIME stand out at the present time, however, and clearly justify this publication of interim results. First, as a *research model* the experiments have proven to be of interest to researchers and academics concerned with theory, design, and analytic methods. Second, as a *program model,* they serve as a frame of reference for the design of NIT programs and the consideration of welfare reform alternatives.

The SIME/DIME effort was above all a piece of practical, applied research. Its underlying theory was developed largely through earlier work, and is implicit in the study design and methodology. Thus, while hypotheses are not stated explicitly, the principles guiding the research emerge upon examination of the experimental variables and the sample composition. The experiments were not intended to elicit specific behaviors in the population, but to offer a setting for observation. Socioeconomic variables that were judged most likely to represent a wide range of participant responses were incorporated; often they were added to the interviews during the course of the experiments. Much of these data are now available in public-use files for outside researchers to use in further analysis.

The research methodology used reflects the rigor with which the study was approached. Attending to undesired economic incentives, identifying and controlling for confounding influences, and systematically monitoring program implementation were necessary to the observation, measurement, and understanding of participant responses. The opportunity to conduct a reasonably "true" social experiment is rare, and appropriate techniques for data collection and analysis were not always available. To carry out the sampling, manage the large amount of longitudinal data, and to verify, store, retrieve, and analyze the information, in many cases required the refinement of existing research methods or the creation of new ones.

At the same time, underlying the experiments was the potential for executing a set of NIT programs. SIME/DIME, in combination with the earlier experiments, has led to new approaches to understanding the structure and operation of welfare programs. Two notable advances in this area have been the development of an empirically tested frame of reference for describing the welfare system, and the continued development of ways of modeling welfare policies and estimating the national impacts of program alternatives.

The design of the experimental research was based on the precise formulation and specification of program parameters. Assuring accuracy and reliability in the experimental results required that elements of program design be defined in controllable terms, and that participant responses to the experimental setting and the influence of external factors be taken into account and monitored. The practical demands of obtaining, analyzing, and using research information dictated the outline of a comprehensive model of welfare policy.

Such a model serves as a context for understanding experimental responses and the connections between policy objectives, program options, and behavioral outcomes. Conceptualizing and measuring the interactions within welfare policy then provides a frame of reference for designing real-world programs. As the trade-offs among cost, work incentives, and benefit adequacy are made clearer, the probability of effectively addressing each of the corresponding perspectives in the policy debate—public finance, attitudes toward work, and social welfare objectives—is raised. An additional advance has been brought about by the need to project the experimental findings nationwide in order to estimate the impacts of proposed federal welfare initiatives. Simulation methods designed for this purpose have relied extensively on the SIME/DIME research.

Taken together, these tools represent a significant contribution to the development of prototypical welfare reform programs, and the capacity for refined analysis of welfare alternatives will be of use for years to come. They have already been used in the analysis and estimates for the Carter Administration's proposed Program for Better Jobs and Income. Other proposed programs can be set in similar terms and modeled for size and impacts.

On balance, this collection of research results indicates the broader role that

SIME/DIME and the earlier income-maintenance experiments will play in future research and in the development of welfare policy. A number of elements of this role has been suggested: a theoretical and methodological basis for large-scale research into questions of social welfare; an empirically grounded framework for considering trade-offs among competing program objectives; and a more sophisticated capability for policy assessment. The potential benefits of these applications are substantial, and their realization is foreshadowed in the sampling of evidence reported here. Discussion of program administration issues, additional analysis of the data, and final estimation of experimental impacts are further steps to be taken in preparation for the use of this research policy and program settings. The task of "summing up" is likely to involve a generation of academicians, policy analysts, program operators and planners, and other participants in the ongoing debates over social welfare. This book offers an initial contribution to this effort.

The book is divided into four parts. The first part is a general introduction to the experimental design, results, and data. The second presents the experimental effects on work behavior for various family members, including results on job satisfaction, the demand for childcare on the part of single mothers, and the incorporation of the labor supply results into a simulation of national welfare reform alternatives. Part III discusses the experimental effects on family behavior, including marital stability, psychological effects, and effects on the demand for children (fertility). Part IV contains five studies of how the benefits were used by the families, including effects on migration, education and training, demand for assets, and the use of subsidized housing programs. An appendix contains a detailed discussion of the SIME/DIME data collection and processing.

JOSEPH G. BELL

Acknowledgments

This volume presents early results based on a series of papers presented at a conference held at Orcas Island, Washington, in May 1978 of one of the country's most ambitious efforts at social experimentation, the Seattle/Denver Income-Maintenance Experiments (SIME/DIME). More than 4800 families participated in these experiments. In addition, at the peak of its operation, more than 200 persons were involved with the day-to-day activities of the experiment, including officials in government agencies, payment specialists, interviewers, data managers, data processors, and researchers. The combined efforts of all these people for more than a decade (1969–1980) contributed to the successful completion of the work upon which this book is based. We do not have room here to list all the persons whose contributions are noteworthy, but a few principal individuals deserve mention.

The technical monitors at the United States Department of Health, Education and Welfare have provided guidance, support, and reviews of our research throughout the entire history of the project. Jodie Allen was instrumental in initiating SIME/DIME and providing support during its early years. Joseph Corbett ably guided the project during most of the operational years. David Greenberg, Gary Burtless, and Douglas Wolf provided invaluable services during later years in reviewing and commenting on SIME/DIME-related research efforts. Many persons in the state governments of Washington and Colorado also contributed to the overall success of the project. We wish to give special thanks to the state directors for SIME and DIME — Mike Linn, Joseph Bell, and Jacob Shockley.

It is very difficult to convey to the reader the complexity of the operations requird to carry out simultaneously a functioning welfare program and an experiment. Mathematica Policy Research (MPR), under subcontract to SRI International (which designed and evaluated the experiment), distributed the payments to the families and conducted the household interviews. A special debt of gratitude is expressed to MPR's late president, David Kershaw, whose untimely death saddened all of us who had worked with him on the experiment. Because of Dave's pioneering work in directing the New Jersey Income-Maintenance Experiment, and because of his dedication to SIME/DIME, MPR performed ably in carrying out its operational activities for SIME/DIME. Key to MPR's successful handling of the experimental operations were Alan Brewster and Gary Christophersen in Seattle, and Mary Scowcroft and Robert Williams in Denver. Also playing a crucial role in experimental operations were the community colleges of Seattle and Denver, which conducted the manpower component of the experiment. Special thanks are given to N. John Andersen and Leroy Fails who managed the Seattle Central Community College's participation, and to Ray Urbas and Paul Kludt who managed Denver's community college participation.

Besides the authors, there are many other persons who played critical roles in the various research operations. Most notable are Martin Gorfinkel for his unique computer interaction data entry system, Virgil Davis for his data base management system, and Charles Thompson for his family master file. A special debt of gratitude is owed to Mordecai Kurz, professor of economics at Stanford University, whose contribution during the design phase of the experiment was a major factor in the overall success of the experiment. We also wish to thank Felicity Skidmore who carefully read the manuscript and offered many helpful suggestions regarding style and consistency.

For almost all of the chapters in this volume, there is an expanded, more technical, unpublished SRI Research Memorandum available. Parts or versions of several chapters have been or will be published elsewhere. Tables in Chapter 3 have been published in *The Journal of Human Resources,* Winter 1978 and Fall 1980. A modified, expanded, and more technical version of Chapters 4, 5, and 9 can be found in *The Journal of Human Resources,* Fall 1980. A more technical and expanded version of Chapter 6 is contained in *Microeconomic Simulation,* edited by Robert Haveman and Kevin Hollenbeck, published by Academic Press for the Institute for Research on Poverty, 1980. A modified version of Chapter 10 has been published in *The Journal of Health and Social Behavior,* May 1979; and a more technical and expanded version of part of Chapter 13 has been published by JAI Press, Inc., 1980, in *Research in Population Economics,* Vol. 2, edited by J. Simon and J. Da Vanzo.

PART I

INTRODUCTION

CHAPTER 1

Design of the Seattle/Denver Income-Maintenance Experiments and an Overview of the Results

MICHAEL C. KEELEY
ROBERT G. SPIEGELMAN
RICHARD W. WEST

SOCIAL EXPERIMENTATION

A decade ago social scientists at the Institute for Research on Poverty of the University of Wisconsin—Madison, the Office of Economic Opportunity, and Princeton University were designing a major social experiment. Before then, a large-scale social experiment was considered to be infeasible, because of the inability to control the environment within which the experiment would take place. The realization that a randomly assigned control group could be used to simulate control over the environment along with the emergence of large, fast computers for the processing of vast amounts of data on experimental observations, combined to make such an experiment feasible. As a result, the New Jersey Income-Maintenance Experiment was launched.

Since then, three other income-maintenance experiments have been undertaken to test the effects of a negative income tax (NIT), along with experiments in housing allowances, educational vouchers, and national health insurance. The Seattle/Denver Income-Maintenance Experiments (SIME/DIME) are the largest and most comprehensive of the income-maintenance experiments.

In this chapter we will describe the conditions underlying such a social experiment, and how SIME/DIME were designed in an effort to maximize the advantages and overcome some of the obstacles facing designers of social experiments. Because social experiments are expensive, we must first establish that benefits derived from improvement in the social programs achieved through the use of experimentally derived information are greater than those derived from information obtained with less costly methods. The annual cost of the Aid to Families with Dependent Children (AFDC) and Food Stamp programs is over $25 billion. The total welfare-related programs, including Unemployment Insurance, cost

3

A GUARANTEED ANNUAL INCOME:
EVIDENCE FROM A SOCIAL EXPERIMENT

over $50 billion. Estimates of the additional costs of new welfare reform programs generally range from $3 billion per year into the $10s of billions. Thus, even an expensive experiment such as SIME/DIME can pay for itself many times over if it provides the basis for more rational decision making in the area of welfare reform.

Although many answers to program-generated questions can be found through the use of cross-sectional or panel survey data that are less expensive than an experiment, where experimentation is possible, there are some very good reasons for using that mode. First, the experimental mode is most appropriate for evaluating programs that are not currently influencing the behavior of the population at risk. Second, experiments in social programs are particularly valuable, because participants in a program tend to be self-selected, i.e., applying for or meeting the criteria for eligibility in a program is largely voluntary. If program participation is the result of such self-selection, then differences between behavior of persons in the program and persons outside it cannot be appropriately attributed to differences in the program itself. For example, if persons entering a particular manpower program are all poor performers in the labor market, then comparing performance of participants and nonparticipants will produce estimates of the effects of the program that are biased downwards.

In addition, in the case of income maintenance, a large segment of the population (primarily two-parent families with one parent working) do not receive significant benefits from the existing welfare system; therefore, we are unlikely to be able to infer the effects of a universal NIT[1] by analyzing participants in existing welfare programs. Comparison of the behavior of welfare and nonwelfare population groups is not likely to be reliable, because the current welfare population is already distinguished from the nonwelfare population by lower employment and labor-market participation rates.

Even if a social experiment is potentially cost effective, it cannot be justified unless critical issues of experimental design and potential bias are dealt with effectively. The critical issues in the design of an income-maintenance experiment are:

1. What are the outcomes of the program to be predicted? Are these outcomes susceptible to quantitative measurement?
2. Can the elements or dimensions of the program be transformed into a well-specified set of experimental treatments? That is, can we be sure that the program is susceptible to experimentation?
3. How does theory guide the design of our experiment? What does our knowledge of economic and sociological theories say about the nature of

---

[1] A negative income tax (NIT) is the conceptual underpinning of the income-maintenance experiments.

the treatments and the information that must be collected in order to undertake the analyses?

4. To what extent are the proposed experimental treatments different from the elements of an actual program? That is, to what extent is the experiment not a true replication of the program being designed or tested?

5. How can the sample be chosen and assigned to treatments in an efficient and cost effective manner in order to obtain the most information with a constrained budget? Will that information be sufficiently reliable to guide the formulation of policy?

6. Can the estimates of experimental effects be extrapolated to cover other populations, other circumstances, or other programs?

The next section discusses the overall design of SIME/DIME and its objectives and includes a discussion of the manpower program component of the design. We then discuss the sample design and the treatment assignment process. After that, we examine the utility of using experimental data in providing answers to the policy questions asked. The penultimate section emphasizes the need for extrapolating the results obtained to a national population. We conclude with a brief introduction to the rest of the book.

DESIGN AND OBJECTIVES OF THE SEATTLE/DENVER INCOME-MAINTENANCE EXPERIMENTS

One important objective of income maintenance is to guarantee satisfactory income support to poor families. However, in discussing program outcomes, it is necessary to distinguish between explicit program objectives and the behavioral effects of the program. These behavioral effects may be totally unintended and yet the success or failure of the program may be critically dependent on them. Concern with potential behavioral effects, in fact, provided the rationale for all the income-maintenance experiments undertaken. The major behavioral effect expected from income maintenance of the NIT variety is change in hours of work. A second important effect is a change in the marital stability of families. Other possible effects, such as changes in geographic mobility, fertility, demand for public housing, and participation in school can also be expected to affect the outcomes of a new income-support program.

Since labor supply response is the critical effect to be evaluated, SIME/DIME were designed with the effect of the program on hours of work as their central measurement objective. Therefore, while other effects also were measured, the experiment was not designed to measure them with maximum efficiency. For a more complete description of the design of SIME/DIME, see Kurz and Spiegelman (1971, 1972).

The Negative Income Tax

An NIT is similar to other income-conditioned transfer programs, such as AFDC, in that it has three basic components: (a) a support level, defined as a sum of money available to the family with no other sources of income over a stated time period; (b) a rate of reduction in support, defined as a tax on the income available to the family from other sources; and (c) the time period over which the support is guaranteed, which implies a certain accounting period for the payment system.

The Maximum Support Level (Guarantee) and Accounting Period

The maximum support level or guarantee in an NIT program is the amount of transfer *guaranteed* to the family over a period of one year (i.e., the total payments they will receive from the program if they have no other income). This annual accounting period adjusts payments to people who have seasonal changes in their income (such as construction workers) in order to provide equity across families with different annual income profiles.[2] These guarantee levels are adjusted using a family index to provide higher absolute guarantees for larger families and lower ones for smaller families (see Table 1.1).[3]

The lowest guarantee level tested in SIME/DIME was set at $3800 for a family of four because it was just sufficient (when the experiment was initially undertaken) to bring the incomes of families with no income from any other source up to the official poverty levels. Moreover, it generally matched the alternative

Table 1.1
Program Guarantee by Treatment and Family Size

Number of family members	Primary family index	$3800 Treatment		$4800 Treatment		$5600 Treatment	
		Primary family[a]	Secondary family[a]	Primary family	Secondary family	Primary family	Secondary family
2	.62	$2356	$1984	$2976	$2604	$3472	$3100
3	.83	3154	2656	3984	3486	4648	4150
4	1.00	3800	3200	4800	4200	5600	5000
5	1.12	4256	3584	5376	4704	6272	5600
6	1.23	4674	3936	5904	5166	6888	6150
7	1.32	5016	4224	6336	5544	7392	6600
8	1.38	5244	4416	6624	5796	7728	6900

[a] A primary family is the only family in a housing unit, or if there is more than one family in the unit, then the primary family is the one principally responsible for financial maintenance of the housing unit. A secondary family is one living with a primary family.

[2] It does, however, create payment adjustment problems for those suffering sudden reductions in their income.
[3] Current research indicates that the indexes used in SIME/DIME may somewhat understate differences in living costs among family types.

guarantee available from the existing welfare alternative—AFDC plus food stamps. The NIT as implemented in SIME/DIME had a broader base than AFDC, because the experimental regulations lacked some of the eligibility constraints preventing many of the working poor from receiving AFDC. However, the financial guarantee of the two options was essentially the same. It was decided, therefore, to include this low guarantee level in the experimental treatment on the grounds that any experimental effects observed for this guarantee could be attributable to nonfinancial differences between the experiment and the AFDC-plus-food-stamps alternative.

The middle support level of $4800 was believed to be the minimum differential (i.e., $1000) that would yield measurable differences in effect due to the financial aspects of the treatment. It is also a program of support just equivalent to the highest level available from the New Jersey experiment, and thus provides an important common point of comparison between the New Jersey results and those of SIME/DIME. A third guarantee level of $5600 was introduced into the experiment to widen the range of feasible support payments, thereby improving our ability to detect responses and to extrapolate them beyond the observed range.

These guarantee levels have been approximately maintained over time in real dollars by the use of an automatic cost-of-living escalator, which is adjusted every quarter. The following figures show the nominal guarantee levels for a family of four at the end of the 3- and 5-year programs, respectively, in Seattle:

Beginning of experiment April 1971	April 1974	April 1976
$3800	$4320	$5200
4800	5460	6560
5600	6360	7650

The Tax Function

The tax function determines how the grant to the family declines from the maximum support or guarantee level in response to other earnings received by the family. A constant rate system is simple to administer and analyze and is easy for the families to comprehend because the tax rate is the same whatever their level of earnings.

A declining tax rate system is one in which the tax rate on the first dollars of earned income is set at a high level and declines as income increases. It can be shown that the declining tax system will tend to push people to work either more or less than they would under a constant tax system, depending on their basic orientation to market work. That is, if they tend to work very little under a constant system, they are apt not to work at all. But if they tend to be work oriented they will work more, because the declining rate system provides workers less work disincentive than a constant tax system. Furthermore, for a given maximum support level (the amount of the transfer when other income is zero) and breakeven point (the income level at which the grant has been reduced to zero), it can be shown that the declining rate system provides a lower program cost to the government than a constant tax rate system. A further advantage of a declining rate system is that it can be integrated into the existing positive tax system without discontinuity in the marginal tax rate at the point where an individual goes from receiving net transfers to paying positive taxes.

SIME/DIME used four different tax systems. Two of these were constant tax systems at 50% and 70%, and two were declining rate systems. One of the declining systems started with an initial tax at 70%, the other with an initial tax at 80%; the average tax rate in both declined at a rate of 2.5% per $1000 of income (equivalently, the marginal rate declined 5% per $1000 of income).[4]

Positive Tax Reimbursement

As part of the NIT payment to the family, all or some of the income taxes paid to the federal or state government or any other taxes that vary with income, primarily Social Security taxes, were reimbursed to the family. This was necessary in order to control the tax rate faced by the families. All receipts from other income-conditioned programs were taxed away at 100%.

Figure 1.1 shows how the NIT plans used in SIME/DIME functioned. The horizontal axis shows gross income (income before taxes or transfer payments such as welfare grants); the vertical axis shows disposable income (income after taxes and with transfer payments). If gross income is zero, the NIT payment is equal to the support level. Without the NIT, a family with gross income A' would have disposable income A after paying positive income taxes; with the NIT payments, that family would have disposable income A''. As is clear from the diagram, the NIT payment has two components: a grant and a reimbursement of positive income taxes. At gross income level G', the NIT grant has declined to zero, but the family still benefits from the program by receiving reimbursement for all positive income taxes paid out. Between the gross income levels G' and B', the family still benefits from the NIT program by receiving partial reimbursement of positive income taxes paid. Families with incomes above the tax breakeven level B' do not receive any benefits of either type. Table 1.2 presents the NIT plans being tested in SIME/DIME, along with the grant and tax breakeven levels of the program.

[4] No experiments were conducted with declining rate systems starting at 50% or with a support level of $5600 combined with the 70% declining tax system, because these would fail to provide for full recovery of the grant before a zero average tax is reached. Also, no constant rate system at 80% was used because it was believed to be too confiscatory to be of programmatic interest.

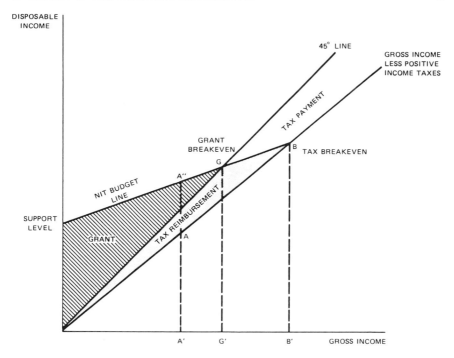

Figure 1.1 An NIT program with positive tax reimbursement. (Note: figure assumes no income outside of earnings and a linear positive income tax system.)

Measurement of Transitory Experimental Effects

One of the major issues of income-maintenance experimentation is the need to estimate long-run responses on the basis of the results obtained in an experiment of limited duration. If it can be assumed that the experimental family would make the same adjustment to the experimental treatment that it would make to an ongoing national program this presents no problem. However, it is likely that the adjustment made to the experiment will be an incomplete reflection of the adjustment that would be made to a program assumed to be permanent.

According to economic theory, the labor supply response to changes in income caused by a temporary NIT would be much less than the response caused by a permanent program, because a temporary program has a much smaller effect on lifetime income. Conversely, the effect of changing the net wage (holding disposable income constant would have a larger effect in a temporary program because in a temporary program it is possible to substitute future as well as current leisure for income. The net magnitude of these two opposing effects depends on their relative magnitudes and is not predictable by theory alone.

In SIME/DIME, several approaches were used to try to take account of the temporary duration of the experiment. First, three treatment durations were

Table 1.2
Treatment Parameters for SIME/DIME (1971 Dollars)

Plan[a]		Grant breakeven level	Tax breakeven level
F1	$(S = 3800, t_e = .5, r = 0)$	$ 7,600	$10,250
F2	$(S = 3800, t_e = .7, r = 0)$	5,429	6,350
F3	$(S = 3800, t_e = .7, r = .025)$	7,367	10,850
F4	$(S = 3800, t_e = .8, r = .025)$	5,302	7,800
F5	$(S = 4800, t_e = .5, r = 0)$	9,600	13,150
F6	$(S = 4800, t_e = .7, r = 0)$	6,867	8,520
F7	$(S = 4800, t_e = .7, r = .025)$	12,000	19,700
F8	$(S = 4800, t_e = .8, r = .025)$	8,000	11,510
F9	$(S = 5600, t_e = .5, r = 0)$	11,200	15,700
F10	$(S = 5600, t_e = .7, r = 0)$	8,000	9,780
F11	$(S = 5600, t_e = .8, r = .025)$	10,360	16,230

Note: These figures are for a family of four with only one earner and no income except for earnings. Positive tax reimbursements include the federal income tax and Social Security taxes. The federal income tax assumes the family takes the standard deduction. State income taxes, which are relevant only for the Denver experiment (there is no state income tax in Washington), are ignored in calculating the tax breakeven levels. The tax breakeven levels are thus slightly higher for the Denver experiment than shown.

[a]S = NIT annual support level; t_e = initial NIT tax rate; r = rate of decline of the average NIT tax rate per 1000 dollars of income.

tested—3, 5, and 20 years. By making treatment duration an experimental variable, it is possible to use directly observed data to measure the effect of varying program duration. Second, pre- and postexperimental data on labor supply will be used to measure changes in behavior that persist after program termination. This measurement will help sort transitory from permanent effects. (See Keeley, 1977, for a detailed discussion of how this may be done.)

The Design of the Manpower Treatments

The final major component of the design was made up of manpower counseling and training subsidies. SIME/DIME were the only income-maintenance experiments to include such a component. The NIT is expected to reduce work effort by lowering the value of market work. The purpose of the manpower treatments was to test whether, and to what extent, increasing job search and improving employability (and thereby the wage rates individuals can command) would counteract the work disincentives of the NIT treatments.

The manpower program is conducted at three levels, $M1$, $M2$, and $M3$. Briefly, $M1$ comprised only counseling services. $M2$ provided counseling services plus a 50% subsidy of the direct costs of any training taken over the life of the experiment. Level $M3$ was counseling plus a 100% subsidy of direct costs of any training over the life of the experiment.

Counseling Element

A counseling option was part of all three major manpower alternatives. Counseling was provided by members of a special counseling staff associated with the community colleges in Seattle and Denver. Any member of an enrolled family, 16 years of age or over and mentally and physically capable of gainful employment, was eligible to take counseling. Although acceptance of counseling was purely voluntary, a contact was made in which each eligible member of the family was encouraged to take advantage of it. Since people are not always aware of what is available, considerable outreach was undertaken in order to encourage the use of the counseling service. We were not concerned in the experiment to test whether or not people would use counseling on the basis of the information they happened to have available to them; rather, we wanted to urge people to use it so that we could be sure they had the information necessary to optimize their training and employment decisions. In fact, by the end of 3 years, 45% of the eligible persons had availed themselves of the counseling service.

In order to implement the counseling component effectively, several experimental goals must be achieved. First, a relevant information set must be determined for each individual based on his or her characteristics, aptitudes, and interests. Second, this information must be imparted in a clear way and must be understood by the recipient. Finally, every individual with the same characteristics, aptitudes, and interests must receive the same treatment (i.e., the same opportunity for self-assessment and the same amount of information relevant to needs). The essence of the counseling program as structured for the experiment was to allow individuals to make efficient decisions in terms of work; however, counselors were not allowed to participate directly in the decision-making process. The individual made his or her own decisions, influenced only by the information provided.

The Training Subsidy

The training subsidies available to those portions of the sample placed in either the $M2$ or $M3$ treatment were delineated, as we have seen, in terms of the percentage of direct costs of training to be covered by experimental payments. There were neither particular training inputs specified in the design nor specific limits on the costs of the training or the length of the training course. The only time limit was that dictated by the total experiment—3 years for most of the sample and 5 years for a smaller subset of the sample. (No manpower treatments were available for the 20-year sample.) This formulation of the training subsidy component has textbook simplicity in that it serves essentially to reduce the price of training without altering the set of training options provided by the market. Thus, the treatment performed the same function as a voucher for education or training. Any course of schooling or training was eligible for subsidy as long as it represented preparation for an occupation or career. Although some schooling that could be considered primarily as consumption (such as flying lessons) was disallowed, the range of subsidized training was wide.

The subsidies were intended to cover all reasonable direct costs of instruction. Reimbursement for tuition was limited to the lowest cost alternative that provided the desired course of instruction. Thus, SIME/DIME would not pay Harvard tuition if the same program was available at the University of Washington. For a variety of reasons, the largest single provider was the community college in each city. Of all those who had a subsidy option, about one-fourth entered a training or education course.

After preparing a research design, our next step was to develop a sample design and a method for assigning enrollees to various aspects of the program. We now turn to these considerations.

SAMPLE DESIGN AND ASSIGNMENT TO TREATMENT

The experimental design just reviewed includes 11 NIT treatments plus a control group, and three levels of the manpower program plus a control group, leading to 48 possible combinations including the no-NIT-no-manpower control group. In addition, length of treatment was an experimental variable. Given that one manpower treatment was omitted for the 5-year subsample, we have a total of 84 possible combinations (plus a special set of four treatments for the 20-year subsample, which is not discussed further).

A crucial design problem was the selection and allocation to treatment of an adequate number of participants so that the data would allow reliable estimates of experimental effects to be generated. The first step in the sample selection process, therefore, was to determine the number of observations required in each of the 84 experimental cells.

Sample Stratification

Once the overall budget constraint for each year of the experiment was set, the number of families required in each of the experimental cells was determined by use of a nonlinear programming model (see Conlisk and Kurz, 1972). The assignment problem started with the basic structuring of the sample along four characteristics: location, race, family composition, and length of treatment.

Location

An important design question for experiments whose final objective is to guide national policy is whether to conduct site-specific experiments rather than drawing a random sample of the U.S. population. How the choice is made depends upon whether site differences with regard to the relevant responses to be examined are or are not expected, and the expected extra cost of managing, monitoring and interviewing on a national scale. If there are significant response differences by site, then site-specific experiments give us limited information for national policy. (If there are significant enough site differences, then no experiment may be feasible, because the sample required to account for all these differences may be too large.) We chose a site-specific approach mainly on feasibility grounds and because the income-maintenance experiments that preceded SIME/DIME had also been conducted at particular sites. Comparison of preliminary results from our two sites and the results for the New Jersey and Gary experiments showed that mean work-effort responses are of the same order of magnitude. This also encouraged us to conclude that we would be able to merge the data from Seattle and Denver in our analysis.

Location did, however, play an important role in SIME/DIME, partly because of the great differences in the rate of unemployment in the two study sites. At the start of the experiment, Seattle had an unemployment rate of 12%, or twice the national average. This posed serious problems for an experiment designed to measure labor supply response. In an environment of low and declining job opportunities, it is difficult to distinguish the effects of changes in labor supply from changes in effective demand for labor. This problem was addressed in SIME/DIME by controlling for changes in the demand for labor through use of information gained in a more favorable labor market. Thus, a second site was selected to provide the information under more normal favorable economic conditions.

Denver was the city selected as the second site, because among all the cities reviewed, it best met the criteria we considered important. First, it had an unemployment rate below the national average, and was experiencing growth in total employment; therefore, the supply of job openings would, it was hoped, be sufficient to measure labor supply response. Second, Denver had a diversified economy that served as protection against future idiosyncratic problems that might arise in an area dominated by a particular industry (such as aerospace in Seattle). Third, Denver was similar to Seattle in terms of the demographic characteristics of its population, as well as in its sociocultural background. Fourth, Denver had the advantage of permitting the experiment to be expanded to study Chicanos as a major segment of the low-income population.

Race

The sample selected was structured so that if racial characteristics significantly affected response, we would be able to measure the responses of each of three differential racial or ethnic groups separately. (The three groups were black, Chicano, and other whites.) Efforts were made to exclude all other minority groups from the sample to preserve sufficient sample homogeneity for analysis. Seattle contains no substantial Chicano population, so only other whites and blacks were included in the Seattle sample. All three groups were represented in the Denver sample, which also accounts for the difference in the sample sizes between Seattle and Denver.

Family Composition

Family composition has many dimensions, such as the ages, sexes, and relationships of the family members, as well as the size of the family and the number of children. These attributes may all be involved in the experimental response. Because of the great potential importance of family structure in interpreting the results, an effort was made to achieve some degree of homogeneity in the population mix by confining the experiment to families with certain characteristics. First, the family, rather than the household, was selected as the basic experimental unit. This selection was based on the premise that the family is more stable and is the resource pooling unit. Second, only families that contained at least one adult and at least one child, or consisted of a married couple with or without children, were brought into the experiment. An unmarried cohabitating couple were eligible for the experiment only if they had at least one dependent child. The sample was then stratified according to whether the unit was headed by a single adult or a couple, with 60% of the budget allocated to the second group. This stratification was undertaken because labor supply responses of these two types of families were expected to be significantly different. It also enabled us to avoid losing participants who had a marital status change that placed them in the single adult category.

Another eligibility restriction was that the male head of the family, or the female head of any family without a male head, must be between the ages of 18 and 58 at the time of enrollment and physically capable of gainful employment.[5]

Length of Treatment

To enable direct estimation of the transitory component of the labor market response, part of the sample was offered the program for 5 years and part for only 3 years. Length of treatment was incorporated into the assignment model by allocating 25% of the budget to the 5-year portion of the experiment, and treating the 3- and 5-year samples as independent. (The small 20-year sample was selected later.)

Application of an Assignment Model

Within each of the 20 strata represented by the two cities, three racial groups, two family types, and two treatment lengths,[6] an allocation of families to treat-

---

[5] The rules permitted a younger person in an eligible family to become an eligible head of family if he or she reached 18 during the experimental period.

[6] There would have been 24 strata if a separate Chicano sample had been selected in Seattle.

ments was made by a mathematical model that allocated families with the objective of maximizing the amount of information on labor supply obtainable with a given budget. The need for such optimization arose because costs per observation differed greatly depending on the generosity of the plan and other income of the family. The cost to the experiment of an experimental family was roughly 3 times that of a control family.

In addition to the stratification variables already mentioned, the sample was stratified by preexperimental normal income. (Normal income is used here as a proxy for permanent income adjusted for family size.) The family's normal income is the expected income excluding the NIT payments and other income-conditioned transfer payments (e.g., AFDC and food stamps) assuming normal circumstances both for the family and for the regional economy in which the family lived and worked. It was measured as the projection of preexperimental income after removing the effect of unusual occurrences such as surgery or pregnancy.

For use in the assignment process, each family income was converted by use of a family size index into the income that provided an equivalent standard of living to a family of four members. Families were then grouped into six income classes, as follows:

Class[7]	Income (family of four equivalent) in 1970-1971 dollars
1	less than 1000
2	1000- 2999
3	3000- 4999
4	5000- 6999
5	7000- 8999
6	9000-10999

Eligibility was limited to one-worker families with a family of four equivalent income below $900, which would be Classes 1-5, plus two-worker families with incomes up to $11,000 (Classes 1-6). The income limits were imposed because it was assumed that families with higher incomes would not, because of the guarantee and breakeven points used, respond measurably to the program.

The Assignment Requirements Table

The assignment model was run with a total budget constraint of $6.3 million (in 1970 dollars) per year for program operations, exclusive of the budget for a Chicano subsample in Denver and fixed costs of research and administration. The budget was first divided equally between Seattle and Denver. A further divi-

[7] In other sections of this volume these classes will be designated as E-levels, i.e., $E1, E2$, etc.

Table 1.3
Enrolled Families by Race and Site

	Seattle		Denver		Total	
Black	901	44%	961	35%	1862	39%
White	1141	56	930	34	2071	43
Chicano	0	0	867	31	867	18
Total	2042	100%	2758	100%	4800	100%

sion of the budget according to the ethnic-racial groups was then made. In each site, 75% was allocated to the 3-year sample and 25% to the 5-year sample.[8] Assignment of sample members to a manpower-only treatment was also made.

The final assignment model selected a total of 5202 families for the sample, of which 4800 were successfully enrolled. The distribution of the enrolled sample by city and race is shown in Table 1.3.

The larger white sample in Seattle reflected the expectation that black families would have a somewhat higher labor market response and family separation rate than white families. The smaller Chicano sample in Denver was due to the absence of the special control group selected for comparisons between Seattle and Denver.

Using the stratification already discussed, the sample members were then placed into one of four treatment groups. Table 1.4 shows the allocation among the four major treatment groupings. Of the total sample, 58% was assigned to some NIT treatment, about half of the remainder to a manpower program only, and the remaining 20% to the null control group. (The null control indicates a group receiving neither NIT nor manpower treatment.) This sample design permits measurement of the separate and combined effects of income maintenance and a manpower program.

Once the sample had been selected according to the appropriate strata and

Table 1.4
Enrolled Families by Treatment and Site

	Seattle		Denver		Total	
Null control	518	25%	523	19%	1041	22%
NIT only	369	18	577	21	946	20
Manpower only	417	20	595	22	1012	21
Manpower/NIT	738	36	1063	39	1801	38
Total	2042	99%[a]	2758	101%[a]	4800	101%[a]

[a]Does not add to 100 due to rounding.

[8] During the experiment we added a 20-year sample to receive only financial treatments, composed of control families and 3-year sample families who had been assigned to NIT treatments but no manpower treatment and had completed their time on the experiment. The 20-year sample has not yet been analyzed.

placed into one of the four treatment groups, the next step was to undertake data collection over time in order to obtain the information needed for the analysis. How the responses were measured will be described after the issues surrounding the use of experimentally generated data have been discussed.

RESEARCH USING EXPERIMENTAL DATA

The basic goal of research using experimental data is to determine the effects of the experiment on individual and family behavior. While experimental effects on many types of behavior can be investigated using data from the income-maintenance experiments, the research has generally concentrated on labor supply and marital stability. Other modes of behavior investigated include migration, human capital formation, fertility, expenditure patterns, occupation changes, wage rate changes, job search behavior, childcare usage, health, and the school performance of children. Although the details of the analysis of these various modes of behavior vary considerably because of causal factors peculiar to each, there is a common methodological basis for most of the analysis. This common basis arises because the researchers are analyzing data generated by an experiment rather than data from a cross-sectional or longitudinal sample survey.

Before the advent of social experimentation on a large scale, researchers typically analyzed existing (usually cross-sectional) data obtained from passive observation, using what is now a fairly well-developed methodology, in order to obtain estimates of the response to an NIT. Unfortunately, in part because of a variety of statistical problems[9] inherent in analyzing such data, the range of estimates in these studies is disturbingly large and of limited usefulness to policymakers. In principle, controlled experiments such as SIME/DIME afford the opportunity to overcome most of the problems inherent in nonexperimental research. This is primarily because, in an experiment, there is a measured stimulus, administered independently of the behavior to be observed, to which (so long as outside influences are adequately controlled or measured) the resulting effects can be attributed with a known degree of statistical confidence. In practice, however, large-scale social experimentation is a relatively new research tool that requires the development of a new and different methodology for analyzing experimental data and for using experimental results to make predictions about the effects of new, permanent nationwide programs such as an NIT.

Experimental data differ in many ways from the previously analyzed nationwide cross-sectional data bases. The experiments typically have highly selected, stratified samples. The experiments test a variety of exogenous treatments of limited duration that are not assigned on a simple random basis; they have a con-

---

[9] For a discussion of these statistical problems see Keeley (forthcoming).

trol population that is not receiving any treatment, yet is subject to nonexperimental but contaminating influences (such as the welfare system); and they follow a given group of people (who divorce, marry, have children, and die) over time. In this section, some of the methodological issues related to analyzing experimental data and extrapolating the results are presented.

Although other kinds of behavioral responses are also of interest, this section focuses on the methodological issues associated with using experimental data to analyze effects of an NIT on hours of work or labor supply. Many of these methodological considerations, however, also apply to the analysis of other behavioral impacts.

As mentioned, the income-maintenance experiments have several interrelated objectives. Most generally, they were funded in order to determine the behavioral effects and the costs associated with the introduction of alternative nationwide NIT programs. Distinguishing nationwide effects from effects on the experimental samples is important, because the highly stratified experimental samples are not representative of the nation as a whole.

An experiment has several advantages over other methods of making such estimates. First and most important, as mentioned, in a controlled experiment the treatment (in this case consisting of changing disposable income and net wage rates) is exogenous. Thus, unlike conventional economic research, there is no question about the direction of causality between changes in income and net wage rates and labor supply response. In addition, the treatment can be measured fairly precisely. Second, in an experiment, individuals are followed over time, and their behavior is known before, during, and after the experimental treatment. This panel feature of experimental data makes them a much more valuable source of information than typical point-in-time or cross-sectional data. Finally, the survey instruments are specifically designed to obtain information on the sorts of behavior being studied. Few other data sources contain such detailed data on the various aspects of market work, e.g., that are the primary focus of the income-maintenance experiments.

Although experimental data have a number of advantages over nonexperimental data for estimating the labor supply responses to alternative nationwide NIT programs, there are a number of characteristics of the design of SIME/DIME and the other experiments that must be accounted for when measuring responses. As mentioned before, because the cost of carrying out a nationwide NIT experiment was believed to be prohibitive, the experimental samples were stratified and site specific.[10] Because of this, a methodology for extrapolating experimental results to the nation was developed. The procedure used in the SIME/

---

[10] A stratified sample is a sample in which certain types of persons are either over- or undersampled from the population from which the sample is being drawn. In SIME/DIME, blacks, Chicanos, single-headed families, low-income families and families on welfare are oversampled.

DIME analysis is first to estimate the parameters of a labor supply response function using experimental data and then to apply these parameter estimates to a national data base to make nationwide predictions.

Measuring Responses to Experimental Treatments

In the SIME/DIME experiments, some persons in the sample were subject to none of the experimental treatments. These persons were subject only to the status quo environment and were known as controls. The remainder of the sample was divided among several experimental treatments, and were known as experimentals. The key advantage of such a procedure arises from the randomness of the assignment to experimental and control status. When the assignment is purely random, i.e., when it does not depend on any characteristics of the individual, controls and experimentals can be assumed to be identical on average, apart from the effect of the experimental treatment. Thus, any difference between the experimentals and the controls can be presumed to result from the experimental treatment. Consequently, the effect of an experimental treatment on the outcome variable of interest, such as labor supply, can be observed by comparing the values of the outcome variable for experimentals with its values for the controls.

It could be asked, "Why have the controls at all? Why not compare behavior of the experimentals during the experiment with the behavior of the experimentals before the experiment?" The answer is simply that having a control group enables the researcher to correct for environmental or other changes that have an effect independent of the experiment, as long as these changes have the same impact on both controls and experimentals. In an experiment there is no need, therefore, for an explicit model describing how these environmental changes affect the outcome variables.

The simplest estimator of the effect of an experiment is the difference between the mean values of the outcome variables for experimentals and controls. This estimator relies on the implicit assumption that, apart from the effects of the experiment, there is no reason to expect any difference between the experimentals and the controls. In an experiment with a purely random design, this assumption can be expected to be approximately valid because persons are randomly assigned to experimental or control status. Of course, one could be unlucky and generate a random assignment with large differences between experimentals and controls; but such an occurrence is very unlikely with large samples.

However, as we have already discussed, persons in SIME/DIME were not assigned to the various treatments in a purely random fashion. Rather, the probability of being assigned to any particular treatment depended on three characteristics of the family: an estimate of the family's normal income level, the race of the family head, and whether the family was headed by a husband and wife or a single person. Each family was determined to be in an income-race-family-structure cell. While assignment to treatment *within* each of these cells was random, different cells had different assignment probabilities. Thus, the actual assignment to treatment in SIME/DIME (as in the other income-maintenance experiments) was not purely random, but rather random within strata defined by normal income, race, and family status.

An important implication of such stratified random assignment is that there is no reason to expect controls and experimentals to be the same on average. This means that, even in the absence of the experimental treatments, the control and experimental groups cannot be expected to have the same average value for labor supply or any other outcome variable.

Because assignment is random within each assignment stratum, however, we know that there are no expected nonexperimental differences between experimentals and controls who are in the same assignment stratum. This means that each person's labor supply in the experimental period can be assumed to be the sum of the mean nonexperimental labor supply for persons in his or her treatment stratum, the mean treatment effect (which would be zero for controls), and an error term. The experimental effect in this model can be estimated using a statistical technique called regression analysis. Regression analysis allows us to estimate the effect of the experiment on hours of work, while accounting for the possibility that a person's hours of work also varies in a way that depends on that person's assignment stratum. Most of the experimental analyses to be discussed in subsequent chapters have been based on modifications of this simple estimator. The modifications generally arise from specific methodological problems. These problems include the method used to assign experimental treatment; participation in welfare programs by experimental sample members; proper measurement of experimental treatment; limited duration of the treatments; differences between the experimental plans and the kind of NIT plans that would exist in a national program; and proper measurement of labor supply. In the remainder of this section, some of these issues are discussed.

Issues Involved in the Assignment to Experimental Treatments

The assignment model resulted in a sample in which families with low normal-income levels (*E*-levels) were more likely to be assigned to treatments with low guarantee levels (or low breakeven levels). Persons with high normal incomes were more likely to be assigned to NIT treatments with high guarantees and breakeven levels. Low normal-income families were less likely and high normal-income families more likely to be assigned to control status. Thus, the distribution of income differs in different NIT treatments, and the distribution of income of controls differs from the distribution of income of persons assigned to any experimental treatment.

As mentioned already, one important implication of this assignment procedure is that simple mean differences in labor supply (or any other variable) between persons eligible for treatment and controls (or between any two different treatments) are not indicative of a response. Instead, at the minimum, all comparisons of differences in labor supply among NIT treatments, including the null treatment, must control for initial differences in labor supply caused by the assignment model. In fact, this may be done relatively easily using multivariate statistical procedures, since all the variables used to assign the families to the treatments are known.

A more serious problem arises, however, if response to an NIT program depends on the same variables as those used in the assignment process. Economic theory indicates that labor supply response is likely to depend on preexperimental income (E-level) because the magnitude of the income change caused by the NIT depends on preexperimental income. This would also be true of any other response that depended on income. At the minimum, expected response above the breakeven level is likely to be smaller than response below the breakeven level; and whether or not someone is above the breakeven level depends to a large extent on preexperimental income—the same variable used in the assignment model. Thus, comparisons of labor supply among the NIT treatments, including the null treatment, must account for the different distributions of preexperimental family characteristics used to assign treatment, so that it can be determined whether differences in response are due to the treatments or to the assignment. In fact, it has been shown (see Keeley and Robins, 1978) that in a model in which the effects of the NIT guarantee level and tax rate are estimated without control for interactions between assignment variables and response, both support and tax effects are about half what they would be if random treatment assignment had been used. The same research has also shown that the distribution of response by income level is greatly affected by the assignment model. Generally, response of low-income persons is smaller with the nonrandom assignment inherent in the SIME/DIME model than it would be with random assignment. Similarly, response of high-income persons is larger. This is because the SIME/DIME assignment model gives smaller treatments to low-income persons and larger treatments to high-income persons than would occur with random assignment. From a policy point of view, such a misleading distribution of responses would lead to serious errors in extrapolating experimental response to the nation as a whole because the national distribution of income differs substantially from the distribution of income in the SIME/DIME sample.

Because response models that ignore this interdependence between assignment and response[11] are not free from bias when experimental treatment is assigned based on preexperimental income level, the approach in the labor supply analysis has been to utilize economic theory to derive a response model that accounts for the interactions between "normal income" and response. See Keeley et al. (1978a) for the details of the response model. (In addition, a variety of

---

[11] Analysis of variance models exemplify such an approach.

other statistical procedures is used when estimating response in order to eliminate artificial differences in labor supply among the different experimental treatments and the control treatment that were caused by the nonrandom assignment process.) This model is outlined in the following section.

Measuring Experimental Treatment

Partly because of the stratified random assignment model used, it is necessary to precisely measure the experimental stimulus received by each family. As was described previously, SIME/DIME is testing 11 different NIT treatments. In principle, treatment effects can be estimated by including a dummy variable for each treatment. With 11 different NIT treatments, three different manpower programs, and two different experimental durations, however, the experimental sample is not large enough to obtain precise estimates of the main effects of each of these treatments, let alone account for all the possible interactions among them as well as interactions with the assignment variables. This means that a researcher is forced to constrain the way the response varies on an a priori basis. Although each NIT treatment is well specified, economic theory indicates that response also depends on the characteristics of the family. Thus, a given treatment represents different stimuli to different families depending on characteristics such as the wage rates of the family members, nonlabor income, tastes for work, family size, and eligibility for and participation in other welfare programs.

To see why this is so, consider Figure 1.2. In this figure a preexperimental budget line AE is depicted along with an NIT treatment, ACF, with support level EF. These budget lines depict the trade-offs between work (or leisure) and disposable income. First, consider a person initially located at point E prior to the initiation of the experiment. Although this person experiences an increase in income and a decrease in the net wage due to the NIT, he does not reduce his labor supply because he is already out of the labor force.[12] Similarly, consider someone above the breakeven level at a position like B. Although he might respond, the probability of a response is low and persons sufficiently far above the breakeven level will not respond. For these persons, the NIT treatment represents no stimulus. However, for persons below the breakeven level, the NIT treatment represents a variety of stimuli depending on hours worked and wage rate. In this context, the actual stimulus is the change in the budget line relevant to that person. Each person has his net wage reduced by a given amount, but the change in income varies from 0 at point C, the breakeven level, to a maximum equal to the guarantee level, EF, at 0 hours of work.

A similar problem occurs for persons who are receiving welfare benefits such as AFDC or AFDC-UP (Aid to Families with Dependent Children of Unemployed Parents). SIME/DIME required that persons receiving payments from the experi-

---

[12] A special statistical technique, called tobit estimation, is used to account for the fact that response cannot be larger than initial hours of work.

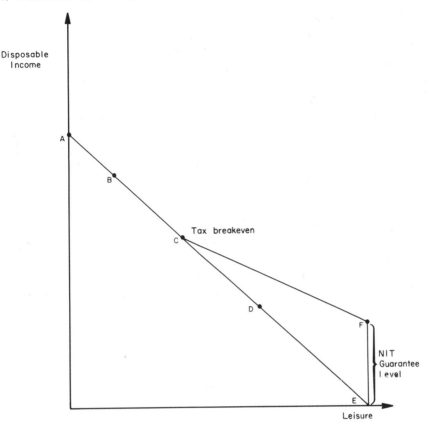

Figure 1.2 Work-leisure trade-off with an NIT.

ments give up welfare payments[13] and this also caused problems in measuring the stimulus. For example, consider a person who is enrolled in a welfare program identical to one of the SIME/DIME treatments that replaced it. In this case the individual undergoes no change in circumstances and essentially is receiving no stimulus. For such an individual, no response is expected. Generally persons previously on welfare receive much smaller treatments than persons not on welfare previously, because the change in budget constraint is smaller for a person on welfare. Therefore, we expect the response of persons previously on welfare to be much smaller.

Finally, in all the NIT treatments being tested in SIME/DIME, as well as in all the other NIT experiments, the guarantee level varies with family size; in the declining tax rates, the tax rate also varies with family size. Thus, different-sized

---

[13] The benefits from welfare programs other than AFDC or AFDC-UP are taxed at 100%.

families with the same income assigned to the same NIT treatment have different changes in their budget constraints and their responses, therefore, can be expected to differ. To summarize, we see that the actual stimulus a family receives depends not only on the NIT treatment to which it is assigned, but also on the number of children and other family members, income, wage rates, hours of work, and participation in welfare programs.

In the labor supply research, the effects of welfare, family size, and differences in initial hours and wage rates on response are controlled by directly measuring the change in each individual's budget constraint that is caused by the NIT. The procedure used measures the change in terms of three variables: whether the person is below or above the breakeven level of income; if the person is below, the change in disposable income at initial hours of work; and the change in the net wage rate caused by the NIT treatment to which that person is assigned.[14] With this formulation, we not only account for the nonrandom assignment, but also derive estimates that may be used to predict labor supply response to NIT programs other than those being specifically tested in SIME/DIME. Also, it is possible to predict response for populations that differ from the SIME/DIME sample in characteristics that affect response such as family size, receipt of welfare, and income.

Extrapolating the Experimental Results

Once unbiased and statistically significant estimates of the effects of exogenous changes in income and wages caused by the NIT on labor supply are obtained, it is still necessary to develop a methodology for predicting the nationwide responses to alternative NIT programs. Nationwide responses will differ from the sample responses because of differences in income, explicit and implicit tax rates, hours of work, wage rates, race-ethnicity, family size, and welfare benefits between the SIME/DIME sample and the national population. The procedures used to extrapolate the SIME/DIME results applies the experimental estimates of response to a national data base, the Current Population Survey. A microsimulation computer program called Micro Analysis of Transfer to Households (MATH), which was jointly developed by Mathematica and SRI, is used to perform the calculations. (MATH is a variant of TRIM, a model developed at the Urban Institute.)

The procedure is to predict, for each eligible person in the national sample, the labor supply response to a given NIT program. A person's response depends on the particular NIT program being considered, and on a variety of socioeconomic characteristics of the person and his or her family. The payment cost for the family may also be determined once the labor supply responses of all family members are known. Aggregate labor supply response and cost are then obtained

---

[14] In an extension of this approach, below and above breakeven level responses are unified. See Robins and West (1978).

by summing up individual responses and costs. The procedure may be repeated to produce analogous estimates for alternative NIT programs and aggregate responses and costs may be compared. This procedure allows the experimental findings to be generalized while accounting for the specifics of the experimental design and the peculiarities of the experimental sample. It also accounts for regional variations in the existing welfare programs and state and local income taxes.

OVERVIEW OF THE REMAINDER OF THE VOLUME

A voluminous body of data was collected during the operational phase of SIME/DIME. Even though analysis of those data will be underway for years to come, this book represents an important preliminary review with interesting policy implications.[15]

Chapter 2, which ends Part I, examines the validity of the data collected by comparing income data reported to SIME/DIME interviewers with comparable income reported to various governmental agencies. The comparisons enable estimates to be made of the extent and magnitude of any discrepancies among the different sources of data.

Part II deals with experimental effects on work behavior. One of the important results of the experiments is that they have confirmed the implications of economic theory. More importantly, however, the experimental data have allowed us to obtain more precise estimates for the magnitude of the predicted changes than were previously possible. Economic theory indicates that increasing disposable income would lead to reduced hours of work, and decreasing the net wage rate, holding disposable income constant, also would lead to reduced hours of work. But theory can only indicate the direction of change, not the magnitude. To estimate the work behavior implications for any specific income-maintenance alternative, it is necessary to have empirical evidence. Such evidence could be inferred from cross-sectional or panel studies that statistically correlate hours of work and the parameters of a welfare program, but the existing (nonexperimental) studies provide estimates that span an uncomfortably wide range. Furthermore, those studies provide no direct evidence regarding the direction of causality (see Cain and Watts, 1973, Table 9-2, pp. 336-337). Experimentation appears to provide the basis for acquiring unambiguous estimates of the effects of various NIT alternatives on hours of work effort, as well as on other types of behavior.

Among the income-maintenance experiments, SIME/DIME covered the widest range of NIT programs and had the largest sample. Therefore, they can provide better estimates of how different guarantee levels and tax rates can be expected

[15] The SIME/DIME Final Report is planned for release late in 1981.

to affect work behavior than were possible with the data from previous experiments.

Chapter 3 discusses the research findings as they relate to labor supply (or hours of work) response. Results from SIME/DIME are used to predict nationwide labor supply effects and costs for six alternative NIT plans. For example, an NIT treatment, characterized by a grant at 75% of the poverty level and a 50% grant reduction rate (which is quite similar to the Carter administration's Tier 1 cash grant programs) would, according to our estimates, provide benefits for 10.6 million families at a total cost, in addition to AFDC and food stamp benefits, of $8 billion in 1974 prices (without state supplementation). Of these costs, 30% result from reductions in hours of work. If the tax rate is raised to 70%, the total additional cost of the program would drop to $2.2 billion in 1974 prices (60% of which is due to reductions in hours of work), but benefits would go to only 5.3 million families. Thus, our research findings can be used to estimate the various trade-offs among program cost, number of beneficiaries, and work effects. In general, our results show that a moderately generous program will not cause massive reductions in hours of work, but that labor supply effects are a substantial portion of total program cost.

Looking at the more detailed results, the research to date indicates that in a two-parent family, husbands and wives each reduce hours of work by about the same amount. However, as a proportion of total hours worked, the reduction is approximately three times larger for wives. Looking at the mean effects of the experiment, it was found that the composite of experimental NIT treatments caused the probability of being employed to decline by 5, 8, and 11 percentage points for husbands, wives, and female heads of families, respectively.

Most of the analysis with regard to labor supply relates to heads of families (husbands, wives, and female heads). However, Chapter 4 examines the effects of the SIME/DIME experiments on the work of persons who were between 16 and 21 years of age at enrollment into the experiment, and who were children, stepchildren, or grandchildren of the heads of their families at enrollment. The most important finding of this study is that the NIT plans induce a substantial reduction in hours of work among persons in this group.

Chapter 5 is concerned with the labor supply response over time. Since the experiments were conducted for a limited time period, and since what is needed are estimates of the labor supply effects of a permanent nationwide NIT program, it is important to account for adjustment over time. Tracing the adjustment process over time shows that work effort response took from 5 to 10 quarters after the start of the experiment to achieve a steady state. According to this study, the 3-year experiment may have been too short to capture fully the effects of a permanent program. For husbands, the reduction in hours of work for the 5-year sample was considerably larger than for the 3-year sample, and the differences were statistically significant. The reduction for wives was also larger for the 5-year sample, although these differences were not statistically significant. There were no duration effects for female heads. If further work substantiates the finding that the 5-year effects are significantly larger than the 3-year effects, then the work effort results used in simulations, at least for husbands, may be revised upward.

Using estimates from the labor supply models, results from the simulation of the Carter administration's suggested welfare reform program, PBJI, are presented in Chapter 6. This chapter illustrates how SIME/DIME findings have been used by policymakers in assessing the merits of alternative welfare reform policies.

In Chapter 7, results from a study of the effects of SIME/DIME on job satisfaction are presented. A theoretical model of the effects of an NIT program on job satisfaction is developed and an empirical formulation of the model is presented in which changes in job satisfaction are related to changes in net wage rates and changes in disposable income. Statistically significant effects of an NIT on job satisfaction are detected for women, but not for men. The effects vary depending on whether or not women adjust their labor force status. For wives, those who changed jobs appeared to be increasing their level of job satisfaction. For single female heads, those who did not change jobs appeared to be decreasing their level of job satisfaction. Job-changing wives also experienced a decline in their wage rates relative to control families.

Chapter 8 examines the factors affecting the choice of work and childcare arrangements for single mothers. With the substantial increase in female labor force participation, as well as the increase in households headed by single females, the effect of childcare on the work-leisure choice has become increasingly important. The results of this study indicate that family structure has a significant impact on both the decision to work and the choice of childcare mode. Because so many familes were eligible for childcare subsidies, the study is unable to detect a significant effect of the SIME/DIME childcare subsidies on the use of market forms of childcare. The direction of the effect of a childcare subsidy is positive, however, suggesting a responsiveness on the part of families to childcare subsidy programs.

Part III consists of three chapters directed to the effects on family behavior. In addition to labor supply effects, the other major focus of the NIT program investigated in the income-maintenance experiments is the effect of such programs on incentives to marry and stay married. Chapter 9 examines the data collected to determine the effect of the experimental NIT programs on the establishment and stability of families. The chapter reports the most publicized and controversial results from SIME/DIME to date. Concern has been expressed by members of the Senate Finance Committee considering welfare reform that SIME/DIME findings on marital stability refute the Carter administration's contention that the Program for Better Jobs and Income (PBJI) helps to stabilize families. As described in Chapter 9, it is difficult to reconcile SIME/DIME findings with the view that an NIT-like welfare reform will increase the stability of two-parent families. The experimental results to date suggest that the immediate impact of such a program would be to increase substantially the rate of marital dissolution. In the experiment, these findings were mitigated only at very high guarantee levels (about $8500 in 1979 dollars).

The findings on marital dissolution ran counter to our expectations that an NIT would stabilize families, which were guided by intuition and accepted dogma. Findings for the first 2 years indicate that an NIT simultaneously acts to stabilize families by providing income support to the existing family, and also destabilizes them by providing support to the wife and her children outside the marriage.

The marital dissolution findings cannot be automatically generalized to the Carter administration's welfare program. First, we do not know as yet whether the marital dissolution rates will persist in the long run if such a program is put into effect. However, even if it does not persist, the short-term effects look strong enough to result in an increase in the proportion of single-headed families for some time. Second, there are some important differences between the NIT under SIME/DIME, and the administration's PBJI. Some of these differences are likely to mitigate the impact on marriage and others to exacerbate it. On the one hand, there are reasons to believe that providing jobs for male heads of two-parent families will help stabilize marriages. On the other hand, under PBJI a female spouse generally must leave the marriage in order to acquire one of the public service jobs; this is likely to increase separation. The existence of the lower tier support for job eligible familes coupled with the work requirement, implies a weaker form of financial support for the two-parent family than is the case under SIME/DIME, and this is likely to be destabilizing. On balance, we cannot say, on the basis of a priori reasoning, whether the PBJI would have more or less effect on marriage stability than SIME/DIME.

Chapter 10 examines the impact of the income-maintenance experiments upon the psychological distress of a large sample of low-income adults living in Seattle and Denver. A well-established empirical generalization in the field of mental health is that psychological distress varies inversely with level of income. However, little is known about the effect of *changes* in income upon psychological status. A somewhat erratic pattern of responses was found that indicates a general tendency for the experiment to increase psychological distress. Scores on an index of distress for white husbands in Denver, black husbands in Seattle, black and white wives in Denver, and black female heads in Denver and Seattle were about 10% higher for treatment than for control families. These effects did not tend to dissipate in the second year of the experiment, which led the researchers to speculate that the experiment increased distress primarily by increasing the number of life events to which the families on the experiment were exposed.

Chapter 11 presents an analysis of the effects of an NIT on fertility. An economic model of fertility is used to derive an empirical model. The parameters of the empirical model are then estimated using data from the income-maintenance experiments. For married females, a large, statistically significant negative effect for the white 5-year sample, a large positive effect for the 5-year Chicanos, and no statistically significant effects for blacks are found. For single females, there was no evidence of a strong fertility response.

Part IV addresses the question of how the benefits received by participants in the income-maintenance experiment are used. In virtually every government income-transfer program designed to raise the standard of living of the family unit, welfare payments are adjusted across families according to their size and composition. The index numbers that are used to scale benefits by family composition go by the name of adult equivalent scales. In Chapter 12 a methodology for developing three alternative adult equivalent scales is presented and estimates of these scales provided, based on the observed behavior of husband-wife families enrolled in SIME/DIME. The indices used in SIME/DIME to adjust guarantee levels for differences in family size may have underestimated the costs associated with maintaining large families. The selection of a family size index seems to have important consequences for family welfare, and we should know to what extent the selected indices compensate for differences in utility, in child maintenance costs, and in nutritional needs.

Chapter 13 presents an analysis of the effects of an NIT on geographical mobility. Theoretical models of migration are developed and parameters of those models are estimated using data from SIME/DIME. It was found that, on the average, being eligible for an NIT treatment caused two-parent white families in both Seattle and Denver to increase their rate of out-migration by 50%.

Chapter 14 presents the effects of the experimental treatments on the desire to obtain increased schooling or training. In addition to the NIT component, as we have noted, the experiment had a substantial manpower component that provided intensive job and career counseling, as well as education or training subsidies. Use of the manpower program by members of families eligible for the program was optional. Any able-bodied person 16 years of age or over who was a member of an eligible family could take full advantage of the options. The experiment operated essentially like a voucher program in that an individual was free to select his or her course of study, restricted only by the boundaries of the experimental objectives; i.e., to be subsidized, the training or education course must enhance the individual's capabilities to perform in the labor market and must be the minimum cost method of achieving those goals. Evidence as to the impacts of this program on labor market behavior will be reported in future weeks. In this book we discuss only the immediate impact of the program in terms of its utilization.

Chapter 14 indicates that the manpower program was used by a substantial fraction of the eligible population: 6350 persons were eligible for counseling, and 4367 of those were also eligible for training subsidies. Of those eligible for counseling, 30% took advantage of the option when first offered, and an additional 15% took counseling later in the experiment. Most of those who took the option later in the program had been ineligible at the beginning (e.g., because they were under the minimum age limit at the earlier date). Of the 1798 individuals who took counseling when initially offered, 1284 wrote a plan of action to carry out some labor market goal, ¾ of which were plans to take training or further education. A total of 675 individuals, about one-third of those who initially started counseling, entered a training or education program, including individuals selecting the General Equivalency Development (GED) as an option.

There is little doubt that knowledge of the availability of the training subsidies increased substantially the likelihood that an individual would take training. Moreover, the 100% training subsidy was more effective than the 50% subsidy. The models estimated indicate high sensitivity to the cost of training on the part of the client population: For heads of families above age 25, a full subsidy increased the number of quarters of schooling attended during the first 2 years of the program by 50% to 300% for heads of families and spouses. These large proportionate increases are particularly striking when it is realized that the amount of the direct subsidy was not large. Those on full subsidy received benefits averaging $956 over 3 years, and those on half subsidy received an average of $382.

Chapter 15 presents an examination of the effects of SIME/DIME on the propensity to hold various kinds of physical and financial assets. Such effects are of potential importance in designing optimal welfare programs because a decrease in the holding (or reported value) of assets, such as homes, are subject to tax under the SIME/DIME payment system. (SIME/DIME taxes an imputed flow of income from assets.) This study, however, finds that most of the effects of the experiment on asset stock demand of those predicted to receive payments were modest.

Chapter 16 investigates the interaction between an income-maintenance program and subsidized housing. Estimates were made of the effects that an NIT would have on the utilization of such housing. In this study, it was found that the financial treatments reduced the likelihood that a family either would remain in subsidized housing (if initially in such housing) or would enter subsidized housing if not there at the beginning of the experiment. This effect was concentrated in small families, probably reflecting the tendency for subsidy values of public housing to increase with family size. This effect might translate into a permanent reduction in the demand for subsidized housing if a national NIT becomes law.

Finally, the Appendix presents a review of the data collection process, from interviewing of participants to the final construction of analytic files. Included in this review are the types of data collected, and a discussion of the steps taken in processing the data.

REFERENCES

Cain, Glen G., and Watts, Harold W. *Income Maintenance and Labor Supply*. Chicago: Rand McNally, 1973.

Conlisk, John, and Kurz, Mordecai. "The Assignment Model of the Seattle and Denver Income Maintenance Experiments." Research Memorandum No. 15, Center for the Study of Welfare Policy, Stanford Research Institute, July 1972.

Keeley, Michael C. "Using Post-Experimental Data to Derive the Effects of a Permanent Income Maintenance Program," Mimeograph. SRI International, 1977.

Keeley, Michael C. *The Economics of Labor Supply: A Critical Review*. New York: Academic Press, forthcoming.

Keeley, Michael C., and Robins, Philip K. "The Design of Social Experiments: A Critique of the Conlisk-Watts Assignment Model." Research Memorandum No. 57, SRI International, November 1978. Revised version in *Research in Labor Economics*, vol. 3, edited by Ronald G. Ehrenberg, JAI Press, forthcoming, 1980.

Keeley, Michael C.; Robins, Philip K.; Spiegelman, Robert G.; and West, Richard W. "The Estimation of Labor-Supply Models Using Experimental Data." *American Economic Review*, December 1978a.

Kurz, Mordecai, and Spiegelman, Robert G. "The Seattle Experiment: The Combined Effect of Income Maintenance and Manpower Investments." *American Economic Review* 61 (May 1971).

Kurz, Mordecai and Spiegelman, Robert G. "The Design of the Seattle and Denver Income Maintenance Experiments." Research Memorandum No. 18, Center for the Study of Welfare Policy, Stanford Research Institute, May 1972.

Robins, Philip K., and West, Richard W. "Participation in the Seattle and Denver Income Maintenance Experiments and Its Effect on Labor Supply." Research Memorandum No. 53, Center for the Study of Welfare Policy, SRI International, 1978.

CHAPTER **2**

Data Validation

HARLAN I. HALSEY

INTRODUCTION

A critical element in the success of any experiment is an understanding of the accuracy of the data on which the conclusions are based. In social experimentation the subjects themselves are usually the source of most of the data. In SIME/DIME the subjects report in periodic interviews, conducted approximately three times a year, and in monthly income and family structure reports. Reporting, however, is a facet of human behavior subject to influences both of the experiment and of society at large. This fact adds an additional element to the potential sources of experimental error—the element of biased reporting. The direct purpose of the SIME/DIME validation study discussed in this chapter is to assess the variance and bias in reported data.

A wider purpose of this chapter is to shed light on income reporting behavior itself. Income data are reported by individuals on many occasions: for example, on state and federal income tax forms; for transfer programs such as AFDC, the Food Stamp program, and public housing programs; for social surveys such as the Survey of Economic Opportunity (SEO), the Survey of Income and Education (SIE), and the forthcoming Survey of Income and Program Participation (SIPP); and for the Labor Department Current Population Survey (CPS). Most such data are self-reported. Notable exceptions include Social Security earnings data and Unemployment Insurance earnings data, which are reported directly by the employer. The accuracy of self-reported data affects public policy decisions on income taxation, unemployment, inflation, government transfers to low-income families, and our knowledge of the income distribution and the unemployment rate.

Over most of the wide range of reported data, either there is little incentive to hide the truth or the report can easily be checked. This is true, for example, of reports of the number and ages of children in a family. Income, however, is an

33

A GUARANTEED ANNUAL INCOME:
EVIDENCE FROM A SOCIAL EXPERIMENT

exception. Income is usually taxed and is often quite easily concealed. As a result, reported income is likely to be subject to both high variance and downward bias. Recent front page articles in the *Wall Street Journal* indicate a growing awareness of tax avoidance through underreporting of income. (See Hill, 1978, and MaLabre, 1979, for examples of newspaper articles.) Peter M. Gutmann (1977), in one of the few published articles on underreporting, has estimated that the fraction of GNP associated with unreported transactions has risen steadily since World War II and now amounts to about 9.4%. C. Northcote Parkinson (1960), a classic source of this insight, has observed that government can tax only up to the cost of tax avoidance. If it is cheaper to avoid the tax than to pay it, the individual will choose to avoid. An SRI study[1] of income reporting to the AFDC program conducted with data from the Denver Income-Maintenance Experiment (DIME) preenrollment interview indicated that, of families that reported income to both sources, only 60% as much income was reported to AFDC as was reported to DIME. An additional 24% of the families reporting income to DIME reported nothing at all to the welfare department. Evidence abounds that income will be underreported when incentive and opportunity coexist. Despite these difficulties, however, reliable data are necessary for public policy analysis as well as for the study of methodological issues.

In the following section, I discuss some of the problems in validating income data. Following that, I summarize the preliminary SIME/DIME validation study. Conclusions follow in the last section.

DIFFICULTIES IN VALIDATING INCOME DATA

Since income data are by far the most difficult to collect, I focus discussion on these data. The difficulties are partly the result of the ways in which income is treated in the United States, and partly because there are many sources of income. Income is often both highly taxed and held in extreme confidentiality. Taxation provides strong incentives to underreport, and privacy makes income difficult to verify.

Although income is treated as one or perhaps two continuous variables in many economic and sociological studies, it can be a composite of many individual payments arising from several different sources. From the validation point of view, income streams are discontinuous. Even where a stream accrues continuously, as do wage earnings, for example, as it is actually paid out, it is quantized into separate payments. While the objective of a survey may be an aggregation into one or two variables, a validity study should concern itself with individual payments because many different aggregations are useful, and because individual streams will often be found to be of particular interest in subsequent analysis.

---

[1] See Halsey *et al.* (1977) for a detailed study of income reporting in the AFDC program.

Income streams are subject to taxation at several levels of government. Taxation is not uniform, however, but varies widely among income sources. In SIME/DIME different types of nonwage income were taxed at 100%, 50%, or at the earned income-tax rate, which varied from 80% to less than 50%. The federal personal income tax also varies by source. Furthermore, certain expenditures (deductions) can be offset against income with the result that some income becomes subject to reduced taxation or escapes taxation altogether. Civil and criminal penalties for underreporting to SIME/DIME and other agencies provide counterincentives for misreporting. The probability of being caught misreporting could be increased by an inconsistent report on an economic survey; thus, the incentives to underreport are extended outside the realm of tax and transfer agency reporting.

Because the person who reports income does so under a variety of incentives, and with a wide range of alternative actions, his decision is an economic one in the ordinary sense. He can decide whether or not to report the existence of an income stream and, if the decision is to report, how much to report. Income reports will differ, therefore, in ways that are consistent with the incentives whenever the opportunity to misreport arises. For this reason, direct source data (which is not without its own problems as a practical matter) are preferable to income tax forms and income reported to tax and transfer agencies for validation purposes.

SIME/DIME interviews were conducted at intervals, and the longer the interval the greater the memory span over which the respondent was requested to recall data. The longer the span, the more difficulty there was for the respondent in reporting data accurately. No doubt with sufficient incentives, respondents could recall income data over a period of years with high accuracy, but this would usually require considerable time and mental effort. Thus, income streams whose payments are infrequent, vary in size, or were terminated some time ago are likely to be reported with poor accuracy relative to income streams whose payments are current, closely spaced, or of equal size. Many nonwage income streams are of the former description while much wage and salary income is of the latter.

Ideally, one would want to validate income payment by payment, rather than in the aggregate, but such detail is expensive and time consuming. More importantly, some corroborative sources record data only in the aggregate, such as is done on federal personal income tax forms or in the unemployment compensation records. In this case, we are forced to aggregate in order to compare, and then we face a variety of difficulties.

Aggregated data are subject to timing error. A payment near an end of the aggregation period may be reported in different periods by the recipient and the source. The longer the period, of course, the smaller this type of error becomes.

Family structure can also be a problem. Some types of nonwage income, such as the AFDC grant, accrue to the family as a whole, not to any individual member. Thus, one must be careful to see that the families match person by person, so that the income accruing to the SIME/DIME family is comparable to the income reported by the corroborating source. The difficulty is exacerbated when comparing income reported by the SIME/DIME family with income reported to transfer agencies such as AFDC. Many AFDC families[2] do not contain the current male head, for example.

Another difficulty is that some public agencies do not retain data for long periods of time or, if they do, the data become increasingly difficult to gain access to as time passes. Regulations, definitions, and personnel undergo continual change, so that it becomes difficult to define what the older data mean. Data processing equipment evolves such that older data tapes may become unreadable, as are the older tapes for Unemployment Insurance and the Food Stamp program. Therefore, for these reasons as well as for the obvious reason that timely corrections cannot be made otherwise, a validity study should proceed concurrently with or very soon after the interview.

In the light of the foregoing discussion, we can make some statements about the expected results of the following study and of validity studies in general. First, the more current, more frequent, and more consistent in size the payments of an income stream, the more likely it is to be reported and the more accurate the report is likely to be. Because of taxation, income is likely to be underreported. The higher the taxation, the lower the likelihood of discovery; and the smaller the penalty, the more substantial the underreporting is likely to be. The penalties for underreporting to government agencies will parallel the SIME/DIME penalties, creating incentives for consistent underreporting. Nonwage income tends to be difficult to validate because its payments are often infrequent and of varying size. Furthermore, many types of nonwage income occur infrequently in the population, so large sample sizes are required to provide a reasonable degree of statistical reliability. Family composition changes can cause difficulties, and these difficulties increase with the length of the aggregation period. Different members of the family may report differently, because the incentives and opportunities to underreport vary among family members.

Since SIME/DIME data will inevitably be found to be in error, the objectives of the validity study should be to assess the size of the bias in the data, and the magnitude of its variance, not to state whether the data are "valid." In the following section we summarize the study conducted on the first 2 years of income data in Seattle and the first year of data in Denver.

---

[2] SIME/DIME families were defined on a functional basis for experimental purposes. The male head is included in the experimental family regardless of whether a legal marriage exists, if he fulfills that role. AFDC families, or support units, were defined by more legalistic or biological criteria. Thus, the current male head was often excluded from the AFDC family if he was not the biological father of the children.

COMPARISON OF SIME/DIME EXPERIMENTAL DATA
WITH PUBLIC AGENCY RECORDS[3]

In 1975 and 1976 we conducted a validity study of the income data collected during the first 2 years of SIME and the first year of DIME. The purpose of this study was to make an early comparison between SIME/DIME data and public agency records for a small sample, to detect gross inconsistencies which could merit further investigation. The study is summarized here, along with the later, more comprehensive study of wage income.

Measures of Income

Income was reported in the SIME/DIME experiment in a highly disaggregated form in two survey instruments: the periodic interview and the income report form (IRF). The periodic interview was administered to all experimental families at approximately 4-month intervals, the IRFs were filled out by the participants and mailed to the payments system by all NIT treatment families[4] either monthly or every 4 weeks. The periodic interview was the principal source of experimental data. The IRFs were primarily operational instruments. For comparison purposes, SIME/DIME data and public agency data were aggregated over time and income type to a common format. This format was a compromise between the length of the period and sample size. Longer periods reduce both the sample size and the errors due to discrepancies in timing of the transfer between public agencies and the sample families.

The public agency source for annual gross earnings is the Internal Revenue Service 1040 and 1040A forms. The public agency source for earnings covered by Unemployment Insurance is earnings reported by the employer to the agency as the basis for unemployment compensation eligibility. The AFDC grant is the cash amount received from AFDC. Unemployment benefit is the cash amount of unemployment compensation received. The food stamp benefit is the difference between the face value of food stamps and their purchase price. Public housing rent is the amount of rent paid by families living in public housing.

Sample Selection

A 10% random sample of originally enrolled families stratified by race and headship, preexperimental normal income, and NIT treatment, was selected from the set of families remaining intact through January 1, 1973 in Seattle

---

[3] For a more detailed discussion of the analysis in this section see Halsey *et al.* (1976).

[4] A small group of control families in Denver filled out IRFs as IRF control families. None of these were included in the validation study.

and in Denver. In this context, intact meant that the family had not changed type of headship either by the breakup of a dual-headed family or by the marriage of a single family head. The size of the Seattle 10% sample was 163 families. The size of the Denver 10% sample was 279 families. The sample sizes reflect the overall size of the experiment, DIME being about half again as large as SIME due to the inclusion of a Chicano group, and the additional 1 year's attrition SIME.

The three-way NIT treatment sample consisted of the subset for whom data was available from three sources: the periodic interview, the IRF, and the public agency source. A three-way data set could not be constructed for controls because most of them did not fill out IRFs. Two-way subsamples were, thus, constructed for NIT treatment families and control families separately, dropping the IRF data requirement. Means and standard deviations were recorded, along with the number of cases excluded and the reason for exclusion.

The three-way sample is small for statistical analysis of many of the income variables. The major reason is the large number of families with zero wage and salary income reported on all instruments. A contributing factor early in the experiment was the nonexistence of IRF data prior to enrollment. Periodic interview data were collected retrospectively from 1970 forward in both sites but IRF data began with the month of enrollment. Enrollment was spread over the first year or so of the experiment, 1971 in Seattle and 1972 in Denver. This caused the greatest reduction in the sample in the annual gross earning category, where a single period of missing IRF data was sufficient to exclude the family record for that year. Since public housing rent did not appear on the IRF, this expense did not appear in the three-way sample statistics.

The two-way subsample sizes are about the same as the three-way sample sizes except for the annual gross earnings category in the start-up years. After start-up, the size more than doubles. The two-way control family subsample is about the same size as the two-way NIT group.

The fractions of the entire 10% sample (163 Seattle families and 279 Denver families) that are useful for validation purpose are relatively small, because the fractions receiving income in any category are small. More families receive wage or salary income than nonwage income. However, the data are not clustered, but cover a wide range. The standard deviation computed over the positive observations is as large as the mean for most of the categories, and the means are not small. The food stamp data, and to some extent, the public housing data exhibit larger mean amounts reported to the periodic interviews than are found in the public agency records. If this is due to overreporting, it implies irrational behavior on the part of NIT treatment families in the case of food stamps, since SIME/ DIME taxed food stamp benefits at 100%. Overreporting rent in public housing would, in contrast, be rational for NIT families, since rent increases are reimbursed 100%. Controls, however, who did not face the same incentives, exhibited reporting differences to about the same degree as the NIT treatment families. This suggests that the problem lay with missing data in the public agency records.

Subsequent investigation of the Food Stamp program records in Seattle and Denver tended to confirm this supposition.

Analysis of Wage Income

Since the reports of income do differ among our three sources we wished to analyze these differences. Biased reporting on either of the SIME/DIME surveys would have implications for the analysis of experimental impacts. Large variations in the differences among the various reports, even if the bias is small, would also need to be taken account of in the impact analysis. Since the purpose of this study was to analyze the SIME/DIME data, our null hypothesis was that the public agency data were correct. Within the experimental data, the interview data were less affected by any direct incentive to misreport, so we adopted them as the standard of comparison.

The study's t-statistics for the difference between pairs of reports, and the correlation between reports, are shown in Table 2.1 for the subsamples described above. These subsamples contain only records in which at least one observation is positive. These tests, of course, address the question of differential reporting accuracy, not absolute reporting accuracy. A family that misreports consistently will still have shown no difference among reports. The earnings covered by Unemployment Insurance are employer reported, however, and are accurate within the constraints of employer misreporting, the accuracy with which records are kept by the Unemployment Insurance Agency, and our success in locating the proper records. These errors are thought to be small in our sample, so the differences between Unemployment Insurance income and SIME/DIME income are considered to be good measures of misreporting in the absolute.

The small mean differences which we find are overwhelmingly in the expected directions. That is, all but one of the t-statistics are negative, indicating underreporting to SIME/DIME relative to the public agency source, or underreporting on the IRF relative to the periodic interview. The differences are statistically significant in 9 of the 30 comparisons, with the largest and most significant differences occurring between the IRF and the public agency reports. These are different at the 95% confidence level in every case except for the Denver 1972 Unemployment Insurance/IRF difference. These mean differences range between —$46 and —$307. As fractions of the mean public-agency reported income they range between —3.47% and —8.55%. The periodic-interview-public-agency differences range between —.32% and —6.55%. The periodic-interview-IRF differences range between +.26% and —3.24%. Relative to the public agency data the SIME/DIME data appear to be quite consistently reported in the mean. Periodic interview data are better than the IRF data, and the IRF and periodic interview data

Table 2.1
Wage Earnings, t-Tests, and Correlation Coefficients

Income type	Sample type	Difference tested[a]	Sample size	t-Statistic	Absolute mean difference	Mean of public source	Proportional mean difference[b]	Standard error	Correlation coefficient
Seattle 1971									
Gross earnings (annual)	3-way NIT	IRF-INT	25	-.94	-126	5643	-2.23%	135	.973
		IRF-PA	25	-2.51*	-235	5643	-4.16%	94	.991
		INT-PA	25	-.90	-109	5643	-1.93%	121	.983
	2-way NIT	INT-PA	57	-.36	-45	6241	-0.72%	125	.963
	2-way control	INT-PA	54	-.48	-91	5809	-1.57%	190	.915
Earnings covered by Unemployment Insurance (quarterly)	3-way NIT	IRF-INT	40	.10	5	1955	0.26%	51	.971
		IRF-PA	40	-4.14**	-118	1955	-6.04%	28	.991
		INT-PA	40	-2.60*	-123	1955	-6.29%	47	.976
	2-way NIT	INT-PA	45	-1.52	-51	1579	-3.23%	34	.976
	2-way control	INT-PA	44	-.51	-18	1436	-1.25%	34	.962
Seattle 1972									
Gross earnings (annual)	3-way NIT	IRF-INT	43	-1.63	-213	7274	-2.93%	131	.968
		IRF-PA	43	-2.72**	-307	7274	-4.22%	113	.977
		INT-PA	43	-.66	-94	7274	-1.29%	144	.962
	2-way NIT	INT-PA	47	-.82	-111	7407	-1.49%	136	.964
	2-way control	INT-PA	45	-.12	-23	7229	-0.32%	182	.933
Earnings covered by Unemployment Insurance (quarterly)	3-way NIT	IRF-INT	53	-2.23*	-47	1450	-3.24%	21	.989
		IRF-PA	53	-3.61**	-124	1450	-8.55%	34	.972
		INT-PA	53	-1.85	-77	1450	-5.31%	42	.958
	2-way NIT	INT-PA	53	-2.00	-81	1471	-5.51%	41	.961
	2-way control	INT-PA	43	-2.39*	-84	1610	-5.22%	35	.966

Denver 1972

Gross earnings (annual)	3-way NIT	IRF-INT	44	-1.37	-144	6740	-2.14%	105	.986
		IRF-PA	44	-2.94**	-295	6740	-4.38%	100	.986
		INT-PA	44	-1.11	-151	6740	-2.24%	136	.977
	2-way NIT	INT-PA	107	-2.00*	-196	6915	-2.83%	98	.970
	2-way control	INT-PA	75	-1.49	-214	7127	-3.00%	144	.931
Earnings covered by Unemployment Insurance (quarterly)	3-way NIT	IRF-INT	117	-.08	-2	1324	-.15%	27	.963
		IRF-PA	117	-1.57	-46	1324	-3.47%	29	.956
		INT-PA	117	-1.12	-43	1324	-3.25%	39	.922
	2-way NIT	INT-PA	119	-1.15	-35	1308	-2.68%	30	.947
	2-way control	INT-PA	70	-1.78	-100	1527	-6.55%	56	.893

Note: Footnotes apply to Tables 2.1-2.5.

[a] IRF = SIME/DIME income report forms; INT = SIME/DIME periodic interview; PA = public agency source.

[b] This is expressed as a percentage of the public source mean.

*Significantly different from 0 at the 95% level of confidence.

**Significantly different from 0 at the 99% level of confidence.

are quite consistent with each other. There is no pattern among the t-statistics, the correlation coefficients, or the mean differences, which suggests that the SIME/DIME control sample reporting differs from that of the NIT treatment sample.

LARGE SAMPLE WAGE INCOME REPORTING

After the June 1976 validity study was completed, a file containing wage income from Federal Individual Income Tax returns and wage income from the SIME/DIME periodic interviews was constructed. The larger sample contains 1138 and 870 observation records from Seattle for 1971 and 1972, respectively, and 1140 records from Denver for 1972. The number of records decreases for Seattle in 1972 because of the requirement that every record contain complete income data from both the federal income tax file and the SIME/DIME data file. The SIME/DIME file size decreases over time because for this study it follows only originally enrolled families. As families leave the experiments, divorce or marry, the originally enrolled sample is reduced in size. In Seattle, 85% of the IRS observations are matched with job file records in 1971 and 68% are matched in 1972. Many fewer matches occur in Denver because the DIME data file used here did not contain data for approximately one-third of the sample that was classified as Chicano. A 100% match is not expected because some people have incomes below the Federal Individual Income Tax filing threshold.

Earnings Comparisons

Scattergrams of earnings reported to the IRS and to SIME/DIME are shown in Figures 2.1a-c. The earnings reported to IRS are wage and salary earnings recorded on Line 9 of the 1040 form. The earnings reported in the SIME and DIME periodic interviews are aggregated over the calendar year. If earnings were accurately or consistently reported to both agencies, then all data points on the scattergrams would fall on the 45° line. The slopes of the regression lines obtained by regressing the SIME/DIME earnings on the IRS earnings are all statistically significantly less than 1.0: Seattle 1971, .906; Seattle 1972, .899; and Denver 1972, .877; and the constant terms are all positive. This is probably the result of error in the independent variable (IRS earnings). More important than the slopes of the regression lines are the estimated standard errors in the DIME earnings. These are large, ranging between $1521 and $1752.

Table 2.2 gives t-statistics and correlation coefficients for the whole sample corresponding to those calculated for the much smaller sample used in the validity study. The mean differences are of the same sign, and approximately the same magnitude as for the smaller sample, but because of the larger sample size the estimates of the standard errors are smaller and most of the t-statistics are

Table 2.2
Wage Earnings, t-Tests, and Correlation Coefficients

Sample type	Difference tested[a]	Sample size	t-statistic	Absolute mean difference	Mean of public source	Proportional mean difference[b]	Standard error	Correlation coefficient
Seattle 1971								
Combined	INT-PA	1105	−5.83**	−282.83	7206.69	−3.92%	48.49	.906
Controls	INT-PA	518	−3.63***	−253.50	7439.80	−3.41%	69.76	.906
NIT	INT-PA	587	−4.58***	−308.71	7000.99	−4.41%	67.45	.906
Seattle 1972								
Combined	INT-PA	856	−4.92**	−302.47	8221.32	−3.68%	61.47	.902
Controls	INT-PA	412	−2.71***	−220.29	8508.90	−2.59%	81.30	.912
NIT	INT-PA	444	−4.15**	−378.72	7954.46	−4.76%	91.35	.892
Denver 1972								
Combined	INT-PA	1109	−2.60**	−125.36	7316.15	−1.71%	48.24	.902
Controls	INT-PA	277	−1.33	−126.61	7667.85	−1.65%	95.31	.908
NIT	INT-PA	832	−2.23**	−124.94	7199.06	−1.74%	55.95	.900

43

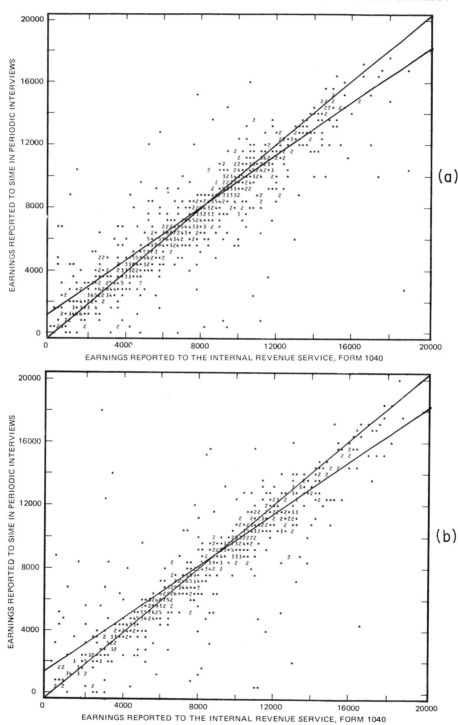

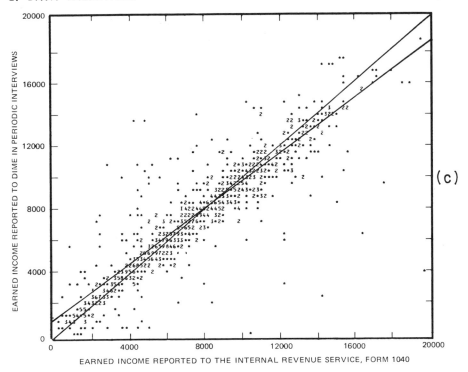

Figure 2.1 Comparisons of earned income: (a) Seattle 1971; (b) Seattle 1972; (c) Denver 1972.

now significantly different from zero at the 99% confidence level. With the larger sample we find statistically significant underreporting on the Periodic Interviews, as expected, but the magnitude, which is on the order of $100 to $300 per year, is probably not large enough to be of behavioral significance.

Analysis of Nonwage Income

The reporting of nonwage income from three income sources (AFDC, Unemployment Insurance, and the Food Stamp program) and one expense source (rent in public housing) is discussed here. In the SIME/DIME experiments, this nonwage income is taxed 100% and changes in the rent in public housing are reimbursed 100%. Because of these taxation incentives, we expect to see the nonwage income underreported and the rent overreported on the IRF and to a lesser degree on the periodic interview, relative to the public agency records. The public agencies are the sources of grant, benefit, and rent amounts, so the issue of underreporting to the public agency does not arise as it does for income data from these agencies or from the IRS.

All data were aggregated into calendar quarters for analysis purposes, and Student's t-statistics of the difference in reports, similar to those for wage income, were constructed. The t-statistics are reported on Tables 2.3, 2.4, and 2.5 for Seattle 1971, Seattle 1972, and Denver 1972, respectively. Generally speaking, the differences are much larger as a fraction of mean income or expense than was found for wage income, and in all cases where the t-statistic is statistically significant, the differences are in the expected direction. The sole exception is the food stamp benefit for Seattle 1971, which is discussed below.

The AFDC grant was underreported to SIME by relatively large amounts. As a fraction of the mean AFDC grant, the underreporting ranges from 19% to 33% in 1971 and from 26% to 31% in 1972. The differences are statistically significant in 1971 but, except for one case, not in 1972. The situation is different in Denver. In spite of larger sample sizes, the reporting difference ranges from +4% to −10% and none of the t-statistics are significantly different from zero. Both the mean differences and their standard errors are much smaller in Denver than in Seattle, indicating more accurate reporting in Denver. This was to be expected, since the DIME experiment started a year later and a strong effort was made to avoid difficulties which had become apparent in SIME.

The IRF-interview differences are never statistically significant in either site, but the mean difference drops dramatically between 1971 and 1972 in Seattle. This may indicate the overcoming of start-up difficulties. Evidently AFDC grants are reported relatively consistently to the experiment. The same consistency is generally observed for unemployment benefits and food stamp benefits. No IRF-interview comparison was made for rent in public housing, since rent was not reported on the IRF.

Unemployment benefits appear to have been underreported in Seattle, while the Denver sample size was too small to be useful.[5] Mean underreporting to SIME ranged between 15% and 45%. In 1971, the underreporting of NIT families to the experiment was statistically significant, but controls' underreporting was not. In 1972, NIT families' underreporting just drops below statistical significance, while controls overreport in the mean but not significantly so.

Food stamp benefits at first appeared to be overreported to the experiment by large amounts but were relatively consistently reported between the experimental instruments. Investigation into the Food Stamp program records indicated that they were in such poor condition that many records seem to have been lost entirely. The statistics were then reconstructed excluding cases in which the Food Stamp program record indicated zero face value of food stamps purchased. In this restricted sample, we find the expected indicators of accurate or underre-

---

[5] Recall that the early 1970s was a period of high unemployment in Seattle due to the Boeing cutbacks, while Denver was booming. In fact, the high unemployment in Seattle was a main reason for the opening of a second site in Denver.

porting; the overreporting disappears. In the 1972 results, the mean differences are negative and significant, ranging between 21% and 47% in Seattle and 14% and 32% in Denver. These statistics are presented below the first sets of results in Table 2.3-2.5.

The analysis of rent in public housing reports indicates a smaller tendency toward overreporting. Although overreporting was the expected response to the experimental incentive for NIT treatment families, the quality of the public housing data was again suspect, so the analysis was done for the sample for whom the public housing authorities reported positive rent paid. In the restricted sample, none of the t-statistics are significant, and the mean differences are small, though still positive, for the NIT treatment families in Seattle. In Denver, the differences, while never statistically different from zero, switch from positive to negative.

While most of the t-statistics are not significant for nonwage income, they are of the expected sign and in the expected range and we can draw several implications from this analysis. First, although the original samples were 163 in Seattle and 279 in Denver, the frequency of nonwage income was very low, so that the analysis samples are very much smaller than the original frame. Many more families would have had to be screened to end up with an analysis sample of sufficient size to produce statistically significant results, say 100-200 observations. Second, the variation in the difference among reports is a larger fraction of nonwage income than it is of wage income; nonwage income is poorly reported relative to wage income, so larger samples are needed for nonwage income if a given minimum accuracy of estimate is to be obtained. Third, public agency sources must be handled with care. Even in cases where the public agency is the direct source of the data, as for income transfers, the data must be carefully checked for accuracy and completeness.

CONCLUSIONS

First, we draw conclusions specific to SIME/DIME, then follow with suggestions of a more general nature. Earned income reported to the experiment was underreported in amounts between $100 and $300 per year relative to income reported to public agencies. This amounts to less than 5% of mean income. Although the underreporting is statistically significant, it is not large enough to be significant in terms of affecting economic behavior. The variance in the error in annual earned income reported to SIME/DIME is on the order of $1000 and, somewhat surprisingly, this variance appears to be constant rather than proportional to income. The wide variance in reported income is large enough to cause behaviorally significant errors in parameter estimates in ordinary least squares re-

Table 2.3
Seattle 1971 Nonwage Income and Expenses

Income type	Sample type	Difference tested[a]	Sample size	t-statistic	Absolute mean difference	Mean of public source	Proportional mean difference[b]	Standard error	Correlation coefficient
AFDC grant (quarterly)	3-way NIT	IRF-INT	22	1.41	61	452	13.50%	44	.775
		IRF-PA	22	-2.22*	-86	452	-19.03%	39	.679
		INT-PA	22	-2.71**	-147	452	-32.52%	54	.615
	2-way NIT	INT-PA	27	-2.68*	-105	441	-23.81%	39	.694
	2-way control	INT-PA	33	-3.10**	-135	490	-27.55%	44	.555
Unemployment benefits (quarterly)	3-way NIT	IRF-INT	16	-.23	-14	422	-3.32%	63	.528
		IRF-PA	16	-2.78**	-140	422	-33.18%	50	.699
		INT-PA	16	-1.89	-126	422	-29.86%	67	.421
	2-way NIT	INT-PA	24	-2.53*	-158	506	-31.23%	62	.296
	2-way control	INT-PA	22	-1.34	-76	498	-15.26%	57	.565
Food stamps net benefit (quarterly)	3-way NIT	IRF-INT	26	.34	2	43	4.65%	6	.937
		IRF-PA	26	2.29*	37	43	86.05%	16	.326
		INT-PA	26	2.14*	35	43	81.40%	17	.322
	2-way NIT	INT-PA	39	3.80**	58	39	148.72%	15	.056
	2-way control	INT-PA	40	2.30*	28	59	47.46%	12	.073

Food stamps net benefit excluding cases where PA reported 0 (quarterly)	3-way NIT	IRF-INT	17	1.55	5	72	6.94%	3	.982
		IRF-PA	17	.55	3	72	4.17%	6	.928
		INT-PA	17	-.21	-2	72	-2.78%	7	.897
	2-way NIT	INT-PA	24	.52	7	76	9.21%	13	.555
	2-way control	INT-PA	26	-1.90	-17	95	-17.89%	9	.589
Public housing expense (annual)	2-way NIT	INT-PA	17	1.78	121	406	29.80%	68	.575
	2-way control	INT-PA	20	1.10	154	464	33.19%	140	-.185
Public housing expense excluding cases where PA reported 0 (annual)	2-way NIT	INT-PA	14	.70	31	493	6.29%	45	.836
	2-way control	INT-PA	15	-1.00	-115	618	-18.61%	114	.259

Table 2.4
Seattle 1972 Nonwage Income and Expenses

Income type	Sample type	Difference tested[a]	Sample size	t-statistic	Absolute mean difference	Mean of public source	Proportional mean difference[b]	Standard error	Correlation coefficient
AFDC grant (quarterly)	3-way NIT	IRF-INT	10	-.32	-23	448	-5.13%	70	.731
		IRF-PA	10	-1.49	-139	448	-31.03%	93	.381
		INT-PA	10	-1.45	-117	448	-26.12%	80	.590
	2-way NIT	INT-PA	9	-1.46	-130	498	-26.10%	89	.493
	2-way control	INT-PA	26	-3.03**	-150	561	-26.74%	50	.687
Unemployment benefits (quarterly)	3-way NIT	IRF-INT	15	.09	4	304	1.32%	50	.541
		IRF-PA	15	-2.07*	-132	304	-43.42%	64	.277
		INT-PA	15	-1.80	-136	304	-44.74%	76	.079
	2-way NIT	INT-PA	15	-1.80	-136	304	-44.74%	76	.079
	2-way control	INT-PA	17	1.34	99	188	52.66%	74	.284
Food stamps (quarterly) net benefit (quarterly)	3-way NIT	IRF-INT	22	1.28	12	73	16.44%	9	.904
		IRF-PA	22	.28	8	73	10.96%	28	-.091
		INT-PA	22	-.16	-4	73	-5.48%	25	.054
	2-way NIT	INT-PA	21	-.08	-2	75	-2.67%	26	-.007
	2-way control	INT-PA	34	1.33	18	65	27.69%	13	.154

Food stamps net benefit excluding cases where PA reported 0 (quarterly)	3-way NIT	IRF-INT	16	.53	2	101	1.98%	5	.966
		IRF-PA	16	-2.52*	-44	101	-43.56%	18	.410
		INT-PA	16	-2.64%	-47	101	-46.53%	18	.463
	2-way NIT	INT-PA	16	-2.53*	-45	99	-45.45%	18	.441
	2-way control	INT-PA	25	-2.26*	-20	92	-21.74%	9	.638
Public housing expense (annual)	2-way NIT	INT-PA	17	2.37*	260	286	90.91%	110	.158
	2-way control	INT-PA	24	.74	82	464	17.67%	112	.161
Public housing expense (excluding cases where PA reported 0 (annual))	2-way NIT	INT-PA	12	.45	37	405	9.14%	81	.675
	2-way control	INT-PA	17	-.63	-81	655	-12.37%	127	.137

Table 2.5
Denver 1972 Nonwage Income and Expenses

Income type	Sample type	Difference tested[a]	Sample size	t-statistic	Absolute mean difference	Mean of public source	Proportional mean difference[b]	Standard error	Correlation coefficient
AFDC grant (quarterly)	3-way NIT	IRF-INT	61	1.12	17	408	4.17%	16	.867
		IRF-PA	61	.24	7	408	1.72%	27	.594
		INT-PA	61	-.37	-11	408	-2.70%	29	.563
	2-way NIT	INT-PA	64	-.29	-9	412	-2.18%	30	.489
	2-way control	INT-PA	37	-.91	-42	430	-9.77%	46	.434
Unemployment benefits (quarterly)	3-way NIT	IRF-INT	4	-1.13	-80	141	-56.74%	71	.905
		IRF-PA	4	.05	6	141	4.26%	115	-.161
		INT-PA	4	.61	85	141	60.28%	139	.212
	2-way NIT	INT-PA	6	1.41	217	94	230.85%	153	-.118
	2-way control	INT-PA	2	0	285	0	—	0	0
Food stamps net benefit (quarterly)	3-way NIT	IRF-INT	59	.40	3	85	3.53%	6	.750
		IRF-PA	59	1.58	17	85	20.00%	11	.275
		INT-PA	59	1.56	14	85	16.47%	9	.434
	2-way NIT	INT-PA	61	1.67	15	84	17.86%	9	.377
	2-way control	INT-PA	40	-2.33*	-29	119	-24.37%	12	.376

Food stamps net benefit excluding cases where PA reported 0 (quarterly)	3-way NIT	IRF-INT	47	.15	1	116	0.86%	6	.840
		IRF-PA	47	-2.15*	-16	116	-13.79%	8	.671
		INT-PA	47	-2.40*	-17	116	-14.66%	7	.726
	2-way NIT	INT-PA	50	-2.81*	-18	112	-16.07%	6	.748
	2-way control	INT-PA	38	-3.94**	-41	128	-32.03%	10	.582
Public housing expense (annual)	2-way NIT	INT-PA	23	1.53	147	451	32.59%	96	.355
	2-way control	INT-PA	9	.80	164	352	46.59%	205	-.197
Public housing expense excluding cases where PA reported 0 (annual)	2-way NIT	INT-PA	14	-.95	-90	740	-12.16%	95	.440
	2-way control	INT-PA	5	-.49	-135	634	-21.29%	274	-.344

gressions, so the analyst must either use care in interpreting such estimates, or use more sophisticated methods.

Nonwage income was reported with a higher variance, as a proportion of mean nonwage income, than earned income. This finding is in agreement with the discussion in the second section about differential problems of recall.

The most important conclusion of the SIME/DIME small sample validity study conducted on early experimental data is that while the bias in reported income is small, the variance is relatively large. Analyses which attempt to utilize SIME/DIME income as an independent variable must take this into account. The results of the small sample validity study are generally confirmed by the large sample income study. The larger sample allows us to draw stronger statistical inferences, however. Mean differences between reported and public source income, which are not statistically significant at conventional confidence levels tend to become so in the larger sample and some of the anomalous effects in the 1972 Denver small sample estimates for controls disappear in the larger sample.

Some general conclusions that we draw from these studies are the following: First the *useful* sample size in a validity study is drastically reduced from the frame size because of the low frequency of positive income streams. This difficulty is exacerbated by the decision to verify income stream by stream rather than in the aggregate, but such disaggregation is necessary if the income streams are to be of use separately. Nonwage income is particularly difficult to validate because some of it tends to accrue in sporadic payments, which are difficult (costly) for the respondent to recall and are relatively easily hidden. Nonreporting is difficult to detect because the frequency of most streams is small in the population. The resulting small samples and large variance made it difficult to go beyond qualitative statements about the accuracy of nonwage income reporting in our 10% sample study. These results highlight the fact that a validation study should be conducted as concurrently as possible with the survey, because the accuracy, ease of access, and even the availability of corroborative sources degrades over time. A 1-year lag is probably the most that should be tolerated.

Another conclusion is that differences in family structure between the family as defined for the survey and the family as defined by each public tax or transfer agency is likely to cause difficulty. Much of the data from public sources is already in aggregate form, aggregated over family members and over time. Both aggregations can cause difficulty in comparisons with survey data.

A third conclusion is that income occupies a special position in economic activity, because it is taxed and because it is so widely held in confidence. As a result, income reporting is a behavioral act, subject to economic incentives. The incentives vary with different streams of income, and as the taxation, penalty, and probability of discovery vary, so does the degree of misreporting. The incentives are overwhelming in the direction of income underreporting. Some effort should go toward redressing this imbalance. Since it is much easier to invalidate overreported income than to discover unreported income streams, an overcorrection of the incentive structures would not be as serious as an equal incentive to underreport. In a sense, data validation is merely an accounting activity, but as usual, an understanding of the underlying process that generates the data can aid in directing effort so as to maximize the information gained for a given cost.

REFERENCES

Gutmann, Peter M. "The Subterranean Economy." *Financial Analysts Journal*, November/December 1977.

Halsey, Harlan; Murarka, Bina; and Speigelman, Robert G. "The Seattle and Denver Validation Study." Unpublished SIME/DIME Research Memorandum, SRI International, June 1976.

Halsey, Harlan; Kurz, Mordecai; and Waksberg, Arlene. "The Reporting of Income to Welfare: A Study in the Accuracy of Income Reporting." Research Memorandum No. 42, The Center for the Study of Welfare Policy, SRI International, August 1977.

Hill, Christian G. ". . . Waitresses . . . ." *The Wall Street Journal*, April 5, 1978, p. 1.

Malabre, Alfred Jr. "The Outlook." *The Wall Street Journal*, March 20, 1978, p. 1.

Parkinson, C. Northcote. *The Law and the Profits*, Boston: Houghton Mifflin, 1960.

PART 11

EXPERIMENTAL EFFECTS ON LABOR SUPPLY

CHAPTER 3

Labor Supply Response of Family Heads and Implications for a National Program

PHILIP K. ROBINS

INTRODUCTION

One of the primary purposes of conducting the Seattle/Denver experiments is to provide information for the design of a national income-maintenance program. Knowledge of the labor supply effects of the experiments is critical because changes in labor supply directly affect program costs and may also alter the structure of the labor force in the United States. Failure to take labor supply adjustments into account when designing a national program may result in incorrect evaluations of the merits of competing proposals.

The feasibility and desirability of any national income-maintenance program depends on its social and economic costs and its ability to satisfy three often contradictory goals. These goals are: (*a*) desirable social and economic incentives, (*b*) an equitable benefit structure, and (*c*) adequate minimum benefits. The cost of such a program, and the importance of the social and economic incentives implicit in its design, depend critically on the effects it may have on individuals' behavior.

In order to make use of the information provided by experimental data in the design of a national program, it is necessary to develop a methodology for extrapolating the experimental results to a national population. In this chapter, we use early findings for heads of families in SIME/DIME to predict nationwide labor supply effects and costs of six alternative NIT programs. These six programs are selected for study because they are within the range of alternatives that appear most likely to be considered for implementation. The methodology used in this chapter consists of estimating the parameters of a labor-supply response function using SIME/DIME data and then simulating the replacement of current transfer programs with an NIT. The simulation uses a national data base, the

59

A GUARANTEED ANNUAL INCOME:
EVIDENCE FROM A SOCIAL EXPERIMENT

March 1974 Current Population Survey (CPS), and applies the experimental response function to this national sample.

The remainder of this chapter is organized as follows. The next section describes the model used to estimate labor supply effects of family heads in the SIME/DIME sample. Following is a discussion of the implications of this model for the labor supply effects and costs of alternative NIT programs at the national level. The final section gives a summary of the findings and discusses policy implications of the results.

A MODEL OF THE LABOR SUPPLY
RESPONSE TO SIME/DIME

An NIT increases the disposable income of all families with gross incomes below the tax breakeven level. (Families with gross income below the tax breakeven level are called program participants.) Economic theory predicts that an increase in income that is not work related (usually termed nonwage income) will induce an individual to reduce the amount of time spent working. As a result of this reduced labor supply, the amount of time spent in leisure activities or work in the home increases. The change in labor supply caused by an increase in nonwage income is called the income effect. In the income-maintenance experiments, nonwage income is increased by the guarantee (or support) level of the program.

In addition to raising the disposable income of participating families, an NIT also imposes a tax rate that is usually higher than the tax rates families would face in the absence of the program.[1] Economic theory predicts that, holding disposable income constant, an increase in the tax rate will induce a reduction in labor supply because of a decrease in the net wage rate, which is a measure of the net economic return from working additional hours.[2] The change in labor supply caused by an increase in the net wage rate (holding disposable income constant) is called the substitution effect.

In estimating the labor supply effects of SIME/DIME, a model is specified that identifies income and substitution effects. Identification of income and substitution effects is important because it enables comparison of the effects of different guarantee levels and tax rates, two of the parameters of an NIT that are under the control of policymakers.

---

[1] For families that would receive public transfers (such as AFDC) in the absence of an NIT, the tax rate may actually be reduced under the NIT.

[2] If w is the gross (before tax) wage rate, t_e is the NIT tax rate, and t_p is the pre-NIT tax rate, the change in the net wage rate caused by the NIT is given by $-w(t_e - t_p)$.

Variables in the Model and the Sample Used

For the analysis of SIME/DIME data, we calculate for each family head the change in disposable income that would occur from the NIT treatment to which the family was assigned if there were no change in labor supply. We also calculate the change in the net wage rate. The change in disposable income is calculated on the basis of earnings and nonwage income in the year prior to enrollment in the experiment[3] and the change in the net wage rate is calculated as the product of a predicted preexperimental wage rate and the difference between the experimental and preexperimental tax rates. The preexperimental tax rates are derived in accordance with the regulations of any tax and transfer programs the family participated in prior to the experiments. For details of the calculations, see Keeley *et al.* (1978a).

Many families enrolled in the experiments were above the breakeven level at enrollment. For these families, the values of the change in disposable income and the change in the net wage rate are set at zero. Even though these values are zero, however, some of the families may respond to the experiment. To measure the response of families above the breakeven level, we define three variables that capture the location of the family relative to the breakeven level. These three variables combine the probability of going below the breakeven level with the income and wage changes that would result if such a movement were to occur. Separate estimates of the above and below breakeven parameters are made for husbands, wives, and single female heads of families. A dummy variable is included to control for differences in response for persons on the declining tax rate treatments. Three dummy variables are also included to capture the effects of the manpower treatments.[4]

The dependent variables are (*a*) hours of work in the second year of the experiment and (*b*) length of spells of employment and nonemployment[5] during the first 4 years of the experiments (3 years of data are used for families on the 3-year financial treatments). The hours of work analysis includes black and white originally enrolled heads of families (Chicanos excluded) for whom data were available for the entire first 2 years of the experiment. The spell analysis includes black and white originally enrolled heads of families, with no change in marital status before the fourth year of the experiments. For the hours of work analysis

---

[3] This change in disposable income calculated on the basis of preprogram labor supply is equal to the NIT payment received at enrollment.

[4] In addition to the experimental variables, the empirical model also includes several nonexperimental variables to account for the assignment process and other determinants of labor supply (age, family structure, etc.). These variables are described by Keeley *et al.* (1978a) and Robins *et al.* (scheduled for publication 1980).

[5] Nonemployment spells consist of time spent unemployed as well as time spent out of the labor force.

this produced a sample of 1592 husbands, 1698 wives, and 1358 single female heads. For the spell analysis the sample was 2157 husbands, 2119 wives, and 1611 female heads.

Results

The estimated effects of the NIT treatments on hours of work for the SIME/ DIME sample are presented in Table 3.1. (See Keeley *et al.*, 1978b, for estimates of the effects of the manpower treatments and the nonexperimental variables.) For families below the breakeven level the income effects are negative and statistically significant for wives and female heads of families and the substitution effects are positive and statistically significant for all three groups. Because the

Table 3.1

Estimated Effects of SIME/DIME NIT Treatments on Annual Hours of Work
(Standard Errors in Parentheses)

	Husbands	Wives	Single female heads
Below breakeven level			
Income effect (per $1000)	− 34	−143**	−101**
	(27)	(44)	(39)
Substitution effect	83**	168*	126*
(per dollar per hour)	(37)	(91)	(66)
Above breakeven level			
Constant effect	− 13	−431*	−345
	(175)	(256)	(291)
Effect of breakeven level	− 6	8	73
(per $1000)	(21)	(30)	(65)
Effect of earnings above	12	48	35
breakeven level (per $1000)	(27)	(42)	(56)
Declining tax rate treatments	− 86**	120	22
	(48)	(78)	(73)
Estimated NIT effects for the average working individual in SIME/DIME below the breakeven level and not on declining tax rate treatments			
Income effect	− 47	−199***	−117**
	(37)	(62)	(46)
Substitution effect	− 56**	− 64*	− 59*
	(25)	(35)	(31)
Total effect	−103***	−263***	−176***
	(33)	(55)	(44)
Percentage effect	− 5%	− 22%	− 11%

*p < .10.
**p < .05.
***p < .01.

NIT experiment raises income and lowers the net wage rate, these estimated income and substitution effects imply an unambiguous negative impact of the experiment on annual hours of work. For the average working individual in the SIME/DIME sample below the breakeven level, and not on declining tax rate treatments, the labor supply effects are −103 hours per year for husbands, −263 hours per year for wives, and −176 hours per year for single female heads. These are percentage effects of −5% for husbands, −22% for wives, and −11% for single female heads of families. For men, the total response is about equally divided between the income and substitution effects; for women, most of the response is due to the income effect. We performed tests to determine whether or not the estimated income and substitution effects differed by race (black, white), site (Seattle, Denver), and experimental duration (3-year, 5-year). The test results suggested that they do not.

For families above the breakeven level, only wives appear to be responding significantly to the experiments. Their response declines in absolute value with distance from the breakeven level. Husbands on the declining tax rate treatments respond substantially more than husbands on constant tax rate treatments.

In addition to causing a reduction in annual hours of work for persons employed, the experiment also reduces the probability of working. (See Robins *et al.*, forthcoming, for a detailed analysis of the effects of SIME/DIME on the probability of working.) The probability of working can be reduced either by lengthening the period of time spent out of work or by shortening the period of time spent working.

Table 3.2 presents estimates of the effects of the experiments on the probability of working and on the length of spells of employment and nonemployment. For husbands, there is a moderate reduction of 5 percentage points in the probability of working, which stems from both shorter periods of time spent working and longer periods of time spent not working. Thus, husbands in the experimental group tend to remain out of work for longer periods of time and tend to work for shorter periods of time than husbands in the control group.

Wives and female heads of families exhibit a somewhat larger reduction in the probability of employment than husbands. The reduction for women stems almost entirely from longer periods of time spent not employed, although single female heads also significantly reduce their length of time employed. One implication of these results is that women in the experimental group who were not employed prior to the experiments were much less likely to seek employment during the experiments than women in the control group, while women in the experimental group who were employed prior to the experiments were only slightly more likely to leave employment than women in the control group. We have not yet analyzed how women spent this additional time out of work. Because most women in SIME/DIME have young children, it is likely that a large part of the additional time was spent in productive activities in the home (such as child rearing), rather than in active job search.

Table 3.2
Effects of SIME/DIME NIT Treatments on Probability of Working and on
Length of Periods of Employment and Nonemployment
(Standard Errors in Parentheses)

	Husbands	Wives	Female heads
Probability of working in the absence of the experiment	.78	.32	.52
NIT treatment effect	−.05*** (.01)	−.08*** (.02)	−.11*** (.02)
Source of the NIT treatment effect			
Percentage change in the length of time spent working	−13%*** (.05)	−8% (.05)	−15%** (.06)
Percentage change in the length of time spent not working	27%*** (.06)	42%*** (.07)	56%*** (.09)

***$p < .01$.
**$p < .05$.

IMPLICATIONS OF THE ESTIMATED NIT EFFECTS
FOR A NATIONAL PROGRAM

The estimated responses to the NIT treatments in SIME/DIME do not have any direct implications for the size of national effects because they are averages over the 11 programs being tested in the experiments and because they do not account for the differences between the experimental sample and the national population. Table 3.3 shows how the distribution of income in the SIME/DIME sample compares to the distribution of income in the United States. As indicated in this table, greater proportions of SIME/DIME families are in the lower income groups, compared to the U.S. population. Moreover, within the experimental sample, control families have higher incomes than experimental families. With the statistical methodology used to estimate the experimental NIT effects, it is possible to correct for these differences and to extrapolate the experimental results to the national population using a technique called microsimulation. The microsimulation model we use in this chapter only predicts national effects on hours of work. It does not yet have the capability of predicting national effects on the length of employment and nonemployment spells.

Microsimulation

Microsimulation consists of applying social program regulations and behavioral assumptions to a microeconomic data base containing disaggregated information

Table 3.3
Distribution of Income in the SIME/DIME Experimental and
Control Samples and in the United States Population

| | Percent in income category | | | | | |
| | Husband-wife families | | | Female-headed families | | |
Income category[a]	Experimentals[b]	Controls[b]	U.S.	Experimentals[b]	Controls[b]	U.S.
<$1,000	9.8%	6.3%	1.1%	39.9%	36.0%	29.0%
$1,000-3,000	8.2	6.3	1.8	16.1	11.8	17.5
$3,000-5,000	9.7	6.9	3.9	13.5	13.1	8.5
$5,000-7,000	12.8	10.3	5.3	18.8	19.6	12.2
$7,000-9,000	18.7	19.5	6.1	8.9	12.2	9.4
$9,000-11,000	17.3	18.5	10.3	1.9	3.8	7.2
$11,000-13,000	10.3	16.0	11.3	.5	1.7	6.5
$13,000-15,000	6.9	7.5	10.4	.3	.6	2.5
$15,000-17,000	3.6	5.2	9.6	.1	.2	1.9
$17,000-20,000	2.2	2.5	13.4	0	0	1.9
>$20,000	.5	1.1	26.1	0	.2	3.3
Total number of families	1023	1158	39.7×10^6	968	654	5.0×10^6

Source: Keeley *et al*. (1978b).

[a] Income is defined as earnings of all family members plus family nonwage income, excluding taxes and public transfer payments. The incomes in the SIME/DIME sample are for the year before enrollment and are inflated to 1974 dollars. The U.S. incomes are from the March 1975 Current Population Survey and cover the year 1974.

[b] Black and white families only. There are approximately 800 Chicano families enrolled in the Denver Experiment, but these families are excluded from the tabulations.

about individuals or groups in order to project program costs and caseloads under varying conditions. To generalize the SIME/DIME results, we use the Micro Analysis of Transfer to Households (MATH) model to assess the effects of a variety of nationwide NIT programs. (See Beebout, 1977, for additional information about the MATH model.) The MATH model reproduces program eligibility requirements and benefit determination schedules. It also estimates behavior of low-income families regarding welfare participation and hours of work. (See Maxfield, 1977, for a description of how the MATH model estimates behavior regarding work effort.)

The tax liability, transfer payment, and amount of employment is determined for each family both before and after the NIT is implemented and the results are summed up to derive the total change in costs, caseloads, and hours of work under alternative plans. The different effects on various family types are also determined. Six NIT plans with varying tax rates and levels of support are simulated using income data from the March 1975 CPS, which are for the year 1974. Thus, the calculations represent what the effects of these plans would have been in

1974. No attempt is made to update the responses or cost estimates to later years.

The six programs for which predictions are made have constant tax rates of 50% and 70% on earnings, and guarantee levels of 50%, 75%, and 100% of the poverty level (i.e., $5000 for a family of four in 1974). Because the poverty level increases with family size, the guarantee level also increases with family size. The nominal guarantee level is assumed to be constant across regions. The NIT plans are assumed to replace the existing AFDC and Food Stamp programs, tax all other nonlabor income at the rate of 100%, and reimburse positive income taxes below the tax breakeven level. All families that are eligible to receive benefits from the program are assumed to participate.

Labor Supply Responses to a Nationwide Program

The average labor supply responses to the six nationwide NIT programs are presented in Table 3.4. The results are reported in two ways: first, as the average responses of all participating families; and second, as the average responses for the U.S. population. The average responses of the U.S. population include the responses of certain nonparticipants, as well as the responses of participants. The nonparticipants assumed to respond are families who previously received welfare benefits and are above the breakeven level of the NIT program. These families increase their labor supply when the welfare programs are replaced by the NIT because they are made worse off (in an income sense) by the program. Other nonparticipants are assumed not to respond to the NIT.

In interpreting the results, it is important to keep in mind that the responses vary not only because of changing guarantee levels and tax rates, but also because of a changing pool of participants. For example, as the tax rate increases (for a given guarantee), the pool of participants decreases. The manner in which the pool changes depends on the distribution of income within the relevant population subgroup. For the programs simulated, the number of participating families (e.g., those who would receive benefits) ranges from 3.3 million to 19.3 million.

For participating husband-wife families, the magnitudes of the average responses are positively associated with both the guarantee level and the tax rate. For participating female-headed families, the responses are positively associated with the guarantee, but do not vary with the tax rate. For both groups, the results indicate fairly sizable reductions in labor supply, ranging from between 10% and 21% for husband-wife families and between 0% and 15% for female-headed families.

The responses averaged over the entire U.S. population are quite small relative to the average responses of participating families, because most families in the United States belong to the categories assumed not to participate in the program. While the magnitude of the average response again increases with the guarantee (as it does for participants), it decreases with the tax rate for both groups. This

Table 3.4
Average Labor Supply Responses for Participating Families and for Families in the United States

	NIT tax rate 50%					NIT tax rate 70%				
	Participating families			All U.S. families		Participating families			All U.S. families	
NIT support level	Change in annual hours of work	% Change	No. of participating families (millions)	Change in annual hours of work	% Change	Change in annual hours of work	% Change	No. of participating families (millions)	Change in annual hours of work	% Change
50% of poverty level[a]										
Husbands	−104	−7.0%		−4	−0.2%	−136	−10.8%		−2	−0.1%
Wives	−92	−23.3		−2	−0.3	−111	−29.9		0	0.0
Total (H+W)	−196	−10.3	2.4	−6	−0.2	−247	−15.1	1.3	−2	−0.1
Female heads	0	0.0	2.3	+16	+1.6	−10	−2.7	2.0	+20	+2.0
75% of poverty level[a]										
Husbands	−106	−5.9		−19	−1.0	−157	−11.2		−9	−0.5
Wives	−110	−22.8		−19	−2.4	−126	−32.5		−5	−0.6
Total (H+W)	−216	−9.5	7.6	−38	−1.4	−283	−15.8	2.8	−14	−0.5
Female heads	−47	−6.7	3.0	−23	−2.4	−47	−9.3	2.5	−12	−1.2
100% of poverty level[a]										
Husbands	−119	−6.2		−47	−2.4	−164	−10.1		−23	−1.2
Wives	−130	−22.7		−50	−6.3	−144	−32.0		−18	−2.3
Total (H+W)	−249	−10.0	15.7	−97	−3.5	−308	−20.6	5.8	−41	−1.5
Female heads	−99	−12.0	3.6	−69	−7.1	−95	−14.9	3.0	−52	−5.3

Source: Keeley *et al.* (1978b).

Note: Average hours of work per year before response, all husbands in the U.S. = 1999. Average hours of work per year before response, all wives in the U.S. = 793. Total number of husband-wife families in the U.S. = 39.8 million. Average hours of work per year before response, female heads in the U.S. = 974. Total number of female-headed families in the U.S. = 4.9 million.

[a] Poverty level is $5000 per year for a family of four in 1974.

67

inverse relationship between the average U.S. response and the tax rate is an interesting and perhaps unexpected result; it is a consequence of the fact that the number of participants decreases by an amount large enough to offset the effect of a larger response among participants. Thus, the total disincentive effect of a nationwide NIT program is smaller under higher tax rate programs, despite the fact that the response of participating families is larger. As we shall see, this result also holds for the costs of a nationwide program.

Because programs with higher guarantee levels and higher tax rates discourage work, a fundamental dilemma would arise in designing an optimal program. Should a program with a low guarantee level and a low tax rate be preferred to a program with a high guarantee level and a high tax rate when both programs cost the same? The low guarantee, low tax rate program has less of a work disincentive effect, but may provide inadequate benefits for persons without earnings. The high guarantee, high tax rate program provides adequate benefits for persons without earnings, but also discourages work effort more for program participants. Because there are significant work effort reductions to the programs simulated, a trade-off exists between benefit adequacy and the incentive to work. How this trade-off is evaluated depends on the value judgments of the policymakers who are charged with designing an optimal national program.[6]

Costs of a Nationwide Program

Estimated annual program costs are presented in Table 3.5. Program costs are defined to be net of the current costs of the AFDC, AFDC-UP, and Food Stamp programs, which would be replaced by the NIT.

Not surprisingly, the costs of a nationwide NIT vary substantially with the parameters of the program. The most expensive plan (guarantee level equal to 100% of the poverty level and tax rate equal to 50%) costs $30 billion more in 1974 dollars than the existing welfare system and has approximately 39% of all husband-wife families and 73% of all female-headed families participating in the program. The least expensive plan (guarantee level equal to 50% of the poverty level and tax rate equal to 70%) involves a net cost *reduction* of $3.9 billion (which represents a 41% savings in welfare program costs) and has approximately 3% of all husband-wife families and 41% of all female-headed families participating in the program. In 1978 dollars, the net cost of these two alternatives would be $40.5 and −$5.3 billion, respectively.

For programs with positive additional costs, the proportion due to the labor supply response varies between 23% and 55%. The magnitude of these additional

---

[6] Our analysis has said nothing about how participants use the additional time spent not working. If the time is used in training or education activities (which could enhance future work opportunities), the trade-off would not pose as serious a problem for the design of an optimal program.

Table 3.5

Program Costs before and after Response, Husband-Wife and Female-Headed Families

NIT support level	NIT tax rate 50%				NIT tax rate 70%			
	Program costs before response (billions)	Change in program costs due to response (billions)	Program costs after response (billions)	No. of participating families (millions)	Program costs before response (billions)	Change in program costs due to response (billions)	Program costs after response (billions)	No. of participating families (millions)
50% of poverty level[a]								
Husband-wife families	$ −.1	$ .3	$ .2	2.4	$ −.8	$ .2	$ −.6	1.3
Female-headed families	−2.9	−.1	−3.0	2.3	−3.3	.0	−3.3	2.0
Total	−3.0	.2	−2.8	4.7	−4.1	.2	−3.9	3.3
75% of poverty level[a]								
Husband-wife families	5.4	2.2	7.6	7.6	1.6	1.1	2.7	2.8
Female-headed families	.2	.2	.4	3.0	−.6	.1	−.5	2.5
Total	5.6	2.4	8.0	10.6	1.0	1.2	2.2	5.3
100% of poverty level[a]								
Husband-wife families	19.0	6.5	25.5	15.7	6.5	3.1	9.6	5.8
Female-headed families	4.0	.5	4.5	3.6	2.6	.4	3.0	3.0
Total	23.0	7.0	30.0	19.3	9.1	3.5	12.6	8.8

Source: Keeley et al. (1978b).

Note: Total number of husband-wife families in the U.S. = 39.8 million. Total number of female-headed families in the U.S. = 4.9 million.

[a]Poverty level is $5000 per year for a family of four in 1974.

costs demonstrates the importance of accounting for labor supply adjustments when designing a national program.

Effects on the Welfare Population

As we have noted, the simulations assume that certain welfare programs (AFDC, AFDC-UP, and food stamps) are replaced by a single income-maintenance program with a uniform benefit structure across the U.S., and that there is no state supplementation of lost welfare benefits. Because of the wide regional variation in benefits under existing welfare programs, it is likely that some families would be made worse off by the replacement of those programs with an NIT. That is, some families that were previously receiving welfare benefits would have their benefits reduced. Table 3.6 presents the number and percentage of welfare families that would be made worse off by the NIT plans, assuming no state supplementation. As indicated in this table, the percentages are quite large, even for the more generous NIT programs. For example, under an NIT program with a support level equal to the poverty level and a tax rate equal to 50%, one-quarter of the welfare families would be made worse off. To compensate families

Table 3.6
Number and Percentage of Welfare Families Made Worse Off by the NIT
(No State Supplementation)

NIT support level	NIT tax rate 50%		NIT tax rate 70%	
	Number made worse off (millions)	Percent made worse off	Number made worse off (millions)	Percent made worse off
50% of poverty level[a]				
Husband-wife families	1.2	79%	1.4	89%
Female-headed families	1.8	93	1.9	95
Total	3.0	87	3.3	92
75% of poverty level[a]				
Husband-wife families	.7	43	1.2	71
Female-headed families	1.4	67	1.6	75
Total	2.1	59	2.8	73
100% of poverty level[a]				
Husband-wife families	.4	23	.7	41
Female-headed families	.5	25	.7	33
Total	.9	24	1.4	37

Note: Welfare is defined as AFDC, AFDC-UP and food stamps.
[a]Poverty level is $5000 per year for a family of four in 1974.

made worse off by the NIT (through some form of state supplementation) would, therefore, result in a substantial increase in program costs.

The reason why so many families would be made worse off by the NIT may be due to the fact that there are provisions in the existing welfare system (especially with regard to the deduction of work-related expenses from income) that enable families to face very low net benefit reduction rates. These low benefit reduction rates imply that welfare grants remain high even when family members work a substantial number of hours. Thus, even though the guarantee level of the NIT may be higher than the guarantee level of welfare, the higher NIT tax rate makes many working welfare families worse off.

SUMMARY AND CONCLUSIONS

There are several important conclusions that emerge from the analysis reported in this chapter. First, and perhaps most important, both the labor supply responses and costs of a nationwide NIT program vary widely with relatively small changes in the program guarantee level or tax rate. The most generous program simulated (a guarantee of 100% of the poverty level and a tax rate of 50%) would cost $30 billion more in 1974 than the existing welfare system cost at that time; the least generous program (with a guarantee of 75% of the poverty level and a tax rate of 70%) would cost only $2.2 billion more. (State supplementation to prevent anyone from being made worse off by the change would add substantially to these cost estimates). Furthermore, adjustments of hours of work in response to these programs account for a substantial fraction of the cost increases, ranging from 23% to 55% of total costs.

Second, although higher tax rates substantially reduce hours of work for program participants, they lead to smaller aggregate reductions in hours of work and smaller program costs than lower tax rates. This is because higher tax-rate programs have lower breakeven levels and, hence, fewer participants than lower tax-rate programs. Thus, adequate minimum benefits (i.e., a high guarantee level) can only be ensured at a feasible cost if the tax rate of the program is high. But under such a program, participants may become dependent on transfers because of the very low economic return from working.

Third, a nationwide NIT program presumably would be more equitable than the current welfare system because categorical eligibility requirements would be eliminated; i.e., working couples would be eligible for benefits. In addition, a nationwide NIT program would reduce the extreme regional variation in current benefit levels. Unfortunately, even a relatively generous NIT program would leave a substantial number of current welfare recipients worse off. To make the welfare system more equitable, either (a) many current welfare recipients would have to have their benefits reduced or (b) a very generous and expensive plan would have to be implemented.

REFERENCES

Beebout, Harold. *The MATH Welfare Model: Executive Summary.* Working Paper E-46, Mathematica Policy Reserach, 1977.

Keeley, Michael C.; Robins, Philip K.; Spiegelman, Robert G.; and West, Richard W. "The Estimation of Labor Supply Models Using Experimental Data." *American Economic Review* 68, no. 5 (December 1978a).

Keeley, Michael C.; Robins, Philip K.; Spiegelman, Robert G.; and West, Richard W. "The Labor Supply Effects and Costs of Alternative Negative Income Tax Programs." *Journal of Human Resources*, 13, no. 1 (Winter 1978b).

Maxfield, Myles Jr. "Estimating the Impact of Labor Supply Adjustments on Transfer Program Costs: A Microsimulation Methodology." Mathematica Policy Research, June 1977.

Robins, Philip K.; Tuma, Nancy Brandon; and Yaeger, Kathryn E. "Effects of SIME/DIME on Changes in Employment Status." *Journal of Human Resources*, scheduled for publication 15, No. 4 (Fall 1980).

CHAPTER 4

Labor Supply Response of Youth

RICHARD W. WEST

INTRODUCTION

The other labor supply chapters in this volume deal exclusively with heads of families (husbands, wives, and unmarried females) (also see Keeley *et al.*, 1977a, b, 1978a, b; Robins and West, 1978a, b). This chapter focuses on the effects of the experiment on the labor supply of young persons who were not heads of families upon enrollment into SIME/DIME. We focus in particular, on persons over 16 years old and under 21 at enrollment who are the children, stepchildren, or grandchildren of the family heads at enrollment. This group is important for several reasons. First, it is the only major group of persons in the experiments other than family heads and young children. Older nonheads, while participating in the experiment, are not present in a sufficiently large number to permit analysis. Second, they were exposed to the experimental treatments at the time when they are likely to be entering the labor market for the first time. Any impact on their labor supply during this crucial period could have important long-run effects by delaying, postponing, or reducing their initial labor market experience. National attention has recently focused on the high unemployment rates observed among young persons. Any impact of the experiments on their behavior is, thus, clearly of interest to policymakers.

The NIT plans which were given to the experimentals can be expected to have an effect on the labor supply of dependent youth. The manner in which this occurs depends on the extent to which these youth are integrated into the family decision-making process. One extreme assumes that they are fully integrated into a decision process that maximizes a *family* utility function. In this case, we can expect the experimentally induced increase in family disposable income and the increase in the tax rate to have a negative effect on the young nonhead's labor supply. (See Keeley *et al.*, 1978b, for a more complete discussion of this model

73

A GUARANTEED ANNUAL INCOME:
EVIDENCE FROM A SOCIAL EXPERIMENT

for heads of families.) At the other extreme, the youth is an independent decision maker but at the same time benefits from being a member of the family. In this case, the experimental effects can be expected to depend on whether the family is able to induce the youth to reimburse the family for the taxes (grant reductions) that the family pays on his or her income.

If the family is able to collect these taxes from the youth, the income of the family (other than the youth) increases, but the youth's income and net wage rate decrease. The net effect of these on the youth's labor supply may go either way, since the increase in family income and decrease in his net wage rate should reduce his labor supply, while the decrease in his income should increase his labor supply. If, in contrast, the family does not collect the taxes from the youth, family income increases while the youth's income and net wage rate are unchanged. In this case, the increase in family income should unambiguously decrease the youth's labor supply.

The manpower plans can also be expected to have an effect on labor supply. First, the counseling plan could enable youth to become more effective at finding jobs. This could decrease the length of their periods of unemployment, and also increase their hours of work if they are able to find jobs with higher wage rates. (A study by West, 1979b, indicates that wage rates of family heads are unaffected by the experiment.) The education and training subsidy could induce youth to take more education and training and consequently work less during that period. Subsequently, however, they could work more if they obtain jobs with higher wage rates because of their increased skills.

THE EFFECTS OF THE NIT TREATMENTS ON THE
LABOR SUPPLY OF YOUTH

In this section, we examine the effects of the NIT treatments on the labor supply of youth during the third year of the experiment (experimental quarters 8-11). We will consider the effects on four different dependent variables: average hours worked per week, the proportion of time working, the proportion of time unemployed, and the proportion of time out of the labor force.[1]

The sample used for this study, as mentioned, comprises males and females

---

[1] Average hours per week is calculated as total hours worked during the year divided by 365/7. The proportion of time worked is calculated as the number of days the person held jobs on which he or she was working at a positive weekly rate divided by 365. Thus, e.g., it excludes periods when the person held a job, but was not working, such as might occur for a school teacher during the summer. However, both average hours worked and the proportion of time worked treat paid vacation and sick leave as work. The proportion of time the youth was unemployed is calculated as the length of periods during which the person did not work, but looked for work, divided by 365. The proportion of time out of the labor force represents the remainder of the period.

aged 16-21 at enrollment, who were either children, stepchildren, or grandchildren of the family head at enrollment. Of 1177 persons originally included in this category, the analysis sample was reduced to 733 because of attrition and missing data. Table 4.1 presents the original sample and shows the cases lost.

The plan of the analysis is as follows. First, we present some simple evidence to indicate whether or not SIME/DIME had any effect at all. Second, we explore the extent to which the response to the treatment varied with family status in the third year of the experiment. Third, we examine the extent to which any labor supply reduction was combined with increases in school attendance.

While several models are estimated to explore these issues, all the models share a common basic structure. Each represents the dependent variable y as a linear function of a set of control variables X, a set of variables representing the NIT treatments F, a set of variables representing the manpower treatments M, and an error term e. Thus,

$$y = X\mathbf{b} + F\mathbf{c} + M\mathbf{d} + e,$$

where $\mathbf{b}, \mathbf{c},$ and $\mathbf{d}$ are vectors of parameters to be estimated.

In order to account for the stratified random nature of the assignment to experimental treatments (see Conlisk and Kurz, 1972; and Keeley and Robins, 1978), variables representing the assignment strata are included in X. These are dummy variables for the normal income level of the youth's family at enrollment, for ethnic group, for being in Denver, and for indicating that the youth's family at enrollment was headed by a single person. Additional variables are included in X to increase the efficiency of the estimates. These additional variables are average hours worked; the proportions of time working and unemployed; average in-school status during the preexperimental year; and the preexperimen-

Table 4.1
Original Sample and Cases Lost Due to
Attrition and Missing Data

	Total	Male	Female
Original sample	1177	612	565
Cases lost due to			
Attrition	378	223	155
Missing data	66	38	28
Remaining cases	733	351	382

Note: The original sample included all persons originally enrolled as the children, stepchildren, and grandchildren of the family heads who were aged 16-21 at enrollment except for those families enrolled in the 20-year sample, and those in families whose equivalent income class used in the assignment process contains only controls. (E-level = 6 for single head families, and E-level = 7 for all families. See Chapter 1.)

tal values of education, weeks of training, number of family members, number of family members aged 0-5, age (piecewise linear with a change of slope at 18), and family income. Separate analyses are performed for males and females.

Dummy variables are used to represent the three manpower treatments. Several representations of the NIT treatments are used.

A Simple Estimate of the Effect of the NIT Plans

A basic question to be answered is whether or not the NIT treatments had any effect on the labor supply of youths. There are good reasons for expecting either some negative effect or no effect at all. On the one hand, since dependent youth are typically considered as marginal workers, they may be especially responsive to economic incentives. On the other hand, as dependent members of families, they are not directly affected by the NIT treatment. While the families receive NIT payments that depend on the youths' earnings (as a component of family income), the youths themselves receive nothing directly. As already noted, unless their work behavior is affected by family income or the families are able to transfer the NIT tax on earnings back to them, young nonheads will not be expected to respond to the NIT treatments.

In order to address the issue of whether or not there is any NIT treatment effect on labor supply, we use the simplest possible representation of the NIT treatments: a dummy variable that takes the value 1 for a person eligible for any of the 11 experimental NIT plans and 0 for the NIT controls. While this model is useful for determining whether or not the experimental NIT plans have any effect on the labor supply, it should be noted that the estimated response cannot be used as an estimate of the effect of any single NIT plan. Rather the estimated response represents an average of the effects of the 11 SIME/DIME plans being tested.

The estimation results for this model for the various dependent variables being considered in this study are presented in Table 4.2. The results indicate that the NIT plans have a substantial and highly significant effect on the labor supply of young male nonheads. Hours of work per week are reduced by 4.63 hours (or about 24%), and the proportion of time worked is reduced by .106 (or 21%). (These percentage effects are calculated by dividing the response by the mean of the variable for controls.) These substantial decreases in work effort are reflected mostly in an increase in time unemployed rather than time out of the labor force. Also presented are results for schooling status, which indicate no evidence that these male youths reduced labor supply in order to increase school attendance. The results for females indicate a somewhat smaller and less significant effect, but in the same direction. Hours worked per week are reduced by 2.78 hours (or 18%), and the proportion of time worked is reduced by .074 (or 17%). As with young males, there is no evidence that work effort was reduced in order to increase school attendance.

Table 4.2
Estimated Experimental Effects
(Standard Error in Parentheses)

Dependent variable	Coefficient	
	Males	Females
Hours worked per week	−4.63***	−2.78*
	(1.67)	(1.62)
Proportion of period worked	−.106***	−.074*
	(.040)	(.042)
Proportion of period unemployed	.067*	.014
	(.035)	(.029)
Proportion of period out of labor force	.039	.060
	(.035)	(.041)
Average in-school status	.035	−.011
	(.047)	(.043)
Sample size	351	382

*$p < .10$.
***$p < .01$.

Since the experiment was temporary, it is not clear that these estimated effects represent the effects of a permanent NIT program. Metcalf (1973, 1974) has shown that in a temporary program the income effect is smaller and the substitution effect larger in magnitude than in a permanent program. The division of the SIME/DIME sample into 3- and 5-year treatments allows us to explore this hypothesis to some degree.

Table 4.3 presents separate estimates of the experimental effect on hours of work and proportion of time working for persons on 3- and 5-year NIT plans. The model is identical to the single dummy variable model except that there are separate dummy variables for the 3- and 5-year treatments. The estimated effects of the 5-year program are somewhat larger for males and considerably larger for females than the effects of the 3-year program. However, the difference between the 3- and 5-year effects is significant only for the proportion of time worked by young females. Thus, while the analysis cannot demonstrate conclusively that the response increases with the duration of the NIT plan, it does demonstrate a distinct possibility that responses to a 5-year program are considerably larger than responses to a 3-year program. Responses to a permanent NIT program may, of course, be larger still.

The analysis of the simple dummy variable model has demonstrated that experimental NIT plans have a considerable effect on the labor supply of dependent youth, especially males. In an analysis reported elsewhere (West 1979a), we attempted, without success, to relate this response to the characteristics of the various experimental NIT plans. In the remainder of this chapter, we analyze the extent to which the response to these plans varies with the characteristics of the youth.

Table 4.3
Estimated 3- and 5-year Effects
(Standard Error in Parentheses)

	Males	Females
Hours worked per week		
5-year effect	−5.78**	−5.35**
	(2.32)	(2.37)
3-year effect	−4.10**	−1.83
	(1.82)	(1.74)
Difference	−1.68	−3.52
	(2.36)	(2.37)
Proportion of period worked		
5-year effect	−.129**	−.163***
	(.056)	(.061)
3-year effect	−.096**	−.041
	(.044)	(.045)
Difference	−.034	−.122**
	(.057)	(.064)

Note: The following probability levels apply to Tables 4.3-4.5.
   *$p < .10$.
   **$p < .05$.
   ***$p < .01$.

Variation in Response by Family Status

Many persons who were dependent youth at enrollment became either heads of families or unrelated individuals during the experimental period. By the 11th experimental quarter, only 48.4% of male youth were still nonheads; 31.1% had become unrelated individuals and 20.5% had become heads of their own families. The figures for females are similar except that females were less likely to be unrelated individuals and more likely to be heads of their own families.[2] These large changes in family status suggest that it is important to account for changes in such status in the analysis of the effects of the experiments on the young nonhead's labor supply, because the NIT treatments may have provided very different incentives to young nonheads in different family statuses during the experimental period. For instance, the guarantee level for an unrelated individual was $1000 on all plans. This is less than half the support level for a two-person family ($2356) on the plans with the smallest guarantee, $3800. Also, a young nonhead who forms his or her own family may be more directly affected by a given program than one who remains in his parental family.

We present separate response estimates for youths in each of the three family

[2] Those who were in the young nonhead sample at enrollment are referred to in that way throughout this chapter, whatever their family status change during the experiments.

statuses, defined on the basis of the family status in experimental quarter 11.[3] This measure of family status is not exogenous with respect to the financial treatments, of course, since family status itself is likely to be affected by the NIT plans. Consequently, the experimental impacts presented in this section cannot be averaged to obtain the overall experimental effect. Rather, they represent only the partial effects of the experiment on the dependent variables other than the effects that operate through changes in family status. The estimates do, however, indicate how the experimental response varies with family status during the experimental period.

The estimates are presented in Table 4.4. The model contains three dummy variables representing persons eligible for an NIT treatment in each of the three family status categories. The model also includes among the control variables dummy variables for each of the family status categories in order to account for the effects of family status on the dependent variables. The results for males indicate that there is a large and significant reduction in work effort for youth who remain nonheads. The reduced work effort is reflected about equally in in-

Table 4.4
Variation of Youth Response by Family Status in Eleventh Quarter
(Standard Error in Parentheses)

Dependent variable	Males			Females		
	Nonhead	Head	Unrelated individual	Nonhead	Head	Unrelated individual
Hours worked	−7.37***	−10.36***	2.16	−6.77***	−2.12	1.90
per week	(2.23)	(3.38)	(2.80)	(2.58)	(2.43)	(3.26)
Proportion of	−.157***	−.286***	.067	−.195***	−.034	.036
period worked	(.054)	(.082)	(.068)	(.067)	(.063)	(.085)
Proportion of	.076	.204***	.011	.051	.025	−.055
period unemployed	(.047)	(.071)	(.059)	(.046)	(.044)	(.059)
Proportion of period	.081*	.082	−.078	.144**	.009	.019
out of the labor	(.047)	(.071)	(.059)	(.065)	(.061)	(.082)
force						
Number in group	170	72	109	141	156	85
Controls	82	29	42	62	68	37
Financials	88	43	67	79	88	48

[3] The longer version of this paper (West, 1979a) also presents estimates based on family status in experimental quarter 7. The quarter 7 definition has the advantage of being determined prior to the dependent variables which represent averages for quarters 8-11. The eleventh quarter definition has the advantage of capturing many more status changes. The results are similar for the two definitions of family status.

creased time unemployed and increased time out of the labor force. For males who become heads of their own families, there is also a substantial reduction in work effort. This reduction is primarily reflected in an increase in unemployment. The response is -7.37 hours (-43%) for those who are still nonheads in the eleventh quarter, and -10.36 hours (-33%) for those who have become husbands by the eleventh quarter. These responses are substantially larger in magnitude than the response estimated for the males who were already heading families at enrollment (see Robins and West, 1978b). There is no significant effect on work effort for youth who become unrelated individuals.

The results for young females show a significant response (of -6.77 hours) only for those who remain nonheads. This reduction in work effort is primarily due to an increase in the amount of time spent out of the labor force.

Thus, the breakdown of response by family status has revealed two important results. The experimental NIT plans induce a reduction in the work effort of young male nonheads who either remain nonheads or become heads of new families; there is no reduction for males who become unrelated individuals. There is a reduction in work effort induced by the experimental NIT plans for young females who remain nonheads, but not for those who become either wives or unrelated individuals.

Schooling

Having determined that young nonheads are indeed working less in response to the experimental NIT plans, it is important to know what they are doing during the additional time they are not working—in particular, whether or not they are decreasing their labor supply in order to increase school attendance. As will be recalled, when estimation results for the simple dummy variable model were presented at the beginning of this chapter (see Table 4.2), estimation results for an average in-school status equation were also presented, and showed no significant impact of the NIT plans on school attendance. It does, however, seem desirable to explore the schooling question in somewhat more detail.

To accomplish this goal, we define four dummy variables that measure combined work and school status. The variables represent four combined states: working and attending school, working and not attending school, not working and attending school, and not working and not attending school. Each variable is defined for each quarter from 8 through 11 and then averaged over the quarters for which information is available. Since the states, defined by the four variables, are mutually exclusive and exhaustive, the four variables sum to one. In Table 4.5, we present estimation results using these variables as dependent variables in two models: the model that allows responses to vary by eleventh quarter family status and the simple dummy variable model. The results for the simple dummy variable model are presented in the rows marked "All"; the responses by family status are presented in the remaining rows.

For young males, the results are consistent with those already reported. The

Table 4.5
Estimated Effects on Combined Work and School Alternatives,
by Eleventh Quarter Family Status
(Standard Errors in Parentheses)

	Work, school	Work, no school	No work, school	No work, no school
Males				
Nonhead	−.057	−.162***	.092*	.126**
	(.049)	(.062)	(.049)	(.052)
Head	−.014	−.266***	.143*	.137*
	(.075)	(.093)	(.074)	(.078)
Unrelated individual	−.046	.038	.018	−.010
	(.062)	(.077)	(.061)	(.065)
All	−.046	−.113**	.082**	.078**
	(.036)	(.046)	(.035)	(.037)
Mean of dependent variable	.171	.411	.180	.238
Females				
Nonhead	−.112**	−.170**	.105*	.177***
	(.048)	(.068)	(.054)	(.066)
Head	−.007	−.038	−.040	.085
	(.046)	(.064)	(.051)	(.062)
Unrelated individual	.011	.006	.049	−.065
	(.061)	(.085)	(.068)	(.083)
All	−.041	−.074*	.030	.084**
	(.030)	(.042)	(.034)	(.042)
Mean of dependent variable	.135	.354	.180	.331

response occurs only among those who remain nonheads or become heads of families. The experimental NIT plans decrease the probability of their working and not going to school and increase both the probability of their not working and going to school, and the probability of not working and not going to school. Thus, it is clear that many young males decrease their work effort even though they do not go to school. However, the increase in the probability of not working and going to school indicates that some of the reduction in work effort occurs among persons who do choose to concentrate on schooling. The responses are somewhat larger for the young males who become heads than for those who remain nonheads. There is no significant net effect on school attendance.

As in our previous estimates for young females, only those young females who remain nonheads exhibit a response to the experimental NIT plans. The results indicate a reduction in the probability of both working and going to school and an almost equal increase in the probability of not working and going to school. Thus, a substantial portion of the work effort response occurs among females who choose to concentrate on schooling. The major part of the work effort response, however, is associated with a reduction in the probability of working and not attending school and an increase in the probability of not working and not attending school. There is, again, no net effect on school attendance. Thus, for both males and females, there is a definite decrease in work effort that is not accompanied by school attendance.

THE EFFECTS OF THE MANPOWER TREATMENTS

We now proceed to present evidence on the effect of the manpower programs on the labor supply of young nonheads. Three different manpower programs are being tested: manpower counseling only ($M1$), counseling plus a 50% subsidy of direct training and education costs ($M2$), and counseling plus a 100% subsidy ($M3$). Dummy variables for each of the treatments are included in the estimated equations for all the models already discussed. Table 4.6 presents the coefficients of the manpower variables for a model that represents the NIT treatments by a single dummy variable. (The NIT treatment results are reported in Table 4.4.) The results clearly indicate that there is no evidence that the manpower programs affect work effort.

SUMMARY AND CONCLUSIONS

Since a wide variety of estimation models and results has been presented in this chapter, it is desirable to summarize some of the key findings. The most im-

Table 4.6
Estimated Effects of the Manpower Treatments
(Standard Error in Parentheses)

Dependent variable	Males				Females			
	M1	M2	M3	F-test	M1	M2	M3	F-test
Hours worked per week	.07	2.30	−1.97	1.10	−1.27	2.08	.61	.67
	(2.32)	(1.97)	(2.37)		(2.24)	(2.04)	(2.22)	
Proportion of period worked	.013	.035	−.055	.80	−.009	.064	.029	.61
	(.056)	(.048)	(.057)		(.058)	(.053)	(.058)	
Proportion of Period unemployed	.014	.019	.032	.15	−.007	.014	−.016	.17
	(.048)	(.041)	(.049)		(.040)	(.037)	(.040)	
Proportion of period out of labor force	−.031	−.049	.024	.87	.009	−.078	−.012	.93
	(.048)	(.041)	(.049)		(.057)	(.052)	(.057)	
Average in-school status	−.006	−.134**	−.010	2.35*	.019	.006	.095	.97
	(.006)	(.056)	(.067)		(.059)	(.054)	(.058)	

Note: The F-test is for the null hypothesis that all manpower effects are zero (3 degrees of freedom).
   $*p < .10$.
   $**p < .05$.

portant result is that the experimental NIT plans definitely induce a reduction in work effort among persons who were young nonheads when the experiment began. Both hours of work per week and the proportion of time worked are reduced. The analysis has also demonstrated that this reduction in work effort is concentrated in particular groups. The response is about −7.7 hours per week (−43%) for young males who remain nonheads and −10.36 hours per week (−33%) for those who become husbands. Of the young females, only those who remain nonheads appear to respond. Their response is −6.8 hours per week (−42%). There is no response for young males or females who become unrelated individuals or for young females who become wives. Also, there is no evidence that the work effort reduction is accompanied by a net increase in school attendance. However, somewhat less than half the response appears to occur among persons who would have worked while attending school in the absence of the experiment, but attend school and do not work under the influence of the experiment. Separate estimates of response for the 3- and 5-year programs indicate that there is a possibility that response increases with experimental duration. Consequently, the response to a permanent program may be even larger than the estimates presented here.

The estimated responses are large in percentage terms and should not be ignored when considering the possible effects of national NIT plans. Furthermore, the response to a national plan could not be reduced by refusing eligibility to young unrelated individuals, since the estimated response comes from groups that would not be excluded by this constraint.

The response by young male and female nonheads who remain nonheads, while large in percentage terms, may not be of great direct importance relative to the estimates for the other youth groups, since these nonheads are generally secondary earners in their families. However, a reduction in work effort during this portion of their life cycles may have continuing effects by reducing their labor market experience and thus possibly reducing their ability to obtain good jobs in the future. Such a long-term effect is purely speculative; there is little empirical evidence to test it.

The reduction in work effort by young male nonheads who become husbands is clearly important. These males are reducing their work effort just at the time when they are undertaking family responsibilities. Not only is their response important in the current period, but the reduction in work effort can also be expected to have long-term effects on their labor supply behavior.

REFERENCES

Conlisk, John, and Kurz, Mordecai. "The Assignment Model of the Seattle and Denver Income Maintenance Experiments." SIME/DIME Research Memorandum No. 15, Center for the Study of Welfare Policy, Stanford Research Institute, July 1972.

Keeley, Michael C., and Robins, Philip K. "Social Experimentation and Nonrandom Assignment." Research Memorandum No. 57, Center for the Study of Welfare Policy, SRI International, November 1978.

Keeley, Michael C.; Robins, Philip K.: Spiegelman, Robert G.; and West, Richard W. "The Labor Supply Effects and Costs of Alternative Negative Income Tax Programs: Evidence from the Seattle and Denver Income Maintenance Experiments. Part 1: The Labor Supply Response Function." Research Memorandum No. 38, Center for the Study of Welfare Policy, SRI International, May 1977a.

Keeley, Michael C.; Robins, Philip K.; Spiegelman, Robert G.; and West, Richard W. "The Labor Supply Effects and Costs of Alternative Negative Income Tax Programs: Evidence from the Seattle and Denver Income Maintenance Experiments. Part 2: National Predictions Using the Labor Supply Response Function." Research Memorandum No. 39, Center for the Study of Welfare Policy, SRI International, May 1977b.

Keeley, Michael C.; Robins, Philip K.; Spiegelman, Robert G.; and West, Richard W. "The Labor Supply Effects and Costs of Alternative Negative Income Tax Programs." *Journal of Human Resources* 13 (Winter 1978a): 1-36.

Keeley, Michael C.; Robins, Philip K.; Spiegelman, Robert G.; and West, Richard W. "The Estimation of Labor Supply Models Using Experimental Data." *American Economic Review* 68 (December 1978b).

Metcalf, Charles E. "Making Inferences from Controlled Income Maintenance Experiments." *American Economic Review* 63 (June 1974): 478-483.

Metcalf, Charles E. "Predicting the Effects of Permanent Programs from a Limited Duration Experiment." *Journal of Human Resources* 9 (Fall 1974): 530-555.

Robins, Philip K., and West, Richard W. "Participation in the Seattle and Denver Income Maintenance Experiments and Its Effect on Labor Supply." Research Memorandum No. 53, Center for the Study of Welfare Policy, SRI International, March 1978a.

Robins, Philip K., and West, Richard W. "A Longitudinal Analysis of the Labor Supply Response to a Negative Income Tax Program: Evidence from the Seattle and Denver Income Maintenance Experiments." Research Memorandum No. 59, Center for the Study of Welfare Policy, SRI International, December 1978b.

West, Richard W. "The Effects of the Seattle and Denver Income Maintenance Experiments on the Labor Supply of Young Nonheads." Research Memorandum No. 60, Center for the Study of Welfare Policy, SRI International, May 1979a.

West, Richard W. "The Impact of the Seattle and Denver Income Maintenance Experiments on Wage Rates: An Interim Analysis." Research Memorandum No. 61, Center for the Study of Welfare Policy, SRI International, May 1979b.

CHAPTER 5

Labor Supply Response of Family Heads Over Time

PHILIP K. ROBINS
RICHARD W. WEST

As indicated in Chapter 1, estimating the labor supply effects of a permanent nationwide NIT was the central objective of SIME/DIME. Several features of the experiments, however, make it difficult to extrapolate the experimental results to the national population. First, the experiments are being conducted in a number of specific geographical sites that may not be representative of the U.S. population. Second, two ethnic minorities, blacks and Chicanos, are oversampled relative to their proportions in the U.S. population. If these minority groups behave differently from the rest of the population and if these differences are not controlled in the empirical analysis, the experimental results would be a misleading indicator of the labor supply response to a nationwide program. Third, the experiments are being conducted for a limited period of time, which may create problems in extrapolating the results to a permanent program.

In the analysis of Chapter 3, which focuses on the second year of the experiments, no statistically significant differences in response by ethnic group, site, and experimental duration are found.[1] Since the panel feature of the data is not fully exploited in that study, additional analysis is required before definitive statements can be made regarding the presence or absence of differences in response among the various groups.

In this chapter we look at the labor supply response to SIME/DIME over time, and we perform tests of differences in response by ethnic group, site, and duration of the treatments. The models we use measure the experimental effect by a single dummy variable. While this approach represents a considerable simplification over the treatment parameterization employed in Chapter 3, we feel that such a specification enables us to perform fairly powerful tests of differences in response among the several groups.

---

[1] The ethnicity tests in Chapter 3 were performed on black and white families only. The Chicano sample was not available for analysis at the time that study was undertaken.

The first section describes the sample and data used in the empirical analysis. The next section presents results from a labor-supply response model in which the experimental effect is allowed to vary freely over time. Then, we present results from a model that imposes constraints on the time pattern of response. The final section of the chapter summarizes the analysis.

A major finding of the empirical analysis is that under the constrained formulation, the labor supply response of husbands does appear to differ significantly by ethnic group, site, and experimental duration. The results indicate that white husbands have a smaller response than black or Chicano husbands, that husbands in Seattle have a smaller response then husbands in Denver, and that husbands on the 3-year program have a smaller response than husbands on the 5-year program.

THE SAMPLE AND THE DATA

SIME/DIME conducted periodic interviews three times a year. As part of these interviews, weekly hours of work were recorded, as well as any changes in weekly hours of work that occurred since the previous interview. These data permit construction of a continuous work history for each individual. For purposes of this study, we have constructed a quarterly time series of hours of work (annualized) for the first 10 quarters of the experiment and for the 4 quarters prior to the experiment.[2]

As with any panel, observations are lost over time. From the first through the tenth experimental quarter, the sample size was reduced by 17% for husbands (1.7% per quarter), by 13% for wives (1.3% per quarter), and by 13% for single female heads of families (1.3% per quarter).[3] In this paper, the tenth-quarter sample is used for the empirical analysis. Thus, we ignore information contained in the data for families that leave the experiment prior to the tenth quarter. Although it should be kept in mind that such a sample selection procedure may lead to biased estimates of the labor supply response to the experiment if the attrition is systematically related to labor supply, an examination of this potential problem concludes that use of the tenth-quarter sample does not lead to a significant bias in the estimated treatment effects (see Robins and West, 1978b, Appendix A).

[2] For most families, however, less than 4 quarters of preexperimental data are available. We convert the available information to an annual total by assuming that behavior in the missing quarters is the same as behavior in the observed quarters. We thus have only one preexperimental observation for each family.

[3] Virtually all the observations lost were because the individual either dropped out of the experiment or could not be found by the interviewers. (A few additional observations were lost because of coding errors.) The subgroups (husbands, wives, and female heads) are defined as of the date of enrollment. The sample sizes differ for husbands and wives because of selective attrition after marital separation.

In the next two sections we present estimates of the labor supply effects we found for the first 10 quarters of the experiments. As has been stressed in previous chapters, observed results such as these cannot be interpreted directly as representing the responses that would be forthcoming from any particular NIT program implemented nationally. (Chapter 3 presents estimates of the labor supply response to particular nationwide NIT alternatives.)

ESTIMATED EXPERIMENTAL EFFECTS

In specifying models of the labor supply response to SIME/DIME, two characteristics of the sample must be taken into account. First, for both experimentals and controls, hours or work followed an upward trend over time for both men and women. During the first 10 quarters of SIME/DIME, average hours of work of the control group increased by 5% for husbands, 20% for wives, and 12% for single, female heads of families. Second, there exists systematic differences in labor supply between the experimental and control groups that are unrelated to the experimental treatment. During the preexperimental year, for example, average hours of work of the control group exceeded average hours of work of the experimental group by 4% for husbands, by 28% for wives, and by 7% for single female heads of families.

The upward trend in labor supply is the result of three phenomena. First, the upward trend for women was primarily due to an increase in their labor force participation rate, following a trend occurring nationwide. Second, for both men and women, the increase in hours of work reflected a steady decrease in the unemployment rate in Seattle. From February 1972 to February 1975 the unemployment rate in Seattle fell from 14.6% to 9%. Finally, the increase in hours of work is partly the result of a peculiar characteristic of the samples in all the income-maintenance experiments: initial truncation by income.[4] By systematically eliminating families with high incomes in the preexperimental period, the sample contains a more than proportionate number of families with temporarily low incomes. As family incomes return to normal, therefore, the average income in the sample inevitably rises. (See Robins and West, 1978a, for further elaboration.) To the extent that hours of work and income are correlated, such truncation of the sample by income would lead to an increase in average hours of work over time.

The systematic differences in labor supply between experimental and control families, as discussed in Chapter 1, are due to the assignment process, which excluded certain income groups from certain NIT treatments, although such famil-

[4] A family was eligible for SIME/DIME if preexperimental income (adjusted for family size) was less than $9000 per year in a family of four with one working head and less than $11,000 per year in a family of four with two working heads. For a discussion of how the experimental sample was chosen, see Kurz and Spiegelman (1972).

ies were represented in the control group. In particular, families with high incomes were not assigned to NIT treatments with low breakeven levels. (It was assumed that these families were above the breakeven level and would not respond to the NIT treatments.) Thus, control families tend to have systematically higher incomes than experimental families.

The above discussion indicates that a labor-supply response model should allow for secular effects, and should correct for potential biases caused by the assignment process as well as for nontreatment differences in labor supply between experimental and control families. As mentioned earlier in the volume, the assignment process used in SIME/DIME allocated families to the various experimental treatments (including control status) on the basis of a variable called "normal income," determined primarily on the basis of preexperimental labor supply corrected for obviously transitory influences. The simplest way to obtain unbiased estimates of experimental effects, therefore, is to regress the change in hours of work on the experimental treatment variable, and the normal income variables. The results of estimating such a model are presented in Tables 5.1-5.3.[5]

For the overall sample, the results indicate that the experiments had a substantial disincentive effect on labor supply. The response of husbands increased (in absolute value) until about the fourth or fifth experimental quarter. Thereafter, the response was relatively stable and ranged from −147 (−8.0%) to −187 (−10.0%) hours per year. For wives the response peaked at experimental quarter 7 at a value of −157 hours (−20.9%) and declined to −113 hours per year (−14.8%) in the tenth quarter. For single female heads, the response increased over time until it reached a value of −205 hours per year (−13.2%) in the tenth quarter.

There are also apparent site differences in response with a larger response in Denver, but again, the differences are not statistically significant. The site differences may be due to ethnic differences (there are no Chicano families enrolled in the Seattle experiment)[6] or to differences in the labor markets of the two cities (average hours of work of control husbands in Seattle are about 17% lower

[5] Several other variables whose presence is likely to increase the efficiency of the estimated treatment effects are also included in the equation. These additional variables are preexperimental hours of work, race and site dummies, age at enrollment, number of family members at enrollment, number of children under 5 years of age at enrollment, AFDC benefits in the preexperimental year, and three dummies for the manpower component of the experiment. Equations are also estimated in which the treatment dummy is interacted with ethnicity, site, and experimental duration dummies. Because preexperimental hours of work are included as an independent variable, we can use experimental hours of work as the dependent variable. (The same results would be obtained if the change in hours of work was used as the dependent variable.)

[6] In the second model to be estimated, which imposes restrictions on the time pattern of response, we test for site differences after excluding Chicano families from the sample.

than average hours of work of control husbands in Denver throughout the entire period of analysis.)[7]

Estimates of responses by duration of the experiment show significant differences for husbands in 3 of 10 quarters. The response of husbands in 5-year families is greater than the response of husbands in 3-year families. Economic theory predicts that under a temporary program the income effect is smaller (in absolute value) and the substitution effect is larger than under a permanent program. (See Chapter 3 and Metcalf, 1973, for a discussion of income and substitution effects.) Thus, the observed responses of 3-year families could be less than, equal to, or greater than the observed response of 5-year families, depending on the size of the income and the substitution effects and the rate of time preference. The fact that the observed responses are larger for 5-year families suggests that the income effect dominates the intertemporal substitution effect.[8] For wives and single female heads the duration differences are not significant (except in the first 2 quarters for wives). However, the estimated responses do tend to show larger responses for persons in the 5-year sample.

RESTRICTIONS ON THE TIME PATTERN OF RESPONSE

The model estimated in the preceding section does not constrain the time pattern of the labor supply response in any way. The estimated experimental effects, although clearly negative, fluctuate considerably in magnitude over time. Consequently, the estimates do not provide a clear picture of the time pattern of response. In this section, we rely on some simple theoretical concepts to impose a relatively restricted structure on the time pattern of response.

Consider a person who is enrolled in an NIT experiment. Upon enrollment there is a sudden and unforeseen change in the person's budget constraint. Both the intercept (support level) and the slope (net wage rate) of the budget constraint are changed. As a consequence of these changes, the person now desires to work a different number of hours. For a variety of reasons it is unlikely that the person will immediately adjust hours of work to correspond with these new desires. Many jobs do not have flexible hours and adjustment may have to wait until a new job is found. Furthermore, the person may not even attempt to find a new job because of the costs associated with changing jobs. However, if the job is lost

[7] Seattle experienced a major recession during the early part of the experiment (mid-1970 to mid-1972). In February 1972, the unemployment rate in Seattle was 14.6%, compared to a 3.8% unemployment rate in Denver. Thus, comparisons of response between these two sites could provide a fairly powerful test of how an NIT would affect economies with substantially different demand characteristics.

[8] The income and substitution effects of a permanent program can be estimated empirically using postexperimental data (Keeley, 1977).

Table 5.1

NIT Treatment Effects on Annual Hours of Work by Experimental Quarter-Tenth Quarter Sample Husbands (Standard Errors in Parentheses)

Experimental quarter	Race					Site			Experimental duration		
	Total	Black	White	Chicano	F-test for ethnic differences	Seattle	Denver	F-test for site differences	3 Years	5 Years	F-test for duration differences
1	-16.8 (31.4)	-6.3 (54.9)	-24.4 (44.0)	-14.6 (72.2)	.03	21.3 (46.8)	-46.9 (41.7)	1.2	-13.9 (34.6)	-22.8 (43.4)	.04
2	-51.5 (32.2)	-53.1 (56.2)	-45.9 (45.1)	-64.3 (74.0)	.02	-7.1 (47.9)	-86.7** (42.7)	1.6	-37.1 (35.4)	-81.5* (44.5)	.96
3	-93.0*** (34.7)	-79.6 (60.5)	-87.5* (48.5)	-131.7* (79.6)	.15	-41.1** (51.6)	-134.0*** (45.9)	1.8	-68.1* (38.1)	-144.7*** (47.8)	2.5
4	-146.7*** (34.82)	-121.1** (60.7)	-128.0*** (48.7)	-242.9*** (79.9)	.90	-108.4** (51.8)	-177.0*** (46.2)	1.0	-118.0*** (38.3)	-206.3*** (48.0)	3.2*
5	-187.3*** (35.1)	-195.6*** (61.3)	-166.0*** (49.2)	-230.1*** (80.6)	.25	-177.3*** (52.2)	-195.2*** (46.6)	.07	-174.2*** (38.6)	-214.3*** (48.5)	.66

6	−160.2*** (35.4)	−108.5* (61.8)	−165.3*** (49.6)	−237.3*** (81.3)	.81	−156.6*** (52.7)	−163.1*** (47.0)	.01	−152.0*** (39.0)	−177.3*** (48.9)	.26
7	−146.7*** (36.7)	−141.5** (64.0)	−112.4** (51.3)**	−249.9*** (84.2)	.99	−125.5** (54.6)**	−163.5*** (48.7)	.28	−130.1*** (40.4)	−181.2*** (50.6)	.98
8	−172.2*** (36.2)	−147.3** (63.2)	−166.0*** (50.7)	−233.1*** (83.1)	.36	−161.3*** (53.9)	−180.8*** (48.0)	.07	−138.8*** (39.8)	−241.7*** (50.0)	4.1**
9	−154.7*** (38.1)	−192.7*** (66.5)	−112.9** (53.4)	−202.4** (87.5)	.63	−120.5** (56.7)	−181.7*** (50.6)	.66	−122.7*** (41.9)	−221.0*** (52.6)	3.4*
10	−183.7*** (38.8)	−193.8*** (67.6)	−123.0** (54.2)	−332.6*** (88.9)	2.1	−140.1** (57.6)	−218.2*** (51.4)	1.0	−165.6*** (42.6)	−221.2*** (53.5)	1.0

Note: Sample size = 2171. The proportion of sample receiving NIT treatment = .57.

Note: The following applies to Tables 5.1-5.3. Control variables include 8 dummy variables for normal income categories, preexperimental annual hours of work, dummy variables for black and Chicano, a dummy variable for Denver, number of family members at enrollment, number of children under 5 years of age at enrollment, AFDC benefits in the preexperimental year, age at enrollment, and three dummy variables for the manpower treatments.

Note: The following probability levels apply to Tables 5.1-5.3.

*$p < .10$.
**$p < .05$.
***$p < .10$.

Table 5.2

NIT Treatment Effects on Annual Hours of Work by Experimental Quarter-Tenth Quarter Sample Wives (Standard Errors in Parentheses)

Experimental quarter	Total	Race				Site			Experimental duration		
		Black	White	Chicano	F-test for ethnic differences	Seattle	Denver	F-test for site differences	3 Years	5 Years	F-test for duration differences
1	−16.7 (26.5)	13.8 (45.3)	−39.2 (37.6)	−12.3 (60.3)	.4	−15.2 (39.6)	−17.9 (34.9)	.00	5.2 (29.1)	−61.9* (36.3)	3.3*
2	−46.3 (29.4)	−116.8** (50.3)	−3.5 (41.7)	−32.3 (67.0)	1.6	−68.2 (44.0)	−29.4 (38.8)	.4	−16.0 (32.3)	−108.9*** (40.4)	5.1**
3	−75.6** (30.4)	−124.0** (51.9)	−17.3 (43.1)	−142.3** (69.2)	1.8	−33.7 (45.4)	−108.0*** (40.1)	1.5	−60.5* (33.4)	−106.8** (41.7)	1.2
4	−74.7** (30.7)	−128.9** (52.5)	−24.0 (43.5)	−110.5 (69.9)	1.4	−38.3 (45.9)	−102.9** (40.5)	1.1	−58.4* (33.7)	−108.3*** (42.1)	1.4
5	−76.7** (31.2)	−96.3* (53.3)	−50.8 (44.3)	−109.7 (71.0)	.4	−89.6* (46.6)	−66.7 (41.2)	.1	−62.5 (34.3)	−106.0** (42.8)	1.0

6	−116.8*** (32.2)	−152.5*** (55.1)	−54.9 (45.7)	−215.9*** (73.4)	2.1	−97.9** (48.2)	−131.5*** (42.5)	.3	−95.4*** (35.4)	−161.1*** (44.2)	2.1
7	−156.9*** (33.4)	−165.8*** (57.1)	−144.2*** (47.4)	−174.4** (76.0)	.08	−130.5*** (49.9)	−177.4*** (44.0)	.5	−138.5*** (36.7)	−194.9*** (45.8)	1.5
8	−141.0*** (33.8)	−126.4** (57.8)	−159.7*** (48.0)	−117.9 (77.0)	.2	−149.6*** (50.6)	−134.3*** (44.6)	.05	−136.5*** (37.2)	−150.2*** (46.4)	.08
9	−124.9*** (34.5)	−118.3** (58.9)	−125.6*** (48.9)	−135.2* (78.5)	.02	−106.1** (51.5)	−139.5*** (45.5)	.2	−107.9*** (37.9)	−160.0*** (47.3)	1.2
10	−113.4*** (34.9)	−118.9** (59.7)	−94.5* (49.6)	−153.4* (79.6)	.2	−81.0 (52.2)	−138.6*** (46.1)	.7	−96.5** (38.4)	−148.4*** (47.9)	1.1

Note: Sample size = 2252. The proportion of sample receiving NIT treatment = .58.

Table 5.3
NIT Treatment Effects on Annual Hours of Work by Experimental Quarter-Tenth Quarter Sample Single Female Heads
(Standard Errors in Parentheses)

Experimental quarter	Total	Race				Site			Experimental duration		
		Black	White	Chicano	F-test for ethnic differences	Seattle	Denver	F-test for site differences	3 Years	5 Years	F-test for duration differences
1	26.8 (34.9)	-1.0 (50.1)	-18.2 (55.3)	220.7*** (85.2)	3.1**	-86.1* (50.3)	127.8*** (47.6)	9.6***	25.0 (37.4)	31.3 (48.6)	.02
2	-30.6 (38.2)	-94.1* (54.9)	-11.4 (60.6)	112.4 (93.3)	1.9	-94.6* (55.2)	26.7 (52.3)	2.6	-33.3 (40.9)	-23.8 (53.2)	.03
3	-90.2** (40.0)	-140.3** (57.5)	-75.6 (63.5)	24.5 (97.8)	1.1	-119.5** (57.9)	-64.0 (54.8)	.5	-77.0* (42.9)	-123.4** (55.7)	.7
4	-66.8* (40.1)	-135.6** (57.7)	8.8 (63.7)	-44.5 (98.1)	1.5	-115.6** (58.1)	-23.2 (54.9)	1.4	-55.2 (43.0)	-96.3* (55.9)	.6
5	-102.6** (40.6)	-161.2*** (58.4)	-38.5 (64.5)	-82.6 (99.3)	1.1	-170.1*** (58.7)	-42.2 (55.6)	2.5	-96.9** (43.5)	-117.0** (56.5)	.1
6	-129.5*** (41.7)	-184.8*** (60.0)	-81.9 (66.3)	-79.8 (102.1)	.8	-198.0*** (60.3)	-68.4 (57.1)	2.5	-122.8*** (44.7)	-146.7** (58.1)	.2
7	-125.8*** (42.5)	-206.2*** (61.1)	-39.6 (67.5)	-94.8 (103.9)	1.8	-162.5*** (61.5)	-93.0 (58.2)	.7	-119.0*** (45.6)	-143.2** (59.2)	.2
8	-178.4*** (42.5)	-215.2*** (61.1)	-111.9* (67.5)	-229.3** (104.0)	.8	-151.7** (61.5)	-202.3*** (58.2)	.4	-174.4*** (45.5)	-188.5*** (59.2)	.06
9	-198.9*** (42.7)	-233.6*** (61.4)	-151.0** (67.9)	-211.2 (104.5)	.4	-210.5*** (61.8)	-188.5*** (58.5)	.07	-195.9*** (45.8)	-206.5*** (59.5)	.03
10	-205.1*** (44.2)	-238.8*** (63.5)	-156.1** (70.1)	-222.5** (108.0)	.4	-225.3*** (63.9)	-186.9*** (60.5)	.2	-212.1*** (47.3)	-187.3*** (61.5)	.2

Note: Sample size = 1656. The proportion of sample receiving NIT treatment = .63.

for reasons outside the person's control or the job becomes undesirable for other reasons, the person may find a new job having hours consistent with his desires.

A variety of models can be specified that do not assume that individuals immediately adjust to the experiment. One such model imposes a constraint on the time pattern of response and is based on the assumption that each person adjusts his hours of work by the proportion, d, of the difference between desired and actual hours of work in every period. We call this model a partial adjustment model. The partial adjustment model enables the estimation of the long-run responses to the experiment as well as the speed at which the adjustment takes place. (See Robins and West, 1978b, for a complete description of the model.)

Table 5.4 presents estimates of the long-run response to the NIT treatments and the speed of adjustments (at half-year intervals.)[9] The results indicate that the long-run NIT treatment effects on hours of work are −191 hours per year for husbands, −140 hours per year for wives, and −265 hours per year for single female heads of families. The corresponding percentage effects are −9%, −20%, and −25%, respectively. The speeds of adjustment are .39 for husbands, .27 for wives, and .22 for single female heads. Thus, from 22% to 39% of the deviation between actual and desired hours is removed each half year. The time periods required for 90% adjustment are 2.4 years for husbands, 3.6 years for wives, and 4.5 years for single female heads.[10]

Table 5.4
Estimates from Partial Adjustment Model
(Estimated Asymptotic Standard Errors in Parentheses)

	Husbands	Wives	Single female heads
Speed of adjustment per half year (λ)	.385*** (.013)	.274*** (.011)	.224*** (.012)
Long-run financial treatment effect	−190.5*** (32.6)	−139.5*** (37.3)	−264.7*** (54.4)

***$p < .01$.

The estimated responses to the NIT treatment appear to be somewhat lower than the quarterly estimates generated from the previous (unconstrained) model. So that the estimated responses may be more easily compared, Figure 5.1 contains graphs of the quarterly responses estimated with the previous model and the calculated half-year responses from the partial adjustment model. Responses using the unconstrained model (Model I) are represented by points and responses using the constrained adjustment model (Model II) are represented by solid lines. As can be seen, the fit of Model II is generally good.

[9] See Robins and West (1978b) for estimates of the long-run responses to the manpower treatments and the effects of the other (nonexperimental) variables in the model.
[10] These figures are calculated as log(.1)/log(1 - λ), where λ is the speed of adjustment.

PHILIP K. ROBINS AND RICHARD W. WEST

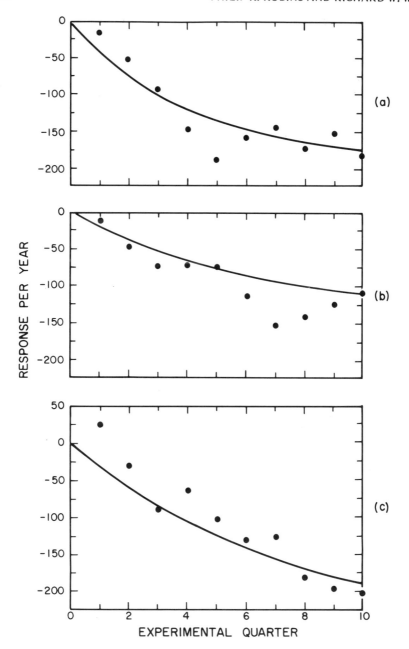

FIGURE 5.1 Comparison of constrained and unconstrained estimates (annual rates): (a) husbands, (b) wives, (c) single female heads. •, Model I; —, Model II.

RACE, SITE, AND EXPERIMENTAL DURATION
DIFFERENCES IN RESPONSE

Having discussed the overall results, we now proceed to discuss differences in the long-run financial treatment effects by race, site, and experimental duration given in Table 5.5. The results indicate that there are no significant differences in response by race, site, or experimental duration for either wives or single female heads. However, for husbands the differences are significant for all three variables. Black and Chicano husbands have a response somewhat over twice the response of white husbands. The response of husbands in Denver is about twice the response of husbands in Seattle.[11] The response of husbands on the 5-year program is 1.6 times the response of husbands on the 3-year program, thus indicating that the bias arising from the temporary nature of the experiment is larger for the income effect than for the substitution effect.

The finding of a significant difference in the estimated response of husbands in the 3- and 5-year samples is important because of its implication for the effects of a permanent program. Presumably, the larger response of 5-year husbands implies that husbands in a permanent program would have an even larger response. However, it is important to note that the estimated difference between the 3- and 5-year program is for some average of the NIT plans tested in SIME/DIME. Since the theoretical biases of a short duration experiment have opposite signs according to whether the response is generated by the substitution effect (which is overestimated) or the income effect (which is underestimated), the total bias of a particular program will vary with the guarantee level and the tax rate of that plan. The plans that might actually be implemented are likely to have lower guarantee levels than the average support level of SIME/DIME. Consequently, the differences between the permanent effects of such a program and predictions from a limited duration experiment may be less than the difference implied by our estimates.

These results are somewhat different from the results using Model I. The results for Model I indicate no race, site, or duration differences for any group. The results of Model II indicate the presence of race, site, and duration differences for husbands, although there are still no significant differences for wives and single female heads. The estimated Model II differences by duration for wives are, however, large and in the same direction as for husbands. It should be noted that we can have greater confidence in the Model II results, because Model II constrains the response over time and thus provides a more powerful test of the null hypotheses of no differences.

---

[11] This result could be due to the fact that there are no Chicanos in Seattle, thus reflecting race rather than site differences. Tests for the black and white sample only (Chicanos excluded), however, indicate that when Chicanos are excluded, the site difference is significant at the 10% level and the Denver response is still twice as large as the Seattle response.

Table 5.5
Ethnic, Site, and Duration Differences in the
Long-Run NIT Treatment Response
(Estimated Asymptotic Standard Errors in Parentheses)

	Husbands	Wives	Single female heads
Total	−190.5***	−139.5***	−264.8***
	(32.6)	(37.4)	(55.4)
Ethnicity			
Black	−270.6***	−148.8***	−284.8***
	(48.1)	(53.1)	(66.6)
White	−112.2***	−116.8***	−196.2***
	(40.5)	(46.4)	(70.9)
Chicano	−255.7***	−175.4***	−359.3***
	(56.9)	(62.2)	(95.5)
x^2	10.436***	.817	2.772
Site			
Seattle	−121.7***	−139.3***	−251.8***
	(42.7)	(48.6)	(68.5)
Denver	−240.9***	−139.6***	−274.4***
	(38.4)	(43.2)	(62.4)
x^2	6.181**	.000	.099
Duration			
3 years	−159.2***	−119.5***	−250.1***
	(35.7)	(40.9)	(58.3)
5 years	−255.9***	−180.4***	−300.5***
	(45.2)	(51.6)	(75.7)
x^2	4.416**	1.338	.466

Note: The coefficients represent the long-run NIT treatment effect. The x^2 statistics are for the test of the null hypotheses of no ethnic, site, or duration differences. Degree of freedom are 2 for the ethnicity tests and 1 for the site and duration tests.
  *$p < .10$.
  **$p < .05$.
  ***$p < .01$.

SUMMARY

This chapter has investigated race, site, and experimental duration differences in the labor supply response to SIME/DIME. Two different models were specified in an attempt to identify such differences. In a model where the experimental effect was allowed to vary freely over time, there was no firm evidence of differences in response by race, site, and experimental duration, although in many cases the differences were large enough to be potentially important in a behavioral sense.

To improve the precision of the estimates, a second model was specified in which the time pattern of response was restricted to follow a geometric form. The results of this model showed significant differences in response by race, site, and experimental duration for husbands, but not for wives or single female heads of families. White husbands had a smaller response than black or Chicano husbands; husbands in Seattle had a smaller response than husbands in Denver; and husbands in the 3-year sample had a smaller response than husbands in the 5-year sample. According to the second model, the estimated length of time required to adjust to 90% of the long-run equilibrium labor supply under the NIT in this model was 2.4 years for husbands, 3.6 years for wives, and 4.5 years for single female heads of families.

REFERENCES

Keeley, Michael C. "Using Post Experimental Data to Derive the Effects of a Permanent Income Maintenance Program." Mimeographed. Center for the Study of Welfare Policy, SRI International, April 1977.

Kurz, Mordecai, and Spiegelman, Robert G. "The Design of the Seattle and Denver Income Maintenance Experiments." Research Memorandum No. 18, Center for the Study of Welfare Policy, SRI International, May 1972.

Metcalf, Charles E., "Making Inferences from Controlled Income Maintenance Experiments." *American Economic Review* 63 (June 1973).

Robins, Philip K., and West, Richard W. "Participation in the Seattle and Denver Income Maintenance Experiments and Its Effects on Labor Supply." Research Memorandum No. 53, Center for the Study of Welfare Policy, SRI International, March 1978a.

Robins, Philip K., and West, Richard. "A Longitudinal Analysis of the Labor Supply Response to a Negative Income Tax Program: Evidence from the Seattle and Denver Income Maintenance Experiments. Research Memorandum No. 59, Center for the Study of Welfare Policy, SRI International, December 1978b.

CHAPTER 6

Using Labor Supply Results to Simulate Welfare Reform Alternatives

DAVID BETSON
DAVID GREENBERG
RICHARD KASTEN

One of the major reasons the income-maintenance experiments were conducted was to provide policymakers with predictions of the costs and effects of alternatives to the existing welfare system. The Seattle/Denver experiments represent perhaps the clearest and most important example of experimental results actually used for this purpose. SIME/DIME have provided information about labor supply behavior that has been incorporated into a large-scale microsimulation model used extensively within the government to evaluate various welfare reform alternatives, including the Carter administration's 1977 welfare reform proposal, the Program for Better Jobs and Income (PBJI).[1] This simulation model, which has become known as the KGB model, was developed in the Office of Income Security Policy, within the Department of Health, Education and Welfare and has been used by HEW, the Department of Labor, and the Congressional Budget Office. The model can use data on a representative sample of the nation's households to simulate the effects and costs of a number of possible components of welfare reform (including new cash transfer programs, changes in the positive tax system, and public service employment), and allows for labor supply responses to all these components. A novel feature of the model is that it provides estimates of potential participation in a guaranteed jobs program.

In this chapter, we describe the KGB model, indicate the critical role the Seattle/Denver labor supply results play in its operation, and illustrate some applications of it.[2] Although uses of the model are principally illustrated through the presentation of results from simulations of the PBJI, it is important to recognize that this program represents only one possible welfare reform alternative.

---

[1] Illustrations of how simulations based on the Seattle/Denver labor supply results were used in the 1977 welfare reform effort may be found in Aaron and Todd (1978).

[2] A more detailed and technical discussion of the model, its applications, and its limitations may be found in Betson et al. (1980) from which this chapter is adapted.

101

A GUARANTEED ANNUAL INCOME:
EVIDENCE FROM A SOCIAL EXPERIMENT

The model has been and continues to be used to analyze a large number of other options. In examining these options, it has been used to investigate a wide range of issues, including the distributional effects of alternative levels of the federal basic benefit, state supplementation levels and funding formulas, benefit reduc-rates, wage rates in public employment programs, and eligibility rules for both cash transfer payments and public service jobs. By providing policymakers with information about the effects of marginal changes in each of these policy param-eters, the model can be used to quantify and highlight the trade offs involved in actual policy choices.

The basic structure of the KGB model is outlined in the first section. The sec-ond section uses the model to develop estimates of the costs and effects of a pro-gram very similar to the PBJI. Major existing weaknesses of the model and plans to remedy these weaknesses are briefly considered in the penultimate section. The final section presents our conclusions.

STRUCTURE OF THE MODEL

In addition to information on labor supply responses from SIME/DIME,[3] the KGB simulation model incorporates three other components: (a) a set of com-puter modules that can be used to simulate changes in tax and transfer policy, (b) a methodology for predicting whether or not particular individual will parti-cipate in guaranteed employment programs, and (c) a stratified random sample survey of the nation's households that is large enough to provide reliable infor-mation at a state level and that provides accurate data on individuals' wage rates, hours of work, and numerous other variables.

Extensive developmental work on microsimulation modules for simulating the costs and effects of modifications in the transfer and positive tax system had been conducted at the Urban Institute and at the Mathematica Policy Research (MPR) before the KGB model was developed. The Urban Institute version of this modeling effort is known as TRIM and the MPR version as MATH.[4] Certain modules from TRIM and MATH were adapted for use in the KGB simulation model. In other cases, however, the required modules were not available and we

---

[3] The initial work that was necessary to utilize the Seattle/Denver behavioral responses estimates for simulation purposes was conducted jointly by Mathmatica Policy Research and SRI, International. See Keeley *et al.* (1978) and Maxfield (1977), and U.S. Department of Health, Education and Welfare (1978). The resulting computer modules was subsequent-ly modified and adopted for use in the KGB model. To use behavioral response estimates from SIME/DIME in a simulation of the national effects of welfare reform, it is obviously necessary to assume that behavioral adjustments by the national population to changes in the welfare system would be similar to those in Seattle and Denver.

[4] A brief history of the evolution of models for simulating changes in tax and transfer policy appears in Beebout (1977). A description of TRIM is found in Beebout and Bonina (1973). A description of MATH can be found in Beebout (1976).

constructed our own. Work on developing a methodology for predicting whether workers will participate in employment programs was performed by Greenberg (1978) and was incorporated into the KGB model after suitable modification.

Although several different available surveys can be used by the KGB model (and indeed have been in other work) simulation estimates reported in this chapter are based on the 1975 Survey of Income and Education (SIE). The SIE sample consists of nearly 200,000 households. The data are relatively recent and contain comparatively good measures of many key variables required for the simulations, including wage rates, household income by source, and hours. Moreover, the SIE provides statistically reliable samples for individual states. This is particularly important because of concern over the fiscal impact that various welfare reform alternatives will have on individual states and interest in the state-by-state distribution of the demand for public employment job slots. Since the SIE data pertain to 1975, the simulation results may be viewed as estimating what the effects and costs of the reforms simulated would have been had they been operative in 1975.

Steps Required For Simulation

Simulation of a proposed alternative to the existing tax and transfer system proceeds in four major steps. First, the prereform economic status of a representative sample of the nation's families is characterized. Some characteristics, such as hours, earnings, and unearned income, can be obtained directly from the SIE data. Others, such as taxes paid and tax rates, are derived from schedules. Still others, including tax rates in current transfer programs and unemployment compensation amounts, are determined from predictive equations.

Second, the values of net wage rates and disposable income are adjusted to what they would be if the simulated reform measure were implemented but work effort and earnings remained unchanged. For workers who are eligible for a public employment job, it is necessary to compute what the values of the variables would be if (a) the worker leaves the conventional labor market to take a public employment job (which we characterize as the pure strategy), (b) the worker remains attached to the conventional job sector and takes a public employment job only when he or she is unemployed (the mixed strategy), or (c) the worker does not participate in public employment at all (the private strategy).

The third step consists of adjusting the values of the postreform variables to account for labor supply responses to changes in wage rates and disposable income under each public employment strategy. The values obtained from the first two steps are used to calculate the changes in net wage rates[5] and disposable in-

---

[5] The net wage rate is simply an individual's nominal wage appropriately reduced to account for the cumulative tax rate he or she faces.

comes that would result from the welfare reform, prior to any labor supply responses. Predictions of the effects on work hours of the reform are then derived by multiplying these calculated changes by the appropriate labor supply parameters estimated from SIME/DIME. Once these labor supply adjustments are computed, they are used to determine the number of hours individuals would work during the postreform period. Given these estimates of the hours family members would work, household earnings, transfer payment receipts, and tax payments can then be recomputed.

The first three steps of the simulation procedure, therefore, provide (a) estimates of postreform income by source for a sample of households and (b) estimates of the postreform hours of work for members of these households. Where a household member is eligible for a public service job, it is necessary to compute alternative sets of postreform income and labor market measures for each of the three public employment strategies listed above.

The fourth step in the simulation involves comparing these measures to determine whether an individual who is eligible for public employment will take such a job whenever he is in the labor force, only when he is unemployed, or not at all. Since this is probably the most novel feature of the simulation methodology, it is discussed in some detail.

Individual Decision on Participation in Public Employment

It seems reasonable to view an individual who is eligible for public employment as engaging in a comparison between the jobs program and his best opportunity within the conventional job sector, and as choosing the alternative that makes his family best off.[6] In general, one would expect that the chosen alternative offers the highest income level at a fixed number of hours worked.[7]

[6] The simulation methodology assumes that this choice is made on the basis of perfect information about the alternatives, an assumption that probably results in an overstatement of the public employment supply population. Unless persons are aware of public employment and know something about it, the program is not a viable alternative for them. Knowledge of the program is likely to be positively related to the publicity given the program, the length of time the program has been in operation, and the size of the program.

[7] For purposes of the simulation, it is assumed that individuals will participate in public employment whenever the program is viewed by them as marginally superior to their best conventional sector alternatives. In actual practice, however, a substantial differential between public and conventional employment may be necessary, if only to overcome inertia. Nevertheless, many of the frictions that exist in labor markets would be reduced over the long run. For example, many persons may not actively consider voluntarily leaving their present job to participate in public employment; but, once they have been terminated or laid off, they may seriously examine public employment as a possible alternative to available conventional job opportunities. Thus, the methodology is best viewed as being based on a static model of economic behavior; the adjustments to the introduction of a public employment program would not take place instantaneously, but only over time. The larger the comparative advantage of public employment, the more rapidly the adjustments would be expected to occur.

An individual is not confined to all-or-nothing choices between public and conventional employment. He may also participate in public employment during his weeks of unemployment, returning to the conventional sector when an opportunity becomes available. This mixed strategy seems, in fact, to be the possibility stressed by most advocates of large-scale public employment programs. Under certain circumstances, however, the mixed strategy may not be a viable alternative. Some unemployed persons may be unwilling to participate in public employment if the program wage is below their usual market wage, and some may be unwilling to relinquish unemployment compensation to accept a public employment job. Moreover, public employment programs may require a waiting period before an unemployed person becomes eligible for participation, and this waiting period may exceed the length of his spell of unemployment. These considerations are explicitly treated by the simulation procedure.

To determine if various persons would participate in given public employment programs and whether they would select the pure or the mixed approach if they do participate, it has been necessary to develop a set of participation tests. These tests assume individuals will chose the strategy that maximizes the expected value of their family's stream of future disposable income after all labor supply adjustments have taken place.[8]

The Components of Disposable Income

Since individuals' decisions to take public service jobs depend on comparisons of family disposable income, it is obviously necessary to obtain information on its components. Moreover, in a simulation of welfare reform proposals, many of these components (such as transfer receipts from various sources and tax payments) are of direct interest in themselves.

As indicated earlier, the first step in the simulation of a welfare reform proposal is to find the values of these income components prior to the reform. Various provisions of the proposed reform (such as eligibility criteria, guarantee levels and tax rates for new transfer programs, and wage rates and hours regulations for public employment programs) then can be used in combination with the estimated labor-supply response parameters to determine how the components would change were the reform implemented.

[8] This assumption has a shortcoming for individuals who are unable to choose freely the number of hours they work in either the conventional sector or the public employment sector. In such cases, family income might be higher if an individual picks one sector over the other, but only because he would work a longer number of hours. If so, the individual must trade off a higher family income against lower hours, and his choice will not be clear. Thus, the assumption that individuals will participate in public employment if this strategy maximizes family disposable income results in some persons being misclassified as public employment participants and others being misclassified as nonparticipants. A procedure that eliminates this problem has been developed and will soon be implemented into the simulation model. Preliminary tests of this procedure suggest that it produces results very similar to those produced by the simpler procedure used for the purposes of this study.

Because the SIE does not contain complete or reliable data on all transfer receipts or tax payments under existing programs or on the tax rates that are associated with such programs, it was necessary to use various estimating procedures for certain transfers. In using these procedures, SIE data on nontransfer income, family size and structure, and personal characteristics were used in combination with the statutory requirements of existing programs and several predictive regression equations. For example, Social Security tax payments and tax rates were estimated from reported earnings in the SIE file and Social Security regulations. Similarly, measures of federal and state income tax payments and marginal tax rates were obtained from SIE data on nontransfer income and from the appropriate tax schedules (although, in the case of federal income tax payments, part of the necessary computer programming was simply duplicated from an existing TRIM module).

Since the transfer payments reported in the SIE file fall short of actual state outlays, it is also necessary to make certain adjustments in order to reach control totals. Reported transfers are used whenever positive, and a fraction of those who reported none are chosen randomly and assigned an imputed amount. AFDC tax rates are based on MPRs regression estimates of actual program experience in individual states. The payment schedules in the appropriate law are used to determine food stamp receipts and benefit reduction rates. The SSI benefit reduction rates are derived from schedules implied in the law.

Unemployment compensation amounts are derived from three regression equations estimated at the Urban Institute specifically for use in the KGB model. These regressions predict for various workers their probability of receiving payments when unemployed, the length of eligibility, and the weekly payment. Individuals are chosen randomly to receive payments on the basis of the probability estimates, and then the predicted length and predicted weekly payment are used to compute their total payments.

It has already been pointed out that the KGB model assumes an individual will choose the public employment strategy that yields the highest future stream of disposable income for his family. If he continues to work in the private sector, however, his future income depends on how much unemployment he will incur, which is something he cannot know with certainty. We assume that he makes his choice on the basis of expected unemployment. Two regression equations from the Urban Institute's Dynasim model, which predict the probability and length of spells of unemployment on the basis of individual characteristics, are used to determine the fraction of a worker's time in the labor force that he or she expects to be unemployed.

Market wage rates for workers are computed directly from the SIE data by dividing annual hours worked into earnings. Those for nonworkers are imputed from regressions estimated on data from the Panel Survey on Income Dynamics. Each imputed wage includes a random error that maintains consistency with the actual distribution of wages.

Annual hours worked prior to the welfare reform are available directly in the SIE. The number of hours that individuals work during the postreform period, however, will be affected by a number of factors. To examine how these factors are treated in the simulation, it is useful to consider an individual's hours worked if he or she (a) does not participate in public employment at all, (b) adopts the pure strategy toward public employment, or (c) takes the mixed approach.

Even if the individual does not consider public employment, his hours will be affected if the proposed reform changes his income or his marginal tax rate. As described earlier, the response to these changes is predicted through the use of estimated labor supply parameters from SIME/DIME.[9]

The hours that an individual works in public employment if he or she becomes a pure strategy participant are estimated in three steps. First, since the individual is no longer subject to involuntary unemployment, the reported hours of unemployment are added to the measure of the hours he or she worked during the prereform period.[10] Second, the individual's labor supply response is calculated in much the same manner as for nonparticipants in public employment, except that any differences between the worker's market wage and the program wage are taken into account. This yields an estimate of the hours the individual is willing to supply to the program, given the program wage rate. The individual's program supply hours are then compared to the maximum hours participants in the program are allowed to work, and the smaller of these two quantities is denoted as program hours worked.

The hours an individual works under the mixed strategy may be computed by summing the worker's hours of conventional sector work (calculation of which has already been described) and the public employment hours he or she works while unemployed. In computing this latter figure, the simulation takes account of any differences between the individual's market wage and the program wage (for most mixed participants, the latter is likely to be smaller) and any losses in unemployment compensation that result from taking the public service job. Losses in unemployment compensation are treated essentially as if they reduce the public employment wage rate. The simulation also ensures that mixed strategy hours conform to the limits on the number of public employment hours that may be worked each week and to the restrictions on the number of weeks unemployed individuals may participate in public employment.

---

[9] Two separate sets of labor supply estimates are actually used to make these calculations. The first, which is based on a logit regression equation, predicts changes in the probability of participating in the labor force. Based on these predicted changes, a random number generator is used to reassign some nonworkers to a worker status. Then the second set of estimates is used to predict adjustments in annual hours for both the new workers and previous workers.

[10] This implicit assumption (that reported unemployment accurately reflects the involuntary loss of time to the labor market) appears consistent with the premise underlying most proposals for public employment programs.

SIMULATION OF THE CARTER ADMINISTRATION'S
WELFARE REFORM PROGRAM

On August 6, 1977, President Carter announced a proposal for welfare reform —the Program for Better Jobs and Income (PBJI). Although the program was ultimately not accepted by Congress, future welfare reform efforts are likely to contain features similar to those found in PBJI. In this section, we illustrate how the KGB model has been applied to practical issues by using it to simulate the PBJI proposal.

Major Features of the Program for Better Jobs and Income[11]

The PBJI proposal was designed to provide the low-income population with access to jobs and to a consolidated cash assistance program that replaced the federal share of AFDC, SSI, and food stamps. It placed considerable emphasis on the desirability of work and included a jobs component designed to reduce the assistance burden from the cash supplement plan as much as possible. Under the program, adults who were expected to work were required to register with an employment and training agency that would seek to locate private sector employment for them. Primary or principle earners in families with children who did not gain sector employment were to be offered a public service job. The public service jobs were to pay at least the minimum wage and were to be full time for all recipients except single parents with young children. Single parents of children under 14 were permitted to choose between full-time and part-time public service jobs.

The cash assistance component of PBJI distinguished between recipients who were expected to work and recipients who might work, but were not required to do so. A separate benefit schedule was maintained for each of these groups: an income support tier for the households that did not include a person expected to work, and an earned-income supplement tier for households that did not include a person expected to work.

Those eligible for the income support tier included the aged, the blind, the disabled, and single-parent families in which the youngest child is under 7. In 1978 dollars,[12] the basic federal cash benefit paid to a single parent with one child with no other income was set at $3000. For each additional child, this basic benefit was raised by $600. The basic benefit for a single-parent family of four, therefore, was $4200, or 65% of the poverty line. These basic benefits were

---

[11] Only the basic essentials of the PBJI are described here. See U.S. Department of Health, Education and Welfare (1977) for a fuller description of the Program. Simulations reported on in this paper are limited to the PBJI, as originally proposed to Congress.

[12] The description of the PBJI is presented here in 1978 dollars. These amounts are deflated to 1975 dollars for use with the SIE in the simulations.

reduced by $.50 for each dollar of earnings in states where supplements are not received and by not more than $.70 in states that supplement federal benefit levels.

The earned-income support tier covered families with a member expected to work, i.e., two-parent families with children, single-parent families with children of school age or above (when the children are 7-13, only part-time work is expected), childless couples, and single individuals. The basic benefit for the spouse and each child in two-parent families was set equal to $1100 and $600, respectively, while the adult expected to work received nothing during an initial 8-week period of job search and nothing thereafter if he or she refused work. The basic benefit for a two-parent family of four was set at $2300, or 36% of the poverty line. If a regular job could not be found and the primary earner was put into a public service job, the worker could keep all of the first $3800 of earned income. Above that level, cash payments were to be reduced by $.50 for each dollar of earnings. This combination of cash supplements and employment opportunities meant that a family of four with one member working full time at the minimum wage would receive a total income of at least 113% of the poverty line.

Single-parent families with all children over 14 were to be treated similarly to two-parent families, but the heads of single-parent families with the youngest child aged 7-13 years were only to be required to work part time while the children were in school. As in the case of two-parent families, the government was to provide public service jobs when regular employment could not be found.

Public service jobs were not to be provided to childless couples and single individuals. These persons were eligible, however, for a basic benefit of $1100 per adult, to be paid during the job search period and continued until a job could be found, but cut off if the individual refused a job paying at least the minimum wage. A reduction of benefits by $.50 for each dollar of earnings was to begin with the first dollar of earnings.

In addition to the jobs and cash components just described, the PBJI would also have amended the earned income tax credit that then existed. Under this provision, poor families with children could receive a refundable tax credit of $.10 for each dollar of earnings up to $4000. The benefit then fell by $.10 for each dollar of gross income beyond $4000. Thus, the benefit was zero for those with no earnings, reached a maximum of $400 for those who earned $4000, and fell to zero when income equaled $8000. Under the PBJI, families were to receive 10% of their first $4000 of private sector earnings plus 5% of any private sector earnings between $4000 and 216% above their federal basic benefit level. The tax credit was then to be reduced by $.10 for each dollar of income above this amount until it phased out and the tax credit was not to apply to earnings from public service jobs, in order to make private employment more attractive than a public service job paying the same wage rate.

Specific Assumptions underlying the Simulation

The simulation results reported here may be viewed as an attempt to answer the following question: What would the effects of PBJI have been in 1975 had the program been operative in that year, had all behavioral adjustments to the program already taken place, and had the Food Stamp program reforms contained in the Food and Agricultural Act of 1977 been in place at the time PBJI was implemented? In keeping with this scenario, we have assumed the following:

1. Demographic composition and economic conditions for calendar year 1975 are accurately represented by the SIE, in particular, an 8.5% unemployment rate for the overall economy.
2. The 1975 tax and transfer system (except for the provisions of the Food and Agriculture Act of 1977) represents prereform conditions facing individuals.
3. States supplement up to the smaller of the following amounts: (*a*) the limits of matching supplementation or (*b*) the state's 1975 AFDC benefit levels plus the bonus value of food stamps for families with children; their 1975 general assistance (GA) amounts for single individuals and childless couples; and their 1975 SSI benefit levels plus the bonus value of food stamps for aged, blind, and disabled filing units.
4. States do *not* grandfather current AFDC, SSI, or GA recipients.
5. The work test functions perfectly for families with children.
6. Sufficient public employment jobs are created so that all eligible workers who want one can obtain one.
7. The program uses an annual accounting period.
8. Any primary earner who was self-employed and had more than a grade school education does not participate in the jobs component of PBJI.
9. Single adults who live with a relative choose whether or not to file as part of their relative's family so as to maximize total transfer benefits.[13]

Results of the Simulation

Discussion of results from the simulation of the PBJI centers on three areas. The first involves eligibility for and participation in the cash component of the program. The second area covers the characteristics of the participants in the jobs component of PBJI. The final area concerns effects of PBJI on disposable income and work effort.

[13] This last assumption attempts to allow for the fact that PBJI leaves the filing unit a matter of choice when single adults reside with a relative's family. The assumption, however, may lead to small overestimates of cash costs and underestimates of job costs because some families would reject their cash-maximizing filing situation in order to permit someone who would otherwise be ineligible to take a public service job.

Participants in the Cash Component of PBJI

The simulation results indicate that, had PBJI existed in 1975, 34.3 million people, or 16% of the total U.S. population, would have been eligible for cash payments of $21.5 billion. However, more persons would have been entitled to benefits than would have actually received them because, for various reasons, some eligible families would fail to participate in the cash program. The KGB simulations attempt to take this factor into consideration, and Table 6.1 permits us to compare the population eligible for cash assistance with the part of this population predicted to participate. In examining this table, it is important to keep in mind that the estimates pertain to persons who would receive cash assistance at any point during the year.[14] Most published statistics on caseloads under current cash programs refer, in contrast, to persons receiving payments during a particular month. Hence, the caseload estimates presented in Table 6.1 are not directly comparable to statistics that report caseloads under current programs.

Table 6.1 indicates that 27.8 million people would have received a cash payment under PBJI in 1975, only 81% of the persons who were eligible to participate. This level of participation would result in a 13% reduction in the annual entitlement of $21.5 billion. The table also implies considerable variation in participation among different recipient groups. For example, participation rates range from 71% for filing units composed of non-ABD (aged, blind, or disabled) childless couples to 89% for filing units of not-expected-to-work families with children.

While filing-unit participation rates range from 71% to 89%, benefits as a percentage of entitlements range from 79% to 94%. Thus, percentage reductions in cash benefits are smaller than corresponding reductions in the number of participants. This is consistent with the expectation that families become less likely to participate in cash assistance programs as their potential benefits from the programs become smaller.

Characteristics of the Public Service Employment Population

One of the primary motivations for the creation of the KGB model was the need to estimate the number and characteristics of persons who would enter public employment programs. Information on this topic appears in Table 6.2, which shows the economic and demographic groups from which participants in the jobs component of PBJI would have been drawn. The table indicates the number of individuals with given characteristics who would have participated in

---

[14] Simulations conducted with monthly data from the SIME/DIME control group imply that moving from an annual accounting period to a monthly accounting period with a 6-month carry forward provision would increase costs by about 2% and the caseload by about 5%.

Table 6.1
Eligibility For and Participation In the Cash Assistance Components of PBJI

Categories of	U.S. population		Eligibles for cash assistance			Participants in cash assistance		
	Persons (millions)	Filing units (millions)	Persons (millions)	Filing units (millions)	Cash entitlements ($billions)	Persons (millions)	Filing units (millions)	Cash payments (billions)
Expected-to-work families with children	103.3	25.1	12.3	2.6	3.7	9.5	2.0	3.0
Single individuals (non-ABD)	26.7	26.7	2.0	2.0	1.4	1.4	1.4	1.1
Childless couples (Non-ABD)	33.3	16.7	1.3	.7	.6	.9	.5	.5
Not-expected-to-work families with children	20.5	6.7	12.7	3.8	10.0	11.4	3.4	9.4
Single individuals (ABD)	11.7	11.7	4.4	4.4	4.8	3.4	3.4	4.0
Childless couples (ABD)	15.3	7.7	1.6	.8	1.0	1.2	.6	.8
Total	210.9	94.6	34.3	14.1	21.5	27.8	11.2	18.7

Table 6.2
Characteristics of the Public Service Employment Participants (in 1000s)

Demographic groups	Pure			Mixed			Total		
	Persons	Slots	Average weeks	Persons	Slots	Average weeks	Persons	Slots	Average weeks
Total	1052	690	34	1792	674	19	2844	1337	24
Sex									
Male	287	229	42	1077	407	20	1364	636	24
Female	765	461	31	715	240	17	1480	700	25
Education									
0-8	279	177	33	341	127	19	620	305	26
9-11	308	197	33	515	197	20	823	394	25
12 and over	465	315	35	936	323	18	1405	638	24
Age									
18-25	249	157	33	502	171	18	751	328	23
26-35	279	177	33	620	228	19	899	404	23
36-45	246	163	34	431	165	20	677	328	25
46-55	178	127	37	189	67	18	367	194	28
Over 55	100	65	34	51	17	17	151	82	28
Private sector wage rate									
Less than $2.10	1043	685	34	196	56	15	1240	742	31
$2.11-$3	9	5	28	468	150	17	478	156	17
$3.01-$5	0	0	0	615	226	19	615	226	19
Over $5	0	0	0	513	214	22	513	214	22
Region									
Northeast	201	119	31	398	172	22	598	291	25
North Central	220	141	33	490	177	19	710	318	25
South	476	325	36	571	188	17	1047	513	25
West	155	105	35	333	109	17	488	214	23

the jobs program, the number of full-time equivalent positions or slots they would have occupied, and the average number of weeks during the year they would have been employed by the program. For example, Table 6.2 indicates that a total of 2.8 million individuals would have participated in the PBJI jobs program sometime during 1975, that they would have required 1.34 million slots, and that their average length of stay in the program during the year would have been 24 weeks.

As described earlier, the KBG model distinguishes between public employment participants who follow the pure strategy and no longer seek conventional sector employment and those who follow the mixed strategy and only accept public service jobs when they are unemployed. The simulation results indicate that 63% of the participants in the public employment component of the PBJI would have been workers following the mixed strategy, but that these persons would have occupied only 48% of the total slots. The average mixed strategy participant would have remained in the program for 19 weeks. While 19 weeks is considerably higher than the average duration of unemployment in 1975 (which was 14.1 weeks), 30.7% of those who were unemployed during the year remained unemployed for more than 15 weeks (U.S. Department of Labor, 1977). Persons in this latter group are the ones most likely to be drawn into public employment.

One provision of the jobs program to which there was considerable objection, especially among feminist groups, was the primary-earner rule. It has been argued that this rule would have served to keep women out of the program. While it is estimated that the rule would have screened out many wives in two-parent families, our projections on the sex of participants in the PBJI jobs program indicates that over half would have been women, and they would have occupied over half of the total program slots.

Public service slots and participants would apparently have been about equally divided between high school graduates and nongraduates. Table 6.2 also suggests that a majority of public employment participants would have been under 35 years of age. However, there appears to be a modest increase in weeks of stay on the program during the year as age increases.

As would be expected, almost all pure strategy participants would have had a market wage rate below the 1975 minimum wage of $2.10.[15] Mixed strategy participants, on the other hand, would mainly have been drawn from relatively higher wage groups.

The number of public service job slots among census regions varied markedly, reflecting regional distributions of wage rates and unemployment. For example,

[15] The 11,000 pure strategy participants with wage rates above the minimum can be accounted for by two factors. First, some states are required to supplement the public employment wage by as much as 10%. Second, certain individuals with very high levels of expected future unemployment will prefer the pure strategy to the mixed, since under the mixed strategy they are forced to incur the public employment waiting period each time they become unemployed.

37% of the participants and 38% of the slots would have been located in the southern census region. It is also useful to note that almost 2/3 of the total slots going to the South consisted of pure participants, while more than half of the total in the rest of the country was accounted for by mixed participants. This difference mainly reflects the relatively high proportion of southern workers who are paid less than the minimum wage.

The Effect of the Program on Disposable Income and Work Effort

The effects of the PBJI on various components of household disposable income can be examined in Table 6.3.[16] As the bottom line of this table indicates, the net increase in total disposable income would have been almost $5 billion. The remainder of the table suggests that this increase results from some fairly dramatic changes in certain components of income, particularly earnings.

Earnings from the public employment component of the program would have equaled $6.2 billion. This increase in income would have been partially offset, however, by a $1.1 billion decrease in private sector earnings, so that the net improvement in earned income would have only equaled $5.1 billion. The $1.1 billion reduction in private sector earnings resulted from workers leaving low-wage private jobs in order to take public service jobs and, to a much lesser extent, from labor supply responses to work disincentives associated with the cash component of the program.

Direct cash assistance payments (including food stamp benefits) to families would have decreased by $1.78 billion. This results, in part, because of changes in eligibility requirements and in rules concerning allowable work-related deductions, and in part, because of the increase in earnings that low-income workers would have attained from public service jobs. The decrease in cash assistance payments would have been partly offset by an expansion of the earned-income tax credit. However, the $2.9 billion increase in tax credits would not only have been paid to cash assistance recipients, but also to households at considerably higher income levels.

The net increase in earnings that would have resulted from public employment would also have produced certain additional effects that are shown in Table 6.3. For example, unemployment compensation payments would have been reduced by $670 million, and tax revenues received by state and federal treasuries would have been increased by a total of $470 million.

As already indicated, when all the outlays are considered, PBJI would have resulted in an increase in disposable income of $5 billion. The net cost to state and federal treasuries of this increase would have been $6.14 billion, an amount that

---

[16] Financing the program would, of course, also have affected disposable incomes. However, these considerations are ignored for purposes of the presentation in this section.

Table 6.3
Direct Effects of the PBJI on Disposable Income (in $1 billions)

Income components	Prereform	Postreform	Change
Private sector earnings	861.13	859.99	−1.14
Public sector earnings	0.0	6.19	+6.19
Other income[a]	169.12	169.12	0.0
Cash assistance	20.92	19.14	−1.78
AFDC (federal and state payments)	9.05	0.0	
SSI (federal and state payments)	5.46	0.0	
General assistance	1.38	0.0	
Bonus value of food stamps	5.03	0.0	
Federal cash benefit and tax			
reimbursement payment	0.0	15.30	
State supplement payment	0.0	3.84	
Unemployment compensation payments	10.75	10.08	−.67
Earned income tax credit	1.17	4.04	+2.87
Taxes	−192.14	−192.61	−.47
Federal income taxes	−123.40	−123.52	
State income taxes	−23.96	−24.01	
Social Security payroll taxes	−44.78	−45.08	
(employee's share)			
Total disposable income	870.95	875.95	+5.00

[a] Other income includes Social Security benefits, railroad retirement, interest, dividends, government and private pensions, veteran's pensions, workman's compensation, and alimony and child support payments.

equals the sum of the change in disposable income and the $1.1 billion reduction in private sector earnings.

Although Table 6.3 indicates many of the changes in the components of disposable income that would have resulted from implementation of PBJI, it masks how these changes would have affected different types of recipients. For example, the net decrease of $1.1 billion in private sector earnings is attributable to a $1.2 billion reduction in the private sector earnings of workers who would have left conventional jobs to become pure strategy participants and a $40 million increase in the earnings of workers who would not have entered public employment but would have increased their private sector hours in response to changes in work incentives. Although the change of $40 million among non-public employment participants appears inconsequential, it represents the net affect of some rather substantial adjustments in hours and private sector earnings that would have taken place within certain subgroups of families.

Table 6.4 families who would have been affected by PBJI are categorized into three subgroups:

1. Families who presently receive AFDC, SSI, GA, or food stamps and who would have continued to receive some form of cash assistance (federal

Table 6.4
Program Effects on the Disposable Incomes of Three Categories of Recipients

Categories of recipients	Number of persons (millions)	Change in (in $1 billion)				
		Disposable income	Private earnings	Public earnings	Cash payments	Earned income tax credit
Current recipients who would continue to receive cash after the reform						
Nonparticipants in public employment	19.9	.29	.58	—	-.65	.41
Pure participants	2.7	.78	-.83	2.33	-.45	-.07
Mixed participants	4.7	.90	.08	2.06	-.98	.08
Total	27.3	1.97	-.15	4.39	-2.08	.42
Current recipients who would not receive cash benefits after the reform						
Nonparticipants in public employment	5.7	-1.63	.65	—	-2.13	.00
Pure participants	.3	.07	-.10	.31	-.10	-.08
Mixed participants	.2	.04	.00	.13	-.06	.00
Total	6.2	-1.52	.55	.44	-2.29	-.08
Families who did not receive cash benefits before the reform						
Nonparticipants in public employment	40.6	3.65	-1.22	—	2.25	2.43
Pure participants	.6	.34	-.27	.53	.16	-.02
Mixed participants	1.9	.56	-.05	.83	.18	.05
Total	43.1	4.55	-1.54	1.36	2.59	2.46

basic benefits and/or state supplement) after the reform.

2. Families who presently receive AFDC, SSI, GA, or food stamps but who would not have received cash assistance after the reform, either because of changes in eligibility rules or because their earnings increase.

3. Families who do not currently receive AFDC, SSI, GA, or food stamps but who would have received cash assistance or an earned-income tax credit after the reform.

Within each of these three categories, families are further divided into those in which the primary earner would not have participated in public employment at all during 1975, those in which the primary earner would have taken a public service job while he or she was unemployed and worked in the private sector during the rest of the year, and those in which the earner would have left the private sector so that he or she could accept a public service job.

Table 6.4 suggests that PBJI would have caused an increase in the hours and earnings of non-public-employment participants who are current recipients of cash benefits but would have resulted in a decrease of non-public-employment participants who do not presently receive cash benefits. This implies, in turn, that current recipients among non-public-employment participants would have been eligible for fewer cash benefits under PBJI than they presently are and, as a consequence, would have increased their work effort. The opposite is, of course, true for non-public-employment participants who would have been new recipients of cash benefits.

Families who engage in public service employment would have increased their overall hours of work. The increased earnings that result from these additional hours have a diminishing effect on the amount of cash benefits received by these groups. The reduction in the private sector earnings of pure participants is a consequence of substitution of public for private work by these persons. Mixed participants would have apparently changed their private sector hours and earnings very little, but their total earnings would have increased substantially as they took advantage of opportunities to work at public service jobs during periods of unemployment.

LIMITS OF AND IMPROVEMENTS IN THE SIMULATION ESTIMATES

The simulation model on which the estimates reported in the last section are based is relatively new and is still evolving. Numerous modifications to improve the model have been made since it was first developed, and more are planned. In this section, we list and briefly discuss some areas requiring further development of the model.

Movements Out of Public Employment

The KGB model makes different assumptions about how long individuals following the pure strategy and those following the mixed strategy remain in public employment. It is assumed that pure participants remain in the program until they retire from the labor force; mixed participants, in contrast, are assumed to stay only until they can find regular employment and the length of time it takes them to do this is assumed to be unaffected by their participation in the program. The assumption that pure participants remain in public employment for the rest of their working lives may be overly restrictive for at least three reasons. First, certain population groups, such as wives and female heads, tend to move into and out of the labor force relatively frequently. Second, public employment may serve as an "aging vat" for some young people, who leave the program when they mature and their opportunities within the regular job sector improve. Third, job opportunities will also improve if the program has an effective training component; as a result, those who receive training will eventually leave. Although there has been some conceptual modeling of these three "dynamic" factors, there has as yet been no attempt to incorporate a dynamic element into the actual simulation model. The conceptual modeling suggests that, while all three factors probably bias simulation predictions about length of stay in public employment, only the third might substantially affect estimates of the annual demand for public employment slots.

There are several reasons why participation in public employment might lengthen the time it takes an unemployed worker who is following the mixed strategy to obtain a regular job. First, job search activities may be more difficult and less efficient while working at a public service job than when not working at all. Second, public employment provides a stable source of income and thereby raises reservation wages and increases search time. Third, some persons may stay in public employment simply to avoid such psychological ordeals as having a job application turned down or being laid off. Finally, some mixed participants may remain in the program simply because of inertia, even when it is demonstrably to their advantage to switch to a private sector job. Crude empirical tests that have been made so far suggest that, if any of these factors is important, an appreciable understatement of the requirements for public employment job slots could result (see Betson et al., 1980). The public employment program itself, however, can do much to offset these factors by allowing time for job search activities (existing evidence suggests that in most cases this would only require a few hours a week), providing extra resources for job search, and requiring participants to take annual unpaid furloughs from public employment. Features such as these were, indeed, incorporated into PBJI.

Work-Related Returns and Expenses

In addition to differing in the money wage and amount of work they offer, public employment and regular employment may vary in their fringe benefits, working conditions, transportation costs, job security, and social status. If any of these differences is large, it should be taken into account in estimating the potential supply populations for public employment programs. However, because of the paucity of necessary data, these factors have not yet been incorporated into the simulation methodology.[17] Nevertheless, it is possible to obtain some idea of the sensitivity of simulation estimates to this omission. This can be done by first conducting a simulation under the assumption that a certain percentage, e.g., 5%, favorable differential in disposable income is required before individuals will be willing to accept a public service job and then reestimating the results under the opposite assumption. Such tests have been conducted (see Betson *et al.*, 1980), and they suggest that, only if large and systematic nonwage differences between regular and public employment exist, will the public employment slot estimates be seriously biased.

Shortcomings of Survey Data

Because of certain inherent limitations, the variables available in survey data only approximate some of the measures that are conceptually appropriate for the simulation model. For example, reported unemployment may not accurately measure true involuntary unemployment, the conceptual variable required by the model. As a result, the model's estimates of mixed strategy participants might include persons who are not truly involuntarily unemployed and, therefore, not willing to accept a public employment job during their weeks of reported unemployment. On the other hand, some persons who have given up on finding a regular job, and consequently do not report themselves as unemployed, might accept

---

[17] In several cases, however, it is possible to say something about the direction of bias that may result. For example, government-controlled public employment jobs probably would be associated with better working conditions, and perhaps superior fringe benefits, than private sector jobs paying equal wages. If so, ignoring these factors will result in understating the relative advantages of public employment. However, potential market wage rates for most persons following the mixed strategy exceed the program wage rate, and many of these persons are probably accustomed to fringe benefits and working conditions that are superior to those found in public employment. It would also appear that jobs in the public employment sector would be more secure than those in the conventional sector and that one will understate the comparative advantages of public employment jobs by not taking this factor into account. This advantage, however, may actually be rather small. Funding levels for manpower programs have varied widely over the years and have largely depended on the current vogue. More importantly, the very existence of a public employment program reduces the risk of accepting a conventional job, since a person who loses his conventional job has the program to fall back on. Failure to take job image or social status into account should not cause much bias in predicting the number of low-productivity workers who will enter public employment, although it does seem likely that relatively skilled workers would feel that they would lose considerable status by taking a public employment position during periods of unemployment. Ignoring this consideration could, therefore, result in an overstatement of the number of mixed participants.

a public employment job. However, estimates of the size of this latter group suggest that it is relatively small (see Betson *et al.*, 1980).

Earnings is another variable inherently difficult to measure with survey data. In many cases, for example, extremely low reported earnings may result from either intentional or unintentional underreporting. Tips and income received through illicit activities are only two examples of earnings components that undoubtedly frequently go unreported to survey interviewers. Such underreporting will cause the KGB model to overestimate the number of persons who would participate in public employment. In the future, we hope to correct at least partially for this problem by utilizing recent estimates of how earnings misreporting differs by income level.[18]

Interaction with Private Sector Markets

Major reform of the nation's welfare system would engender a complex series of adjustments in private sector labor and product markets. Two such adjustments, changes in labor supply and employer demand responses to the impact of public employment on market wage levels, are explicitly treated in the simulation model.[19] Others probably should be, but considerable further theoretical and empirical work will be required first. For example, workers who reduce their supply of hours to the conventional sector, either to take a public employment job or to increase their leisure time, will be partially replaced by the unemployed, especially during periods of high unemployment.[20] If a substantial fraction of these unemployed persons reside in low-income families, the simulation model will overestimate both the need for cash assistance payments and the number of mixed strategy participants. Moreover, if the supply of labor available to conventional employers shrinks, wage (and possibly price) levels will increase. Ideally, the simulation estimates should also take account of these changes.

Accounting Periods

Most welfare reform proposals condition the size of cash transfer payments, and eligibility itself, on income flows over some previous period. The length of this proposed accounting period is generally set at substantially less than a year. However, since simulation models usually use household surveys that only pro-

[18] Preliminary exploration with corrections for misreporting suggests that such data errors may cause the number of persons predicted by the KGB model to follow the pure strategy to be considerably overstated.

[19] The model allows for the possibility that private sector employers may offer some workers, who otherwise would follow the pure strategy, higher wages in order to retain them. See Greenberg (1978) for an explanation.

[20] For an exploration of this possibility within a microsimulation context, see Greenberg (forthcoming).

vide data on annual incomes, they tend to underpredict transfer payments that would be received by families with relatively high annual incomes but with low incomes during part of the year. To assess the effects of accounting periods of alternative lengths, we have modified the KGB simulation model so that it can utilize available data on the monthly income flows of the control group families in SIME/DIME.

Extensions of the Model

It would be very useful if the KGB model could take account of behavioral adjustments to welfare reform programs in addition to labor supply, such as changes in marital stability and geographic mobility patterns. It would also be desirable to be able to simulate policy porposals in areas, such as day care and health insurance, that closely interrelate with cash transfer and jobs programs. Such extensions of the model, however, are ambitious and must await further work on many of the issues discussed in the preceding subsections.

CONCLUSIONS

This chapter has described the KGB model, a microsimulation model that has been used to analyze various alternative welfare reform options. It is principally through their incorporation into this model that labor supply results from SIME/DIME have been utilized in the policymaking process. Simulation results were reported for one specific welfare reform option, the Carter administration's PBJI, so that the capabilities of the KGB model could be illustrated. But by concentrating on one such program, this paper has ignored one of the most important uses of the KGB model or any other microsimulation model. This involves using microsimulation methodology to analyze the effects of marginal changes of a single policy parameter in the context of a given overall program.

We have noted in considerable detail that, although progress has been made in improving the KGB model, much remains to be done. Results from the model must, therefore, be treated as suggestive rather than definitive. Considerably more confidence can be placed in the simulations that predict the marginal effects of a change in a given program than in the predictions of the overall costs and size of a new welfare program. Nevertheless, even predictions of the effects of major new policy initiatives go far to decrease the range of uncertainty that would exist in the absence of a formal simulation effort.

REFERENCES

Aaron, Henry, and Todd, John. "The Use of Income Maintenance Experiment Findings in Public Policy, 1977-78." *Industrial Relations Research Association Proceedings*, 1978.

Beebout, Harold. *Micro-simulation As a Policy Tool: The MATH Model.* Policy Analysis Series No. 14, Mathematica Policy Research, Washington, D.C., February 1977.

Beebout, Harold, and Bonina, Peggy. *TRIM: A Micro-simulation Model for Evaluating Income Policies.* Working Paper 971-04, Urban Institute, Washington, D.C., January 1973.

Beebout, Harold, ed. *MATH Technical Description.* Mathematica Policy Research, Washington, D.C., July 1976.

Betson, David; Greenberg, David; and Kasten, Richard. "A Micro-Simulation Model for Analyzing Alternative Welfare Reform Proposals: An Application to the Program for Better Jobs and Income." In *Microeconomic Simulation,* edited by Robert Haveman and Kevin Hollenbeck. Academic Press, New York, 1980.

Greenberg, David H. *Employers, the Unemployed, and the Effects of Transfer Programs on Hours of Work.* Technical Analysis Paper, Office of Income Security Policy, U.S. Dept. of Health and Human Services (forthcoming).

Greenberg, David H. "Participation in Guaranteed Employment Programs: An Exploratory Simulation." In *Public Service Employment, Supported Work, and Job Guarantees: Analytic Issues and Policy Implications,* edited by John Palmer. Washington D.C.: The Brookings Institute, 1978.

Keeley, Michael C., *et al.* "The Estimation of Labor Supply Models Using Experimental Data." *American Economic Review,* December 1978, pp. 873-887.

Maxfield, Myles Jr. *Estimating the Impact of Labor Supply Adjustments on Transfer Program Costs: A Microsimulation Methodology.* Mathematica Policy Research, Washington, D.C., March 1977.

U.S. Department of Health, Education and Welfare. *Better Jobs and Income Act, H.R. 9030: A Summary and Sectional Explanation.* September 13, 1977.

U.S. Department of Health, Education and Welfare. Office of the Assistant Secretary for Planning and Evaluation, Office of Income Security Policy/Research. *The Seattle/ Denver Income Maintenance Experiment: Midexperimental Labor Results and a Generalization to the National Population,* February, 1978.

U.S. Department of Labor, Bureau of Labor Statistics. *Handbook of Labor Statistics,* 1977.

CHAPTER 7

Job Satisfaction

PHILIP K. ROBINS

INTRODUCTION

Chapters 3 and 5 have shown that heads of families reduce their labor supply in response to the experimental NIT treatments. Reductions in labor supply are generally considered to be an undesirable effect of an NIT, primarily because of the increased costs associated with such a decline and the corresponding reduction in gross national product (GNP). However, reductions in labor supply can have desirable effects. For example, the reduction might take the form of increased production in the home (Gronau, 1977), which although not included in GNP is generally considered productive effort, or it might take the temporary form of a job change in order to improve the work environment. It is of considerable importance, therefore to study the nature of the labor supply response to an NIT as well as the characteristics of any changes in the work environment that may occur.

This chapter analyzes the effects of SIME/DIME on job satisfaction (or perceived job quality), using data from a job satisfaction survey given to family heads. The only previous attempt to study the effects of an NIT program on job satisfaction was by Spilerman and Miller (1977) for the New Jersey Income-Maintenance Experiment. Spilerman and Miller analyze a sample of male family heads who change jobs. They find that an NIT increases the job satisfaction of younger males who were initially more educated and in better occupations while it decreases the job satisfaction of older, less educated males who were initially in lower level occupations. Spilerman and Miller do not study effects on the job satisfaction of women or of persons who do not change jobs.

In the first section of this chapter, the model used to analyze the effects of an NIT program on job satisfaction is presented and estimated. The most important finding of the empirical analysis is that only women appear to significantly alter their level of job satisfaction in response to an NIT. The effects differ between wives and single female heads, however, being positive for wives and negative for single female heads. In the next section, a further examination of the

125

data reveals that the experimental response is concerted among wives who change jobs during the period analyzed and among single female heads who remain in the same job. These findings suggest that the changes for wives represent changes in job attributes (caused by job exit), while the changes for single female heads represent changes in attitudes toward working. The effects of an NIT on job mobility and on the wage rates of job-changing wives are also investigated. The final section summarizes the chapter.

A MODEL OF THE EFFECTS OF NEGATIVE INCOME TAX ON JOB SATISFACTION

The methodological approach used to analyze the effects of an NIT on job satisfaction assumes there is a trade-off between the pecuniary and nonpecuniary benefits from working. When workers select jobs, they take this trade-off into account. Each worker is assumed to possess a maximum wage, which is a reflection of his or her productivity and which represents the wage the person would receive from a job with no nonpecuniary benefits. The greater the nonpecuniary benefits are from a given job, the lower the wage rate that is received. For purposes of analysis, the amount of nonpecuniary benefits associated with a particular job is termed job satisfaction.

An NIT, as we have seen, simultaneously increases income by providing a guarantee and decreases the net wage rate by taxing earnings. (It is assumed that the tax rate of the NIT is higher than the cumulative tax rates of the programs it replaces.) As a result of these changes, an NIT affects a worker's optimal combination of pecuniary and nonpecuniary benefits. In general, it is not possible to predict a priori whether the combined effect of these changes will increase or decrease a person's preferred wage rate and the level of job satisfaction. As described by Robins (1977), the guarantee (or change in disposable income) associated with the NIT should lead to an increase in job satisfaction and a decrease in the observed wage rate. The effect of the NIT tax rate on these variables is ambiguous, however, making the total effect uncertain. In the empirical analysis presented here, income and tax rate effects are estimated separately in order to test the implications of the theoretical model. The basic formulation of the empirical response function relates the change in job satisfaction to both the change in disposable income and the change in the tax rate caused by the experimental NIT treatments.

Estimation of the Model

To test the model just described, observations are required on job satisfaction prior to and during the experiments. Job satisfaction is defined as equal to the total value of the nonpecuniary benefits of working, or, more succinctly, the value of the amenities on one's job. These include the monetary value of fringe benefits, geographic location, and other aspects of an individual's working conditions that are not reflected in the person's observed wage rate. Unfortunately, data on these job attributes are not available in the SIME/DIME data. Hence, we are not able to provide a direct test of the model in the sense of matching the concept of job satisfaction with observed job attributes.

As an alternative, we make use of a measure of job satisfaction that is based on an individual's perception of the value of the attributes of the job. Such a measure is known to be inadequate because perceptions are clouded by the psychological state of an individual, which depends, in part, on the individual's value system. However, if the error in this measure of job attributes is random, it leads to less precision but not to biases in the estimated parameters. Thus, a strong case can be made that any significant empirical results obtained by using this measure of job quality should be taken quite seriously.

Data and Specification of the Empirical Model

At periodic intervals during SIME/DIME, family heads were asked to reveal feelings about their present jobs. For the analysis reported here, we use responses to the question[1]:

Talking about your current job, would you say you

(a) *like it very much*
(b) *like it*
(c) *think it is OK*
(d) *do not like it*
(e) *hate it*

These responses were coded into a dummy variable that takes on the value of 1 if the response is (a) or (b), and 0 for the other responses.[2]

Because our model is a change model, we need both a pre and postexperimental measure of job satisfaction. Unfortunately, although two measures of job satisfaction are available for each person, neither is a preexperimental measure.[3] Thus, both are likely to contain experimental effects. To obtain a measure of job

---

[1] An alternative question, relating to aspects of the job other than the wage rate, was also asked but only in later interviews. Since we are interested in obtaining measures of job satisfaction at two different times for this study, we are forced to use the question that includes opinions about the hourly wage rate rather than the preferable measure that excludes opinions about the hourly wage rate. As it turns out, the measures are quite similar, their correlation being .76 for husbands, .80 for wives, and .84 for single female heads. Empirical results using both measures are also quite similar.

[2] It is felt that persons who state that they like their job are generally satisfied while persons displaying an indifferent feeling or a dislike for their job are generally dissatisfied. A polytomous variable, taking on five values, was also tested but the results were virtually identical to those using the dichotomous variable.

[3] The job satisfaction measures used in this study come from the following interviews: for male heads, the second periodic (postenrollment in Denver) and the fifth periodic; for spouses of male heads, the third periodic and the sixth periodic; for female heads of families, the second periodic (postenrollment in Denver) and the sixth periodic.

satisfaction that is free from experimental effects, the earlier of the two measures for control families is regressed on a set of observed characteristics, and the resulting empirical equation is used to predict the level of job satisfaction for the entire sample (experimentals and controls).[4] The predicted job satisfaction variable is included on the right-hand side of the response function rather than estimating the model in first difference form.[5]

In addition to predicted job satisfaction, the change in disposable income, and the change in the tax rate,[6] several additional variables are included in the empirical specification. First, about ¼ of the experimental families were initially above their breakeven level. Depending on their labor supply response to the experiment, such families may or may not experience a change in disposable income and/or tax rates. To measure the response of these families, a dummy variable is included in the empirical specification that takes the value of 1 if the family was initially above the breakeven level. Families initially above the breakeven level are assigned a 0 change in disposable income and a 0 change in the tax rate. Second, as was described in Chapter 1, families were enrolled for either 3 years or 5 years. To measure the effects of length of the program on experimental responses, a dummy variable is included in the empirical specification that takes the value of 1 if the family is enrolled for 3 years, and 0 if the family is enrolled for 5. Third, because of the nonrandom allocation of families to experimental treatments, we include the following assignment variables in the model: 7 dummy variables for normal income categories (E-levels), a race dummy, a site dummy, and family size. Fourth, we include a set of control variables to correct for other differences between experimental and control families and to increase the precision of the estimated experimental effects: age, education, number of preschool age children, welfare status prior to enrollment, and the city's unemployment rate. Finally, we include 3 dummy variables to represent the manpower treatments.

Sample

The sample consists of a subset of persons enrolled in the experiment who were employed at enrollment, employed at the time of the latest job satisfaction

[4] The variables used to predict job satisfaction include a measure of work experience, occupational prestige scores, earnings, race, marital status, and industry. See Hamermesh (1976) for a discussion of why these variables are likely to affect job satisfaction. Appendix A presents the results of the estimated job satisfaction equations.

[5] The rationale for including the predicted value of job satisfaction on the right-hand side of the impact equation is similar to the rationale given by Keeley *et al* (1976, Appendix B) for estimating labor supply impact equations.

[6] See Keeley *et al*. (1978) for a discussion of how the change is disposable income and the change in the tax rate are calculated from the data.

survey, and who remained in an intact family between the two interview time periods.[7] Control families are included in the sample to increase the precision of the estimated experimental effects.

The reason for restricting the sample to workers is that job satisfaction is only observed for persons who are employed. The impact of income maintenance on changes in employment status, a related issue, is investigated later in the chapter to provide some indication of how the sample selection process itself is influenced by the treatments. Nonintact families are exluded from the sample because data were not yet available for them. Overall, then, the results should be interpreted as representing estimates of the effects of the experiment on job satisfaction, conditional on being employed and remaining in an intact family.

Results

Table 7.1 presents the estimated experimental effects on job satisfaction for husbands, wives, and single female heads of families. The effects of the predicted job satisfaction variable are also reported. (Coefficients of the assignment, control, and manpower variables are reported in Appendix B to this chapter.)

The results indicate that only the job satisfaction of wives and single female heads is significantly affected by changes in any of the experimental variables. However, the effects differ for the two groups. For wives, a $1000 increase in income raises the level of job satisfaction by 10 percentage points, or by about 13% (.095/.707). For single female heads of families, a $1000 increase in income reduces the level of job satisfaction by 11 percentage points, or by about 13%. In the next section, we attempt to reconcile these apparently contradictory findings.

Before turning to a discussion of how the contrasting results for wives and single female heads of families may be reconciled, however, let us briefly discuss some other aspects of the results in Table 7.1. First, there appears to be a significant relationship between the nonexperimental and experimental measures of job satisfaction. Second, the insignificant coefficients of the tax rate variable indicate that the empirical results shed no light on the theoretical ambiguity of this variable. Finally, only in the case of single female heads does there appear to be a significant overall experimental impact on job satisfaction. Since the experiment increased both disposable income and the tax rate, the sign of the effect of any given income-maintenance program for single female heads depends on the size of the income and tax rate changes. For example, a program that increased disposable income by $500 and increased the tax rate by 50 percentage points would increase the job satisfaction of single female heads of families by 6 per-

---

[7] An intact family is one that does not move out of the Seattle or Denver areas and does not experience a change in marital status (such as divorce, separation, or remarriage) during the observation period.

Table 7.1
Experimental NIT Impact on Job Satisfaction
(Standard Errors in Parentheses)

Variable	Husbands	Wives	Female heads
Predicted nonexperimental job	.573***	.373*	.227
satisfaction	(.139)	(.200)	(.206)
Change in disposable income	.002	.095*	−.105***
(per $1000)	(.023)	(.051)	(.035)
Change in the tax rate	.037	−.287	.220
(per 100 percentage points)	(.110)	(.228)	(.148)
Above breakeven	−.022	.108	−.113
	(.055)	(.092)	(.857)
3-year program	−.026	−.085	.033
	(.040)	(.073)	(.060)
Sample size	1069	343	464
F-test for all treatment			
variables	.365	1.045	2.183*
F-test for change in disposable			
income and change in tax rate	.167	1.611	4.563***
Mean of dependent variable	.703	.729	.681
Mean of predicted non-experimental			
job satisfaction	.666	.707	.831

Note: The following probability levels apply to all tables in this chapter.
   *p < .10.
  **p < .05.
 ***p < .01.

centage points; a program that increased disposable income by $1000 and increases the tax rate by 25 percentage points would decrease job satisfaction by 5 percentage points. Similar results would hold for wives, although the overall experimental impact is not significant for this group.

FURTHER ANALYSIS

Because an NIT also affects labor supply, our use of a sample restricted to workers (during the experiment) may have created a selectivity bias in the estimated treatment effects on job satisfaction. For example, if only dissatisfied workers respond to an NIT by leaving employment, then the remaining experimental families would, on average, be more satisfied than controls. Inclusion of a predicted measure of job satisfaction as an independent variable in the impact equation is an attempt to control for such selectivity bias, but the explanatory power of the equation generating the prediction is quite low. A direct investigation of the effect of the experiment on leaving employment may provide some additional information on the job satisfaction responses of workers.

There is also another potentially important issue that warrants investigation. Presumably, individuals are most likely to alter their level of job satisfaction by changing jobs, assuming that job satisfaction is a measure of job attributes. (It is also possible, though less likely, to alter job attributes without changing jobs.) This means that if significant institutional rigidities exist in the labor market that prevent individuals from making marginal adjustments to exogenous shocks (e.g., the high cost of changing jobs), then we would expect to observe a change in job satisfaction only for those workers who actually change jobs during the experiment. On the other hand, if our measure of job satisfaction is contaminated by changes in psychological attitudes toward a job, then a worker forced to remain in disequilibrium because of an exogenous shock, may also change his or her level of job satisfaction. (For another view, see Beaver, 1974, who uses dissonance theory as an explanation for changes in attitudes of persons on the same job.) To investigate these possibilities, we estimate the effects of the experiment on retaining or changing jobs and the resulting effects on job satisfaction for both classes of workers.

Effects on Job Mobility

Tables 7.2-7.4 present estimates of the impact of the experiment on the probabilities of leaving employment, retaining the same job, and changing jobs between enrollment and the time of the job satisfaction survey. (See chapter Appendix C for coefficients of the nonexperimental and manpower treatment variables in these equations.) The coefficient of the predicted nonexperimental level of job satisfaction is also reported, along with the results of a regression where the change in disposable income is interacted with the predicted level of job satisfaction.

Before discussing the results, it is interesting to note that, overall, men exhibited less job mobility than women. Of those employed at enrollment, only 10% of the husbands were not working at the time of the job satisfaction survey (roughly a year and a half later), vs 27% of the wives and 20% of the single female heads. However, among those who remained employed, almost 60% of the single female heads kept the same job, vs 54% of the husbands and 52% of the wives.

Tables 7.2-7.4 reveal four interesting effects. First, it appears that job satisfaction was negatively related to job mobility for women, but not for men. Women who were more satisfied with their current jobs were more likely to retain them and less likely to either change jobs or leave employment during the period studied, although the effect on changing jobs is not statistically significant. Second, the experiment increased the probability of leaving employment for husbands and single female heads of families, but not for wives. (These results are consistent with those reported in Chapter 3.) The response for husbands arises

Table 7.2
Experimental NIT Impact on Leaving Employment
(Standard Errors in Parentheses)

Variable	Husbands		Wives		Female heads	
Predicted nonexperimental job satisfaction	−.079 (.084)	−.054 (.097)	−.461*** (.160)	−.536*** (.178)	−.106 (.150)	−.183 (.154)
Change in disposable income (per $1000)	.048*** (.014)	.076 (.055)	.030 (.038)	−.060 (.100)	.009 (.024)	−.116* (.063)
Change in the tax rate (per 100 percentage points)	.012 (.067)	.014 (.067)	−.171 (.178)	−.179 (.179)	−.295*** (.106)	−.293*** (.106)
Above breakeven	.021 (.034)	.021 (.034)	.020 (.076)	.020 (.076)	.003 (.065)	−.006 (.064)
3-year program	−.077*** (.024)	−.077*** (.024)	−.101* (.059)	−.101* (.059)	.009 (.043)	.003 (.043)
Interaction between change in disposable income and predicted job satisfaction (per $1000)		−.040 (.077)		.130 (.136)		.158** (.073)
Sample size	1191		471		579	
F-test for all treatment variables	4.184***	3.532***	1.097	1.069	3.330***	3.531***
F-test for change in disposable income and change in tax rate	5.149***		.732		8.30***	
Mean of dependent variable	.101		.268		.199	

132

Table 7.3
Experimental NIT Impact on Retaining a Job
(Standard Errors in Parentheses)

Variable	Husbands		Wives		Female heads	
Predicted nonexperimental job satisfaction	.045 (.139)	-.009 (.159)	.628*** (.175)	.668*** (.194)	.337* (.188)	.374* (.194)
Change in disposable income (per $1000)	-.028 (.023)	-.087 (.090)	-.065 (.041)	-.017 (.110)	.029 (.030)	.087 (.079)
Change in the tax rate (per 100 percentage points)	-.053 (.110)	-.056 (.110)	-.022 (.195)	-.018 (.195)	.304** (.133)	.303** (.133)
Above breakeven	.050 (.056)	.049 (.056)	-.052 (.083)	-.052 (.083)	.013 (.081)	.015 (.081)
3-year program	.025 (.040)	.025 (.040)	.157** (.064)	.157** (.064)	-.025 (.054)	-.023 (.054)
Interaction between change in disposable income and predicted job satisfaction (per $1000)		.086 (.127)		-.070 (.148)		-.075 (.092)
Sample size	1191		471		579	
F-test for all treatment variables	.752	.704	1.823*	1.556	1.606	1.449
F-test for change in disposable income and change in tax rate	.877		.135		3.892***	
Mean of dependent variable	.484		.384		.473	

mainly from the income effect, while for single female heads of families, it arises from the tax effect. Third, the length of the experiment is strongly related to job mobility for husbands and wives. Both spouses were more likely to leave employment if they were enrolled for 5 years than if they were enrolled for 3. Wives in the 5-year sample were also much less likely to remain in the same job. Fourth, there appears to be a differential response by degree of job satisfaction for single female heads of families leaving a job. The effect is counterintuitive, however, which suggests there may be some selectivity bias for this group.

Effects on Job Satisfaction for Job Changers and Job Stayers

Tables 7.5 and 7.6 present estimates of the impact of the experiment on job satisfaction for job changers and job stayers. As before, no discernible impact is detectable for husbands. For wives and single female heads, however, the results are quite revealing. They suggest that, for wives, only job changers responded to

Table 7.4
Experimental Impact on Changing Jobs
(Standard Errors in Parentheses)

Variable	Husbands		Wives		Female heads	
Predicted nonexperimental job satisfaction	.034 (.137)	.063 (.157)	−.167 (.178)	−.132 (.198)	−.231 (.183)	−.190 (.189)
Change in disposable income (per $1000)	−.020 (.022)	.012 (.089)	.035 (.042)	.077 (.111)	−.038 (.029)	.027 (.077)
Change in the tax rate (per 100 percentage points)	.040 (.109)	.042 (.109)	.193 (.199)	.196 (.199)	−.009 (.130)	−.010 (.130)
Above breakeven	−.071 (.055)	−.070 (.055)	.031 (.084)	.031 (.084)	−.011 (.079)	−.009 (.079)
3-year program	.052 (.049)	.052 (.039)	−.056 (.066)	−.056 (.066)	.017 (.053)	.019 (.053)
Interaction between change in disposable income and dicted job satisfaction (per $1000)		.046 (.125)		−.060 (.151)		−.083 (.090)
Sample size	1191		471		579	
F-test for all treatment variables	.573	.500	.523	.462	.470	.533
F-test for change in disposable income and change in tax rate	.217		.612		1.105	
Mean of dependent variable	.416		.348		.328	

the experiment, while for female heads of families, only job stayers responded.[8] Wives who changed jobs increased their level of job satisfaction by 16 percentage points, or by 23%, for each $1000 increase in income, but decreased their level of job satisfaction by 7 percentage points, or by 10%, for each 10 percentage point increase in the tax rate. Thus, wives who changed jobs appeared to be able to alter their level of job satisfaction in a manner consistent with the earlier theory. It is likely that this change in job satisfaction represents a change in job attributes.

In the case of single female heads, those who remained on the same job decreased their level of job satisfaction by 14 percentage points, or by 17%, for each $1000 increase in income, and increased their level of job satisfaction by 4 percentage points, or by 4%, for each 10 percentage point increase in the tax rate. Those who changed jobs did not appear to be altering their level of job satisfaction in response to the experiment. Since the income effect for job stayers is negative, it appears that this change in job satisfaction represents a change

[8] It also appears that there is a closer association between pre- and postexperimental job satisfaction for job stayers than for job changers.

Table 7.5
Experimental Impact on Job Satisfaction for Job Changers
(Standard Errors in Parentheses)

Variable	Husbands	Wives	Female heads
Predicted nonexperimental job satisfaction	.712*** (.214)	.023 (.305)	.063 (.041)
Change in disposable income (per $1000)	.016 (.034)	.157** (.079)	−.078 (.051)
Change in the tax rate (per 100 percentage points)	.008 (.160)	.707* (.360)	−.152 (.257)
Above breakeven	−.048 (.085)	.057 (.144)	−.113 (.155)
3-year program	−.008 (.058)	−.015 (.110)	.020 (.098)
Sample site	494	163	190
F-test for all treatment variables	.756	1.205	.576
F-test for change in disposable income and change in tax rate	.948	2.915*	1.176
Mean of dependent variable	.700	.724	.695
Mean of predicted nonexperimental job satisfaction	.654	.677	.796

in attitudes toward a job rather than a change in job attributes. Single female heads who were unable (or unwilling) to make marginal adjustments in response to an NIT may be voicing their disequilibrium by decreasing their level of job satisfaction, rather than by exiting from the job in an effort to increase it.

Effects on Wage Rates for Job Changers

One of the theoretical implications of the model discussed in the first section is that the observed wage rate depends on the amount of job satisfaction (job attributes) associated with a particular employment situation. If leisure and job satisfaction are strong substitutes and if job satisfaction is a normal good, then an NIT will induce some persons to choose more satisfying, but lower paying jobs.[9] Since our empirical results indicate that job satisfaction increases under an NIT for wives who change jobs, we should observe a decrease in their wage rates (or at least an increase that is smaller for experimental families than for control families).

[9] The wage rate will fall only if there is no investment in human capital (through education or training), which could tend to raise wage rates.

Table 7.6
Experimental Impact on Job Satisfaction for Job Stayers
(Standard Errors in Parentheses)

Variable	Husbands	Wives	Female heads
Predicted nonexperimental job satisfaction	.477*** (.183)	.537* (.287)	.358 (.228)
Change in disposable income (per $1000)	−.019 (.032)	.012 (.074)	−.144*** (.049)
Change in the tax rate (per 100 percentage points)	−.109 (.153)	−.144 (.310)	−.371* (.193)
Above breakeven	.022 (.074)	.105 (.125)	−.183* (.109)
3-year program	−.053 (.057)	−.117 (.104)	.046 (.079)
Sample size	575	180	274
F-test for all treatment variables	.344	.300	2.389*
F-test for change in disposable income and change in tax rate	.403	.040	4.574***
Mean of dependent variable	.704	.733	.672
Mean of predicted nonexperimental job satisfaction	.677	.735	.855

To test this hypothesis, we compute the average wage rates of experimental and control wives, before and after a job change, and calculate an experimental effect.[10] The estimated experimental effect is −$.24 per hour (or $500 per year for a full-time worker). Thus, the NIT treatments apparently induced wives to seek slightly lower paying jobs in exchange for greater job satisfaction.[11]

SUMMARY

In this chapter, the effects of an NIT program on job satisfaction have been analyzed using data from a survey given to family heads in SIME/DIME. Statis-

---

[10] The experimental effect is given by $\bar{w}_a^e - \bar{w}_b^e - (\bar{w}_a^c - \bar{w}_b^c)$, where $\bar{w}_a^e$ = the average wage rate of experimental wives after the job change, $\bar{w}_b^e$ = the average wage rate of experimental wives before the job change, $\bar{w}_a^c$ = the average wage rate of control wives after the job change, and $\bar{w}_b^c$ = the average wage rate of control wives before the job change. The values of $\bar{w}_a^e$, $\bar{w}_b^e$, $\bar{w}_a^c$, and $\bar{w}_b^c$ are $2.81, $2.54, $3.06, and $2.55, respectively.

[11] In real terms (adjusting for inflation), the average wage rate of experimental wives decreases by $.05 after the job change.

tically significant effects on job satisfaction are estimated for women, but not for men. The effects vary, depending on whether or not women adjust their labor force status. For wives, only those who changed jobs appeared to be altering their level of job satisfaction. For single female heads of families, only those who did not change jobs appeared to be altering their level of job satisfaction. For each $1000 increase in income generated by the experiment, job-changing wives increased their level of satisfaction by 17%. These wives also experienced about a 10% decline in their wage rate relative to control families. Thus, for a subset of employed women (those who are married), an NIT program appears to induce a shift to jobs that pay less but provide greater nonpecuniary benefits. Unmarried women with children who remain on the same job apparently become less satisfied as a result of the NIT, but do not attempt to change their work environment.

REFERENCES

Beaver, Steven. "The Effect of Income Maintenance on Attitudes: Preliminary Findings from Seattle." Unpublished paper, Center for the Study of Welfare Policy, SRI International, November 1974.

Gronau, Reuben. "Leisure, Home Production, and Work—the Theory of the Allocation of Time Revisited." *Journal of Political Economy* 85, no. 6 (December 1977): 1099-1123.

Hamermesh, Daniel S. "Economic Aspects of Job Satisfaction." In *Essays in Labor Market and Population Analysis*, edited by O. Ashenfelter and W. Oates. New York: John Wiley and Sons, 1976.

Hodge, Robert W.; Siegel, Paul M.; and Rossi, Peter H. "Occupational Prestige in the United States, 1925-1963." *American Journal of Sociology* 70 (November 1964):286-302.

Keeley, Michael C.; Robins, Philip K.; Spiegelman, Robert G.; and West, Richard W. "The Estimation of Labor-Supply Models Using Experimental Data." *American Economic Review* 68 (December 1978): 873-887.

Keeley, Michael C.; Robins, Philip K.; Spiegelman, Robert G.; and West, Richard W. "The Estimation of Labor Supply Models Using Experimental Data: Evidence from the Seattle and Denver Income Maintenance Experiments." Research Memorandum No. 29, Center for the Study of Welfare Policy, Stanford Research Institute, August 1976.

Kurz, Mordecai, and Spiegelman, Robert G. "The Seattle Experiment: The Combined Effect of Income Maintenance and Manpower Investments." *American Economic Review* 61 (May 1971):22-29.

Kurz, Mordecai, and Spiegelman, Rogert G. "The Design of the Seattle and Denver Income Maintenance Experiments." Research Memorandum No. 18, Center for the Study of Welfare Policy, Stanford Research Institute, May 1972.

Robins, Philip K. "Job Satisfaction and Income Maintenance: Evidence from the Seattle and Denver Income Maintenance Experiments." Research Memorandum No. 45, Center for the Study of Welfare Policy, SRI International, October 1977.

Spilerman, Seymour and Miller, Richard E. "The Impact of the Experiment on Job Selection." In *The New Jersey Income Maintenance Experiment Labor Supply Responses*, Vol. II. Edited by Harold W. Watts and Albert Rees. New York: Academic Press, 1977.

APPENDIX A. PREDICTED JOB SATISFACTION (CONTROL SAMPLE)

	Husbands	Wives and single female heads
Work experience[a]	.004**	.004*
	(.002)	(.002)
Occupational prestige score[b]	.003*	.006***
	(.002)	(.002)
Earnings in prior years	.012	.013
($1000s)	(.008)	(.011)
1 if black	—	−.109***
	—	(.040)
1 if married	—	.020
	—	(.043)
Industry dummies		
Agriculture-mining	.253	—
	(.192)	—
Construction	.126	—
	(.085)	—
Transportation	.065	—
	(.068)	—
Trade	.146***	—
	(.055)	—
Finance	.248**	—
	(.126)	—
Services	.154***	—
	(.053)	—
Government	.187***	—
	(.067)	—
Manufacturing	—	—
Constant	.330***	.395***
	(.085)	(.087)
Mean of dependent variable	.675	.680
Sample size	625	518
R^2	.042	.054
F-statistic for overall regression	2.710***	5.811***

Note: Standard errors are in parentheses for Appendixes A-C. The following probability levels apply to Appendixes A-C.

   *$p < .10$.

   **$p < .05$.

   ***$p < .01$.

[a]Defined as age minus years of education minus 5.

[b]A scale ranging from 9 (bootblacks) to 82 (physicians) developed by Hodge, Siegel, and Rossi (1964) for ranking occupations by social standing. The prestige score was originally designed for use with the 1960 U.S. Census Occupational Codes and was adapted to the 1970 codes used in the SIME/DIME surveys.

APPENDIX B. COEFFICIENT ESTIMATES OF NONEXPERIMENTAL AND MANPOWER TREATMENT VARIABLES IN THE JOB SATISFACTION IMPACT EQUATION

	Total workers		
	Husbands	Wives	Female heads
Normal income			
1 = Income not determined	.563	−.181	.272
	(.474)	(.179)	(.197)
1 = $0-$1,000	−	−	−
1 = $1,000-$3,000	.666	.461	.224
	(.471)	(.340)	(.140)
1 = $3,000-$5,000	.731	.022	.148
	(.461)	(.090)	(.135)
1 = $5,000-$7,000	.656	.149**	.056
	(.460)	(.070)	(.136)
1 = $7,000-$9,000	.696	.081	.155
	(.461)	(.062)	(.140)
1 = $9,000-$11,000	.683	−	.193
	(.462)	−	(.201)
1 = $11,000-$13,000	.738	−.027	−
	(.476)	(.139)	−
Denver (1 if Denver)	−.247	−.116	−.177
	(.286)	(.229)	(.262)
Age	.003	.005*	.002
	(.002)	(.003)	(.003)
Race (1 if black)	−.031	−.098*	−.086
	(.030)	(.053)	(.055)
No. of family members	−.010	.002	.000
	(.011)	(.018)	(.019)
No. of children aged 0-5	.016	.040	.022
	(.020)	(.041)	(.040)
AFDC (1 if on AFDC prior to enrollment	.024	.078	−.004
	(.060)	(.128)	(.058)
City unemployment rate	−.057	−.039	−.073
	(.064)	(.053)	(.061)
1 = M1 (counseling only)	.042	−.035	−.012
	(.040)	(.066)	(.060)
1 = M2 (counseling + 50% subsidy)	.007	−.078	.042
	(.036)	(.066)	(.056)
1 = M3 (counseling + 100% subsidy)	.040	−.043	−.062
	(.044)	(.079)	(.069)
Education	.006	.004	−.004
	(.006)	(.013)	(.014)
Sample size	1069	343	464

APPENDIX C. COEFFICIENT ESTIMATES OF NONEXPERIMENTAL AND MANPOWER TREATMENT VARIABLES IN THE JOB MOBILITY IMPACT EQUATIONS

Table 7.C.1
Probability of Leaving Employment

	Husbands	Wives	Female heads
Normal income			
1 = Income not determined	−.481**	−1.095**	−.058
	(.223)	(.476)	(.131)
1 = $0-$1,000	−	−	−
1 = $1,000-$3,000	−.280	−.551	−.104
	(.217)	(.480)	(.092)
1 = $3,000-$5,000	−.351**	−.841*	−.055
	(.212)	(.448)	(.089)
1 = $5,000-$7,000	−.402**	−.837*	−.151*
	(.211)	(.446)	(.091)
1 = $7,000-$9,000	−.496**	−.937**	−.152
	(.212)	(.447)	(.095)
1 = $9,000-$11,000	−.448**	−.906**	−.172
	(.212)	(.447)	(.147)
1 = $11,000-$13,000	−.537**	−1.033**	−
	(.225)	(.464)	−
Denver (1 if Denver)	.179	−.292	−.352
	(.176)	(.250)	(.191)
Age	.001	−.002	−.004
	(.001)	(.003)	(.002)
Race (1 if black)	.000	−.088**	−.033
	(.018)	(.043)	(.040)
No. of family members	−.013**	−.014	−.011
	(.007)	(.015)	(.013)
No. of children aged 0-5	−.015	.064**	.002
	(.012)	(.032)	(.029)
AFDC (1 if on AFDC prior to enrollment	.023	.004	.048
	(.036)	(.105)	(.042)
City unemployment rate	.044	−.038	−.052
	(.040)	(.060)	(.044)
1 = $M1$ (counseling only)	.009	−.082	−.058
	(.025)	(.056)	(.045)
1 = $M2$ (counseling + 50% subsidy)	.033	.013	−.048
	(.022)	(.054)	(.041)
1 = $M3$ (counseling + 100% subsidy)	.021	.096	.095*
	(.027)	(.063)	(.049)
Education	.001	−.021*	−.015
	(.004)	(.011)	(.010)
Sample size	1191	471	579

Table 7.C.2
Probability of Retaining a Job

	Husbands	Wives	Female heads
Normal income			
1 = Income not determined	.400	.739	.048
	(.367)	(.520)	(.165)
1 = 0-$1,000	—	—	—
1 = $1,000-$3,000	.231	.446	.121
	(.358)	(.524)	(.115)
1 = $3,000-$5,000	.286	.535	.032
	(.349)	(.489)	(.111)
1 = $5,000-$7,000	.308	.513	.242**
	(.348)	(.487)	(.114)
1 = $7,000-$9,000	.374	.584	.173
	(.348)	(.488)	(.119)
1 = $9,000-$11,000	.443	.506	.046
	(.349)	(.488)	(.185)
1 = $11,000-$13,000	.518	.749	—
	(.370)	(.506)	—
Denver (1 if Denver)	−.591**	.253	.390
	(.290)	(.273)	(.240)
Age	.009***	.007**	.009***
	(.002)	(.003)	(.003)
Race (1 if black)	.015	.132***	.152***
	(.030)	(.047)	(.050)
No. of family members	−.028**	.010	.016
	(.011)	(.016)	(.017)
No. of children aged 0-5	.007	−.041	.018
	(.020)	(.035)	(.036)
AFDC (1 if on AFDC prior to enrollment)	−.089	.015	−.056
	(.059)	(.114)	(.053)
City unemployment rate	−.123**	.033	.064
	(.065)	(.061)	(.056)
1 = $M1$ (counseling only)	−.058	−.033	−.009
	(.040)	(.061)	(.057)
1 = $M2$ (counseling + 50% subsidy)	−.022	−.012	.016
	(.036)	(.059)	(.052)
1 = $M3$ (counseling + 100% subsidy)	−.009	−.047	−.053
	(.045)	(.068)	(.061)
Education	−.002	.013	.008
	(.006)	(.012)	(.012)
Sample size	1191	471	579

Table 7.C.3
Probability of Changing Jobs

	Husbands	Wives	Female heads
Normal income			
1 = Income not determined	.081	.356	.011
	(.362)	(.529)	(.161)
1 = $0-$1,000	—	—	—
1 = $1,000-$3,000	.050	.105	.017
	(.353)	(.533)	(.113)
1 = $3,000-$5,000	.065	.306	.023
	(.344)	(.498)	(.108)
1 = $5,000-$7,000	.094	.325	−.092
	(.344)	(.496)	(.111)
1 = $7,000-$9,000	.122	.353	−.021
	(.344)	(.496)	(.116)
1 = $9,000-$11,000	.005	.400	.125
	(.345)	(.497)	(.180)
1 = $11,000-$13,000	.020	.284	—
	(.366)	(.515)	—
Denver (1 if Denver)	.412	.040	−.038
	(.286)	(.278)	(.234)
Age	−.010***	−.005*	−.004
	(.002)	(.003)	(.003)
Race (1 if black)	−.015	−.044	−.119**
	(.030)	(.048)	(.048)
No. of family members	−.014	.004	−.005
	(.011)	(.016)	(.016)
No. of children aged 0-5	.009	−.023	−.020
	(.020)	(.035)	(.036)
AFDC (1 if on AFDC prior to enrollment)	.066	−.019	.008
	(.059)	(.117)	(.052)
City unemployment rate	.079	−.009	−.013
	(.064)	(.067)	(.054)
1 = $M1$ (counseling only)	.049	.050	.067
	(.040)	(.062)	(.055)
1 = $M2$ (counseling + 50% subsidy)	−.011	−.001	.032
	(.035)	(.060)	(.051)
1 = $M3$ (counseling + 100% subsidy)	−.012	−.049	−.042
	(.044)	(.070)	(.059)
Education	.003	.007	.007
	(.006)	(.012)	(.012)
Sample size	1191	471	579

CHAPTER 8

Labor Supply and Childcare Arrangements of Single Mothers

C. ERIC MUNSON
PHILIP K. ROBINS
GARY STIEGER

INTRODUCTION

Childcare has become an increasingly important public policy issue in recent years. Discussions of welfare reform emphasize developing comprehensive childcare programs that can be integrated into a more general system of providing tax relief for low- and moderate-income families (Lewis, 1973; Krashinsky, 1973). As more women enter the labor force and take advantage of available subsidies, it is important that the effects of various programs on labor supply and childcare demand be fully understood. In this chapter, we examine the effects of an NIT on the demand for childcare and the labor supply of single mothers.

The SIME/DIME experiments are expected to affect labor supply and use of childcare through two mechanisms. First is the direct and rather well-known work disincentive effect resulting from the high marginal tax rates and increased levels of nonwage income for families receiving NIT payments (see Keeley et al., 1978a,b, and Chapters 3 and 5 in this volume). In addition to the NIT component, SIME/DIME include a program for childcare subsidies similar to those available under the AFDC program. The principal difference between the SIME/DIME and AFDC programs is that SIME/DIME allow reimbursement of childcare expenses irrespective of family income level. In a study of working wives, Robins and Spiegelman (1978) found that subsidization of certain forms of childcare led to increased use of those types of care. Similar results were obtained for single female heads in the SIME/DIME sample (Kurz et al., 1975).

The availability of childcare subsidies raises net wage rates of users of subsidized modes of care. Increased returns from working are likely to bring additional workers into the labor force and induce current workers to increase their labor supply. This effect on labor supply can offset the disincentive effects of the NIT.

A GUARANTEED ANNUAL INCOME:
EVIDENCE FROM A SOCIAL EXPERIMENT

Thus, explicit measurement of any effects of the SIME/DIME childcare subsidy component on work effort is of primary concern.

The demand for childcare and the mother's labor supply is estimated simultaneously using a statistical procedure known as the multinomial logit model. (See Munson *et al.*, 1980, for the application of the model.) Data from a survey of childcare utilization are combined with data on labor supply to estimate the parameters of the model for single female heads of households. The first two sections describe the nature of childcare services and subsidies in Seattle and Denver, and the sample used for the analysis. The following section presents the theoretical framework and the estimation technique. The final section discusses the empirical results and their implications.

CHILDCARE AVAILABLE IN DENVER AND SEATTLE

Childcare services can be provided in a variety of institutional settings. In this section, we discuss the modes for which information was obtained during the SIME/DIME interviews and explain the aggregation criteria for our analysis. We then outline the various subsidies available to users of childcare, including those provided by SIME/DIME, AFDC, and other programs in Seattle and Denver.

Childcare Modes

Families in our sample responded as follows when asked if they used any of the seven modes of care:[1]

Day care center	6.6%
Licensed family day care home	4.5
Hired sitter	5.8
Friend or relative	20.4
Care by another person in the household	15.2
Self-care	19.8
No regular care	41.8

[1] The percentages total more than 100% because some families use more than one mode of care. These families are treated henceforth as if they are using only the mode for which they report the greatest number of hours. The modes were defined during the interviews as follows: *day care center*: a licensed facility not in a private home providing care for 12 or more children; *licensed family day care home*: a licensed facility providing care for fewer than 12 children, usually in a private home; *hired sitter*: someone other than a relative or friend who is paid to provide childcare; *friend or relative*: any friend or relative from outside the family unit; *care by another person in the household*: anyone in the family unit except the male head (if one is present); *self-care*: child cares for self; *no regular care*: mother reports no care by any of the sources above.

We aggregate these seven modes for analysis into market and nonmarket categories to reflect whether a family can receive a subsidy for the type of childcare used. In both sites, the primary requirement for subsidization is a monetary payment to someone who is not a member of the family unit. Thus, we define market modes as care in a day care center, in a licensed family day care home, or by a hired sitter on the assumption that these modes always require a monetary payment to the provider. Any care by a friend or relative (excluding members of the family unit) for which a monetary payment is made is also considered to be market care. Nonmarket care includes care by friends and relatives at zero price and all other forms of care not included in the market mode.[2]

Childcare Subsidies

Families living in Seattle and Denver can reduce their net costs of childcare through several subsidy programs. Subsidies are available from SIME/DIME, from AFDC under Title IVa of the Social Security Act, from Title XX of the Social Security Act for families with low incomes who do not qualify for AFDC, and from the federal income tax regulations. The subsidies are distributed by reimbursement of a family's expenses, direct payments to childcare vendors, or through the federal income tax structure by allowing work-related childcare expenses to be deducted from income in computing tax liability.[3] Our sample is composed primarily of low-income families who are unlikely to itemize deductions. Because of this, we ignore the possible effects of the deductibility of work-related childcare expenses through the federal income tax system.

The SIME/DIME and AFDC programs offer essentially identical subsidies for qualifying one-parent families. The major difference is that the AFDC subsidies are only available to those below a certain income limit whereas the SIME/DIME subsidies are available to experimental families irrespective of income level. Table 8.1 shows the maximum reimbursable amounts available to qualifying AFDC and SIME/DIME families at the time of the childcare survey. (See Kurz et al., 1975, for a discussion of the available subsidies.) Qualifying SIME/DIME families' childcare expenses in excess of the reimbursable maximums may be deducted from income, subject to a $5 daily limit.

Low-income families who do not qualify for AFDC are eligible for work-

---

[2] To the extent that the childcare subsidy programs cause income transfers among friends, they will appear to induce a shift to market care when in fact there is no impact on modal choice. Both the AFDC and the SIME/DIME subsidies allow reimbursement for work-related care by relatives not residing in the child's home. It is therefore quite likely that some observed market care is merely the result of a friend or relative getting paid for services that would have been provided at no charge in the absence of a subsidy program.

[3] Current IRS regulations allow a tax credit for 20% of childcare expenses. At the time of the childcare surveys, expenses were deductible from income.

Table 8.1

Maximum Childcare Subsidies Available to All AFDC and
One-Parent SIME/DIME Families

Type of arrangement	Maximum subsidy amount per day[a]	
	Seattle	Denver
Formal care		
Day care center		
1st child	$5.31	$8.00
2nd child	4.75	8.00
3rd child	3.26	8.00
Per additional child	3.00	8.00
Family day care home		
1st child	5.31	3.00
2nd child	4.75	2.25
3rd child	3.26	1.70
Per additional child	3.00	1.70
Informal care		
Inside user's home		
1st child	7.50	3.00
2nd child	none	2.25
3rd child	none	1.70
Per additional child	2.50	1.70
	(4th child only)	
Outside user's home		
1st child	5.31	3.00
2nd child	4.75	2.25
3rd child	3.26	1.70
Per additional child	3.00	1.70

Note: The subsidies shown are the maximum allowed at the time of the Seattle eighth and Denver ninth periodic interviews (November 1973-June 1974 in Seattle, and November 1974-June 1975 in Denver).

[a] A day represents 10 hours of care.

related childcare subsidies under Title XX of the Social Security Act. Full reimbursement of childcare expenses is available when family income is below the levels shown in Table 8.2. When family income exceeds these levels, a fee proportional to the excess income is assessed for childcare services.[4]

In addition to the subsidies for work-related childcare, SIME/DIME provide reimbursement through their manpower treatments. Families eligible for training and education subsidies are also eligible for childcare reimbursement during the

[4] In Seattle, the tax rate is 100%, i.e., the fee charged to the family equals the amount by which family income exceeds the maximum. In Denver, the tax rate is 10%; a single parent with three children and gross monthly income of $500 would pay $11.30 per month for day care services.

Table 8.2
Maximum Family Income to Qualify for Full
Childcare Subsidy Under Title XX

Number of persons living in home[a]	Maximum monthly gross income	
	Denver	Seattle
1	$264	$355
2	330	416
3	387	466
4	459	504
5	525	543
6	597	579
7	648	600
8	702	600
9	750	600
10 or more	802	600

[a]Exclusive of the female family head.

hours the parent is out of the home. Those enrolled in the 100% subsidy plan are eligible for full reimbursement of training-related childcare costs; families in the 50% subsidy plan are eligible for 50% reimbursement.

THE SAMPLE

The sample used for analysis consists of originally enrolled single female heads of households who did not marry and who had children under the age of 13 at the time of the childcare survey. All results must be interpreted as conditional on being single, having young children, and having remained in the experiments through the time of the childcare survey.

The data on childcare utilization were collected via interviews administered approximately 2½ years after enrollment (between November 1973 and July 1974 in Seattle and between November 1974 and June 1975 in Denver). Women with children under 13 were asked a series of questions about childcare. Those who were working and using childcare regularly at the time of the interview were asked detailed questions about their childcare arrangements and costs, number and ages of children receiving care, hours of childcare, satisfaction with childcare arrangements, and reasons for not using the specific modes of care they did not choose. Those who were not working or were not using childcare regularly were given an abbreviated interview. Our sample consists of 818 originally enrolled women who responded to the childcare survey.

In addition to possible biases caused by attrition and marriages, the sample may be biased because of experimental effects on fertility.[5] We have assumed that fertility has negligible effects on our estimates.

Table 8.3 compares the means of selected characteristics for experimental and control families in our sample by work status at the time of the childcare survey. Women are defined to be working if they have positive hours of market work during the week of the childcare interview or during any of the 3 weeks immediately prior to the interview. Information on the mode of childcare used prior to enrollment is not available, but net expenditures on childcare during the preexperimental year are reported as one proxy for preprogram childcare use.

ESTIMATION TECHNIQUE

We assume an individual chooses one of four mutually exclusive and exhaustive combinations of work behavior and childcare modes. Consider the following four choices available to a given individual:

1. Work and use market care
2. Work and use nonmarket care
3. Not work and use market care
4. Not work and use nonmarket care.

The multinomial logit model, which we employ in this chapter, allows us to estimate the effect of a change in a given variable on the odds of choosing one alternative relative to another.[6] The estimated coefficients can then be used for given values of the independent variables to calculate the probabilities that spe-

---

[5] It seems likely that the experiment affected the probability that a family would have children, although the effect might be smaller for single female heads than for two-parent families. A study of the experiment's impact on fertility revealed significant effects for married women. Effects for single female heads were qualitatively similar but were not statistically significant (see Keeley, 1978, and Chapter 11 in this volume). A sample selected on the basis of children present at the time of enrollment would yield different results if fertility were affected by the experimental treatment. It would be possible to investigate differences between the results for our sample, which includes families with children under 13 at the time of the survey, and a sample based on whether the children present at enrollment would be less than 13 years old on the date of the interview. Of the 818 families included in our analysis sample, 29 had only children less than 3 years of age or no children between the ages of 3 and 13 at the time of the childcare survey and would not have been included in the alternative sample. The remaining 789 families all would have been included if the selection criterion had been based on ages of children present at enrollment.

[6] The multinomial logit model was developed by Theil (1969) and by McFadden (1974). It is also possible to model the choice of childcare mode and hours worked in a continuous rather than a discrete framework (see Heckman, 1974). We chose the multinomial logit approach primarily because the computational costs are much lower than for estimating a set of simultaneous equations for truncated continuous dependent variables. A detailed description of the application used here is given by Munson et al. (1980).

Table 8.3
Means of Selected One-Parent Family Characteristics by Work and Experimental Status

	Female head working (N=375)			Female head not working (N=443)			Total sample (N=818)		
	Experimentals	Controls	Difference	Experimentals	Controls	Difference	Experimentals	Controls	Difference
Preexperimental year childcare expenses net of subsidies	$199	$263	−$64	$102	$38	$64	$148	$161	−13
Preexperimental year income	$3583	$3893	−$310	$1505	$1663	−$158	$2483	$2874	−391
Preexperimental year hours of work	1257	1221	36	510	371	139	862	833	29
Number of family members	3.51	3.50	.01	3.80	3.64	.16	3.67	3.56	.11
Age structure									
1=Children 0-4 years old	.22	.28	−.06	.49	.42	.07	.36	.35	.01
1=Children 5 years old	.14	.10	.04	.19	.15	.04	.17	.12	.05
1=Children 6-12 years old	.85	.85	.00	.77	.80	−.03	.81	.83	−.02
1=Children 13-17 years old	.46	.34	.12	.38	.38	.00	.42	.36	.06

cific alternatives will be chosen. Computation of conditional probabilities (such as the probability that a mother will use market care, given that she works) is also straightforward.

The variables used in our empirical analysis and the coefficient estimates of the multinomial logit model are described in the Appendix to this chapter. The model depicts the current probability of a given alternative as depending on the preexperimental probability of the alternative and the experimental impact on net wages, disposable income, and price of childcare. Since data on the preexperimental mode of childcare are not available, we include as a proxy in the empirical specification a set of variables associated with the preexperimental decision to use market care, such as preexperimental expenditures on childcare and family structure.[7]

EMPIRICAL RESULTS

In this section, we summarize the implications of the estimated coefficients reported in the chapter Appendix. To illustrate these effects, the vector of estimated coefficients and selected values of the explanatory variables are used to solve for the predicted probability of each alternative. Using the coefficients reported in Table 8.A.2, the predicted probabilities in Table 8.4 are computed for the given value of each specified variable and the mean values of all other variables, in order to depict a "typical" response. The effects shown in Table 8.4 can therefore be interpreted as the response of an average family to the given change. The first column in Table 8.4 shows the effects of the independent variables on the probability of working. The second column shows the effects on the probability of using market care given that the mother is working.

The family structure effects are best interpreted as the marginal effect of an additional child in the given age group for a family with the average number of members in each other age group. They indicate that an additional preschool child increases the probability of using market care, given that the mother works, by 12 percentage points. This effect is almost entirely due to a 10 percentage point reduction in the probability of working. The probability of both working and using market care is unaffected by the number of preschool children. One explanation may be that women who stop working to care for young children

---

[7] An alternative specification of the model would recognize the almost universal availability of full subsidies for child care among families in our sample. The SIME/DIME subsidy is available to families regardless of their income and thus represents a significant departure from other subsidy programs. Therefore, we could estimate the probability of choosing an alternative as a function of experimental-control status while controlling for all other factors that might affect the choice of childcare mode or the decision to work. Estimated coefficients of this "program effect" model are quite similar to those presented in the Appendix of this chapter, and are discussed by Munson *et al.* (1980).

Table 8.4
Predicted Probabilities for Selected Characteristics of One-Parent Families
(Asymptotic Standard Errors in Parentheses)

	Probability of working	Probability of market care given work
Family structure		
No children 0-4 years old	.476	.380
	(.027)	(.038)
One child 0-4 years old	.369[a]	.504[a]
	(.031)	(.052)
No 5-year-old children	.442	.408
	(.024)	(.035)
One 5-year-old child	.361	.576
	(.055)	(.086)
One 6-12-year-old child	.427	.464
	(.024)	(.036)
Two 6-12-year-old children	.432	.366[a]
	(.030)	(.043)
No teenager or older person	.399	.507
	(.028)	(.044)
One teenager or older person	.440	.406[a]
	(.024)	(.035)
Preexperimental annual net childcare expenses		
$100	.430	.414
	(.023)	(.035)
$200	.426	.450[a]
	(.023)	(.035)
Hours worked in the preexperimental year		
800	.419	.434
	(.022)	(.035)
900	.436[a]	.432
	(.026)	(.034)
Nonwage income in the preexperimental year		
$1000	.454	.426
	(.028)	(.040)
$2000	.424	.434
	(.022)	(.035)
Experimental treatment effects		
Change in net hourly wage rate		
−$.30	.432	.424
	(.023)	(.035)
−$.40	.427	.434
	(.022)	(.035)
Change in annual disposable income		
$500	.438	.438
	(.024)	(.036)
$1000	.420	.429
	(.023)	(.036)

Table 8.4 (Continued)
Predicted Probabilities for Selected Characteristics of One-Parent Families
(Asymptotic Standard Errors in Parentheses)

	Probability of working	Probability of market care given work
Childcare subsidy effects		
SIME/DIME		
No subsidy	.461	.415
	(.086)	(.093)
Full subsidy	.410	.443
	(.047)	(.057)
SIME/DIME manpower program		
No subsidy	.455	.428
	(.024)	(.036)
Full subsidy	.298[a]	.462
	(.048)	(.086)
Race		
Black	.443	.417
	(.031)	(.043)
Chicana	.396	.324[a]
	(.056)	(.075)
White	.427	.524
	(.041)	(.057)
City		
Seattle	.330	.536
	(.033)	(.055)
Denver	.516[a]	.357[a]
	(.032)	(.040)
Predicted probability at means of all variables	.428	.433
	(.022)	(.034)

[a]Indicates that the difference in predicted probabilities associated with the change in the specified variable is greater than 1.96 times the standard error of the difference in predicted probabilities. For instance, an "average" single female head with one child under 5 is .124 more likely to use market care, given that she works (column 2). The standard error of the difference is .058, less than half the difference.

were using nonmarket modes of care, while those who work and use market care would continue to do so even with an additional young child. Older children seem to increase the probability of working but reduce the probability of using market care.

There are several significant race and site effects. The probability of working is higher in Denver, but the probability that a working mother will use market care is lower. Working blacks are 10.7 percentage points and Chicanas 20 percentage points less likely than whites to use market care (although only the white-Chicana difference is significant). There are no significant race differences in the probability of working.

The effects of families' prior behavior are captured by the preexperimental childcare expenses, hours worked by the head, and nonwage income variables. Families who spent an additional $100 on childcare during the year prior to enrollment were slightly (but significantly) more likely to use market care if the head worked. The preexperimental level of work effort does not affect the probability of using market care but is significantly positively associated with the probability of working. The effect of nonwage income is consistent with the assumption that both leisure and market childcare are normal goods, although none of the effects are statistically significant.

The effects of the NIT treatments are estimated by the change in net hourly wage rate and change in annual disposable income variables. The first shows that the probability of working may have been reduced when the NIT treatment caused a more severe reduction in net wages or a larger addition to net disposable income. However, neither of these effects is statistically significant.

The effects of the childcare subsidy are captured with two variables, one showing eligibility for a subsidy through the NIT treatments, the other showing eligibility through the manpower treatments. Both variables show that eligibility for the subsidy may increase the probability of using market care, given that the mother works, but neither difference is statistically significant. The lack of strong evidence of a price effect on use of market care may be because most families in our sample qualify for some form of work-related subsidy, either through SIME/DIME or AFDC.

We hypothesized that a subsidy for work-related childcare would increase work effort because it would raise mothers' net wage rates, but the empirical analysis does not support this hypothesis. However, for women eligible for full reimbursement of training and education-related childcare expenses through the SIME/DIME manpower treatments there is a significant reduction of work effort. Presumably this represents a strong impact on the probability of enrolling in education or training programs. (A test of manpower program effects would require a six-state model and was not attempted.)

The predicted probabilities for the family structure variables in Table 8.4 represent the predicted effect of an additional child on the probabilities of work or use of market care for families that are average in all other respects. Table 8.5 shows the estimated probabilities for specific family structures. These probabilities are computed at the means of all variables except the family structure variables, which are set to either 0 or 1; the result is the set of predicted probabilities for specific types of families. Our model predicts the probability that a working mother with one child under 5 years old will use market care is .677. The probability rises to .714 if the child is 5 years old, and falls to .457 if the child is over 5 but under 13. Working mothers with two children, one of whom is a teenager, are less likely to use market care (by about 10 percentage points). Clearly, the effects of family structure on use of market care are important.

The effects of family structure on work effort are also seen in a slightly dif-

Table 8.5
Predicted Probabilities for Selected Family Structures
(Asymptotic Standard Errors in Parentheses)

	Probability of working	Probability of market care given work
Mother and one child		
Less than 5 years old	.377	.677
	(.048)	(.064)
5 years old	.405	.714
	(.066)	(.079)
6-12 years old	.457	.457
	(.038)	(.055)
Mother with teenager plus one other child		
Less than 5 years old	.400	.583
	(.042)	(.064)
5 years old	.426	.624
	(.065)	(.087)
6-12 years old	.501	.359
	(.034)	(.045)

ferent light in Table 8.5. The probability that a mother with one child will work still appears to be sensitive to the age of the child. This result can be compared to the finding in Table 8.4 that an additional preschool child significantly reduces the probability of work. The effect in Table 8.4 results from the combination of changing the family structure and increasing the number of children. In Table 8.5, the number of children is held constant but the age of the child is varied.

CONCLUSION

We have investigated factors affecting single mothers' choice of work and childcare arrangements. Family structure is found to have a significant impact on the decision to work and the choice of childcare mode; preschool children inhibit work and increase the probability of using market care. Older children increase the probability of work and reduce the probability that market care will be used. Previous labor supply is strongly positively associated with the current probability of work, but has no discernible effect on choice of childcare mode. Previous expenditures on childcare positively affect the probability of market care, given that the mother works, but are not significantly related to the probability of working. Because so many families in the sample were eligible for full reimbursement of work-related childcare expenses, we have been unable to detect a significant effect of the childcare subsidy on the probability of using market care. The direction of the effect of a childcare subsidy on the use of market care is positive, however, suggesting a responsiveness on the part of families to childcare subsidy programs.

APPENDIX. VARIABLES USED IN THE ANALYSIS

The explanatory variables and their mean values are listed in Table 8.A.1. Several of the variables in this table require explanation. Normal income is constructed by assigning the mean of the appropriate income class to each family. (See Kurz and Spiegelman, 1972, for a description of income classes.) A better treatment of the assignment process would have been to use a complete set of dummy variables; in this case, the dummy variables are collapsed into a single variable in order to reduce computational costs. If the income class for a specific family is unknown, the mean over all income classes is assigned.

The change in annual disposable income (ΔY) is constructed by subtracting disposable income before the NIT experiment from income available under the NIT, evaluated at preexperimental hours of work. For control families and experimental families with preexperimental earnings above the tax breakeven level of earnings, ΔY is set to 0. The variable as constructed measures the impact of the NIT treatments on family income at initial hours of work for families with preexperimental earnings below the tax breakeven level.

The change in net hourly wage rate, Δw, is calculated by first regressing observed wage rates for workers on a vector of demographic variables.[8] The coefficients are then used to compute a predicted wage rate for all persons, and the product of the predicted wage and the difference between preexperimental and predicted experimental tax rates (evaluated at preexperimental hours of work) is called Δw. The variable is set to 0 for all control families and for experimental families with preexperimental earnings above the tax breakeven level. As constructed, Δw measures the predicted change in an individual's net wage rate caused by the NIT treatments for female heads with earnings below the tax breakeven level.[9]

Two variables are used to measure the effect of a childcare subsidy. The first

[8] We follow the method of Keeley et al. (1978a). The estimated wage equation for women who worked during the year prior to enrollment is

$$W_0 = 1.03 + .08E + .05X - .001X^2 - .20D + .14B - .02C,$$
$$\quad\;\; (.018) \;\; (.013) \;\; (.0004) \;\; (.07) \;\; (.07) \;\; (.11)$$

where W_0 is the preexperimental net wage rate, E is years of education, X is experience (age minus education minus 5), $D = 1$ if Denver, $B = 1$ if black, and $C = 1$ if Chicana. Standard errors are in parentheses. Adjusted R^2 is .088.

[9] In our sample, 25 families had preexperimental earnings above the breakeven level. We assume no response by these families to the experimental treatment.

Table 8.A.1
Variables Used in Logit Analysis

Variable	Mean
Independent	
Normal income ($1000s)	3.366
Denver (1, if in Denver)	.562
Black (1, if black)	.520
Chicana (1, if Chicana)	.169
AFDC (1, if AFDC received preexperimentally)	.632
Number of family members	
aged 0-4	.438
age 5	.153
aged 6-12	1.313
aged 13 and over	.724
Childcare expenses net of subsidies in the	
preexperimental year ($1000s)	.153
Education/10	1.166
Age/100	.335
Hours worked in the preexperimental year (1000s)	.852
Change in annual disposable income ($1000s)	.782
Change in net hourly wage rate	−.391
Nonwage income in the preexperimental year ($1000s)	1.894
Manpower program subsidy (50%) (1, if eligible for 50%	
subsidy for training and education)	.243
Manpower program subsidy (100%) (1, if eligible for 100%	
subsidy for training and education)	.163
SIME/DIME childcare subsidy (1, if on financial	
treatment program)	.647
Predicted probability of eligibility for non-SIME/DIME	
reimbursement of childcare expenses	.207
Dependent	
Proportion working and using market care	.185
Proportion working and using nonmarket care	.274
Proportion not working and using market care	.046
Proportion not working and using nonmarket care	.495

Note: sample size = 818.

is a dichotomous variable equal to 1 if the family is eligible for reimbursement under SIME/DIME. Since our sample consists of single female heads, all NIT treatment families are eligible for the childcare subsidy.

Some control families are also eligible for reimbursement of work-related childcare expenses under provisions of AFDC or Title XX of the Social Security Act. A dichotomous variable reflecting participation in AFDC or qualification for the Title XX subsidy could be used but would be endogenous; an instrumental variable is used instead. A linear probability model is estimated to predict eligibility for childcare subsidies (see Munson *et al.*, 1980, Appendix). The estimated coefficients are used to calculate the predicted probability of being eligi-

Table 8.A.2
Multinomial Logit Estimates of the Work-Child Care Model
(Asymptotic Standard Errors in Parentheses)

	Using market care and working relative to using nonmarket care and working	Using market care and not working relative to using nonmarket care and not working	Working and Using Market care relative to not working and using market care	Working and using nonmarket care relative to not working and using nonmarket care
Normal income ($1000s)	.01 (.06)	.08 (.10)	.02 (.11)	.10* (.06)
Denver	-.73*** (.28)	-.13 (.42)	.49 (.45)	1.09*** (.24)
Black	-.43 (.27)	-.14 (.42)	-.03 (.45)	.26 (.24)
Chicano	-.83** (.41)	-.66 (.75)	-.02 (.80)	.19 (.33)
AFDC	.41 (.35)	.28 (.62)	-.02 (.65)	-.41 (.30)
Number of children				
aged 0-4	.51** (.23)	.74*** (.27)	-.85*** (.29)	-.62*** (.21)
age 5	.67* (.37)	.86** (.42)	-.79* (.46)	-.61* (.34)
aged 6-12	-.41*** (.16)	.16 (.20)	-.37 (.23)	.20 (.13)
aged 13 and over	-.41*** (.15)	-.41 (.30)	.33 (.32)	.33*** (.11)
Net childcare expenses in the preexperimental year ($1000s)	1.48*** (.41)	-.23 (.93)	.88 (.92)	-.83** (.42)

Table 8.A.2 (Continued)

	Using market care and working relative to using nonmarket care and working	Using market care and not working relative to using nonmarket care and not working	Working and Using Market care relative to not working and using market care	Working and using nonmarket care relative to not working and using nonmarket care
Education/10	.10	4.08***	-1.87*	2.12***
	(.65)	(1.01)	(1.07)	(.50)
Age/100	-3.94**	1.34	-1.22	4.07***
	(1.82)	(3.19)	(3.39)	(1.48)
Hours of work in the preexperimental year (1000s)	-.07	-.34	.98**	.72***
	(.21)	(.44)	(.45)	(.18)
Change in annual disposable income ($1000s)	-.07	-.15	-.05	-.13
	(.15)	(.23)	(.25)	(.12)
Change in net hourly wage rate	-.43	.48	-.52	.39*
	(.29)	(.43)	(.46)	(.26)
Nonwage income in the preexperimental year ($1000s)	.03	.01	-.11	-.14
	(.10)	(.14)	(.15)	(.08)
Childcare subsidy (SIME/DIME)	.11	-.06	-.08	-.26
	(.54)	(1.22)	(1.23)	(.55)
Childcare subsidy (other programs)	.06	-1.24	1.01	-.29
	(.90)	(1.65)	(1.70)	(.84)
Manpower program dummy (100%)	.14	-.20	.41	-.75***
	(.36)	(.48)	(.53)	(.29)
Constant	1.47	-7.59***	3.81	5.25***
	(1.40)	(2.41)	(2.53)	(1.24)

Note: Coefficients give the estimated effect of each variable on the natural logarithm of the odds of being in the first state relative to the second state.

*p < .10.

ble for the AFDC or Title XX subsidy, and the probability of eligibility is used as an independent variable in the analysis.

The estimated coefficients for the experimental impact model are shown in Table 8.A.2. The model is estimated with the coefficients for "not working and not using market care" set to 0 but, for ease of interpretation, the coefficients are presented differently. The first two columns show the effects of the explanatory variables on the log of the odds of using market care relative to using nonmarket care for workers and nonworkers, respectively.[10] The third and fourth columns show the effects on the log of the odds of working for users of market care and users of nonmarket care respectively.

REFERENCES

Heckman, J. J. "Effect of Child-Care Programs on Women's Work Effort." *Journal of Political Economy*, March-April 1974, pp. S136-S163.

Keeley, M. C. "The impact of Income Maintenance on Fertility: Preliminary Findings from the Seattle and Denver Income Maintenance Experiments." Research Memorandum No. 49, Center for the Study of Welfare Policy, SRI International, March 1978.

Keeley, M. C., *et al*. "The Estimation of Labor Supply Models Using Experimental Data," *American Economic Review*, December 1978a, pp. 873-887.

Keeley, M. C. *et al*. "The Labor Supply Effects and Costs of Alternative Negative Income Tax Programs." *Journal of Human Resources* 13, no. 1 (Winter 1978b).

Krashinsky, M. "Day Care and Welfare." *Studies in Public Welfare*, pp. 166-209. Joint Economic Committee, Subcommittee on Fiscal Policy. Washington, D.C.: U.S. Government Printing Office, 1973.

Kurz, M., and Spiegelman, R. G. "The Design of the Seattle and Denver Income Maintenance Experiments." Research Memorandum No. 18. Center for the Study of Welfare Policy, SRI International, August 1972.

Kurz, M.; Robins, P. K.; and Spiegelman, R. G. "A Study of the Demand for Child Care by Working Mothers." Research Memorandum No. 27. Center for the Study of Welfare Policy, SRI International, August 1975.

Lewis, V. "Day Care: Needs, Costs, Benefits, Alternatives." *Studies in Public Welfare*, Paper No. 7. Washington, D.C.: U.S. Government Printing Office, July 1973.

McFadden, D. "Conditional Logit Analysis of Qualitative Choice Behavior." In *Frontiers of Econometrics*, edited by P. Zarembka. New York: Academic Press, 1974.

Munson, C. E.; Robins, P. K.; and Stieger, G. "The Labor Supply and Child Care Demand of Single Mothers in the Seattle and Denver Income Maintenance Experiments." Research Memorandum No. 69, Center for the Study of Welfare Policy, SRI International, January 1980.

Robins, P. K., and Spiegelman, R. G. "An Econometric Model of the Demand for Child Care." *Economic Inquiry* 16 (January 1978):83-93.

Theil, H. "A Multinomial Extension of the Linear Logit Model." *International Economic Review* 10 (October 1969):251-260.

---

[10] Note that the coefficients in the first column are estimated using observations on workers and nonworkers and therefore differ from estimates using only a sample of workers.

PART

EXPERIMENTAL EFFECTS ON
FAMILY BEHAVIOR

CHAPTER 9

Marital Dissolution and Remarriage

LYLE P. GROENEVELD
NANCY BRANDON TUMA
MICHAEL T. HANNAN

Policy analyses of proposals to replace the current welfare system with an NIT program usually focus on two issues. First, how does the proposed program alter the incentives to work? Second, how does the program alter incentives to marry and stay married? With regard to labor supply responses, it has been widely agreed that changes in the welfare system alter levels of work effort, and that such changes constitute a major component of the net increase in costs under an NIT scheme. Unitl recently there has been no similar consensus among the social science community that alternative welfare arrangements might substantially alter marital behavior. Hence, policy analysts have tended to understate the importance of marital stability responses to the long-run cost of an NIT program. However, this situation seems to be changing. The stabilization of marriage was a central point in President Carter's message to Congress on his Program for Better Jobs and Income (PBJI). (See Chapter 6 for a description of PBJI.)

This chapter has three main purposes. The first is to state the issues involved; in particular, why one would expect an NIT to have an effect on marital stability. The second is to present the results of the SIME/DIME marital stability studies.[1] Our final purpose is to address the policy relevance of the SIME/DIME findings by comparing our findings with the results from the other income-maintenance experiments and then discussing their implications for welfare reform.

THE EXPECTED EFFECT OF A NEGATIVE INCOME TAX PROGRAM ON MARITAL STABILITY

There are several reasons why one might expect an NIT program to affect marital stability. First, an NIT program might remove the incentives to marital

---

[1] As will become clear, the experimental design and the marital stability analyses are complex. Complete discussions of our findings are found in the papers cited at the conclusion of this paper.

163

A GUARANTEED ANNUAL INCOME:
EVIDENCE FROM A SOCIAL EXPERIMENT

dissolution inherent in the present system. AFDC prohibits benefits to families in which the father is present. The AFDC-UP program eases this restriction somewhat, but only if the father is employed less than some maximum number of days in a period. It is the number of days he is employed, not the adequacy of the family income, that determines eligibility under the AFDC-UP program. An NIT program with benefit levels determined by family income would do away with these restrictions and thereby eliminate any effect of these incentives on marital disruption rates.

As an example of these incentives, President Carter's August 6, 1977 message to Congress on PBJI notes that "in Michigan a two-parent family with the father working at the minimum wage has a total income, including tax credits and food stamps, of $5922. But if the father leaves, the family will be eligible for benefits totaling $7076." Similar, though perhaps less dramatic, examples can be cited for other states. However, no one has yet shown that such financial inducements have important effects on marital dissolution rates. Most research correlates state welfare benefit levels with the number of female-headed households, while controlling for other factors such as the level of unemployment or female wages (Honig 1974, 1976; Minarik and Goldfarb, 1976; Ross 1975). When using data aggregated at the state or SMSA level, one cannot disentangle the effects of welfare programs on families from selective migration to areas with high benefit levels. Also, the effect of the benefit levels on the number of female-headed families cannot be distinguished from the effect of the number of female-headed families on the benefit levels.

Even if the current welfare system does not promote marital instability, an NIT program may still alter marital dissolution rates by altering levels of family income. Many studies have shown that the probability of marital dissolution is highest for the lowest income families. This relationship permits several interpretations. According to one (the culture-of-poverty thesis) the relationship between income and marital instability reflects cultural differences between the poor and the rest of society. This position argues that the poor have high rates of marital dissolution, not because they lack material resources but because they lack appropriate values and personality traits. If so, altering income levels will not greatly affect marital stability in this population.

Other interpretations of this relationship suggest that an NIT program will stabilize marriages. One holds that changes in income affect the strains to which marriages are exposed and the ability of the families to cope with a variety of problems and dissatisfactions. Another interpretation contends that personal and social worth are evaluated primarily through consumption activities in our society. Heads of families who cannot provide certain levels of consumption for their families are viewed as failures by themselves and others. One response to such failure is flight from the marriage. Income supplement programs that substantially improve living standards might reduce the pressures toward dissolution. We refer to effects of this sort as income effects. We expect that the income effects of an NIT program would tend to lower the rate of marital dissolution.

Another possible effect has been overlooked in most discussions of welfare reform. Early in our research we suggested that an NIT program would alter the structure of dependence in marriages (Hannan *et al.*, 1974). An NIT program guarantees support to unmarried as well as married people. Consequently it alters the level of resources available outside marriage and thereby alters the dependence of the members on marriage. We refer to this as the independence effect. If the NIT program increases the level of resources outside marriage, the independence effect tends to raise the probability of marital dissolution.

This independence effect is, of course, the defect that critics see in the current system. To understand why an independence effect would be stronger under an NIT program than in the present welfare system we need to consider the issue of welfare stigma and more generally, the idea of a welfare discount.

It is often argued that the current welfare system stigmatizes recipients and that an NIT program would reduce the stigma. If participation in the current system is perceived as degrading, both its income and independence effects are muted. Families receiving payments would not experience the full income-effect because of strains induced by stigma. Likewise, dependent spouses would not experience the full independence effect of the welfare system. In particular, women who believe that receiving welfare is degrading may choose to remain in unsatisfying marriages rather than go on welfare. This suggests that NIT payments have stronger income and independence effects than payments of the same amount from the current welfare system. Another way of putting this is to say that payments from the current welfare system are discounted in their effects on marriage relative to NIT payments.

There are other nonpecuniary differences between current welfare and NIT plans that may result in welfare being discounted. Participation in the NIT program involves less effort than going on welfare. For instance, the experimental NIT plans had a simpler and presumably less alienating bureaucracy. The rules of the NIT plan are carefully explained to the participants. Information about eligibility rules and support levels for welfare are probably not known as well. Each of these three factors (stigma, transaction costs, or lack of information) suggests that the effects of the current welfare system may be discounted.

What, then, can be said about the expected impact of an NIT program on marital dissolution rates? For an NIT scheme that is more generous than the present welfare system, as is the case with SIME/DIME, it is not possible to predict the direction of the impact a priori. If the income effects dominate, the NIT will lower the dissolution rate. If the independence effects are stronger, the reverse will hold. Even a less generous program may have both income and independence effects if the changes in the operation of the program affect the rate at which welfare benefits are discounted.

DESIGN OF THE STUDY

We will describe analyses separately by race and marital status, controlling for site and normal family income. The control and treatment groups should be alike in all other respects, except for small chance differences, because of the random assignment. We do control for other variables in our analysis to increase the precision of findings. But we stress that the validity of the findings does not depend on our ability to control other variables; the experimental design takes care of this.

The experiments began in 1970-1971 in Seattle and in 1971-1972 in Denver. About 40% of the 4800 families were placed in the control group. Of the remainder, 75% received a 3-year NIT treatment; the rest were given a 5-year treatment. We interviewed families at the beginning of the experiment and three times a year thereafter. These interviews recorded all changes in family composition, including marital dissolutions and marriages. We used exactly the same procedure to obtain these records from control and experimental families. This chapter analyzes changes that occurred during the first 2 years of the experiments.

We did not require that couples be legally married to be included in the study. For families with children, we considered two persons to be married if they lived together, pooled resources, and claimed the relationship to be permanent. For couples who were not legally married and did not have children, we required an affidavit stating that the relationship was a legal union or a common-law marriage. We obtained mostly long-term unions using this definition of marriage. Between 85% and 90% of the couples at the beginning of the experiment had been married for more than 2 years. We treat a marriage as having ended when one partner moves out of the household and the members report that they have permanently separated. So the outcomes we study are not legal divorces; they are endings of marital unions. Therefore, we report effects of an NIT program on the marital dissolution rate, not on the rate of legal divorce. We note that NIT effects on the marital dissolution rate are more important than effects on the divorce rate insofar as the dollar cost of an NIT program are concerned.

We concentrate on the experimental impacts on dissolution, with only brief mention of impacts on remarriage. There are 2771 couples who met our definition of married at enrollment. Table 9.1 reveals some important characteristics of the originally married sample. The mean duration married at enrollment is 9.42 years. This, when compared with the mean ages of husbands (33.49 years) and wives (30.66 years) indicates that our definition of marriage did not result in a sample with a large number of temporary unions. The families enrolled in SIME/DIME belong to the lower 50% of the income distribution; however, many of the families are not "poor." Only 11% of the sample attrited during the first two years. This low attrition rate gives us increased confidence in our findings.

Table 9.1

Characteristics of the Originally Married Sample

Variable	Mean or proportion
Husband's age	33.49
Husband's education (in years)	10.90
Wife's age	30.66
Wife's education (in years)	11.03
Duration married at enrollment (in years)	9.42
Number of children	2.30
Preexperimental family disposable income	$6208
Proportion with at least one child under 10 years old	.75
Proportion who reported receiving AFDC in the year before the experiment	.16
Proportion of wives employed preexperimentally	.48
Proportion white	.47
Proportion black	.34
Proportion Chicano	.19
Manpower treatment	
Control group	.42
Counseling only	.19
Counseling plus 50% subsidy	.24
Counseling plus 100% subsidy	.14
Financial treatment	
Control group	.45
$3800 support level	.18
$4800 support level	.23
$5600 support level	.14
Proportion of sample enrolled for 5 years on financial treatment	.18
Proportion attriting before 2 years	.11

BASIC FINDINGS FROM SIME/DIME

We found that the NIT plans destabilized marriages. As Table 9.2 shows, the experimental group had a larger fraction of disrupted marriages than the control group for all three racial-ethnic groups. The unadjusted figures in Table 9.2 indicate that dissolutions were 66% more likely among the white experimentals than controls, and 22% more likely among Chicano experimentals than controls. This table does not, of course, take into account differences between the control and NIT treatment groups that might affect the rates of marital dissolution.

Table 9.3 reports the experimental impact, controlling for the variables used in assigning families to treatments and for several other variables that may affect dissolution (for details see Hannan et al., 1976a,b, 1977; Tuma et al., 1976). Throughout this chapter, we report impacts estimated for the 5-year sample. The

Table 9.2
Proportion of Marriages at Enrollment that End in
Dissolution Within 2 Years
(Number of cases in parentheses)

	Blacks	Whites	Chicanos
Control group	.152	.101	.140
	(435)	(605)	(200)
Financial treatment group	.232	.168	.170
	(504)	(692)	(335)

effects for 3-year families are approximately 80% of the 5-year effects. Entries on Table 9.3 are percent increases in the dissolution rate due to the experiments. For whites and blacks the impact is positive and statistically significant. For those groups, therefore, we can say with some confidence that the experimental-control difference was not due merely to chance.

This finding is consistent with a model in which the independence effects dominate the income effects for the NIT plans tested. Does it imply, therefore, that all NIT schemes will increase dissolution rates in populations like those we studied? To answer this question we must consider some more complex analyses. Our most provocative findings concern the pattern of impacts by level of income guarantee. The lowest guarantee level holds particular interest since it differs little in financial terms from the existing level of support available from the AFDC and Food Stamp programs. If benefits of the current welfare programs are not discounted, this NIT plan should have no independence effect. However, dissolution rates for families on this treatment greatly exceeds that of the control group which leads us to conclude that the independence effects of welfare programs are indeed discounted relative to those of the NIT programs tested. This finding makes clear the need to understand the stigma and information content of NIT schemes in order to compare their effects with the existing system.

The impacts for the three guarantee levels are presented in Table 9.4. Note a curious result: for each racial-ethnic group, the plan that has the highest guarantee (140% of the poverty line) has the smallest impact, and it is not statistically significant for any racial-ethnic group. Indeed it appears from this table that at the highest guarantee level the income and independence effects are approxi-

Table 9.3
Change in Marital Dissolution Rate Due to NIT Treatment

	Blacks	Whites	Chicanos
Percentage (adjusted)	61%**	58%**	−4%
Number of cases	939	1297	535

$**p < .05$

Table 9.4
Percentage Change in Marital Dissolution Rate by
Level of Income Guarantee

Guarantee level	Racial-ethnic group		
	Black	White	Chicano
90% of poverty line	69%**	96%***	60%
125% of poverty line	93***	55*	−28
140% of poverty line	21	12	−35
Number of cases	939	1297	535

*$p < .10$.
**$p < .05$.
***$p < .01$.

mately equal. The independence effects do, however, dominate at the lower guarantee levels.

The basic results of the experimental analysis in Tables 9.3 and 9.4 are robust. We have found no technical problem that explains the findings. The problem of attrition deserves particular mention. We lost track of some families, and others refused to participate after a time. A family's decision to remain in the study was probably affected both by the benefits received from the experiment and by marital events. If control families were more likely to leave the experiment at the time of a marital dissolution, our records would undercount dissolutions for this group, which would inflate experimental-control differences. Fortunately, the attrition rates in SIME/DIME are low, about 11% over 2 years. In studies of rare events such as marital disruptions, even small attrition rates may give misleading results. Further investigations (Hannan et al., 1976a) showed that our results are not very sensitive to attrition. Even if all the controls who left the experiment had an unrecorded marital dissolution, the experimental-control difference would still be positive for whites and blacks. The difference between the low guarantee group and the controls is still the most robust of all the basic findings.

The effects of an NIT on the proportion of families headed by females depend on its effects on both dissolution and remarriage rates. Thus, before discussing refinements to our analysis of marital dissolution we briefly discuss our findings on remarriage to which neither the scientific nor the policy literature gives much attention. The increased dissolution rates we observed do not necessarily imply increased costs under an NIT program. What matters is the composition of families, particularly the number of female-headed families.

For whites and blacks, the NIT treatment had weak and insignificant total impacts on rates of remarriage (Table 9.5). However, more refined analyses (Tuma et al., 1976) reveal an experimental response that depends on the duration of singleness. The NIT treatment lowered remarriage rates of recently single

Table 9.5
Change in Remarriage Rate Due to NIT Treatments

	Blacks	Whites	Chicanos
Percentage	3%	−30%	−75%***
Number of cases	902	750	318

***$p < .01$.

women relative to comparable controls; but, for those single a longer period (more than about 4 years), the NIT treatment increased the remarriage rate. These experimental-control differences are statistically significant only for the 140% of poverty line treatment for whites and blacks, and for the 125% program for blacks. Unlike the findings on dissolution, programs that differ most from the nonexperimental environment induce the largest response.

For Chicanos the NIT treatments lower remarriage rates. The rate of remarriage for those on NIT treatment is approximately one-fifth that of the controls (Table 9.5). We have puzzled over the strength of the experimental response for this group. It appears to reflect differences between groups in the nonexperimental environment. The remarriage rates of Chicano controls are much higher than those of comparable white and black controls. The NIT treatment lowers the remarriage rate of Chicano experimentals so that they are close to those for black and white controls. We suspect, therefore, that a understanding of the strong response of Chicanos to the NIT treatment awaits an explanation for their much higher rates of remarriage as controls.

The models we use permit calculations of the total effect of various NIT plans on the equilibrium proportion of families headed by females. Our calculations indicate that the guarantee levels used in the experiment would yield slight increases in the fraction of female-headed families for blacks, since the remarriage response partially offsets the dissolution response. For both whites and Chicanos, however, the fraction of families headed by females would increase substantially (see Hannan *et al.*, 1977, for details).

Responses to the experiment may vary over time. There may be a delay in response due to learning and adjustment to a new situation; or there may be a burst of responses because marriages on the brink of dissolution are given a push. The response of whites is significantly higher over the first 6 months than over the remaining 18. Thus, the average 2-year response may overstate the long-run response for whites. For the black and Chicano samples the pattern is less clear, though it appears that the response is delayed for 6 months. This delay may indicate a lack of trust in the experiments or a period of testing prior to taking action. In any case, for the black and Chicano samples, the 2-year average response may underestimate the full effect.

We also considered the implications of the view that we observe merely short-run effects of switching from one form of income support to another. Suppose that an NIT alters rates of dissolution and remarriage for only 2 years. Can the marital response to the program be safely disregarded? Our claculations show that it takes a long time, on the order of 10 years, for the fraction of households headed by females to return close to its pre-NIT level following the two years of altered dissolution and remarriage rates like those we estimate (see Tuma *et al.*, 1977 pp. 25-42, for details). Thus, it can be expected to take a reasonably long time for the impact of an NIT program on marriage to manifest itself fully; it will also take a long time for transitory impacts to recede.

INCOME AND INDEPENDENCE EFFECTS ON THE RATE OF MARITAL DISSOLUTION

We have studied the seeming paradox of the guarantee levels. Recall that the 90% of poverty level guarantee has a larger impact on dissolution than the 140% guarantee. Moreover, the former is statistically significant while the latter is not. Why does a small financial change from the control environment have a strong impact when a bigger change does not? We have argued that income maintenance has both income and independence effects. Perhaps each of the treatments studied substantially increases independence but only the 140% of poverty line plan strongly reduces strains within the family (due to the income effect). That is, the 90% of poverty line plan may have only an independence effect, while the 140% plan may have offsetting income and independence effects.

We sought to explain this pattern of experimental-control differences with a model of the income and independence effects of the various NIT plans. Briefly, our model assumes that the income and independence effects are nonlinear functions of income. (See Hannan *et al.*, 1977, 1978, for a discussion of the model and the evidence supporting it.)

Figure 9.1 graphs the estimated income effect for black couples with children and white control couples with two and three children. Throughout our analysis we have found that the income effects differ by race and family size. Recall that we estimate multiplicative rather than the more common additive models. Therefore, in our models the effect of a variable such as family income is represented as a multiplier of the base rate predicted by all other variables in the model, which we denote by $\bar{r}$. Thus, the vertical axis of Figure 9.1 gives the dissolution rate in units of $\bar{r}$, which depends on other characteristics of the family.

In Figure 9.1 we see a backward S-shaped relationship between family income and the dissolution rate. All four curves are flat for very low family incomes and steeper for incomes in the range of $5600-15,000. For family incomes above $15,000, which are beyond the range of most of our sample and not pictured in Figure 9.1, the curve is again flat, indicating that changes in income will have little effect on the dissolution rate for high income families. The curves for three

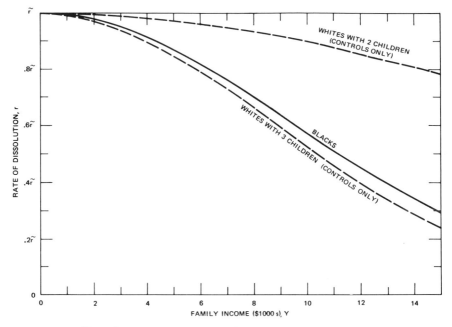

Figure 9.1   Estimated income effects. See text for definition of $\tilde{r}$.

children are steeper than for two children and the curves are steeper for whites than for blacks. A steeper curve means a larger percentage change in the dissolution rate for a given change in family income.

Most of the families in our sample have disposable income between $4000 and $7500 for the year before the experiment. The average increase in their income from the NIT treatment was $1056 for the low guarantee level, $1608 for the medium level, and $2016 for the high level. The response of black families to NIT may be seen directly in Figure 9.1 in which a family moves along the curve the horizontal distance of the change in their income due to the NIT. For a black family with an initial disposable income of $6000, for example, a payment of $1500 decreases the rate from $.81\tilde{r}$ to $.71\tilde{r}$—a 12% decrease.

The response for white experimental families is more complex and cannot be pictured so easily. For this group we found that the effect of the change in income from the NIT treatments was larger than the effect of the initial income on the dissolution rate. Furthermore, the change in the dissolution rate depended not only on the magnitude of the change but also on the initial level of income. In terms of a graph such as Figure 9.1, we found that the response of whites to the NIT could not be represented in terms of movement along a line for controls, but involved a change in the shape of the line as well. (See Hannan et al., 1978 for a fuller discussion of the white response). For a white family with three children and $6000 annual disposable income, a $1500 change in income decreases the rate from .81$\bar{r}$ to .74$\bar{r}$—a 9% decrease. These decreases in the dissolution rates would be offset by increases due to the independence effect.

The estimated independence effect has an S-shape. When the income available to the wife outside her marriage (independence income, which includes welfare and earnings) is low, increases in independence income have little effect on the dissolution rate. When the independence income is somewhat higher, however, increases in independence income can increase the dissolution rate substantially. For women with high independence income, changes of the size expected in an NIT program have little effect on the dissolution rate.

Figure 9.2 shows the shape of the independence effect estimated for white couples with 2 or 3 children and black couples with children. As with the income effect, the independence effect differs by race. For whites, the effect differs by family size and we present the effects for families with two or three children. For blacks we found an independence effect only for families with at least one child under 10 years old (72% of our sample). When we controlled for the presence of young children we found that the independence effect did not depend on the number of children in the family.

As in Figure 9.1 the vertical axis of Figure 9.2 expresses the rate as a multiplier of the portion of the rate determined by other variables, which here include the income effects. We denote the portion of the rate determined by these other

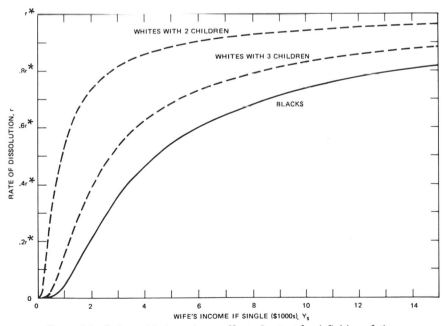

Figure 9.2   Estimated independence effects. See text for definition of $r*$.

variables as r^*. Again, the fact that the multipliers of r^* are less than 1 is a constraint imposed by our model and has no substantive importance.

As discussed in the preceding, it is necessary to assume that current welfare benefits are discounted in order to explain the observed pattern of guarantee level effects. We experimented with several discounts and found that the exact discount made little difference as long as it was greater than 0. Figure 9.2 presents the independence effects with a 50% welfare discount for all women. (That is, we assume that for a married woman considering her economic position outside her marriage, $2 of welfare (AFDC and food stamps) are worth $1 of earnings or NIT payment.)

Most women in our sample have preexperimental independence incomes between $1000 and $4000. The mean increase in annual independence income from the NIT with welfare discounted by 50% is $1603 for women with the 90% of poverty level guarantee, $2258 for women with the 125% guarantee, and $2872 for women with the 140% guarantee. Because most women are in the range of independence income where the independence effect is steepest, changes of this magnitude have large effects on the dissolution rate. Consider, for example, a black woman with children whose initial independence income is $2000. A $2000 increase in her independence income from an NIT would change her dissolution rate from $.23r^*$ to about $.48r^*$, an increase of over 100%. For a white woman with three children and initial independence income of $2000, a $2000 increase from an NIT program increases her dissolution rate from $.42r^*$ to $65r^*$, a 55% increase. In contrast, a $2000 increase in independence income for a black woman with children and with initial independence income of $4000 would increase her dissolution rate from $.48r^*$ to $.61r^*$, a 27% increase. For a white woman with three children and with initial independence income of $4000, a $2000 increase in independence income would increase her dissolution rate from $.65r^*$ to $.75r^*$, a 15% increase. Of course, both of these examples ignore the offsetting income effect, which would depend on the level of family income before the NIT program and the change in family income due to the NIT program.

In order to understand the overall effect of an NIT program it is necessary to examine the pattern of combined income and independence effects. Figure 9.3 illustrates the results of the combined income and independence effects. As in Figures 9.1 and 9.2, the effect is given as a multiplier of the portion of the rate determined by other variables, denoted $\check{r}$. The horizontal axis is the wife's independence income. Plots for four different levels of family income are drawn. We choose the income and independence effects for blacks with children because the results are clearer graphically. The same patterns of effects can also be demonstrated for whites.

Consider a couple in Figure 9.3 whose family income is $4000 and wife's independence income is $4000, represented by point A in Figure 9.3. If an NIT plan increased the wife's independence income by $1000, the couple would move along the curve to point B, increasing the dissolution rate. If the NIT plan

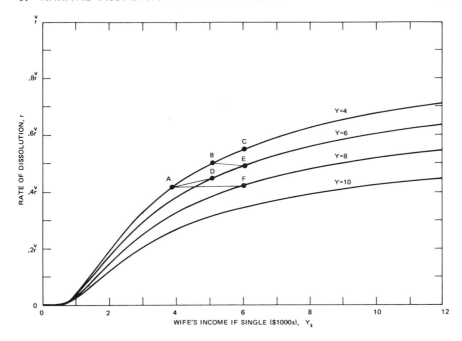

Figure 9.3 Estimated income and independence effects for black couples with children. Y denotes family income. See text for definition of $\check{r}$.

increased the family income by $2000, they would move down to point D, still with a net increase in the dissolution rate. With a more generous NIT plan that increased the wife's independence income by $2000 and family income by $4000, the couple would move from point A to point F. This would still be a slight net increase in the dissolution rate, but a much smaller increase than in the first case. Next, consider a couple with the same family income but with the wife's independence income at $5000. If an NIT plan increased the wife's independence income by $1000 and family income by $2000, the couple would move from point B to point E, a net decrease. These examples illustrate how an NIT program can increase or decrease the dissolution rate through the combined effects of income and independence.

FINDINGS OF OTHER INCOME-MAINTENANCE EXPERIMENTS

Each of the other income-maintenance experiments (New Jersey, Rural, and Gary) has reported analysis of impacts on marital dissolution. Most reported analyses find no significant experimental effects. However, Sawhill *et al.* (1975) report significant effects of the experimental treatments on marital dissolution which are similar to the SIME/DIME findings: The experimental treatment increased the rate of marital dissolution relative to the controls.

There are several reasons why the results of SIME/DIME should carry more weight in any policy discussion than the results of the other experiments. First, large samples are essential for the study of impacts on rare events like marital dissolutions. The other three experiments are hampered by relatively small samples. The SIME/DIME sample contained more families than the other three experiments combined.

SIME/DIME also covers a longer time period than the other experiments. The other three experiments lasted 3 years. In SIME/DIME, approximately ¾ of the experimental families were enrolled for 3 years and one-fourth for 5 years. (Approximately 170 Denver families were enrolled for 20 years.) To the extent that a longer term experiment should more closely approximate the impact of a permanent program, the results from SIME/DIME should provide better predictors of the effect of a permanent NIT program than the results from the other experiments.

A third reason to give more weight to the SIME/DIME findings is that there were major changes in the rules regarding marital status and program eligibility during both the New Jersey and Gary experiments. In New Jersey, the welfare system available to the control families changed, permitting families with unemployed fathers to receive AFDC, and the AFDC support level also changed substantially. In the Gary experiment, families on an NIT plan were told that any single-person family formed as a result of a marital dissolution would not be eligible for the NIT. Though this rule was changed at the end of the first year, it limits the usefulness of any study of marital impacts.

A fourth reason to give greater weight to the SIME/DIME findings is methodological. The methodology used in the SIME/DIME marital stability analysis allows the observation period to be different for each case. Consequently, cases can be included that end prematurely, such as families who participate in the experiment for a time and then drop out. The marital history up until the date of attrition is used in the analysis (See Tuma *et al.*, 1979 for a discussion of the methodology used in the SIME/DIME marital stability analysis.) The methodologies to analyze the other experiments necessitated the elimination of cases that were not observed for the entire period under consideration. Thus, those analyses are subject to attrition bias much more than the SIME/DIME analyses, and are less representative of the initial experimental population.

For all these reasons SIME/DIME offers the best opportunity to evaluate the effects of NIT alternatives on marital stability. We now turn to consider the implications of these findings for policy.

POLICY IMPLICATIONS

Our model of the income and independence effects implies that projecting the impact of an NIT program for some populations is even more complex than our earlier discussion indicates. Because income and independence affects are nonlinear, a family's response depends on its income and the wife's independence income when the NIT program starts, as well as on the generosity of the program. Our estimates show that NIT plans such as those used in SIME/DIME increase the dissolution rate for some families, and reduce it for others.

We addressed this problem by using our model for the income and independence effects of NIT payments, and found that the impact of an NIT differs according to the race and ethnicity of the family, the number of children, and a variety of other demographic and background characteristics. We must, therefore, calculate impacts separately for each combination of characteristics. We cannot be exhaustive here, but will illustrate the impacts of various NIT programs on rates of marital dissolution for white couples who are 25 years old, have been married for 5 years, have 11 years of education, and have two children. We vary both family income prior to the NIT program, and the wife's pre-NIT independence income (i.e., her expected income from earnings and welfare if her marriage is dissolved). As will become clear, the latter plays a crucial role in determining the NIT impact on dissolution rates. We consider two cases typical of those we studied: (a) wives who would not be employed upon becoming single and (b) wives who would earn $3000 per year as single women. In each case we assume, in line with both the discussion earlier and our empirical findings, that welfare is discounted. In particular, we assume that the independence effect of each dollar of welfare payments is half that of a dollar of earnings or a dollar from the experiments.

We consider plots of the dissolution rate for white families with two children under various programs by levels of pre-NIT family disposable income. In Figures 9.4 and 9.5, the curve for controls shows how the dissolution rate declines with family income. To the extent that an NIT plan increases family income, it shifts families to the right on such curves and thereby tends to lower the dissolution rate. The income effect of any given program depends on family income in two ways. First, the payment a family receives depends on the level of their income. The lower their family income, the larger the change in their income due to an NIT. Second, magnitude of the effect of a unit change in income effect is strongest for families with moderate incomes and weaker for families with either very low or high incomes. The independence effect of any particular NIT program is constant across levels of pre-NIT independence. If there were no income effects, the NIT plans would simply shift the control curve upwards. Because the NIT plans have both income and independence effects, their curves are generally shaped differently from the control curve. Only at family income levels above the breakeven level (the region in which families receive no NIT payments or tax reimbursements) do the NIT curves parallel the control curve.

Figure 9.4 contains the predicted curves for white families with two children in which the wives would have no earnings after leaving the marriage. All NIT plans depicted in Figure 9.4 increase the rate of dissolution. For most levels of family income, the guarantee of 90% of poverty level increases the rate more

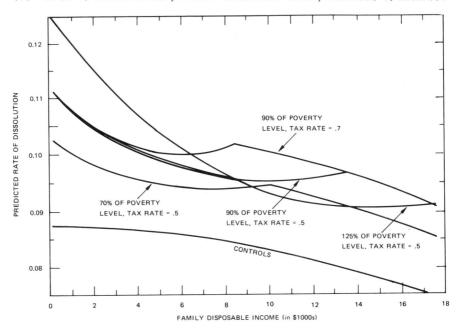

Figure 9.4   Predicted marital dissolution rate for white couples with two children, wife's gross earnings = $0.

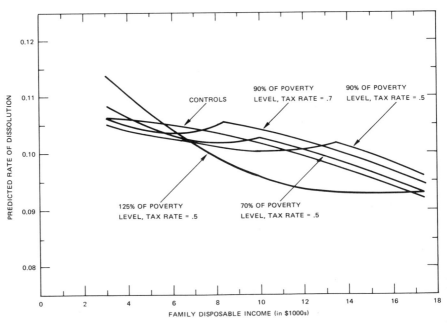

Figure 9.5   Predicted marital dissolution rate for white couples with two children, wife's gross earnings = $3000.

than either the 70% of poverty level or the 125% of poverty level guarantee. For the 90% of poverty level guarantee, increasing the tax rate from .5 to .7 increases the dissolution rate.

It is easiest to understand the shape of the curves in Figures 9.4 and 9.5 by working from right to left. Consider the curve for a guarantee of 90% of poverty level and a tax rate of .5 in Figure 9.4. Above $13,000 of disposable family income, this curve coincides with the curve for the 90% of poverty level and .7 tax rate plan, and parallels the control curve. The distance between the NIT curve and the control curve is due to the independence effect. Because the family is above the breakeven level in this region and receives no NIT payments, there is no income effect. The breakeven level for the guarantee of 90% of poverty level and .5 tax rate plan is represented by the cusp at approximately $13,000. To the left of the cusp there is an income effect offsetting the independence effect. Still proceeding right to left we observe that the dissolution rate declines as family income declines, reaching a minimum at approximately $9500. Between $9500 and $13,000 we observe that, as payments decrease with increasing income, the income effect decreases and is dominated by the independence effect. To the left of $9500 the dissolution rate increases monotonically as family income decreases. The shape of the curve in this region reflects the nonlinearity of the income and independence effects and the dependence of the income effect on the level of family income as well as on the NIT-induced change in family income. The other NIT plan curves in Figures 9.4 and 9.5 may be interpreted in the same way. The 125% of poverty level plans have a breakeven level that is greater than $15,000 and the cusp, therefore, does not appear on the graphs.

Notice that in Figure 9.5 the control rate is higher than in Figure 9.4. This reflects the higher pre-NIT independence effect for women who would earn $3000 if single compared with women who have no single earnings. In Figure 9.5 all four of the NIT plans shown are below the control curve when family income is below $7000. Each NIT curve crosses the control curve before the breakeven cusp (this is also true of the 125% of poverty level plan, although it is not shown in Figure 9.5). For lower income families, all four NIT plans decrease the marital dissolution rate for families where the wife would earn $3000 if single and raise the marital dissolution rate for higher income families. The more generous plans lower the rate for a broader range of family incomes than the less generous plan.

Several generalizations can be drawn from these figures (and others not shown here). First, the NIT impact on marital dissolution is mainly concentrated in those families with the most dependent wives. For working wives (who, we assume, would remain working upon becoming single), the introduction of an NIT changes the financial alternatives to an existing marriage only slightly and thereby has less impact on decisions to end a marriage. Second, the high guarantee and low tax programs yield the lowest dissolution rates, due to the offsetting income and independence effects.

The role of the welfare discount is important in the discussion of these figures.

As we mentioned earlier, the exact discount used makes comparatively little difference when we are estimating the income and independence effects. As long as some discount is used our results account for the pattern of support level effects. However, the size of the discount plays an important role in generating the curves in Figures 9.4 and 9.5, because it affects the vertical distance between the control curves and the NIT curves. (It also affects the shape of the control curve and the NIT curves above the tax breakeven, but this is of less importance.) A larger discount implies that an NIT scheme has a larger independence effect, and consequently a greater distance between the control and the NIT curves. Had we used a 25% discount in Figures 9.4 and 9.5 rather than 50%, the control curve and the NIT curves would be closer together. Because the independence effect is nonlinear there is no easy was to project the results from one discount rate to another, but the general implications remain the same.

The welfare discount has important policy implications. We have seen that the effect of an NIT program on marital stability depends on the generosity of the program, and on the characteristics of the families affected. The change also depends on the size of the welfare discount. We include the welfare discount in our analysis to capture the effects of stigma, lack of information, and transaction costs that are part of the present welfare system. The necessity of the welfare discount in our analysis suggests that efforts to improve the current welfare system by reducing the stigma or transaction costs of receiving aid will affect marital stability even if benefit levels are not changed. For example, our analysis indicates that a change in AFDC administration that reduced the stigma (such as operating the program through the IRS or the Social Security administration) would increase the rate of marital dissolution.

CONCLUSION

We conclude with a brief summary of what we have learned from SIME/DIME about the effects of an NIT program on marital stability. First, we have learned that the experimental implementation of a set of NIT plans increased the rate of marital dissolution. Further, we know that the size of the increase depends on the generosity of the plans and the characteristics of families. The hypothesized income and independence effects appear to be operating in the experiments. These effects are nonlinear and depend on the level of incomes, as well as on the NIT-induced changes in incomes.

Second, we are aware that projecting the SIME/DIME results to a national NIT program is complicated. The complications arise not only in the complexity of our findings but also from the problems inherent in projecting a short-term experiment in two cities to a permanent national program.

We are presently working on a methodology to make such projections. Even without such a methodology the findings from SIME/DIME can be of use to policymakers. It appears unlikely that a national NIT program would be neutral with respect to marital stability; thus, the financial and social costs of changes in marital dissolution rates must be considered in evaluating any proposed welfare reform. In addition, our analysis has shown that the nonpecuniary aspect of welfare reform may have important effects on marital stability that also need to be considered.

REFERENCES

Hannan, M. T.; Beaver, S. E.; and Tuma, N. B. "Income Maintenance Effects on the Making and Breaking of Marriages: Preliminary Analysis of the First Eighteen Months of the Denver Income Maintenance Experiment." Unpublished manuscript, SRI International, Menlo Park, California, 1974.

Hannan, M. T.; Tuma, N. B.; and Groeneveld, L. P. "The Impact of Income Maintenance on the Making and Breaking of Marital Unions: Interim Report." Research Memorandum No. 28, Center for the Study of Welfare Policy, SRI International, June 1976a.

Hannan, M. T.; Tuma, N. B.; and Groeneveld, L. P. "Income and Marital Events: Evidence from an Income-Maintenance Experiment." *The American Journal of Sociology*, May 1976b, pp. 1186-1211.

Hannan, M. T.; Tuma, N. B.; and Groeneveld, L. P. "A Model of the Effect of Income Maintenance on Rates of Marital Dissolution: Evidence from the Seattle and Denver Income Maintenance Experiments." Research Memorandum No. 44, Center for the Study of Welfare Policy, SRI International, February 1977.

Hannan, M. T.; Tuma, N. B.; and Groeneveld, L. P. "Income and Independence Effects on Marital Dissolution: Results from the Seattle-Denver Income Maintenance Experiments." *The American Journal of Sociology* (November 1978):611-633.

Honig, Marjorie. "AFDC Income, Recipient Rates, and Family Dissolution." *Journal of Human Resources* 9 (Summer 1974):303-322.

Honig, Marjorie. "A Reply." *Journal of Human Resources* 11, no. 2 (Spring 1976):250-260.

Minarik, Joseph J., and Goldfarb, Robert S. "AFDC Income, Recipient Rates, and Family Dissolution: A Comment." *Journal of Human Resources* 11, no. 2 (Spring 1976): 243 250.

Ross, H. L., and Sawhill, I. V. *Time of Transition: The Growth of Families Headed by Women*. Washington, D. C.: The Urban Institute, 1975.

Sawhill, I. V.; Peabody, G. E.; Jones, C. A.; and Caldwell, S. B. *Income Transfers and Family Structure*. Washington, D. C.: The Urban Institute, 1975.

Tuma, N. B.; Groeneveld, L. P.; and Hannan, M. T. "First Dissolutions and Marriages: Impacts in 24 Months of the Seattle and Denver Income Maintenance Experiments." Research Memorandum No. 35, Center for the Study of Welfare Policy, SRI International, August 1976.

Tuma, N. B.; Hannan, M. T.; and Groeneveld, L. P. "Variation Over Time in the Impact of the Seattle and Denver Income Maintenance Experiments on the Making and Breaking of Marriages." Research Memorandum No. 43, Center for the Study of Welfare Policy, SRI International, February 1977.

Tuma, N. B., Hannan, M. T.; and Groeneveld, L. P. "Dynamic Analysis of Event Histories." *The American Journal of Sociology*, January 1979, pp. 820-854.

CHAPTER 10

Income and Psychological Distress

PEGGY THOITS
MICHAEL T. HANNAN

For social policy reasons, the experiments undertaken to assess the effects of an NIT have focused on the labor supply responses and the marital stability of experimental subjects. However, program effects upon recipients' overall quality of life are also of policy interest. This chapter examines the impact of SIME/DIME upon one indicator of life quality—psychological distress.

Past studies of the relationship between income and psychological disorder have typically been static, or cross-sectional, in nature. Little is known about the effect of changes in income upon psychological state. An experimental environment offers a valuable opportunity to examine the effect of a positive change in financial circumstances upon psychological well-being. In this chapter we review briefly several competing explanations of the relationship between income and psychological distress. From two theories that can be applied to the experimental situation we then derive competing hypotheses regarding the effect of an NIT upon psychological distress. Finally, we estimate the effects of SIME/DIME upon distress and discuss the theoretical and policy implications of the results.

THEORETICAL BACKGROUND

A good deal of literature over the past 50 years has demonstrated that psychological distress varies inversely with level of income: the greater the individual's income, the less will be his or her reported psychological distress[1] (Brad-

---

[1] We restrict our attention to prevalence studies in this review, as this chapter is also a prevalence study. Prevalence refers to all active cases during a specified time period or in a particular population, regardless of the actual time of illness onset. Thus, prevalence rates include continuing and recurring as well as new cases of disorder. The prevalence studies cited

183

burn, 1969; Bradburn and Caplovitz, 1965; Dohrenwend and Dohrenwend, 1969; Gurin *et al.*, 1960; Lemkau *et al.*, 1942; Parker and Kleiner, 1966; Phillips, 1966; Srole *et al.*, 1962; U.S. Department of Health, Education and Welfare, 1970). This inverse relationship between distress and income is but one instance of the general finding that psychological distress varies inversely with social class (see Dohrenwend and Dohrenwend, 1969, and Kleiner and Parker, 1970, for reviews of this literature).

Several explanations of this relationship have been advanced. Two explanations that have received the most attention are the social selection and the social causation hypotheses. The social selection hypothesis (Dunham, 1965) suggests that individuals have drifted down into a low-income position because their mental illness has impeded social interaction or effective functioning at a job. According to this hypothesis, psychological disorder is causally prior to and predictive of a low-status position in society. Because the social selection hypothesis treats psychological distress as a dependent variable, further consideration of the selection hypothesis is not appropriate for this paper. However, the social causation hypothesis is suggestive for our purposes. Social causation theorists (Dohrenwend and Dohrenwend, 1969; Kohn, 1968) reverse the selection explanation. They argue that psychological disturbance is not a cause but a result of social status. They reason that the lower income individual has fewer resources with which to resolve the ordinary crises that seem particularly common in the lower class (accidents, job lay-offs, unexpected car repairs, etc.). These unresolved problems may overtax the individual's capacity to cope and thus produce symptoms of psychological distress. According to this hypothesis, then, the inverse relationship between income and psychological distress is situational—due to a lack of material, social, and psychological resources.

The social causation, or resource, hypothesis attempts to account for the observed inverse relationship between level of income and psychological distress. It does not address the question of how a change in income affects distress. However, we can follow the implications of the hypothesis and make a prediction regarding the possible impact of an NIT. The resource hypothesis suggests that an increase in or stabilization of income will facilitate coping with the exigencies of living. An increase in the ability to cope should decrease levels of psychological distress. Thus, an implication of the resource hypothesis is that receipt of NIT payments should decrease the psychological distress of experimental subjects relative to controls.

An alternative hypothesis is suggested by recent literature on life events of life crises. This literature addresses directly the question of the effects of change.

in the text employ a variety of definitions of distress, or mental illness, many of which are compatible with our own. By psychological distress, we mean here a general state of unpleasant arousal which is accompanied by physiological symptoms such as nervousness, upset stomach, and dizziness. Such arousal, if intense, is assumed to impair the daily functioning of the individual.

Life events are defined as "objective events that disrupt or threaten to disrupt the individual's usual activities" (Dohrenwend and Dohrenwend, 1969, p. 133). These events require the individual to readjust his or her behavior substantially. Readjustments are assumed to cause stress in the individual, regardless of the desirability of the event. Intense or prolonged stress in turn may eventuate in physical or psychological disorder. Several studies demonstrate a positive relationship between life events and distress: The more life events a person experiences, the more psychological distress he or she exhibits or reports (Brown and Birley, 1968; Myers et al., 1971, 1972, 1974; Paykel, 1974).

The change in financial circumstances due to SIME/DIME may be a life event in itself. Furthermore, it has been shown that the experiments significantly increase the divorce rate of NIT subjects (Hannan et al., 1977; Tuma et al., 1976), their rate of unemployment (Robins and Tuma, 1977), and their rate of geographic mobility (Keeley, 1976). Divorce, unemployment, and migration are additional examples of disruptive life events. Thus, one could hypothesize that the NIT treatments would, at least initially, increase the psychological distress of financial subjects relative to the controls. Note that a counterintuitive implication of the life events hypothesis is that people may rationally make choices that are distress producing. One consequence of a major change toward a life-style that is more satisfying is a short-run increase in distress.[2]

To summarize, two explanations of the relationship between income and distress have clear implications for the impact of an income-maintenance program upon psychological distress. The resource hypothesis implies that the experiment will facilitate coping and thus decrease the distress of experimental subjects relative to controls. The life events hypothesis suggests that participation in SIME/DIME is a life event and causes other life changes and may increase the distress of experimentals relative to controls.

---

[2] We have excluded consideration of a fourth hypothesis, the societal reaction hypothesis, the societal reaction hypothesis, for the following reasons. The societal reaction, or labeling, hypothesis (Scheff, 1966) argues that the low-income individual is more often classified mentally ill because he or she lacks the social and financial resources to resist labeling by agents of social control (e.g., the courts, social workers, psychiatrists). This hypothesis cannot be tested in the present study because we measure psychological state only with self-reports of distress symptoms; we have no records of court, hospital, or mental health clinic dispositions. However, following the labeling approach, one could make an alternative argument—that receiving income maintenance stigmatizes the individual. In society's eyes, the person joins the ranks of the "disreputable poor" (Matza, 1971). Stigmatization in turn may produce symptoms of psychological distress. We believe that SIME/DIME protect experimental subjects from such labeling by others. In contrast to control subjects who may receive AFDC, welfare, or food stamps, experimental subjects are not required to report to a welfare office in order to qualify for payments. All income reporting and payment transactions are handled by mail. Thus, program participation is much less visible to others than participation in other welfare programs. In our judgment, the societal reaction or labeling explanation is thus not applicable to the income-maintenance situation.

Two previous NIT experiments have reported social psychological outcomes. In New Jersey (Middleton and Allen, 1977), experimentals reported somewhat higher rates of psychsomatic symptoms overall than did controls. Furthermore distress was weakly but positively related to the levels of actual payments received by the experimentals. However, none of these experimental effects was significant. In the Rural Experiment (Middleton, 1976), a similar pattern emerged. This time the effects were statistically significant. Overall, experimentals had significantly higher distress scores than the controls. The amount of payment received also had a significant direct effect upon distress. The results of these two experiments, though not conclusive, are consistent with the life events hypothesis that an increase in income will cause an increase in the level of distress. The SIME/DIME sample was larger and more ethnically diverse than these previous experiments and thus presents a good opportunity to test these hypotheses further.[3] We turn now to a description of the experimental design, the methods employed, and the results.[4]

METHODOLOGY

Sample and Data

A sample of approximately 7500 adult heads of household participating in SIME/DIME provides the basis for the analysis reported here. The design requirements produced a sample consisting of three marital types: married men, married women, and divorced or separated women (hereafter termed "singles"). Divorced and separated men are not analyzed in this study as there are too few of them ($N = 63$) for meaningful statistical comparison.

Sample families were followed wherever they moved within the continental United States and families were interviewed every 4 months during the duration of the treatments and for a 2-year period thereafter. The interviews provided a continuous record (with dated changes) of family composition, marital status, and labor supply. They also provided attitudinal data and information regarding health status and psychological distress. Data collection procedures were identical for experimentals and controls; however, as in all panel studies, sample attrition was a problem. This chapter analyzes only those individuals present when each psychological distress measurement was taken. The effect of attrition upon our experimental results is discussed at a later point in the chapter.

---

[3] The measure of psychological distress and the methodology used here differ in minor ways from the Rural and New Jersey studies of psychological effects.

[4] Since the general design elements can be found in Chapter 1, we will only add those design issues relevant to psychological distress.

Measurement of Psychological Distress

The psychological distress index used in SIME/DIME is a close variant of the MacMillan Health Opinion Survey index (MacMillan, 1957). The instrument consists of a series of psychophysiological symptom items. The MacMillan index has been employed in several prevalence studies (Gurin et al., 1960; Jackson, 1962; Leighton et al., 1963; Myers et al., 1971; Srole et al., 1962; U.S. Department of Health, Education and Welfare, 1970). Validity studies have shown that this instrument, and variants of it developed by Gurin et al. (1960) and Langner (1962), significantly discriminate psychiatric patients and nonpatient community residents (Leighton et al., 1963; MacMillan, 1957; Manis et al., 1963; Spiro et al., 1972; Tousignant et al., 1974). However, the instrument primarily taps neurotic symptomatology; it is less sensitive to psychotic symptoms (Leighton et al., 1963; Schwartz et al., 1973). The cases identified by the index are likely to be individuals whose psychological state impairs their everyday functioning to some degree and not individuals who are actively psychotic.

The MacMillan index and its variants have been severely criticized in recent reviews (Seiler, 1973; Spiro et al., 1972; Tousignant et al., 1974). The three most serious difficulties are (a) the scale lacks diagnostic specificity, (b) a physical health bias may be present, and (c) social desirability may also bias responses. However, none of these problems mitigates against the use of the index here. First, since our purpose is to assess levels of distress in our sample and not the prevalence of particular psychiatric disorders, lack of diagnostic specificity is not a handicap. Second, although differences in the scores may reflect variations in the state of physical health, it is nevertheless true (and most commentators overlook this) that physical and psychological health are strongly correlated (Eastwood and Trevelyan, 1972; Hinkle and Wolff, 1957; Shepherd et al., 1966.)[5] Thus, physical symptoms on the scale are probably useful indicators of psychological distress rather than items which bias scores. It is important to remember that this index, containing both physical and more psychological symptoms, has been repeatedly shown to discriminate successfully between psychiatric patients and nonpatients. Thus, the index has strong criterion validity. Furthermore, the items appear to have the face validity as indicators of preceived distress. For these reasons, the index seems appropriate to employ in assessing the prevalence of psychological distress in our sample. Finally, although it is possible that subjects may respond with socially desirable answers to the symptom items, this bias simply lessens variance in the scores and forces us to draw more conservative conclusions. Desirable answers may vary by sex, socioeconomic status, or race-

---

[5] In this sample, number of reported physical health problems and distress are correlated .30 for married men, .32 for married women, and .37 for single women. All correlations are significant at the .01 probability level or better.

ethnicity, but these variables are controlled in the analysis. In summary, none of the problems with the MacMillan index seem to be serious. The index has been shown to be positively and significantly associated with stressful conditions (Seiler, 1973). We concur with several authors (Myers *et al.*, 1971; Seiler, 1973; Spiro *et al.*, 1972; Tousignant *et al.*, 1974) who conclude that the instrument is indeed interpretable as a measure of mild psychological impairment, or psychological distress.

The items on the distress index are shown in Table 10.1. Symptomatic responses are given values of 3 or 4; symptom-free responses have values of 1. The items are summed and the total score ranges from a low of 18 (little or no distress) to 71 (high distress). Cronbach's (1951) Alpha, a measure of internal consistency for the scale, is satisfactorily high, ranging from .80 to .85 for all groups analyzed.

The psychological distress index was administered four times. The administrations of the index were staggered by sex to preclude contamination from spouse's responses. For both sexes an interval of about 16 months separates the first administration from the second. Data from the first two administrations only are available to us now. For male heads, the first measure (Time 1) was taken approximately 4 months after enrollment in the experiment and the second (Time 2) was taken approximately 20 months into the experiment. For female heads, the Time 1 measure was generally taken 8 months after enrollment except for single females in Seattle, who answered the distress questions at the same Time 1 as the males. The Time 2 measure for them occurred 24 months after enrollment.

Analysis Strategy

Impact Analysis

In this chapter we seek to answer the following question: What total effect do experimental NIT treatments have on levels of psychological distress? Our concern is with the existence and direction of effects rather than with modeling the processes that produce them. Our intent is to produce some basic findings that will become the object of further theoretical and empirical work. Thus, we adopt a very simple analysis strategy. We relate measured distress during the experiment only to variables that are exogenous to the experiment. More concretely, we regress levels of distress at Time 1 and Time 2 on experimental treatment variables, on variables that determine assignment to experimental treatments, and on other variables measured at enrollment that are known to affect distress (age, education, occupation, etc.). This strategy relies heavily on the experimental nature of the study. When the assignment variables are held constant, the control group and the experimental groups should not differ systematically on

Table 10.1
Psychological Distress Index

	Never	Seldom	Sometimes	Often
1. How often do your hands tremble enough to bother you?	1	2	3	4
2. How often do you smoke?	1	2	3	4
3. How often do your hands or feet sweat so that they feel damp and clammy?	1	2	3	4
4. How often are you bothered by your heart beating hard?	1	2	3	4
5. How often do you have cold sweats?	1	2	3	4
6. How often do you feel that you have several different ailments in different parts of your body?	1	2	3	4
7. How often do you lose your appetite?	1	2	3	4
8. How often has ill health affected the amount of work you do?	1	2	3	4
9. How often do you have weak spells?	1	2	3	4
10. How often do you have spells of dizziness?	1	2	3	4
11. How often do you tend to lose weight when important things are bothering you?	1	2	3	4
12. How often are you bothered by nervousness?	1	2	3	4
13. How often have you been bothered by shortness of breath when you were not exercising?	1	2	3	4
14. How often do you tend to feel tired in the mornings?	1	2	3	4
15. How often do you have trouble getting to sleep and staying asleep?	1	2	3	4

	Never	Not very much	Pretty often	Nearly all the time
16. How often are you bothered by having an upset stomach?	1	2	3	4

	Never	A few times	Many times
17. How often have you been bothered by nightmares or dreams which frighten or upset you?	1	2	3

	Very good spirits	Good spirits	Low spirits	Very low spirits
18. In general, would you say that most of the time you are in:	1	2	3	4

Note: All questions are similar to those on the MacMillan Health Opinion Survey (Mac-Millan, 1957) with the exception of number 18.

initial levels of distress. If they differ later in the experiment, we can attribute the difference to the experimental treatment(s).

An alternative strategy might be to perform panel analysis, i.e., to regress distress at Time 2 on treatment variables, assignment variables, background variables, and distress at Time 1. This strategy would yield estimates of change in psychological distress, rather than simple experimental-control group differences. We have not adopted this strategy for several reasons. First, we have no a priori expectations regarding the timing or nature of the experimental effects. Neither the resource hypothesis nor the life events hypothesis specifies the lag between a change in financial circumstances and its initial effect upon distress. Nor does either theory indicate whether we can expect a one-time impact or cumulative effects over time. To determine the adjustment period and the nature of the impacts, then, it is in our interest to examine the total impacts of the experiment upon distress at Time 1 and Time 2. Panel analysis would partial out any treatment effects upon distress at Time 1, thus underestimating the total impact of the experiment upon distress at a later time point. Given our interest in the nature of treatment effects, this result is clearly undesirable. Furthermore, panel analysis produces other statistical problems. Of particular concern are biased estimates of experimental effects due to (*a*) the autocorrelation of the two distress measures and (*b*) attrition from the experiment. Following the first strategy outlined in the preceding (essentially an analysis of variance strategy) allows us to infer that experimental treatments cause a change in psychological state wherever we find significant differences between control and experimental subjects at each time period.

Independent Variables

Each regression contains the same set of nonexperimental variables, which we refer to as the "background function." As mentioned in the preceding, the background function contains all variables used in assignment to experimental treatments as well as several other variables that the literature shows to be related to distress. The latter are included to reduce the sampling variability of estimated experimental impacts. The background function includes:

Assignment variables
Denver   (0,1)
Black   (0,1)
Chicano   (0,1)
Marital status of head (0 = single, 1 = married)
Normal preexperimental family income: Expected income of the family in the year prior to the experiment, assuming normal family circumstances and adjusted for family size. It includes all money and in-kind earnings from paid work and family business, but omits all transfer payments. There

are seven categories and a residual category for families not assigned to an income level. This set of categorical variables is used in our analysis instead of actual earnings because it was used in the assignment of families to experimental treatments. Each income category appears as a dummy variable (0,1) except the last two categories ($9000+) which serve as the omitted comparison group. (For single women, the last three categories serve as the comparison group [$7000+].)

Other variables

Age at enrollment

Education at enrollment (years of formal schooling)

Parent: family has one or more children (0,1)

Occupational status at enrollment:

　　0 = not employed

　　1 = service and private household worker

　　2 = laborer, farm laborer, farm owner and manager

　　3 = operative

　　4 = craftsperson

　　5 = sales and clerical worker

　　6 = manager

　　7 = professional and technical worker

Spouse's occupational status at enrollment: as above

　　(for those married at enrollment)

Working at enrollment (0,1)

Spouse working at enrollment (0,1) (for those married at enrollment)

We represent the NIT treatments in two ways. In preliminary analysis (not reported here), we found that length of time in the experiments interacted with the effect of the NIT treatment and with race-ethnicity. Consequently, we present the experimental treatments as follows:

F3xWhite	White 3-year financial subject (0,1)
F5xWhite	White 5-year financial subject (0,1)
F3xBlack	Black 3-year financial subject (0,1)
F5xBlack	Black 5-year financial subject (0,1)
F3xChicano	Chicano 3-year financial subject (0,1)
F5xChicano	Chicano 5-year financial subject (0,1)

With the inclusion of these six interaction terms, differences between the racial-ethnic groups become nonsignificant and the samples can be pooled. Thus, we first report results from a simple model of experimental effects, in which we utilize the six racial-experimental interaction dummies. (Analysis not reported here indicates that replacing these variables with a larger set of support level and tax rate dummies does not improve the fit of the model.)

The more complex model we report is one in which we add a variable that estimates the yearly NIT payment a family would receive if they did not change their preenrollment behavior (including labor supply and family composition). We refer to this variable as "payment." In short, payment measures the magnitude of the change in disposable income a family experiences upon being assigned to an NIT treatment.

The general form of the models we estimate is

$$\text{Distress} = \underline{a}\underline{X} + \beta\underline{F3xRace} + \gamma\underline{F5xRace} + \delta\text{PAY} + \mu, \tag{1}$$

where $\underline{X}$ denotes the set of background variables, $\underline{F3xRace}$ and $\underline{F5xRace}$ are the sets of 3- and 5-year racial-experimental interaction dummies, PAY is the payment variable, and μ is a random disturbance term. In the simple model, δ is constrained to be 0. In this case, the total experimental effect is measured by β and γ. In the more complex model, the total effect is given by β, γ, and δ.

As stated previously, the model in (1) is estimated with ordinary least squares regression. The dependent variable approximates the distribution appropriate for the assumptions underlying the usual regression sampling theory (normal distribution). Moreover, since assignment to experimental treatment is random, conditional on the background variables included in the model, the seven experimental treatment variables should be independent of the disturbance. Under these conditions, ordinary least squares gives best linear unbiased estimates of experimental effects. As already mentioned, analysis is performed on all individuals who answered the distress index at each administration.

RESULTS

For precision in the estimation of experimental effects, it is necessary to control for the influences of background variables that are known to be, or seem likely to be, related to psychological distress. Furthermore, an examination of background effects seems desirable, since little is known about which variables cause psychological distress within the lower class; most studies have utilized cross-class comparisons. In the following section, we briefly discuss the effects of background characteristics upon psychological distress, controlling also for the effect of the experiments. Then we turn to a detailed examination of the experimental effects.

Effects of Background Characteristics

Since preliminary analysis revealed significant site, sex, and marital status interactions, we present our results throughout the paper by site for three subgroups: married men, married women, and single women. Due to this format, the effects of site, sex, and marital status are not readily apparent in most tables. In Table 10.2 our findings with respect to these three background characteristics will be described and then we will turn to an examination of the other background characteristics shown in Table 10.4.

Considering site effects first, we see an odd pattern in Table 10.2. In Denver, for each subgroup, mean scores varied little from Time 1 to Time 2. In Seattle, however, distress scores were quite high at Time 1, then decline at Time 2 to values comparable to those in Denver. Our first interpretation was that this effect was due to an unfortunate variation in the skip logic of the health interview. In all other health interviews, if a respondent reported being permanently and totally disabled, the remaining health and psychological distress questions in the interview were skipped. Thus, a psychological distress score for a disabled respondent received a missing value and the respondent was dropped from statistical analysis. However, in Seattle at Time 1 disabled persons were not identified and the disabled answered the psychological distress items. Thus, the Seattle Time 1 samples include the permanently and totally disabled, while all other samples do not. Since physical and psychological health are strongly correlated (see footnote 5) the physically disabled should have higher distress scores, and these elevated scores should be reflected in the mean scores for Seattle at Time 1. At Time 2, the disabled are not present in the Seattle samples, so the mean scores should be similar to those in Denver at Time 2.

We therefore recomputed the means for Seattle at Time 1 based on the samples present at Time 2 (thereby eliminating all permanently disabled persons as well as those who attrite between Time 1 and Time 2). The resulting mean scores

Table 10.2
Mean Psychological Distress Scores of Control and Experimental Subjects
at Time 1 and Time 2

	Denver		Seattle	
	Controls	Experimentals	Controls	Experimentals
Married men[a]				
Time 1	27.9 (624)	28.4 (840)	34.5 (506)	35.2 (564)
Time 2	28.0 (546)	28.6 (708)	27.5 (374)	28.4 (423)
Married women[a]				
Time 1	29.7 (607)	29.6 (797)	32.0 (484)	32.3 (548)
Time 2	30.0 (547)	30.6 (734)	30.2 (394)	31.2 (443)
Single women[a]				
Time 1	29.9 (380)	31.1 (648)	37.8 (344)	38.8 (468)
Time 2	30.0 (339)	31.2 (589)	30.8 (270)	32.5 (377)

Note: Psychological distress scores range from a low of 18 (little or no distress) to a high of 71 (high distress). Numbers in parentheses refer to total number of respondents.

[a]"Married" refers to married or cohabitating individuals. "Single" referes to divorced, separated, or widowed individuals.

Table 10.3
Percent of Married Men Experiencing One or More
Periods of Involuntary Unemployment

	Denver	Seattle
Preexperimental year 1	23.1%	24.8%
Experimental year 1	32.5	41.8
Experimental year 2	33.7	37.2

Note: These results are based upon a sample of husbands who had not attrited nor experienced a marital dissolution during the 2 years.

were from .2 to .6 points lower than those shown in Table 10.2. They were, however, still considerably higher than those in Denver at Time 1. Extensive inquiries have failed to identify other procedural variations in Seattle and Denver that would explain these site differences.

It is possible that the employment situation in Seattle at Time 1 was responsible for these elevated distress scores. Table 10.3 reports the percentage of husbands involuntarily unemployed in each site by experimental year. (Figures for wives and for single women closely approximate the patterns evident in Table 10.3 for husbands.) In both sites, workers experienced a sharp increase in unemployment during the first experimental year, but for Seattle this increase was nearly two times that in Denver. Moreover, from the first year to the second, the involuntary unemployment rate remained fairly stable in the Denver sample while it declined somewhat in the Seattle sample. (These sample unemployment rates reflect similar changes in the total unemployment rates of the two metropolitan areas at those times.) The distress scores in Table 10.2 appear to covary with these unemployment rates. Mean distress remained fairly constant in Denver from Time 1 to Time 2, while in Seattle mean distress was high at Time 1 and declined at Time 2 to levels comparable to those in Denver. Since previous literature has shown an inverse relationship between indicators of economic change and psychiatric dysfunction (Brenner, 1973; Liem and Liem, 1978), it seems reasonable to assume that the patterns of site differences evident in Table 10.2 were due to the changing unemployment situations in the two cities.

Moving on to examine sex differences, we see in Table 10.2 that within each site, married and single women had somewhat higher mean distress scores than married men at Time 1 and Time 2. (The only exception occurred in Seattle at Time 1: married men had higher distress scores than women.) This finding is consistent with a large literature which indicates that females have significantly higher rates of neurosis and psychophysiological distress than males (see reviews by Dohrenwend and Dohrenwend, 1976, and by Gove and Tudor, 1973).

With respect to marital status, only married and single women can be compared. This is done in Table 10.2, and a pattern emerges: at both time periods, single women had somewhat higher distress scores than married women. This re-

Table 10.4
Effects of Background Variables and Financial Treatment upon
Psychological Distress at Time 1

Variable	Married men		Married women		Single women	
	Denver	Seattle	Denver	Seattle	Denver	Seattle
Age	−.02	.01	−.03	−.07**	−.005	−.02
Black	−2.13***	−2.21***	−1.20	−.94	−1.34	.11
Chicano	−1.70**	−	−.99	−	−2.38*	−
Normal income level						
Unclassified	−1.92	4.08**	−2.63	3.19	2.38	3.83**
$000-999	6.92***	4.81***	2.90	7.17***	.71	2.98**
$1000-2999	1.69*	4.10***	.02	3.69***	.86	1.90
$3000-4999	.11	3.19***	−1.21	1.24	.63	.49
$5000-6999	−1.20**	1.14	−.91	.52	.51	.12
$7000-8999	−.57	.84	−.86	−.20	−	−
Education	−.11	−.55***	−.23**	−.73***	−.41***	.50***
Parent	−1.48*	−1.16	−1.10	−.04	−	−
Occupation	−.18	.37**	−.21	.18	−.10	.02
Spouse's occupation	−.25	−.07	.08	−.07	−	−
Working	−1.14*	−3.02***	.50	−2.43**	−.80	−1.98*
Spouse working	1.10	1.19	−.63	.17	−	−
Financial treatment x race						
F3xWhite	−.57	−.11	−.42	−.16	.32	.97
F5xWhite	2.58***	.64	2.28**	.81	−.73	1.60
F3xBlack	.71	1.71**	−.15	.41	1.73*	.70
F5xBlack	.59	−.98	2.02**	−.19	1.99*	−.003
F3xChicano	.42	−	−.85	−	.97	−
F5xChicano	.05	−	−1.40	−	.60	−
Constant	34.14***	41.79***	35.72***	42.63***	35.87***	43.59***
R^2	.06	.13	.03	.09	.03	.07
Adjusted R^2	.05	.11	.01	.08	.01	.05
F-test for equation	4.54***	8.33***	1.87***	5.67***	1.86**	3.99***
Number of cases	1432	1064	1371	1020	988	790

Note: The following note and probability levels apply to Tables 10.4 and 10.5. All regression coefficients are unstandardized. A positive regression coefficient indicates increased distress; a negative coefficient indicates decreased distress. "Married" refers to married or cohabitating individuals; "single" refers to divorced, separated, or widowed persons.

    *$p < .10$.
    **$p < .05$.
    ***$p < .01$.

sult is consistent with the literature. Most studies report that rates of disorder for the unmarried (i.e., the never married, separated, divorced and widowed) exceed rates for married persons (Gove, 1972; Knupfer et al., 1966; Mechanic and Greenley, 1976; Meile and Haese, 1969; Phillips, 1966; Srole et al., 1962; Zolik and Marches, 1968).

Up to this point we have not mentioned the slight experimental-control dif-

ferences evident in Table 10.2. Experimental subjects' mean scores were generally equal to or somewhat higher than the scores of comparable controls. In no
case was the mean distress score of an experimental group substantially lower
than its comparable control group. These patterns suggest that we may find
some evidence for the life events hypothesis in the regression analyses to follow.

As mentioned previously, sex, site, and marital status were found to have significant effects on psychological distress at one or both time periods in initial regression runs. We then tested for interaction effects. The F-tests for overall
homogeneity of slopes (Johnston, 1972) revealed that the background equations
for each site, sex, and marital status group were significantly different from one
another. Analysis was thereafter performed by subgroup. The background equations for each subgroup are displayed in Table 10.4. The estimates shown were
obtained using the simple form of the model described in equation (1). Because
the effects of background characteristics were found to be generally stable from
Time 1 to Time 2, only results at Time 1 are shown. We turn now to an examination of these background characteristics.

Looking at age first, we see that in most groups distress decreased with age.
This effect is significant only for Seattle wives, however. This pattern of results
runs counter to some of the literature. In general, prevalence studies indicate
that rates of psychological disorder increase with age (Bradburn, 1969; Gurin *et
al.*, 1960; Leighton *et al.*, 1963; Lemkau *et al.*, 1942; Srole *et al.*, 1962). But
there are several exceptions to this finding. Some studies report a curvilinear relationship (Phillips, 1966), some report no relationship (Bradburn and Caplovitz,
1965; Meile and Haese, 1969), and some find relationships between age and disorder that vary depending upon the measure of disorder employed (U.S. Department of Health, Education and Welfare, 1970; Warheit *et al.*, 1975). Our results
throw little light on this confusion of findings. In general, age appeared to have a
a slight negative influence on distress in our sample. The relationship between
age and distress may be somewhat attenuated here because adults over the age of
60 were excluded in the initial screening process.

With respect to race-ethnicity, we have an unexpected finding. In all but one
group (Seattle single women), blacks had lower distress scores than whites (the
omitted comparison category). This effect is large and significant among married
men, reducing their distress scores by roughly two points. Similarly, in Denver,
Chicanos exhibited much lower distress scores than whites. The effect is significant for both married men and single women. Whites, then, reported more psychological distress than blacks or Chicanos. Turning to the sparse literature on
racial-ethnic differences in psychological status, we find inconsistent patterns.
Some studies indicate no differences between whites and blacks (Dohrenwend
and Dohrenwend, 1969, Leighton *et al.*, 1963; U.S. Department of Health, Education and Welfare, 1970). Others report that whites have higher rates of psychological disorder than blacks (Pasamanick *et al.*, 1959; Warheit *et al.*, 1975). Our
results do not resolve these inconsistencies since our white samples were relative-

ly poorer compared to all whites than were our blacks compared to all blacks in the two cities. Thus, our finding of a racial difference may reflect the fact that the SIME/DIME black samples were more representative of blacks in the two cities than were the white samples. With respect to Chicanos, we are not aware of any studies of the prevalence of psychological distress in this group, so a comparison of our results to previous findings is not possible.[6]

As discussed in the introduction, income repeatedly has been found to be inversely related to psychological distress. This relationship is clearly evident in the pattern of income effects for all three Seattle groups. Individuals at low pre-experimental income levels[7] had significantly higher distress scores than individuals in the omitted comparison categories ($9000-$12,999). At successively higher income levels distress scores decreased. This pattern also holds for Denver men and single women, although no coefficient is significant for singles and one coefficient significantly reduces distress rather than increases it for men. The relationship does not hold for Denver married women. However, in general, the higher the income level the lower the distress score of the individual.

The literature indicates that education is also inversely related to psychological impairment: the higher the educational level, the lower the rates of impairment (Bradburn and Caplovitz, 1965; Bradbur, 1969; Dohrenwend and Dohrenwend, 1969; Gurin *et al.*, 1960; Meile and Haese, 1969; Parker and Kleiner, 1966; Phillips, 1966; U.S. Department of Health, Education and Welfare, 1970). Table 10.4 substantiates this relationship. In all groups education is inversely related to distress with coefficients that are significant for all groups except Denver married males.

In preliminary analyses we examined the influence of the number of children on psychological state. No significant effects were found. However, inclusion of a dummy variable for parenthood reveals that, among the SIME/DIME sample, being a parent reduced psychological distress, significantly so for Denver hus-

---

[6] There are a few incidence studies of the rates of psychopathology among Chicanos relative to whites and blacks. Jaco (1960) concluded that Chicanos in Texas had significantly lower rates of hospitalization for psychosis than whites or blacks. Taking issue with Jaco's generalization from these findings, Fabrega *et al.* (1968) present evidence that hospitalized Chicanos exhibit more serious psychopathology than white or black patients, suggesting that Chicano families are more tolerant of deviant behavior and tend to delay hospitalization until absolutely necessary. Lower incidence rates of psychosis in this ethnic group, then, may reflect cultural differences in treatment-seeking behavior rather than real differences in the rates of mental illness. Hospital rates, however tell us nothing about the prevalence of psychiatric disturbance in the general community. Anthropological observations made by Madsen (1969) in a Chicano community in Texas suggest that Chicanos do have lower rates of mental illness than whites, but these observations cannot be taken as anything more than suggestive.

[7] It is important to remember that our variable for this characteristic indicates the individual's state at the beginning of the experiments. Marital status, employment status, occupation, and income level may change during the experimental period, but such changes may be due to the impact of the experiments. Thus, in order to assess total experimental impacts and to avoid simultaneity bias, only states at enrollment are used.

bands. (Because all single women were parents by deliberate experimental design, no coefficient is computed for this variable in the singles' regressions.) Parenthood has generally nonsignificant effects on psychological state. We are not aware of any other work that has examined the effect of children on psychological health.

For occupation, another indicator of social class,[8] we find an unexpectedly mixed pattern of results. The literature leads us to expect an inverse relationship between occupational status and psychological distress. However, this pattern appeared only in Denver; in Seattle, the greater the occupational status, the somewhat greater the distress. Only the coefficient for married men in Seattle is significant. Spouse's occupational status was not significantly related to distress in these samples.

Although occupational status had small and nonsignificant effects, we see that working itself generally decreased psychological distress. The reduction was large and significant for all groups in Seattle and for married men in Denver.[9] This finding is consistent with previous literature which demonstrates an inverse relationship between employment and psychological disturbance (see review by Liem and Liem, 1978). There is some suggestion here that the wife's employment increases the distress level of married men, but, in general, the spouse working has no significant effects on psychological state.

In summary, in these low-income groups we find that being female, separated or divorced, white, low income, of low educational status, and unemployed all significantly raised psychological distress. Other variables (age, parenthood, occupation, spouse's occupation) had no important relationships with psychological distress. It is possible that these latter variables showed no relationship to distress due to sample selection by socioeconomic status and family structure.

Although most variables in the background function affect psychological well-being in the directions expected from previous literature, it is important to note that all adjusted R^2's in Table 10.4 are quite small. Very little variance in distress is explained by the background and treatment variables in the regressions. Thus, we must refrain from overstating the importance of any of these variables as causes of psychological distress.

Experimental Effects

We turn now to a more detailed examination of experimental treatment effects on distress at Time 1 and Time 2. Using the simple form of the model de-

---

[8] The reader might wonder if education, income, and occupation are highly correlated. In these lower class samples they are not. Correlations between variables range from .01 to .20 in value. Thus, multicollinearity is not a problem with the results of income, education, and occupation.

[9] Occupational status and working are highly correlated (r = .75-.85). Multicollinearity affects efficiency and thus makes significant results more difficult to obtain. However, extreme correlation between two variables does not produce biased regression coefficients.

scribed in equation (1) we estimated the effects of the 3- and 5-year financial treatments (F3 and F5) interacted with race-ethnicity. Table 10.5 reports these results for Time 1 and Time 2. We also estimated the more complex model, which adds payment to each regression equation, and found results that were very similar to those in Table 10.5. We summarize the findings of the more complex model in the discussion that follows.

Table 10.5
Effects of the 3- and 5-Year Financial Treatments upon Psychological Distress, Controlling for the Effects of Background Variables

	Denver		Seattle	
	Time 1	Time 2	Time 1	Time 2
Married men				
F3xWhite	−.57	−.004	−.11	−.07
F5xWhite	2.58***	3.14***	.64	−.53
F3xBlack	.71	−.12	1.71**	2.58***
F5xBlack	.59	.07	−.98	−.74
F3xChicano	.42	.94	−	−
F5xChicano	.05	.39	−	−
F-test for set of experimental treatments	2.36**	2.25**	1.82	2.72**
Increase in R^2 due to set of treatments	.01	.01	.01	.01
Number of cases	1432	1228	1064	793
Married women				
F3xWhite	−.42	.15	−.16	1.38*
F5xWhite	2.28**	1.97*	.81	1.67
F3xBlack	−.15	−.82	.41	.42
F5xBlack	2.02*	2.47**	−.19	−.90
F3xChicano	−.85	.40	−	−
F5xChicano	−1.40	1.54	−	−
F-test for set of experimental treatments	2.21**	2.11**	.23	1.77
Increase in R^2 due to set of treatments	.01	.01	.002	.01
Number of cases	1371	1251	1020	820
Single women				
F3xWhite	.32	.29	.89	−.08
F5xWhite	−.73	−.43	1.40	2.12
F3xBlack	1.73*	2.36**	.58	3.09***
F5xBlack	1.99*	2.79**	−.03	−.15
F3xChicano	.97	−1.02	−	−
F5xChicano	.60	.41	−	−
F-test for set of experimental treatments	.89	1.37	.41	3.22**
Increase in R^2 due to set of treatments	.004	.01	.002	.02
Number of cases	988	889	777	615

We examine the results for married men in Table 10.5 first. White husbands on the 5-year treatment in Denver and black husbands on the 3-year treatment in Seattle responded with significantly increased distress (compared to controls, the omitted comparison group). Their responses were evident at both Time 1 and Time 2 and appeared to become larger over time. All other racial-treatment groups showed inconsistent and nonsignificant effects.

In general, among married women in Table 10.5 distress appeared to increase from Time 1 to Time 2 for these groups. White and black wives on the 5-year treatment in Denver exhibited significantly increased distress at both time points. White wives on the 3-year treatment in Seattle showed a significant response at Time 2 in the same direction. (Denver white wives on the 5-year treatment are the exception. Their distress coefficient remains fairly constant.) No other pattern of effects can be identified among the remaining groups of wives.

Among single women in Table 10.5 we see that significant experimental impacts were concentrated in black groups. Black singles on the 3- and 5-year treatments in Denver responded with significantly increased distress at both time points. Black singles on the 3-year program in Seattle exhibited significantly increased distress at Time 2. Again, impacts appeared to have increased over time in these groups. There is no apparent pattern of effects among the other subgroups of singles.

In general, there were scattered significant effects by site, duration of treatment, and race-ethnicity. All significant coefficients are positive, indicating that when the NIT treatments had an impact, they increased the psychological distress of experimentals relative to controls. (These results are similar to those in the New Jersey and Rural Experiments.) Significant responses occurred early in the experiments (Time 1 measures were taken 4 to 8 months after enrollment) and appeared to increase over time. In Denver, significant impacts appared primarily among subjects on the 5-year treatment. In Seattle, significant effects appeared only among 3-year experimental subjects. These significant effects appeared only for blacks and whites; Chicanos show no significant responses.

As mentioned in the preceding, we estimated the more complex model described by equation (1) by adding the payment variable to each regression. Recall that controlling for payment essentially controls for the magnitude of the financial change experienced by a family upon assignment to an experimental treatment. The payment coefficient was nonsignificant in all groups and showed no consistent direction of effect. (This finding differs from the significant positive effect found in the Rural Experiment.) Control for the magnitude of the change in disposable income did not alter the pattern reported in Table 10.5 of treatment effects for married men or for single women. Among married women, however, two changes occurred. Along with white and black wives, Chicana wives on the 5-year treatment exhibited a significant increase in distress at Time 2. But the positive response of black wives on the 3-year treatment in Seattle at Time 2 ceased to be significant, although the coefficient remained large and positive

(1.19). In summary, the magnitude of a financial change appears to be less important than the change itself. Most significant positive treatment effects remain when the magnitude of the financial change is controlled. These findings and those reported in Table 10.5 thus, are consistent with the life events hypothesis. However, we must be cautious in interpreting the importance of these results, as in no regression did the set of experimental treatments add more than 2% to the amount of explained variance in psychological distress.

A Note on Attrition[10]

Most panel studies face the problem of sample attrition and the SIME/DIME experiments were no exception. By Time 2 (approximately 2 years into the experiments), roughly 24% of each sample group had missing observations on psychological distress. This rate is fairly high, so there is a possibility that attrition biases our estimates of experimental impact. This problem is especially serious if the probability of attrition depends on experimental treatment or level of psychological distress. To determine the extent to which attrition biases our results we approached the problem in two ways.

First, for each subgroup we estimated the impacts of background and treatment variables upon psychological distress at Time 1 using only the sample of individuals who were still present at Time 2 (call these individuals "stayers"). If the characteristics of those who attrite at a later time account for our Time 1 findings, then reestimation excluding those individuals should result in different findings. We found that the results obtained when using the samples of stayers replicated our original Time 1 findings. Where initial treatment coefficients were positive and significant, they remained so, and where nonsignificant, they remained so. These results indicated that our estimates of experimental effects were not seriously biased by attrition.

In our second approach, we estimated a model of attrition for each subgroup. The dependent variable was a dummy indicating attrition between Time 1 and Time 2. Logit analysis was performed to test for the effects of background characteristics, treatment variables, Time 1 distress, and distress-treatment interaction terms upon the probability of attrition. In no case did the results obtained by this analysis cast doubt upon our initial significant experimental impacts. In two cases (white single women in Seattle and black married women in Seattle), in fact, attrition bias may have led us to underestimate any experimental impact upon distress. Highly distressed experimentals tended to attrite more than less

---

[10] See the Appendix of Thoits and Hannan (1977) for a detailed presentation of the attrition problem and analysis results. The background function in the Appendix differs somewhat from the one employed in this paper; however, these differences should not affect the analysis substantially. Attrition analysis was performed only for whites and blacks, since data on Chicanos were not available at that time. We summarize that analysis here.

distressed individuals, thereby making experimental impact in the direction of increased distress very difficult to find.

Taken together our replication of original Time 1 findings using only samples of Time 2 stayers and our examination of attrition patterns using logit analysis lead to the same conclusion for all male and female groups: The attrition results do not invalidate the experimental impacts on psychological distress.

CONCLUSION

The objective of this study was to determine the impact of the SIME/DIME NIT treatments upon the psychological distress of the experimental group. Two alternative hypotheses regarding the posited effect were proposed. The resource hypothesis suggested that the experiment would decrease financial subjects' distress by enabling them to better cope with the exigencies of life. The life events hypothesis implied that the NIT treatment itself and other life events accompanying this financial change (divorce, unemployment, return to school, etc.) would raise the psychological distress levels of financial subjects relative to controls.

In no case did we find the experiments significantly decreasing distress. Thus, there is no support for the resource hypothesis in our results. In the majority of groups examined, the experiments had no significant effects upon distress. But several groups did respond and it was always with significantly increased distress, as predicted by the life events hypothesis. The heightened distress of these experimental subjects is consistent with the results of two previous experiments, the New Jersey and Rural Experiments. We conclude that there is some support for the life events hypothesis in our findings.

How we can account for the fact that the experiment did not affect the distress levels of most groups examined here? Although the guarantee levels in SIME/DIME generally exceeded the aid available from AFDC, food stamps, or other public assistance programs, the payments were not high in absolute terms. The predicted payment to experimental families averaged only $1180 per year, a mean increase in income of about 20%. Thus, the change in the standard of living may not have been large enough to have had a perceptible effect upon distress.

Given the preceding considerations, it is perhaps surprising to find that the experiment did significantly raise the distress levels of some subgroups—an effect that did not appear to be a short-run reaction to a change in financial circumstances. The effect was evident not only within the first year, but 2 years after enrollment as well. And the effect appeared to increase over time. These findings suggest that an increase in or stabilization of income may cause other stressful life changes to occur and distress levels to elevate.

The policy implications of these findings are uncertain at present. Given that distress scores of particular groups of experimental subjects are raised only two to three points on average and that the experimental treatments explain a very small percentage of variation in psychological distress, they can hardly be viewed as alarming. However, it is impossible to estimate the costs to society of the somewhat distressing effects of NIT. We hope in the future to collect hospital and mental health agency records to assess whether experimentally induced stress caused increased utilization of psychiatric facilities.

REFERENCES

Bradburn, Norman. M. *The Structure of Psychological Well-Being.* Chicago: Aldine, 1969.

Bradburn, Norman M., and Caplovitz, David. *Reports on Happiness.* Chicago: Aldine, 1965.

Brenner, M. Harvey. *Mental Illness and the Economy.* Cambridge Mass.: Harvard University Press, 1973.

Brown, G. W., and Birley, J. L. T. Crises and Life Changes and the Onset of Schizophrenia. *Journal of Health and Social Behavior* 9 (1968):203-214.

Cronbach, L. J. "Coefficient Alpha and the Internal Structure of Tests." *Psychometrika* 16 (September 1951):297-334.

Dohrenwend, Bruce P., and Dohrenwend, Barbara S. *Social Status and Psychological Disorder.* New York: John Wiley and Sons, 1969.

Dohrenwend, Bruce P., and Dohrenwend, Barbara S. "Sex Differences and Psychiatric Disorders." *American Journal of Sociology* 81, no. 6 (1976):1447-1454.

Dunham, H. W. *Community and Schizophrenia.* Detroit: Wayne State University Press, 1965.

Eastwood, M. R., and Trevelyan, M. H. "Relationship between physical and psychiatric disorder." *Psychological Medicine* 2 (1972):363-372.

Fabrega, H., Jr.; Swartz, J. D.; and Wallace, C. A. "Ethnic Differences in Psychopathology. II. Specific Differences with Emphasis on a Mexican-American Group." *Journal of Psychiatric Research* 6 (1968):221-235.

Gove, Walter. "The Relationship between Sex Roles, Mental Illness, and Marital Status." *Social Forces* 51 (1972):34-44.

Gove, Walter, and Tudor, Jeannette F. "Adult sex roles and mental illness." *American Journal of Sociology* 78 (1973):50-73.

Gurin, G.; Veroff, J.; and Feld, S. *Americans View Their Mental Health.* New York: Basic Books, 1960.

Hannan, Michael; Tuma, Nancy B.; and Groeneveld, Lyle P. "Income and Marital Events: Evidence from an Income Maintenance Experiment." *American Journal of Sociology* 82 (May 1977):1186-1211.

Hinkle, L. E., and Wolff, H. G. "Health and the Social Environment." In *Explorations in Social Psychiatry*, edited by A. M. Leighton, J. A. Clausen, and R. N. Wilson, pp. 105-137. New York: Basic Books, 1957.

Jackson, Elton F. "Status Consistency and Symptoms of Stress." *American Sociological Review* 27, no. 4 (1962):469-480.

Jaco, E. Gartley. *The Social Epidemiology of Mental Disorders.* New York: Russell Sage Foundation, 1960.

Johnston, J. *Econometric Methods.* 2d ed. New York: McGraw-Hill, 1972.

Keeley, Michael C. "The Impact of Income Maintenance on Geographical Mobility: Preliminary Analysis and Empirical Results from the Seattle and Denver Income Maintenance Experiments." Stanford Research Institute, Center for the Study of Welfare Policy, 1976.

Kleiner, Robert J., and Parker, Seymour. "Social Structure and Psychological Factors in

Mental Disorder: A Research Review." In *Social Psychology and Mental Health*, edited by H. Wechsler, L. Solomon, and B. M. Kramer, pp. 203-218. New York: Holt, Rinehart and Winston, 1970.

Knupfer, G.; Clark, W.; and Room, R. "The Mental Health of the Unmarried." *American Journal of Psychiatry* 122 (February 1966):841-851.

Kohn, Melvin. "Social Class and Schizophrenia: A Critical Review." In *The Transmission of Schizophrenia*, edited by D. Rosenthal and S. Kety, pp. 155-187. Oxford: Pergamon Press, 1968.

Langner, T. S. "A Twenty-Two Item Screening Score of Psychiatric Symptoms Indicating Impairment." *Journal of Health and Human Behavior* 3 (1962):269-276.

Leighton, Dorothea C.; Harding, J. S.; Macklin, D. B.; MacMillan, A. M.; and Leighton, A. H. *The Character of Danger: Psychiatric Symptoms in Selected Communities.* New York: Basic Books, 1963.

Lemkau, P.; Tietze, C.; and Cooper, M. "Mental Hygiene Problems in an Urban District." *Mental Hygiene* 26 (1942):100-119.

Liem, Ramsay, and Liem, Joan. "Social Class and Mental Illness Reconsidered: The Role of Economic Stress and Social Support." *Journal of Health and Social Behavior* 19 (June 1978):139-156.

MacMillan, A. M. "The Health Opinion Survey: Technique for Estimating Prevalence of Psychoneurotic and Related Types of Disorder in Communities." *Psychological Reports* 3 (1957):325-339.

Madsen, William. "Mexican-Americans and Anglo-Americans: A Comparative Study of Mental Health in Texas." In *Changing Perspectives in Mental Illness*, edited by S. C. Plog and R. B. Edgerton, pp. 217-241. New York: Holt, Rinehart and Winston, 1969.

Manis, Jerome; Brawer, M. L.; Hunt, C. L.; and Kercher, L. C. "Validating a Mental Health Scale." *American Sociological Review* 28 (February 1963):108-116.

Matza, David. "Poverty and Disrepute." In *Contemporary Social Problems*, 3d ed., edited by R. K. Merton and R. Nisbet, pp. 601-656. New York: Harcourt Brace Jovanovich, 1971.

Mechanic, David, and Greenley, James R. "The Prevalence of Psychological Distress and Help-Seeking in a College Student Population." *Social Psychiatry* 11 (February 1976): 1-14.

Meile, Richard, and Haese, Phillip. "Social Status, Status Incongruencies, and Symptoms of Stress." *Journal of Health and Social Behavior* 10 (1969):237-244.

Middleton, Russell. "Psychological Well-Being." *Final Report of the Rural Negative Income Tax Experiment*, vol. 5, chap. 7. Institute for Research on Poverty, University of Wisconsin, Madison, 1976.

Middleton, Russell, and Allen, Vernon. "Social Psychological Effects." In *The New Jersey Income Maintenance Experiment*, vol. III. Edited by H. Watts and A. Rees, chap. 8. New York: Academic Press, 1977.

Myers, Jerome; Lindenthal, J. J.; and Pepper, Max. "Life Events and Psychiatric Impairment." *Journal of Nervous and and Mental Disease* 152, no. 3 (1971):149-157.

Myers, Jerome; Lindenthal, J. J.; and Pepper, Max. "Life Events and Mental Status: A Longitudinal Study." *Journal of Health and Social Behavior* 13 (1972):398-406.

Myers, Jerome; Lindenthal, J. J.; and Pepper, Max. "Social Class, Life Events, and Psychiatric Symptoms: A Longitudinal Study," In *Stressful Life Events: Their Nature and Effects*, edited by B. S. Dohrenwend and B. P. Dohrenwend, pp. 191-205. New York: Wiley, 1974.

Parker, S., and Kleiner, R. J. *Mental Illness in the Urban Negro Community.* New York: Free Press, 1966.

Pasamanick, Benjamin; Roberts, D. W.; Lemkau, P. W.; and Krueger, D. B. "A Survey of Mental Disease in an Urban Population: Prevalence by Race and Income." In *Epide-*

miology of Mental Disorder, edited by B. Pasamanick, pp. 183-196. Washington, D.C.: American Association for the Advancement of Science, 1959.

Paykel, E. S. "Recent Life Events and Clinical Depression." In Life Stress and Illness, edited by E. K. E. Gunderson and R. H. Rahe, pp. 134-163. Springfield, ILL.: Charles C. Thomas, 1974.

Phillips, Derek L. "The 'True Prevalence' of Menal Illness in a New England State." Community Mental Health Journal 2 (1966):35-40.

Robins, Philip K., and Tuma, Nancy Brandon. "The Effects of a Negative Income Tax on Job Turnover." Center for the Study of Welfare Policy, Stanford Research Institute, 1977.

Scheff, Thomas J. Being Mentally Ill. Chicago: Aldine, 1966.

Schwartz, Carol C.; Myers, K.; and Astrachan, B. M. "Comparing Three Measures of Mental Status: A Note on the Validity of Estimates of Psychological Disorder in the Community." Journal of Health and Social Behavior 14 (September 1973):265-273.

Seiler, Lauren. "The 22-Item Scale Used in Field Studies of Mental Illness: A Question of Method, a Question of Substance, and a Question of Theory." Journal of Health and Social Behavior 14 (September 1973):252-264.

Shepherd, M.; Cooper, B.; Brown, A. C.; and Kalton, G. W. Psychiatric Illness in General Practice. London: Oxford University Press, 1966.

Spiro, H. R.; Siassi, I.; and Crocetti, G. "What Gets Surveyed in a Psychiatric Survey: A Case Study of the MacMillan Index." Journal of Nervous and Mental Disease 154, no. 2 (1972):105-114.

Srole, Leo; Langner, T. S.; Michael, S. T.; Opler, M. K.; and Rennie, T. A. C. Mental Health in the Metropolis: The Midtown Manhattan Study. New York: McGraw-Hill, 1962.

Thoits, Peggy, and Hannan, Michael. "Income and Psychological Distress: The Impact of an Income Maintenance Experiment." Technical report, Center for the Study of Welfare Policy, Stanford Research Institute, July 1977.

Tousignant, M.; Denis, G.; and Lachapelle, R. "Some Considerations Concerning the Validity and Use of the Health Opinion Survey." Journal of Health and Social Behavior, 1974, pp. 241-252.

Tuma, Nancy Brandon; Groeneveld, Lyle P.; and Hannan, Michael T. "First Dissolutions and Remarriages: Impacts in 24 Months of SIME/DIME." Research Memorandum No. 35, Center for the Study of Welfare Policy, Stanford Research Institute, 1976.

U.S. Department of Health, Education and Welfare. Selected Symptoms of Psychological Distress. Public Health Service Publication No. 1000, Series 11, no. 37. Washington, D.C.: U.S. Government Printing Office, 1970.

Warheit, George; Holzer, Charles E.; and Arey, Sandra A. "Race and Mental Illness: An Epidemiologic Update." Journal of Health and Social Behavior 16 (1975):243-256.

Zolik, E., and Marches, J. "Mental Health Morbidity in a Suburban Community." Journal of Clinical Psychology 24 (January 1968):103-108.

CHAPTER 11

Demand for Children

MICHAEL C. KEELEY

INTRODUCTION

In the United States, the federal income tax, many state income-tax systems, and the array of programs that make up the welfare system may have important effects on parental decisions regarding the timing, number, and quality of children. This is in part because virtually all welfare or public transfer programs have benefit structures that depend on family type (i.e., married, female-headed, single individual) and family size. Similarly, the federal income tax rate and many state and local tax rates are determined by family size and type. (In many tax systems both the marginal and average tax rates depend on family and type.) Tax and transfer programs are likely to affect the demand for children because they affect disposable income and because they both directly and indirectly affect the costs of having and raising children. Understanding the relationship between public policy and fertility decisions is important because changes in fertility rates have important effects on the rate of population growth and on the age structure of the population, and both of these demographic factors in turn have significant influences on social, economic, and political phenomena.[1]

Recently, there has been interest in replacing the existing public welfare system with a nationwide NIT. An important question arises in designing such a program; specifically, what would the impact of an NIT on fertility be? This is important because the children of the poor are more likely to be poor themselves (when reaching adulthood) and, consequently, the eventual size of the poverty population may depend on the effects of an NIT on fertility. (See, e.g., the theoretical work of Becker and Tomes, 1977, and the empirical work of Bowles, 1972, and Brittain, 1977.) Furthermore, the budgetary costs of an NIT

---

[1] For example, Easterlin (1978) argues that the baby boom of the 1950s led to substantially lower real lifetime incomes of the cohorts born during the period.

A GUARANTEED ANNUAL INCOME:
EVIDENCE FROM A SOCIAL EXPERIMENT

would depend on the magnitude of a fertility response because in most NIT programs under consideration, the benefit structure depends on family size. This chapter deals with the effects of alternative NIT programs on fertility, using data from the first 3 years of the SIME/DIME experiments.

The first section of this chapter is a theoretical discussion of the effects of an NIT on fertility. The next section presents the data and the empirical results. The last section draws some conclusions.

THE THEORETICAL EFFECTS OF A NEGATIVE INCOME TAX ON FERTILITY

Parents' decisions regarding the number of children and expenditures on children are the result of a complex decision-making process. These decisions are subject to constraints regarding income, time, knowledge, and contraceptive technology. Economic theory provides a means of analyzing the effects of changes in these constraints on fertility and on expenditures on children. (See Willis, 1973; Becker and Lewis, 1973; and Keeley, 1975.) The effects of an NIT on fertility can be analyzed using this framework because an NIT has direct effects on some of these constraints.

The household production model, pioneered by Becker (1965), provides a framework in which fertility decisions can be systematically analyzed. The household production model stresses that many, if not most, market goods and services are not demanded in and of themselves, but as inputs into the production of more basic household commodities. Health, education, prestige, companionship, and children are examples of commodities that are not typically available in the market per se. Although these commodities have no explicit market prices, shadow prices may be derived that depend on the prices and quantities of the inputs used to produce the commodities and on the structure and technology of the household. These shadow prices, in conjunction with income and preferences, determine the quantities of various commodities that will be produced in the home and the allocation of resources used to produce these commodities. Since children are produced in the home and investments in child capital are made in the home, the costs of children in terms of both quantity and quality are affected by the technology of production, which in turn is affected by a variety of socioeconomic variables. Since both quantity and quality of children presumably yield positive utility and have positive costs, the income of the household as well as the shadow price of children affect fertility.

In addition, changes in the prices of other commodities may have effects on fertility if they are substitutes for or complements to children. To summarize, economic theory suggests that changes in the cost of children (caused by changes in the costs of having and raising them), changes in the costs of other commodities, and changes in income may all lead to changes in fertility.

An NIT has three basic effects on the budget constraint that may have important effects on fertility. First, in all 11 of the SIME/DIME NIT treatments and in virtually all proposed welfare reforms, the guarantee level is positively related to family size. That is, all else equal, larger families receive larger payments and are guaranteed a larger minimum annual income. This scaling by family size results in an implicit subsidy for additional children because the cost of additional children is substantially reduced. Thus, this subsidy should lead families to have more children. The increase in number of children in turn would make it more expensive for the family to provide each of their children with a given level of goods and services, leading to a reduction in the average expenditure per child. Consequently, the outcome of increasing the subsidy component (holding constant the other effects of the NIT) would not only be an increase in quantity but also a relatively large decrease in quality.

Second, an NIT increases the disposable income of families below the break-even level. Normally, increases in income would lead to increases in all commodities. Theory does suggest that the increase in income should lead to an increase in total stock of child "capital" but not necessarily increases in the number of children. For example, an increase in income may lead people to have fewer children but yet spend much more on each child. In fact, if expenditures per child are strongly related to income, number of children may decrease with income because the cost of an additional child is higher when expenditures per child are higher. That is, if the quality per child is assumed to be the same for all children in a given family, then the price of increasing quantity is greater than the level of quality per child. Consequently, the net effect of an increase in income caused by an NIT is uncertain.

Finally, the high implicit tax rate of the NIT reduces the opportunity cost of time. That is, it reduces the cost of time involved in having and raising children. However, it also reduces the cost of time in other nonmarket pursuits. The reduced cost of time leads to a reduction in the cost of both numbers and quality of children. Existing evidence suggests that this decrease in cost of time should increase fertility, although theoretically the effect depends on the substitutability of quality and quantity, and the substitutability of children with other commodities whose cost also depends on the cost of time.

To summarize, the net effect of an NIT on fertility is not theoretically determinant. Although the subsidy effect alone does lead to an increase in fertility, the income effect and the cost-of-time effect are of unknown sign. The empirical analysis presented in the next section seeks to assess the net effect, utilizing data on fertility from the first 3 years of SIME/DIME.

THE DATA AND EMPIRICAL RESULTS

One of the most serious drawbacks of existing empirical research on fertility using nonexperimental data is that fertility is simultaneously determined along with labor force participation, education, income, and marriage and it is very difficult to statistically identify a behavioral model of fertility. By using experimental data many of these problems may be avoided, because changes in income, net wages, and the child subsidy are known to be exogenous. There are, however, a new set of statistical problems associated with properly analyzing the effects of the experiments. Perhaps the most important features of the experiment that need to be considered are the measurement of experimental treatment, the sample selection procedure, the process used to assign treatment, (see Keeley and Robins, 1978) and the limited duration of the treatment.

Variations in Support Level with Family Size

In Table 11.1 the actual variation of guarantee with family size for each of the three guarantee levels is presented. For example, for a family of two on the $5600 program, an additional child would increase the support level by $1176. The increment in support level, however, declines as family size increases.

The whole change in the guarantee level represents an additional payment for all families on constant tax rate plans below the breakeven level. For families on the declining tax plans, this is only true for persons with no earned income, because the declining tax rates depend positively on family size. The reduction in the grant due to the higher tax is a function of the family size index and earnings. For example, a family of two with $6000 in earnings would have its grant

Table 11.1
Support Levels and Changes in Support Level by Family Size
and Experimental Plan

Family size	Family size index	$3800		$4800		$5600	
		Support level	Change in support level	Support level	Change in support level	Support level	Change in support level
1		1000		1000		1000	
			1356		1976		2472
2	.62	2356		2976		3472	
			798		1008		1176
3	.83	3154		3984		4648	
			646		816		952
4	1.00	3800		4800		5600	
			456		576		672
5	1.12	4256		5376		6272	
			418		528		616
6	1.23	4674		5904		6888	
			342		432		504
7	1.32	5016		6336		7392	
			228		228		336
8	1.38	5244		6624		7728	

reduced by $368 due to the higher tax if it were to have an additional child. Note that this exceeds the increase in guarantee level for famuies of seven for all programs and for families of six on the $3800 program. Thus, for some families, the NIT subsidy for an additional child could be negative.

The Sample

For purposes of the analysis presented in this chapter, only originally enrolled husband-wife families and female-headed families are considered. The resulting sample includes 2194 married women (681 black, 1061 white, and 452 Chicana) and 1392 single women (667 black, 503 white, and 222 Chicana). Because the income cutoff varied positively with family size, large families were more likely than small ones to be enrolled.[2] This factor may have led to the selection of a sample with somewhat unusual fertility patterns.

In a previous paper (Keeley, 1978), it was shown that the mean number of children present in SIME/DIME families was much larger than in a comparable national sample. Similarly, very few childless families were enrolled in SIME/ DIME. This was because childless families are more likely to have two full-time workers and consequently higher incomes, and because the income cutoff varied positively with family size. Because of these sample selection criteria, the fertility of the SIME/DIME sample was somewhat low because high-parity women have lower fertility rates than low-parity women.

If response to an NIT depends on parity, then it is important to control for initial parity in the response function so that predictions of response in different samples can control for differences in parity. This would be of particular importance in extrapolating SIME/DIME results to a national sample.

Measuring the Experimental Impact

If it is assumed that there is no abortion, any experimental impact on fertility can occur only after a considerable delay. This is because both conception and pregnancy take time. For an "average" woman, an experimental impact will not be observed for 13 months (9 months of pregnancy plus 4 months to conceive) (see Michael and Willis, 1973). Because of this delay between the time a woman decides to have a birth and the occurrence of a birth, an experimental impact cannot be expected until late in the experiment. However, with effects on abortion, there is no such delay, so experimental impacts can occur any time during the experiments. In this study, fertility is measured during two different periods: during the first year after enrollment and during a period covered by the second and third years of the experiments.

[2] The same family size index reported in Table 11.1 is used. Thus, a family of eight, for example, with two working heads should have had an income of less than $15,180 in order to be enrolled. This can be compared to an income cutoff of $11,000 for a similar family of our.

Although some considerations suggest that, for the purposes of fertility decisions, the family is the appropriate decision-making unit, there are difficulties in analyzing the response of families. The primary difficulty is that there is considerable family change due to divorce, marriage, and remarriage during the time period being studied. It is possible to analyze fertility response conditional upon no family change, but such a conditional analysis does not give the total reduced form effect of experimental treatments, since experimental treatments affect family change. For the purposes of this study, analysis is carried out on samples of all originally enrolled married females and single females categorized by their marital status at the time of enrollment regardless of subsequent marital status.

The fertility of women over 40 is close to zero because of biological reasons and consequently no experimental effect is expected for them. Thus, all women over 40 at enrollment are excluded from the analysis.

Experimental-Control Differences in Fertility Rates[3]

In this section, experimental-control differences in fertility rates, controlling for assignment, background, and manpower treatment variables, are presented. Estimates of experimental-control differences may be interpreted as estimates of response to the mean program conditional upon the particular assignment of treatment. Separate estimates are obtained for persons assigned to 3- and 5-year programs. This model is the most constrained of all response models and thus is most likely to have statistically significant coefficients.[4]

In Table 11.2, estimates of experimental-control differences in fertility rates for married females are presented. Estimates of the effects are presented separately for the first year of the experiments (Period 1) and the second and third years (Period 2). Experimental effects are measured as ratios of fertility rates. For example, during Period 2, the ratio of .57 for 5-year white experimentals to controls indicates that white 5-year experimentals had a fertility rate equal to 57% of the white controls' fertility rate. Similarly, the ratio of 3-year experimentals to 5-year experimentals for this group indicates that 3-year experimentals

[3] In the remainder of this chapter, the term experimental refers to persons receiving an NIT treatment.

[4] The actual model estimated is

$$\ln r_p = \alpha_0 + \beta C_p + \gamma_p FGTO + \delta_p YRS3, \qquad p = 1,2,$$

where C is a vector of control variables; $FGTO = 1$, if experimental family, 0 otherwise; $YR3 = 1$, if 3-year experimental family, 0 otherwise; $\alpha, \beta, \gamma, \delta$ are coefficients to be estimated; and p refers to the period as defined previously. The coefficient of $FGTO$, γ_p, is a measure of the experimental impact of the NIT treatment on the log of the birth rate (after controlling for assignment and background variables) for persons assigned to the 5-year sample. The sum, $\gamma_p + \delta_p$ gives the impact for persons in the 3-year sample. A maximum likelihood procedure developed by Tuma (1976) and Tuma et al. (1978) is used to obtain these estimates. The computer program used is described in Tuma and Crockford (1976).

Table 11.2
Experimental-Control Differences in Fertility Rates for
Married Females 40 and Under

	Black	White	Chicana
Average annual birth rate	.092	.091	.097
Number of individuals	681	1061	452
x^2 (for the equation)	166.12***	189.71***	130.34***
Degress of freedom	65	65	61
x^2 (for treatment effects during period 2, 2 degrees of freedom)	.08	5.69*	4.83*
Period 1 (1st year)			
FGTO (coefficient)	−.4334	.3615	−.5394
Ratio to 5-year experimentals to controls	.65	1.43	.58
t-statistic	(1.18)	(1.14)	(1.17)
YRS3 (coefficient)	.3844	−.3612	.03108
Ratio of 3-year experimentals to 5-year experimentals	1.47	.70	1.032
t-statistic	(1.02)	(1.16)	(.069)
Period 2 (2nd and 3rd years)			
FGTO (coefficient)	−.001926	−.5584*	.7996**
Ratio of 5-year experimentals to controls	1.00	.57	2.23
t-statistic	(.006)	(1.88)	(2.14)
YRS3 (coefficient)	−.06979	.6329**	−.6009*
Ratio of 3-year experimentals to 5-year experimentals	.93	1.88	.54
t-statistic	(.202)	(2.262)	(1.79)

Note: The ratio is equal to the exponential of the coefficient and given the percentage effect of a 0-1 variable on the birth rate. For example, a ratio of 2.23 for Chicanas indicates that experimentals for the 5-year sample have births at a rate 2.23 times that of identical controls.

Note: Probability levels for all tables in this chapter are as follows:

*$p < .10$.
**$p < .05$.
***$p < .01$.

had a fertility rate 1.88 times that of 5-year experimentals, and hence, 1.07 ($1.07 = 1.88 \times .57$) times that of controls. The t-statistics presented in parentheses indicate the statistical precision (or confidence) with which the effects are estimated. As expected, there were no statistically significant effects during Period 1. During Period 2, there were large significant negative effects for whites and positive effects for Chicanas of the 5-year treatment sample. For example, white 5-year experimentals had a fertility rate during the first through third year of the experiment equal to 57% of comparable controls, and 5-year experimental Chicanas had a fertility rate 2.23 times as large. The magnitude of these effects was considerably lower in absolute value for 3-year experimentals (1.08 for whites and 1.20 for Chicanas). The effects during Period 2 were jointly significant (at the .10 level) for whites and Chicanas, but no significant effects were found for blacks. The fact that experimental effects were observed only during Period 2 lends support to the hypothesis that these were in fact behavioral responses although there is no readily apparent explanation for widely differing responses of blacks, whites, and Chicanas.

In Table 11.3, similar estimates were presented for single females 40 and under at the time of enrollment. For this group, however, none of the coefficients are significant even at the .10 level of probability. Tests for the joint significance of treatment effects during Period 2 are not significant at even the .10 level for any of the racial-ethnic groups.

As an additional measure of treatment effects, the fertility of participants in SIME/DIME is distinguished from the fertility of nonparticipants. A participant is defined to be an individual who was below the breakeven level and received payments. (Whether or not an individual is receiving payments was determined by self-reporting.) Although participation is to some extent an endogenous variable, this endogeneity is less important when analyzing fertility response than when analyzing labor-supply response, which is directly related to participation.

Table 11.3
Experimental-Control Differences in Fertility Rates for
Single Females 40 and Under

	Black	White	Chicana
Average annual birth rate	.045	.038	.064
Number of individuals	667	503	222
χ^2 (for the equation)	87.65***	68.62***	55.44***
Degrees of freedom	51	51	49
χ^2 (for treatment effects during Period 2)	2.60	4.58	1.02
Period 1 (1st year)			
FGTO (coefficient)	−.09588	−.674	−1.317
Ratio	.91	.51	.27
t-statistic	(.13)	(.76)	(1.28)
YRS3 (coefficient)	.7281	.7526	.3043
Ratio	.48	2.10	1.36
t-statistic	(.93)	(.89)	(.36)
Period 2 (2nd and 3rd years)			
FGTO (coefficient)	.3035	.07097	−.09017
Ratio	1.36	1.07	.91
t-statistic	(.77)	(.13)	(.12)
YRS3 (coefficient)	−.6472	−.9522	.5064
Ratio	.52	.39	1.66
t-statistic	(1.56)	(1.63)	(.82)

Table 11.4
Participant-Nonparticipant Differences in Fertility Rates for
Married Females 40 and Under

	Black	White	Chicana
Average annual birth rate	.092	.091	.097
Number of individuals	681	1061	452
χ^2 (for the equation)	169.10***	110.49***	67.24***
Degrees of freedom	65	32	30
Period 2 (2nd and 3rd years)			
P23 (coefficient)	−.0198	−.4262	1.00***
Ratio	1.020	.65	2.72
t-statistic	(.055)	(1.38)	(2.70)
P23*YRS3 (coefficient)	−.2412	.4739	−.5547
Ratio	.79	1.61	.57
t-statistic	(.63)	(1.51)	(1.56)

Note: These results are estimated using a 1=period model.

(See Robins and West, 1978, for an analysis of determinants of participation and an analysis of the effects of participation on labor supply.)

An individual was considered to be a participant if she participated in both the second and third years of the experiment. Participation in a given year is defined as receiving a payment in excess of the minimum payment during any quarter during that year. Thus, an individual must have received payments in excess of the minimum payment during both the second and third years of the experiment to be considered a participant.

In Table 11.4 participant-nonparticipant differences in fertility rates for married females 40 and under are presented. Participants in the 3-year sample are distinguished from participants in the 5-year sample by interaction with a dummy variable for 3-year treatment, YRS3, with the participation dummy, P23. Thus, the estimates produced by this model are directly comparable to the experimental-control estimates presented in Table 11.2. The results are generally similar, although the only significant coefficient in the participation model is that of Chicanas in the 5-year sample. The response of these Chicana participants, in fact, is considerably larger than that of the 5-year sample of Chicanas eligible for treatment (2.72 vs 2.34 in ratio terms).

In Table 11.5, similar results are presented for single females. The only coefficients jointly significant are those for whites. Although participants in the 5-year sample showed no significant response, participants in the 3-year sample showed a large reduction in fertility (32% that of nonparticipants). Similarly, black participants in the 3-year program showed a smaller reduction in fertility (68% that of nonparticipants). In terms of magnitude, however, the results are roughly comparable to those presented in Table 11.3.

Table 11.5
Participant-Nonparticipant Differences in Fertility Rates for
Single Females 40 and Under

	Black	White	Chicana
Average annual birth rate	.052	.036	.064
Number of individuals	673	485	221
χ^2 (for the equation)	53.71***	34.87***	26.98***
Degrees of freedom	25	25	24
χ^2 (for treatment effects, 2 degrees of freedom)	3.37	6.35**	1.46
Period 2 (2nd and 3rd years)			
P23 (coefficient)	.4245	.05142	−.4131
Ratio	1.529	1.053	.6616
t-statistic	(1.08)	(.09)	(.54)
P23*YRS3 (coefficient)	−.8097*	−1.177*	.7432
Ratio	.4450	.3082	2.103
t-statistic	(1.83)	(1.80)	(1.10)

Estimates of Parameterized Treatment Effects

In this section, coefficient estimates of parameterized treatment effects are presented. The experimental treatment is parameterized in terms of the following six variables, which are all calculated based on preenrollment data.

ΔG The change in the annual grant of the NIT that would occur if the family had on additional child, holding constant hours of work. This variable is defined to be 0 if the family with one additional child is above the breakeven level and is 0 for controls (measured in dollars per year).

ΔY The change in annual disposable income due to the NIT, holding constant family size and hours of work. This variable is defined to be 0 for those above the breakeven level and for controls (measured in dollars per year).

ΔW The change in the net wage caused by the NIT evaluated at preexperimental income. This variable is also 0 for those above the breakeven level preexperimentally and controls (measured in dollars per hours).

$\Delta Y *EMPSTF$ The change in disposable income multiplied by the preexperimental employment status of the female.

$\Delta W*EMPSTF$ The change in the net wage multiplied by the preexperimental employment status of the female.

$FABOVE$ A dummy variable equal to 1 for experimental families above the NIT breakeven level preexperimentally.

By parameterizing the experimental treatment in terms of these variables it should be possible to measure income and price effects. The coefficient of ΔG gives the subsidy effect, which should be positive, ΔY gives the income effect which is ambiguous in sign, and ΔW gives the price of time effect, which is theoretically ambiguous in sign but is expected to be positive. The interaction terms allow for differential effects depending on the wife's work status. An increase in income for a nonworking wife should be more negative than an increase in income for a working wife because for a nonworking wife the increase in income also increases the value of time in the home. Similarly, a change in the net wage has no effect on the value of time for a nonworking wife.

In Table 11.6, the coefficient estimates of this model are presented for married females 40 and under. The only significant coefficient is the coefficient of ΔG for Chicanas, which is positive as expected. This coefficient indicates that a $1000 subsidy would increase the fertility rate by 2.83 [2.83 = exp (1.041)] times what it would be without any subsidy.

In Table 11.7, similar estimates are presented for single females under 40. The

Table 11.6
Parameterized Treatment Model for Married Females 40 and Under

	Black	White	Chicana
Average annual birth rate	.092	.091	.097
Number of individuals	681	1061	452
χ^2 (for the equation)	172.75***	190.48***	135.21***
Degrees of freedom	73	73	69
Period 2 (2nd and 3rd years)			
ΔG (coefficient)	−.0006327	−.0004648	.001041
Ratio	.9994	.9995	1.001
t-statistic	(1.27)	(1.24)	(1.70)
ΔY (coefficient)	.0001837	−.00002756	.000062
Ratio	1.0	1.0	.9999
t-statistic	(1.03)	(.196)	(.30)
ΔW (coefficient)	−.1915	−.2995	.3284
Ratio	.8257	.7412	.7412
t-statistic	(.47)	(.92)	(.92)
$\Delta Y*EMPSTF$ (coefficient)	−.0002085	−.0000231	.000064
Ratio	.9998	1.0	1.0
t-statistic	(.76)	(.11)	(.11)
$\Delta W*EMPSTF$ (coefficient)	−.5195	−.2434	−.05113
Ratio	.5948	.7839	.9502
t-statistic	(.74)	(.47)	(.067)
$FABOVE$ (coefficient)	.5396	.4025	.4791
Ratio	1.715	1.496	1.615
t-statistic	(1.19)	(1.31)	(.90)

Table 11.7
Parameterized Treatment Model for Single Females 40 and Under

	Black	White	Chicana
Average annual birth rate	.052	.036	.064
Number of individuals	673	485	221
χ^2 (for the equation)	53.45***	37.76	36.48
Degrees of freedom	29	29	28
χ^2 (for treatment effects during Period 2, 6 degrees of freedom)	3.11	9.24	10.96*
Period 2 (2nd and 3rd years)			
ΔG (coefficient)	.000251	.000337	.001284
Ratio	1.000	1.000	1.001
t-statistic	(.44)	(.41)	(1.26)
ΔY (coefficient)	−.000353	−.000585	.001195**
Ratio	.9996	.9994	1.001
t-statistic	(1.13)	(1.24)	(2.16)
ΔW (coefficient)	−.2267	.5023	2.834***
Ratio	.7972	1.653	17.01
t-statistic	(.46)	(.58)	(2.74)
$\Delta Y*EMPSTF$ (coefficient)	.000299	.000599	−.001467**
Ratio	1.000	1.001	.9985
t-statistic	(.84)	(1.18)	(2.10)
$\Delta W*EMPSTF$ (coefficient)	.1636	.4739	−1.790
Ratio	1.178	1.606	.1670
t-statistic	(.30)	(.47)	(1.44)
$FABOVE$ (coefficient)	−11.83	−12.38	−.1521
Ratio	.000007	.000004	.8589
t-statistic	(.03)	(.02)	(.12)

only significant effects are for Chicanas. The grant coefficient ΔG is positive but not statistically significant. The income effect is positive and large (a $1000 increase in income increases fertility 3.30 times). The positive ΔW coefficient indicates that the higher the tax rate of the NIT the greater the reduction in fertility, an unexpected result. Finally, the income-employment status interaction indicates a negative income effect for women who were employed preexperimentally.

The general lack of significant estimates presented in Tables 11.6 and 11.7 may be due in part to the aggregation of 3- and 5-year samples, since the previous results suggest smaller (in absolute value) responses for persons in the 3-year sample. In order to test this hypothesis, the model was reestimated excluding the 3-year experimentals. Unfortunately, perhaps because of the small sample sizes, the resulting coefficient estimates were not generally significant (see Keeley, 1979).

CONCLUSIONS

Both the number of children and quality per child in a given family are in part the result of choices made by the parents under various time and money constraints. An NIT can be expected to affect both the numbers and quality of children because an NIT affects disposable income as well as the relative prices of numbers, quality, and nonmarket time.

The empirical analysis presented focuses on the fertility of women 40 and under during the second and third years of the experiment. For married females, there is evidence of a large statistically significant negative effect for the white 5-year sample, a large positive effect for the 5-year Chicanas, and no statistically significant effect for the 5-year blacks. Whites and Chicanas, in the 3-year sample had much smaller responses in absolute value. It is not known, however, whether this change in fertility would result in a change in completed family size or whether it simply represented a change in the timing of births. Efforts to estimate separate income and price effects were not generally successful. With the exception of the Chicanas, none of the estimated coefficients are significant. This may in part be due to the aggregation of 3- and 5-year samples, since other results suggest smaller (in absolute value) responses for persons in the 3-year sample. However, estimates of the model with the 3-year experimentals excluded do not give notably different results.

For single females (at the time of enrollment) there is no strong evidence of any fertility response to financial treatment in models that compare experimentals to controls. There is, however, some evidence of a negative 3-year effect for blacks and whites. None of the coefficients in the parameterized treatment model is significant for either blacks or whites, although the coefficients of this model are jointly significant for the Chicanas.

REFERENCES

Becker, Gary S. "A Theory of the Allocation of Time." *Economic Journal*, September 1965.

Becker, Gary S., and Tomes, Nigel. "A Theory of the Distribution of Income and Intergenerational Mobility." Mimeographed. University of Chicago, 1977.

Becker, Gary S., and Lewis, H. G. "On the Interaction between the Quantity and Quality of Children." *Journal of Political Economy* 81, (April 1973).

Bowles, Samuel. "Schooling and Inequality from Generation to Generation." *Journal of Political Economy* 80, no. 3 (May/June 1972).

Brittain, John A. *The Inheritance of Economic Status*. Washington, D. C.: The Brookings Institution, 1977.

Easterlin, Richard A. "What Will 1984 Be Like? Socioeconomic Implications of Recent Twists in Age Structure," *Demography* 15, (November 1978).

Keeley, Michael C. "A Comment on 'An Interpretation of the Economic Theory of Fertility." *Journal of Economic Literature* 13, no. 2 (June 1975).

Keeley, Michael C. "The Impact of Income Maintenance on Fertility: Preliminary Findings from the Seattle and Denver Income Maintenance Experiments." SRI Research Memorandum No. 49, March 1978.

Keeley, Michael C. "Taxes, Transfers, and Subsidies and Demand for Children: The Impact of Alternative Negative Income Tax Program." SRI Research Memorandum No. 65, June 1979.

Keeley, Michael C., and Robins, P. K. "The Design of Social Experiments: A Critique of the Conlisk-Watts Assignment Model." Research Memorandum 57, SRI International, November 1978; also in *Research in Labor Economics*, Vol. 3, edited by Ronald G. Ehrenberg, JAI Press, forthcoming.

Michael, Robert, and Willis, Robert. "Contraception and Fertility: Household Production under Uncertainty." In *Household Production and Consumption*, edited by N. Terleckyj. New York: Columbia University Press, 1973.

Robins, Phillip, and West, R. "Participation in the Seattle and Denver Income Maintenance Experiments and Its Effect on Labor Supply." SRI Research Memorandum no. 53, March 1978.

Tuma, Nancy. "Rewards, Resources, and the Rate of Mobility: A Nonstationary Multivariate Stochastic Model." *American Sociology Review* 41 (1976):338-360.

Tuma, Nancy, and Crockford, Douglas. "Invoking RATE." Research Memorandum draft, SRI International, Center for the Study of Welfare Policy, 1976.

Tuma, Nancy B.; Hannan, Michael T.; and Groeneveld, Lyle P. "Dynamic Analysis of Marital Stability." Mimeographed. SRI International, December 1977.

Willis, Robert J. "A New Approach to the Economic Theory of Fertility Behavior." *Journal of Political Economy*, Part II, 812 (March/April 1973):514-565.

PART IV

USING NEGATIVE INCOME
TAX BENEFITS

CHAPTER 12

Welfare Payments and Family Composition

TERRY R. JOHNSON
JOHN H. PENCAVEL

INTRODUCTION

In those government income transfer programs designed to raise the standard of living of the family unit (e.g., AFDC, Food Stamp, and Unemployment Insurance programs), index numbers are often applied to the benefits formulas that result in welfare payments varying across families according to their size and composition. These index numbers go by the name of adult equivalent scales since, by convention, they are normalized with respect to a given number of adults. For instance, if a family of two adults is eligible to receive x dollars in a given income transfer program, while a second family of two adults and one child (but otherwise identical in those respects relevant to the program) is entitled to receive $(1 + m)x$ dollars, then one child is considered as "equivalent" to an "mth" of two adults as far as that program is concerned. In Table 12.1 we present a variety of adult equivalent scales. Although these scales may appear to be quite similar, the differences in the implied guarantee level can be substantial. For example, an income transfer program with a guarantee level of $3800 per year for a reference family of two adults and two children would provide $4104 for a family of two adults and four children using the index given in Column 1, whereas the corresponding benefit level using the scale given in Column 7 would be $5510.

The extreme sensitivity of the benefit level to the scale used suggests an important policy question: In designing a national NIT program, how should the guarantee level be scaled by family size and composition? Since all of the NIT experiments have scaled the guarantee level by family size, it is surprising that the issue of what is an appropriate indexing scheme has not received any systematic treatment from researchers associated with those experiments. In this chap-

A GUARANTEED ANNUAL INCOME:
EVIDENCE FROM A SOCIAL EXPERIMENT

Table 12.1
Alternative Adult Equivalent Scales

	1	2	3	4	5	6	7	8	9
2 adults, no children	.78	.64	.60	.68	.63	.55	.55	.62	.63
2 adults, 1 child	.80	.70	.82	.84	.89	.79	.78	.83	.82
2 adults, 2 children	1.00	1.00	1.00	1.00	1.00	1.00	1.00	1.00	1.00
2 adults, 3 children	1.06	1.18	1.16	1.16	1.10	1.19	1.23	1.12	1.15
2 adults, 4 children	1.08	1.32	1.32	1.32	1.20	1.36	1.45	1.23	1.29

Note: The column numbers refer to the following scales.
1   Kapteyn, Arie, and van Praag, Bertrand. " A New Approach to the Construction of
    Family Equivalence Scales." *European Economic Review* 7, no. 4 (May 1976):
    313-336. (In this scale, the man is 27 years old and the woman 25 years old.)
2   From Orshansky (1965).
3   From Jackson (1968). (The age of the head is 35-54 years with the older or oldest
    child aged 6-15 years.)
4   From Bojer (1977).
5. Seneca, Joseph J., and Taussig, Michael K. "Family Equivalence Scales and Personal
    Income Tax Exemptions for Children." *Review of Economics and Statistics* 53,
    no. 3 (August 1971):253-262. (This is their estimated "necessities" scale evaluated
    at an income of $10,000 for the reference family.)
6   Washington, State of. *Food Stamp Program*, January 1974.
7   Colorado, Denver. *Aid to Families with Dependent Children Program*, July 1960.
8   Kurz, M.; Spiegelman, R. G.; and Brewster, J. A. "The Payment System for the Seat-
    tle and Denver Income Maintenance Experiments." Research Memorandum No.
    19. Center for the Study of Welfare Policy, Stanford Research Institute, June
    1973.
9   Mean values of scales 1 through 8.

ter, we outline a methodology for developing alternative adult equivalent scales
and provide estimates of these scales based on data from SIME/DIME.

The logic behind the scaling of benefits to family size and composition is rare-
ly spelled out convincingly. Since a husband and wife are not obliged to have
children, why index welfare benefits to family size any more than index benefits
to some other characteristic that the family can choose to acquire? One response
to this takes note of the fact that the children themselves have not been a party
to this choice, but then we must ask: Is it the welfare of the parents that is the
object of scaling benefits to family size or the welfare of the children? We know
of no information on the extent to which supplementary benefits are spent on
items that are largely consumed by parents as distinct from items that are more
specific to the children. The tacit assumption for treating the family as the relevant unit for redistributing income seems to be that the head of the family inter-
nalizes the welfare of different family members and acts as a benevolent despot
with respect to expenditures within the family (see Samuelson, 1956). We will

not attempt to evaluate these important and difficult questions. We simply observe that the prevailing sentiment appears to be that, since expenditures on necessities such as food and clothing rise with the number and perhaps the age of children,[1] families eligible for receiving welfare benefits require additional financial assistance to meet these costs of satisfying the minimum requirement of children. Assuming, then, that welfare payments are to be adjusted according to the number of children in the family, in this chapter we address some of the issues that arise in determining adult equivalent scales.[2] Our procedure in this chapter, therefore, is not to challenge the notion that families with children require greater welfare benefits than childless families so that the former can meet some of the expenditures associated with raising children. Instead, we will examine the logical implications of this notion and offer some estimates of these scales that are derived from the behavior of the SIME/DIME families.

Essentially there are three methods for estimating adult equivalent scales. The first uses information obtained from adults on how much extra money they require to meet the minimum costs of raising a child. An example of an adult equivalent scale derived in this way is shown in Column 1 of Table 12.1. For well-known reasons, the problems in interpreting the answers to such questions leave economists reluctant to place much weight in the derived deflators.

A second procedure involves determining minimum or adequate nutritional requirements for different family types. This procedure was adopted by Orshansky (1965) in her determination of poverty levels and they subsequently formed the basis of the Social Security administration's equivalent scales. Orshansky's scale is given in Column 2 of Table 12.1. Her procedure shares some of the characteristics of the previous method; except that, instead of asking families to estimate the minimum cost of raising a child, the Orshansky procedure at one remove reduces to asking a group of nutritionists to estimate the minimum expenditures on food required to raise a child. In both cases the estimate of minimum requirements is likely to involve not merely a physiological concept of requirements, but also a social concept.

The third procedure and one that has greater appeal to economists is to rely on the observed pattern of expenditures across families of different sizes and composition. Most frequently, these procedures expand upon Ernst Engel's original idea of drawing inferences from the fraction of family income spent on food. For instance, Jackson (1968) estimates adult equivalent scales based on the assumption (supported by considerable evidence) that the income elasticity of demand for food is .5, independent of family size and composition. In addition, she makes the strong assumption that families spending the same propor-

---

[1] By "necessities" we mean commodities with income elasticities of demand of less than unity. For evidence and discussion of the association between estimated income elasticities and household size, see Bojer (1977), Leser (1976), and Prais and Houthakker (1955).

tion of their income on food attain an equivalent level of total consumption. Based on these assumptions, she calculates an adult equivalent scale as $(\alpha_j/\alpha_r)^2$ where α_r is the fraction of income spent on food by the reference family of two adults and no children, while α_j is the corresponding food share in the budget of a family consisting of two adults and j children. Her computed indexes are given in Column 3 of Table 12.1. It is not a sufficient explanation to account for the similarity of the scales in Columns 2 and 3 in terms of the fact that the consumption of food lies behind each. This similarity is suggestive of something of a social or behavioral nature in the nutritionists' evaluation of minimum requirements.

One feature shared by all of these scales is their exclusive attention in their construction to the consumption of commodities. Yet if these scales are supposed to reflect the relative costs of meeting the minimum requirements of children, then it is curious that they omit reference to one of the most important factors in attending to the welfare of children, namely, the fact that caring for children requires the input of parental time.[3] Thus, in forming comparisons between, e.g., a family of two adults with no children and a family of two adults with one child, it seems inappropriate to ignore the fact that in the second family at least one parent (by convention, principally the wife) will have to devote time to raising and caring for the child. This is because her time has earnings potential that, in the childless family, could be allocated to the market place.[4] A casual glance at the data presented in Table 12.2 supports the proposed association between the working behavior of each adult in husband-wife families and the number of children in the family.[5] These data correspond to the second year of the experiment for control families only, in both Seattle and Denver. Rows 1b and 1c present the fraction of husbands and wives, respectively, who worked any hours in the labor market during the year (we call this the employment rate), while Row

---

[2] There is also, of course, the issue of the consequences of these adult equivalent scales. That is, any scheme that involves differential payments to families according to some characteristic they possess, by the same token poses differential incentives for the potential population of recipients to acquire or dispose of this characteristic. In the present context this general observation implies that differences in the size and structure of families may not be independent of these adult equivalent scales. Although this is an eminently testable proposition (to the best of our knowledge one that has not been investigated explicity), its examination is beyond the scope of this chapter.

[3] Vickery (1977) had made the same point though her procedure for handling the time dimension is very different from ours. Also relevant is the paper by Garfinkel and Haveman (1977).

[4] There are, of course, other options—the use of mothers-in-law or the hiring of babysitters—but the principle remains: Scarce resources have to be spent in childcaring that could be allocated to other purposes.

[5] Although these numbers are suggestive of an association between work behavior and family size, the reader should be reminded that such cross-tabulations ignore the influence of all other variables that affect hours of work.

Table 12.2
Work Behavior and Number of Children

No. of children:	0	1	2	3	4	5-6	Total sample
1. Employment rate							
(a) No. of families	105	152	230	164	82	44	777
(b) Husband	.857	.941	.935	.976	.915	.932	.932
(c) Wife	.571	.599	.600	.573	.549	.432	.575
(d) Husband and wife	.476	.579	.574	.555	.524	.409	.543
2. Hours worked							
(a) No. of families	50	88	132	91	43	16	422
(b) Husband	1584	1967	1949	2084	2027	2166	1957
(c) Wife	1413	1355	1090	1262	1070	897	1210
(d) Husband and wife	2997	3322	3039	3346	3097	3063	3166

Note: The employment rate measures the fraction of husbands (or wives) who worked a positive number of hours in the second year of the experiment. Row 1d measures the fraction of families in which both the husband and the wife worked positive hours during the year. The hours worked data measure annual hours of work for those families in which both the husband and the wife worked at all during the year. Row 2d is simply the sum of rows 2b and 2c in any column.

1d measures the fraction of families in which both the husband and the wife worked some time during the year. Rows 2b and 2c measure the average hours worked by the husband and the wife for those families in which both the husband and the wife worked positive hours during the year.

The employment rate of wives with either one or two children is slightly larger than that of childless wives, but beyond that the employment rate falls with the number of children. The employment rate of husbands with children is almost 10 percentage points lower than the rate for husbands with one child. This relationship between the husband's work behavior and number of children is also evident from the hours data where husbands with one child work almost 400 hours more per year than husbands without children. As for wives, hours worked fall as the number of children increase from zero to one and from one to two, but then from two children to three children the wife's hours rise considerably. Though this may appear surprising at first sight, it is consistent with the fact that raising children in some families is assisted by the presence of older children. That is, it is not merely the number of children, but their age composition that is relevant for the wife's hours of market work. Thus, in the three-child families, one of these three children may be old enough to assume some of the responsibilities of caring for the younger children, which in turn releases some of the mother's time for her to redirect to the market.

In this chapter we build on this apparent relationship between the parents' hours of work and the number and ages of their children in order to derive various adult equivalent scales. Our procedure is to follow the conventional one in economics of distinguishing objects of choice from constraints (or predetermined variables) and of assuming that families make their choices so as to do the best they can with what they have. Naturally, what is classified in the category of constraints and in the category of decision variables depends upon the particular questions under examination. Since in this chapter we take our cue from current government programs and concern ourselves with the construction of adult equivalent scales given the number of children, we treat the size and composition of the family as predetermined. This is in the spirit of existing welfare programs that identify families requiring assistance on the basis of some short-term criteria (such as weekly or annual earnings) and take such lifetime decisions as the size of family as given for the purposes of the program. No doubt on other occasions this assumption should be relaxed and fertility decisions integrated with consumption and work decisions. Instead of assuming all families of a given size and structure have the same fixed minimum requirements for necessities (which is the tacit assumption underlying the scales given in Columns 2 and 3 of Table 12.1), we assume that all families of a given size and structure have the same preferences for consumption and work and that, in response to differences among families in relative prices and wages facing them, they will substitute among commodities and work time to maximize their welfare.[6] Of the many possibilities we could choose for modeling family preferences, we have selected a functional form that permits us to distinguish between (*a*) an adult equivalent scale that compensates families of different sizes for the costs of satisfying minimum requirements, and (*b*) an adult equivalent scale that compensates families of different sizes for the costs of achieving some reference level of welfare, which may be greater than the welfare enjoyed at the "minimum requirements" level.

DEVELOPMENT OF ALTERNATIVE ADULT EQUIVALENT SCALES

In this section we describe and estimate three alternative adult equivalent scales that involve slightly different concepts of compensation. (See the chapter Appendix for a more technical discussion of the construction of these scales.) Our approach to the construction of adult equivalent scales appropriate to an NIT program relies on the observed expenditures and working behavior of the SIME/DIME husband-wife families.[7] We infer from their behavior what expenditures can be regarded as those satisfying minimum requirements and distinguish these from those "discretionary" expenditures meeting wants above the mini-

---

[6] In the empirical work we relax this assumption and allow for differences in preferences for consumption and for work by recognizing that individuals are creatures of habit and that current choices depend on previous consumption and work decisions.

[7] Although SIME/DIME also enrolled a large number of single female-headed households, we have not yet analyzed their behavior to estimate adult equivalent scales. The results reported in this chapter, therefore, refer to husband-wife families only.

mum level. We assume that the minimum required-consumption expenditures are the same for all families of a given size and composition and we estimate how much consumption requirements change with family size.

Correspondingly, we infer from their working behavior the extent to which each adult chooses to work less than his or her maximum feasible working hours given the time needed for rest and caring for children. That is, income is spent not only in consuming commodities in the conventional sense, but also in consuming leisure time (in other words, some income is foregone by not working the maximum feasible number of hours). Again, we assume that all husbands in a family of the same type have the same maximum feasible hours of work, but that this earnings potential may change with family size. We also assume that all wives in a family of the same type have the same maximum feasible hours of work, but recognize that their earnings potential may fall with family size since time has to be subtracted from the labor market for caring for children. For both the husband and the wife we estimate the extent to which the earning potential of each parent is affected by the presence of children. Thus, in general, we characterize families as having to make necessary consumption expenditures and as having to devote certain minimum amounts of time to the raising and caring for children. The actual level of well-being enjoyed by these families is measured by the extent to which their consumption expenditures and leisure time exceed these commitments.

One could imagine the role of adult equivalent scales in an NIT program as serving one of a number of purposes. One purpose is to do no more than scale the payments in order to compensate families with children for the increase in their minimum necessary consumption expenditures. This type of compensation is quite conventional and we present our own estimates of this type of adult equivalent scale in Column 2 of Table 12.3. For ease of comparison we present the adult equivalent scale used in SIME/DIME in Column 1 of this table. As is evident from a comparison of Columns 1 and 2, our estimates are strikingly similar to the adult equivalent scales used to adjust the guarantee level with respect to family size in SIME/DIME.

An adult equivalent scale may also be devised to take account of the loss in potential earnings that occurs when adults (principally wives) divert time from work to raising children. This sort of compensation is less conventional than the first but no less real. To make the point through a different route, suppose that all women—those with and those without children—work the same number of full-time hours, so that those women with children have to pay for the services of day-care centers to take responsibility for the supervision of their children during their working hours. If the guiding principle of any adult equivalent scale is to compensate families for child-related expenditure requirements, then it would necessarily take account of at least some of these expenditures on the services of day-care centers. If, however, it is appropriate to compensate families for their dollar expenditures in purchasing the time of others to care for their

Table 12.3
Estimates of Adult Equivalent Scales

	1	2	3	4
2 adults with no children	.62	.58		.32
2 adults with 1 child	.83	.84	.65	.76
2 adults with 2 children	1.00	1.00	1.00	1.00
2 adults with 3 children	1.12	1.11	1.23	1.16
2 adults with 4 children	1.23	1.20	1.41	1.29
2 adults with 5 children	1.32	1.27	1.55	1.39

Note: The reference utility level in Column 4 was taken to be a childless family facing mean gross wage rates on an NIT program involving a tax rate of .50 and a guarantee level of $3800. Similarly, changes in discretionary full income (the basis for the statistics in Column 3) was normalized with respect to a family with two children receiving a guarantee level of $3800. Since the scale in Column 3 is based on *changes* in discretionary full income across family composition, no element can be completed for the first row. For the scales presented in Columns 3 and 4, the first child is assumed to be less than 10 years of age while the second child is assumed to be between the ages of 11 and 16. The scales given in Columns 1 and 2 do not distinguish between the ages of children.

children, then surely it is also appropriate to compensate in part those mothers who forego some labor income and spend their own time (rather than buying the time of others) in such child-related responsibilities. Otherwise, the scales are tacitly penalizing those mothers who reallocate either their market work time or their pure leisure time to the raising of their children. Hence, the logic of an adult equivalent scale that does no more than compensate families for the costs of satisfying the minimum requirements of children implies that child-related expenditures of time should be treated symmetrically with child-related consumption expenditures. Thus, if the support level in an NIT program were used to compensate families for these increases in minimum consumption expenditures and these losses in foregone earnings, then the level of discretionary full income across families of different size and consumption, but facing the same wage rates and prices, is left constant; we call scales derived in this way *constant-discretionary full income adult equivalent scales*.

Our estimate of this scale is presented in Column 3 of Table 12.3. Clearly, it implies a much greater per child compensation than the consumption-specific scale in Column 2 since it incorporates not merely the increase in minimum consumption expenditures with respect to children, but also the loss in earnings potential. If a family of two adults and two children were granted a guarantee level of $3800 per year, then a guarantee of $3800 (1.23) or $4674 would have to be provided to a family with one more child in order to compensate this family fully for the increased minimum consumption requirements plus the decreased earnings potential that is associated with this extra child. This is $456 more than would be needed to compensate families merely for the additional minimum consumption requirements [$4674 − 1.11 (3800)]. Observe that the compensation required increases with the number of children at a decreasing rate, a characteristic that sometimes goes by the name of economies of scale in family size.

An adult equivalent scale may also be directed to a somewhat different end, one which recognizes that the well-being of a family should neither be equated to its actual income nor to its discretionary income, but that it should depend upon both the goods consumed and the leisure time enjoyed by the family. With well-being gauged in this way, the well-being or utility of, e.g., a two-adult, two-child family on a particular NIT program may serve as the reference point for scaling NIT payments with respect to family size. The question then arises as to what support level a second family with two adults and three children has to receive, such that, after attending to the needs of the extra child, this second family's well-being or utility is no different from the first. An adult equivalent scale that leaves the well-being or utility of families of different sizes and composition no different from that of the reference family is designated a *constant-utility adult equivalent scale*.

Our estimate of this scale is presented in Column 4 of Table 12.3 where the reference utility level corresponds to a family on the $F1$ experimental program, i.e., a program with a support level of $3800 and a tax rate of .5. The estimates in Column 4 indicate that, if a two-adult, two-child family receives $3800, then to maintain the level of welfare constant, a family with three children should receive $3800 (1.16) or $4408. This compensation, which maintains utility constant, is greater than that implied by Column 2, which only compensates families for their consumption requirements. On the other hand, the constant-utility scale implies less child-related compensation than the constant-discretionary full income scale, which in addition to minimum consumption requirements, also compensates families for their loss in earnings potential.

To illustrate our results in a slightly different manner, we present in Table 12.4 the implied guarantee levels for families with various numbers of children based on the adult equivalent scales given in Table 12.3 and assuming that a two-

Table 12.4
Implied Support Levels Based on Adult Equivalent Scales
Given in Table 12.3

	1	2	3	4
2 adults with no children	$2356	$2204		$1216
2 adults with 1 child	3154	3192	$2470	2888
2 adults with 2 children	3800	3800	3800	3800
2 adults with 3 children	4256	4218	4674	4408
2 adults with 4 children	4674	4560	5358	4902
2 adults with 5 children	5016	4826	5890	5282

adult, two-child family would receive $3800. In Column 1 we present the guarantee levels used in SIME/DIME (calculated by multiplying the scale given in Column 1 of Table 12.3 by $3800). The guarantee levels based on the conventional notion of simply meeting the increased consumption expenditures of children (Column 2) are remarkably similar to the SIME/DIME levels. The guarantee levels provided in Column 3 correspond to compensating families with children fully for their loss in total feasible work time to maintain dicretionary full income constant. There are large differences between the guarantee levels given in Columns 2 and 3. For example, a family with two adults and five children would be eligible for $5890 if discretionary full income was held constant, but only $4826 if families were just compensated for meeting the minimum consumption expenditures of children—a difference of $1064. Finally, in Column 4 we present the guarantee levels assuming that the utility of families of different sizes remains constant. This form of compensation results in levels that lie between those given in Columns 2 and 3. Thus, the table shows how sensitive the levels are to the method of compensation used.

CONCLUSION

Although the main focus of SIME/DIME is directed to measuring the work disincentive effects of an NIT program, the data collected with respect to this issue can also be employed fruitfully for other purposes. One such purpose has been demonstrated in this chapter, namely, the construction of adult equivalent scales. Such scales are a feature of practically all welfare programs and would almost certainly figure in any national NIT program.

We have presented three scales in this chapter, each one corresponding to a slightly different concept of compensation. Our procedure has not been to contest the tacit proposition that underlies these scales, namely, that parents require some form of compensation for the additional costs of raising children. Instead, we have addressed the logical implications of this proposition: These child-related costs do not merely cover the increased consumption expenditures associated with larger families; they also include the redirection of parental time away from leisure or from work in the labor market to the caring for and supervision of children.

Adult equivalent scales based on the conventional notion of simply meeting the increased minimum consumption expenditures of children imply less compensation for children than scales that take account of the value of time reallocated to the caring for children. The constant-discretionary full income scale constructed in this chapter goes so far as to compensate families with children fully for their loss in total feasible work time and this yields a scale that increases faster with respect to family size than any other of which we are aware. A scale that lies midway between the conventional consumption-specific index and the constant-discretionary full income scale is our constant-utility adult equivalent scale, which indexes benefits such that the utility of families of different sizes is maintained constant.

In the literature on adult equivalent scales, a great deal of attention has been devoted to measuring child-related consumption expenditures. By contrast, our impression is that the time costs of children have not merely escaped quantification, but have not even been recognized in principle as a relevant dimension of the construction of adult equivalent scales. Our purpose in this chapter has been to remedy this deficiency and to provoke a discussion of these issues by the relevant policymakers.

APPENDIX

The purpose of this appendix is to set out in slightly more technical language the characteristics of our model. Our starting point is the following representation of husband-wife preferences for consuming commodities and for working,

$$U(x, h_1, h_2) = B_0 \log \left(\frac{x}{m_0} - \gamma_0 \right) + \sum_{i=1}^{2} B_i \log \left(\gamma_i - \frac{h_i}{m_i} \right) \tag{1}$$

with each $B_i > 0$, with $\sum_{i=0}^{2} B_i = 1$, and where x stands for the consumption of commodities, h_1 the hours worked by the husband, and h_2 the hours worked by the wife. The m's are parameters that vary across families according to the number and perhaps the age of children. For the reference family, e.g., two adults with no children, $m_i = 1$ for $i = 0, 1, 2$. The preference specification (1) is the Stone-Geary utility function augmented by household composition factors in the spirit of Barten's (1964) formulation. It is observationally equivalent to the following form of the utility function, which brings out more clearly the implications of the household parameters.

$$U(x, h_1, h_2) = \widetilde{U}(x, h_1, h_2)$$
$$+ (B_0 \log m_0^{-1} + B_1 \log m_1^{-1} + B_2 \log m_2^{-1})$$

where

$$\widetilde{U}(x, h_1, h_2) = B_0 \log(x - m_0 \gamma_0) + \sum_{i=1}^{2} B_i \log(m_i \gamma_i - h_i).$$

Since $\widetilde{U}(\cdot)$ is a linear transformation of $U(\cdot)$, any proposition concerning U will also hold for $\widetilde{U}$.

Though it is by no means necessary to adhere to this interpretation, the utility function may be given some intuitive meaning by following Samuelson's (1948) proposal and by interpreting the γ_0 parameter as the physiological and psychological minimum consumption of commodities. With respect to commodities, therefore, the family only derives utility from consuming goods in excess of the minimum. Our parameterization of household composition is consistent with the approach of Orshansky, Jackson, and others discussed in the main body of this chapter in that it specifies the minimum subsistence parameter γ_0 as varying across families according to differences in m_0. The effect on utility of proportional increases in consumption above the subsistence level (i.e., proportional increases in $x - m_0\gamma_0$) is given by B_0.

Correspondingly, γ_1 may be interpreted as the maximum feasible hours of work of the husband and m_1 as a multiplier that either inflates or deflates γ_1 according to the characteristics of the household. A similar interpretation holds for the wife's parameter γ_2 and, given the wife's dominant role in childcaring, we would expect m_2 to behave such that the wife's maximum feasible hours of work are lower for families with children than for those without. B_1 and B_2 measure the increase in utility associated with small proportional decreases in hours worked below the maximum feasible hours of work. Finally, the husband and wife's household-budget restraint is described by the equation $px = w_1h_1 + w_2h_2 + y$, where p is the price of commodities, w_1 and w_2 are the after-tax wage rates of the husband and wife, respectively, and y denotes the household's after-tax flow of income from sources other than the sale of their labor. The problem for the family is that of selecting x, h_1, and h_2, the decision variables, in some purposive fashion subject to the constraints they face.

Before proceeding, it is appropriate to pause and consider the manner in which household structure is being parameterized in this model. Because the form of the dependence of each m_i parameter on the household composition variables has yet to be specified, it is clear that no assumption concerning "constant returns to family size" has even tacitly been made. On the other hand, our treatment of the household composition variables as exogenous is an assumption that a model with a longer time horizon would want to dispense with. This is, of course, an objection that can also be raised with respect to the wage rate and nonlabor income variables as well. The usual response to this objection (namely, with the appropriate assumptions with respect to the intertemporal separability of the objective function, the lifetime decision-making process can be decomposed into a series of more convenient shorter period decisions) can be applied to the household composition variables in addition. Moreover, our characterization that, without appropriate compensation and with other things equal, the well-being of families with children is less than that of childless families, fits comfortably with the underlying notions of the use of adult equivalent scales in government welfare programs. Our procedure is not to contest the principles that underpin the use of these scales in such programs, but to draw out the logical implications of these principles and to present some estimates of these scales that rest on observed behavior.

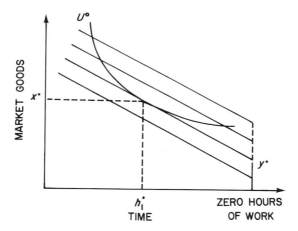

Figure 12.A.1   Constrained expenditure minimization: choice of hours of work and market goods to minimize nonwage income for a given level of utility.

There are a number of alternative yet equivalent ways of characterizing the family's choice of x, h_1, and h_2. For our purposes, it is perhaps most convenient if we first rewrite the budget constraint as $px - w_1 h_1 - w_2 h_2 = y$ so that, for any given p, w_1, and w_2, we can imagine a level of nonlabor income, y, accompanying any particular choice of x, h_1, and h_2. Suppose now we set some reference level of utility, say, U^0, and ask what levels of x, h_1, and h_2 and therefore, with p, w_1, and w_2 given, what level of y—will attain this level of welfare U^0 or more. Clearly one could imagine the family choosing a large x and small h_1 and h_2—and therefore, high y—that yields U^0 or more. But suppose we restrict the possibilities more by posing for the family the artificial problem of selecting x, h_1, and h_2 that corresponds to the lowest level of y subject to attaining at least the level of welfare U^0. A graphical depiction of this minimization problem is shown in Figure 12.A.1, where in order to accommodate the two dimensions, the woman is assumed not to work. The lowest level of y subject to attaining at least U^0 for given prices is given by $y*$ and the corresponding choice of commodities and working hours is given by $x*$ and $h_1 *$.[8]

Clearly, the minimum level of y will be higher, the greater the reference level of utility U^0. Moreover, as is suggested from the budget identity, $px - w_1 h_1 - w_2 h_2 = y$, the minimum level of y will be greater, the higher the prices of com-

---

[8] Here we have described, of course, the minimizing dual of the more conventional optimizing problem of selecting x, h_1, and h_2 to maximize utility subject to the budget constraint. The graph makes it clear that the optimal values of the decision variables determined by one problem are the same as those determined by the dual. A more careful discussion of the role of household composition in demand analysis appears, for instance, in Muellbauer (1974).

modities (p) and the lower the wage rates (w_1 and w_2) earned by the husband and wife. This relationship between the minimum level of y and the particular values of U^0, p, w_1, and w_2 may be called the net expenditure function or net cost function ("net" because y is equal to expenditures on commodities net of family labor income) and may be written for families of a type and composition indexed by M as $y = E(p, w_1, w_2, U^0; M)$. In the special case of our augmented Stone-Geary utility function, the net expenditure function takes the form

$$y = m_0\gamma_0 p - \sum_{i=1}^{2} m_i\gamma_i w_i + U^0 \left(\frac{m_0 p}{B_0}\right)^{B_0} \prod_{i=1}^{2} \left(\frac{m_i w_i}{B_i}\right)^{B_i}. \tag{2}$$

The minimizing level of y depends not only on prices, wage rates, and the reference utility level, but also on the household composition parameters m_i. This implies that, even for families purchasing commodities at the same prices p and earning incomes at the same wage rates w_1 and w_2, the minimizing level of y that attains U^0 will be different for families of varying sizes. These differences across families are the consequences not merely of varying family "needs" in the consumption of commodities (the m_0 parameter), but also of differences in time requirements in the caring for children (the m_1 and m_2 parameters).

Since the net expenditure function forms the basis of our calculations of adult equivalent scales, it is important to dwell on its meaning. In fact, it offers an appealing intuitive interpretation. First, observe that $m_0\gamma_0 p$ expresses the family's expenditures on commodities necessary to satisfy the "subsistence" level of consumption and, if m_0 rises with family size, then necessary consumption expenditures rise with the number of children. The terms $m_1\gamma_1 w_1$ and $m_2\gamma_2 w_2$ may be interpreted as the maximum feasible labor earnings of the husband and wife respectively. To anticipate our results somewhat, if m_2 falls with family size but m_1 rises with family size, then the wife suffers a loss in her earnings potential by having to divert time from the market place to the caring of their children while the husband's earnings potential is increased. Hence, if, as family size increases, m_0 and m_1 rise but m_2 falls, then maximum feasible income, $y + m_1\gamma_1 w_1 + m_2\gamma_2 w_2$, may either increase or decrease while minimum consumption expenditures, $m_0\gamma_0 p$, necessarily rise with the number of children. The combined effect of children in affecting the earnings potential of the parents and in increasing the minimum necessary consumption expenditures is captured by $m_0\gamma_0 p - \sum_{i=1}^{2} m_i\gamma_i w_i$ which is exactly the first two terms on the right-hand side of equation (2). The extent to which minimum necessary consumption expenditures fall short of maximum feasible labor income, $y = m_0\gamma_0 p - \sum_{i=1}^{2} m_i\gamma_i w_i$, is expected to decline as family size increases, implying that discretionary expenditures are lower in larger families.

The second term on the right-hand side of equation (2) may be written

$$\lambda U^0, \quad \text{where} \quad \lambda = (m_0 p)^{B_0}(m_1 w_1)^{B_1}(m_2 w_2)^{B_2} B_0^{-B_0} B_1^{-B_1} B_2^{-B_2}.$$

Now λ is simply a geometric index of commodity prices and wage rates where the weights in this index are the B_i parameters that in the discussion of equation (1) were related to the marginal utility of consumption and of work time. Hence, equation (2) implies that the discretionary income y, minus the discretionary income $\bar{y}$ required to attain U_0, is proportional to this reference utility level where the factor of proportionality (λ) depends upon prices, wage rates, and family composition.

We have made use of this cost function to present two types of adult equivalent scales. We define a reference family of two adults and two children on the NIT experiments who are receiving a support level of S dollars and whose utility is given by U^0. Consider a second family facing the same commodity prices and wage rates, but with a different number of children. By substituting into equation (2) the values of the relevant family size variables of the second family, we derive y^*, which is that guarantee level required by the second family to attain U^0, given the second family's number and age of children. A constant-utility adult equivalent scale is given by $I_u = y^*/S$ and this is presented in Column 4 of Table 12.3 where S is set equal to $3800.

A second adult equivalent scale exploits the interpretation of the parameters as subsistence consumption (γ_0) or as maximum feasible hours of work (γ_1 and γ_2) by asking not what guarantee level a second family must receive to attain the utility level of the reference family, but rather by asking what level a second family must receive to cover the increased subsistence consumption expenditures and to compensate for the reduction in earnings potential as family size increases. Minimum consumption expenditures are $m_0\gamma_0 p$ and they increase with the number of children as m_0 rises. Maximum labor earnings are given by $\sum_{i=1}^{2} m_i\gamma_i w_i$ and (if m_1 and m_2 fall as family size increases) these potential earnings decline as m_1 and m_2 fall. Let us define $F = y + \gamma_1 m_1 w_1 + \gamma_2 m_2 w_2 - \gamma_0 m_0 p$ as discretionary full income, the difference between maximum feasible income and minimum consumption expenditures. Discretionary full income falls with family size and let this reduction between a reference family of two adults and two children and, e.g., a two-adult, three-children family be given by ΔF. Suppose the guarantee level in an NIT scheme were adjusted to compensate families fully for declines in discretionary full income as family size increases. Then, if S were the guarantee level received by the reference family of two adults and two children, then a constant-discretionary income adult equivalent scale is given by $I_d = \sum_i \frac{\Delta F_i}{S}$, where i refers to the number of children. This index is presented in Column 3 of Table 12.3, where S is set equal to $3800. Hence, I_d is an adult equivalent scale that compensates families for differences in the full value of their net resources in terms of both the increased consumption expenditures and reduced earnings potential that accompany the raising and caring for children. By contrast, I_u determines the adult equivalent scale that leaves the welfare of the reference family constant.

The parameters of the net expenditure function [equation (2)] were estimated by fitting the husband's and wife's hours of work equations to the data drawn from the first and second years of SIME/DIME. Though a full discussion of these data and of the maximum likelihood procedures we have used is presented elsewhere,[9] we should mention here that our estimation strategy does take account of the fact that some 53% of wives are not observed working in the second year. We have also investigated a number of different ways of expressing the dependence of the m_i parameters on the family size and composition variables. Data presented in Table 12.1 indicated that the actual hours of work of women were not related in a simple linear fashion to the number of children. Because of these data and because of the attention in the literature to some sort of economies of scale in consumption with respect to family size, we were led to the following relationships between the m_i deflaters and family size and composition.

$$m_0 = 1 + \mu_0 \log(1 + C)$$
$$m_1 = 1 + \mu_1 N,$$
$$m_2 = 1 + \mu_{21} N_1 + \mu_{22} N_2 + \mu_{23}(N_1 N_2),$$

where C denotes the total number of children, N takes the value of unity if there are any children at all in the family and 0 otherwise, N_1 takes the value of unity if there are any children at all aged up to 10 years and 0 otherwise, and N_2 takes the value of unity if there are any children at all aged from 11 to 16 years and 0 otherwise. The logarithmic relation between m_0 and C permits economies of family size in consumption while the form of the m_1 and m_2 functions posits that it is the presence or absence of children in particular age groups as distinct from the number of children that affects hours of work.

The maximum likelihood point estimates of these parameters and of the other parameters of the net expenditure function are

$$
\begin{array}{lll}
B_0 = .870, & \gamma_0 = 5614.2, & \mu_0 = .662, \\
B_1 = .030, & \gamma_1 = 2149.9, & \mu_1 = .014, \\
B_2 = .100, & \gamma_2 = 2051.1, & \mu_{21} = -.230, \\
& & \mu_{22} = -.242, \\
& & \mu_{23} = .185.
\end{array}
$$

One natural procedure for evaluating these parameter estimates is to consider their implied labor supply elasticities, which, evaluated at the sample means of workers only, are

$$\frac{w_1}{h_1}\frac{\partial h_1}{\partial w_1} = .090, \qquad \left(\frac{w_1}{h_1}\frac{\partial h_1}{\partial w_1}\right)^* = .109, \qquad \frac{y}{h_1}\frac{\partial h_1}{\partial y} = -.012,$$

$$\frac{w_2}{h_2}\frac{\partial h_2}{\partial w_2} = .297, \qquad \left(\frac{w_2}{h_2}\frac{\partial h_2}{\partial w_2}\right)^* = .366, \qquad \frac{y}{h_2}\frac{\partial h_2}{\partial y} = -.119,$$

[9] The data and estimating procedures are described by Johnson and Pencavel (1979).

$$\frac{w_2}{h_1}\frac{\partial h_1}{\partial w_2} = -.010, \qquad \left(\frac{w_2}{h_1}\frac{\partial h_1}{\partial w_2}\right)^* = -.003,$$

$$\frac{w_1}{h_2}\frac{\partial h_2}{\partial w_1} = -.216, \qquad \left(\frac{w_1}{h_2}\frac{\partial h_2}{\partial w_1}\right)^* = -.022,$$

where the asterisk denotes the utility-constant (or compensated) elasticities. These estimates accord well with previous estimates of labor supply elasticities in that the responses of the wife are considerably larger than those of the husband. Further examination of these estimates is contained elsewhere.

The estimates of the μ's are also consistent with our prior expectations. The consumption requirements of the family rise with the number of children and its quantitative implications are brought out in the text. The estimate for μ_1 of .014 indicates a small positive influence of the presence of children on the husband's maximum feasible hours of work. By contrast, the wife's maximum feasible hours of work are reduced considerably by the presence of children. The similarity of the estimates of μ_{21} and μ_{22} indicates that the presence of a child aged 0-10 years has about the same effect in reducing the wife's maximum feasible hours of work as the presence of a child aged 11-16 years. The interesting implication of the estimate for μ_{23} of .185 is that the simultaneous presence of a younger and an older child partially offsets the decline in the wife's maximum feasible hours of work, a consequence presumably of the assistance given the wife by the older child in caring for the younger child.

REFERENCES

Barten, A. P. "Family Composition, Prices, and Expenditure Patterns." In *Econometric Analysis for National Economic Planning*, edited by P. Hart, G. Mills, and J. Whitaker, pp. 277-297. Colston Society, 16th Symposium. London: Butterworth, 1964.

Bojer, H. "The Effect on Consumption of Household Size and Composition." *European Economic Review* 9, no. 2 (May 1977):169-193.

Garfinkel, I., and Haveman, R. "Earnings Capacity, Economic Status, and Poverty." *Journal of Human Resources* 12, no. 1 (Winter 1977):49-70.

Jackson, Carolyn A. "Revised Equivalence Scale for Estimating Equivalent Incomes or Budget Costs by Family Type." BLS Bulletin No. 1570-2. U.S. Department of Labor, November 1968.

Johnson, T. R., and Pencavel, J. H. "Utility-Based Hours of Work Functions for Husbands, Wives, and Single Females Estimated from Seattle-Denver Experimental Data." Unpublished manuscript, SRI International, August 1979, 58 pp.

Leser, C. E. V. "Income, Household Size and Price Changes 1953-1975." *Oxford Bulletin of Economics and Statistics* 38, no. 1 (February 1976):1-10.

Muellbauer, J. "Household Composition, Engel Curves, and Welfare Comparisons Between Households: A Duality Approach." *European Economic Review* 5 (1974):103-122.

Orshansky, Mollie. "Counting the Poor: Another Look at the Poverty Profile." *Social Security Bulletin*, January 1965, pp. 7-9.

Prais, S. J., and Houthakker, H. S. *The Analysis of Family Budgets*. Monograph No. 4. Department of Applied Economics, University of Cambridge, 1955.

Samuelson, P. A. "Some Implications of 'Linearity'." *Review of Economic Studies* 15 (2), no. 38, (1948):88-90.

Samuelson, P. A. "Social Indifference Curves." *Quarterly Journal of Economics* 70, no. 1 (February 1956):1-22.

Vickery, C. "The Time-Poor: A New Look at Poverty." *Journal of Human Resources* 12, no. 1 (Winter 1977):27-48.

CHAPTER 13

Migration

MICHAEL C. KEELEY

INTRODUCTION

Migration is an important equilibrium mechanism in a changing economy. Migration tends to reduce interregional differences in real wage rates, property values, and unemployment rates. In addition, migration is an important determinant of the geographical population distribution.

Recently, there has been interest in replacing the existing complex public welfare system in the United States with a nationwide NIT. One important policy issue in designing such a program is the impact of alternative NIT plans on the rate of migration and the geographical distribution of the population. Any substantial redistribution of the population, especially the low-income population, caused by a change in the welfare system, would have important consequences for regional economic growth and development. It would also have important fiscal effects on local government because tax revenues and expenditures probably would be affected. A second important policy issue concerns the implications of welfare reform on migration to and from depressed regions with high unemployment rates. A final policy issue involves not only selecting appropriate guarantee levels and tax rates but, in addition, determining whether or not regional variations in the benefit levels corresponding to regional variations in the cost of living are appropriate.

Although existing studies of the determinants of geographical migration that use nonexperimental data provide useful information regarding these policy issues, they do not provide direct evidence regarding the likely impacts of a nationwide NIT on migration. In this chapter, SIME/DIME data are used to analyze the effects of alternative NIT plans on both the rate of migration and the destinations of those who migrate. These data are ideal for investigating the impact of alternative NIT programs on migration, because all sample members who move

A GUARANTEED ANNUAL INCOME:
EVIDENCE FROM A SOCIAL EXPERIMENT

(within the United States) continue to be interviewed and continue to receive their NIT treatments. The first section discusses the theoretical effects of an NIT on migration. The second section presents the results of the empirical analysis. The final section contains the conclusions.

THE THEORETICAL FRAMEWORK

The decision of a family to migrate, like many choices, is influenced by the expected costs and benefits, both pecuniary and nonpecuniary, of the consequences of the choice. Economists traditionally have stressed the importance of wage differentials or other pecuniary gains as one of the prime motives for migration and there is considerable empirical evidence that wage differentials are an important factor (see, e.g., Sjaastad 1962, DaVanzo 1972, Schwartz 1973, 1976, Greenwood 1975a,b, 1976). Viewed as a response to wage differentials, migration may be regarded as an investment in human capital because it may lead to a stream of benefits over time and because it entails current costs. Viewed in this way, the probability of migrating is positively related to the present value of the investment, which is equal to the discounted sum of net benefits. Thus, the decision to migrate is similar to other investment decisions and depends on the rate of return to the investment.

An NIT influences the decision to migrate, according to the above human capital model, because it affects the costs and benefits of an investment in migration. An NIT program is characterized by a guarantee level, which is the grant that a family receives if it has no other income, and a tax rate, which is the rate at which the grant declines as other income increases. (See Chapter 1 for a more detailed discussion of the overall experimental design.)

An NIT program has several effects on the benefits and costs and hence on the rate of return to an investment in migration. First, assuming hours of work or labor supply is fixed, the tax rate of an NIT reduces the rate of return if the monetary costs of migration are not deductible from income (which they are not in SIME/DIME). This is because the tax rate reduces the income differential and hence the gain from migration, but does not correspondingly reduce the costs of migration unless they are deductible from income. If the monetary costs are deductible, then the tax rate of an NIT program reduces gains and costs proportionately and does not affect the rate of return to migration. Thus, the tax effect (without deductibility of costs) would tend to reduce the rate of migration and the responsiveness of people to move for monetary incentives, and this would imply that depressed regions would become even more permanent.[1] The guarantee level of the NIT, assuming fixed labor supply and a perfect capital market,

---

[1] This effect is one strong argument for allowing job-related moving costs to be deductible from income in any nationwide NIT program.

would not affect migration. However, it is likely that low-income persons especially, would have difficulty borrowing the funds to finance a move and thus the income-increasing aspects of the NIT should facilitate self-financing of migration. This effect would tend to offset the negative tax effect.

The assumption that the NIT does not affect hours of work is, of course, unrealistic (see, e.g., Keeley *et al.*, 1978a,b). Both the guarantee and tax components of an NIT reduce desired hours of work and this would reduce the profitability and hence the rate of migration. For example, if desired hours of work are zero over the range of feasible wage rates likely to be obtained by migrating, there is no point to moving for purely financial reasons.

One final aspect of the NIT that may easily be incorporated into the human-capital investment framework is its effect on risk. Both the guarantee and tax components of an NIT reduce the variability of disposable income. This effect on reducing the risk of migration should increase migration if low-income people are, on average, risk averse. Thus, the human capital model indicates two negative influences: the tax effect and the reduced labor supply effect. The model also shows two positive influences: the reduced risk and increased availability of financing effects. Consequently, the net effect of an NIT on the rate of migration according to this model is indeterminant. However, given that the rate of return to investing in migration is positive, the destination choice should not be affected by the NIT.

An alternative, but not mutually exclusively way of viewing migration is to emphasize the nonpecuniary characteristics of different regions. In particular, one reason people move is to improve the quality of their environment. Generally, there is a negative trade off between the real wage level and the environment of a region. That is, locations with more desirable environments have lower real wage rates. This is because a region with a superior environment and equal or better wage rates would continue to attract new population until either wages fell or congestion reduced the quality of the environment. Thus, migration is one important way individuals can substitute nonmonetary consumption (the environment) for income or market consumption.

An NIT increases the desirability of environmental consumption relative to market consumption because the high tax rate of the NIT reduces the return from market work but does not tax consumption of the environment. Thus, in much the same way as high tax rates encourage people to select jobs with lower wage rates and greater nontaxable fringe benefits, it also encourages people to move to more desirable locations with better climates, physical attractiveness, parks and other recreational facilities, for example. Not only does the tax effect of an NIT increase the demand for the environment, but the income effect of an NIT would also tend to lead to an increase in consumption of the environment. Consequently, based on this model it is ecpected that an NIT would lead to an increase in the rate of migration, since migrating is one way of improving one's environment. It should be noted that in a permanent NIT program, for each individual, this effect would be a once-and-for-all effect and would not lead to a permanently higher rate of migration for a given individual.[2] Thus, this model of migration predicts that an NIT would lead to a redistribution of the population to regions with better environments and lower wages. A resolution of the different implications of this model and the human capital model is, however, a task left to the empirical analysis in the next section.

A final theoretical issue concerns whether or not there should be regional cost-of-living differentials in a national NIT program. From the point of view of strict equity, economics has little to say except that with existing technology and information it would be nearly impossible to construct a meaningful regional cost-of-living index. (See Peskin, 1977, for a detailed discussion of this problem.) However, from an efficiency point of view, economic considerations indicate that resources would be wasted unless a uniform nationwide payment system were adopted.[3]

Currently, there are large interregional differences in welfare eligibility rules and benefit levels that induce noneconomic migration. That is, even though individuals who move increase their personal welfare, the welfare of society is reduced since the resources invested in migration serve no beneficial economic function. In fact, they tend to reduce total national real income since persons are induced to consume in areas in which consumption is more expensive and less efficient (assuming that high benefits are paid in high cost-of-living areas). Thus, the imposition of a uniform nationwide NIT program would eliminate this perverse incentive to migrate and would lead to a spatial distribution of the population in which each person's real income could be made larger. A uniform nationwide NIT program would provide incentives for people to move to lower cost-of-living areas. Such migration serves a beneficial economic function since the sum of each individual's increase in welfare is equal to the societal increase in welfare. Thus, unlike the current system, an increase in one individual's welfare would not result in the decrease in someone else's welfare. Such a policy might lead to a redistribution of the low-income population and it is to this question that we now turn in the analysis of the SIME/DIME data on migration.

EMPIRICAL ANALYSIS

SIME/DIME tested 11 different NIT programs. As mentioned in Chapter 1, guarantee levels of $3800, $4800, and $5600, normalized for a family of four

[2] The aggregate rate of migration, however, would increase since new individuals would be continually entering a permanent NIT program. In addition, changes in the environment or changes in individual characteristics over time might lead to a permanent effect on the rate of migration.

[3] This is because the cost of making a given payment is independent of the cost-of-living in a particular region.

persons at 1970-1971 prices, were combined with four different tax systems: two with constant tax rates of 50% and 70% of earned income, and two with tax rates that declined as income increased. Part of the sample were enrolled for 3 years, part for 5, and a small subset (not included here) for 20 years. In this section, the effects of these treatments on rates of migration and destination are investigated.

From an operational point of view, a person was considered to have moved out of the area if he or she moved out of the greater Seattle or Denver metropolitan area and remained out of the area long enough to miss a periodic interview.[4] Detailed accurate records of the dates when persons moved were kept in hard copy files in both Seattle and Denver, although information on dates of moves only entered the interviewing system if a postmove interview and a postmove module were completed. An important advantage of this procedure is that information on an individual's moving data is known even if he or she dropped out of the experiment after moving out of the area and before receiving a postmove interview. Thus, attrition that is associated with moving does not lead to a loss of information regarding the date of a move. Of course, destination data are not known unless a postmove interview was actually completed.

Although some previous nonexperimental analysis suggests that the family is the appropriate decision-making unit, the analysis presented in this chapter concerns the response of individuals. The primary reason for this is that there was considerable family change due to divorce, marriage, and remarriage during the time period studied. If the family was used as the unit of analysis, then response would have to be measured conditional upon the family remaining intact. Since there is considerable evidence that SIME/DIME affected family stability (see Chapter 9), such a conditional analysis might lead to seriously biased estimates of the total effects on geographical mobility if mobility were related to family status. Thus, all analysis is carried out on individuals classified by their original marital status regardless of subsequent marital status. This method also leads to larger samples than would be obtained if the analysis were restricted to an intact sample.

The sample used for the rate of mobility analysis consists of all originally enrolled family heads. The sample for the destination analysis consists of 181 married males, 201 married females, and 121 single females. Data for Chicanos were not available at the time the analysis of the impact on the rate of mobility was conducted. They are, however, included in the analysis of destination choice.

---

[4] In Seattle, moving is defined as moving out of the four-county area that includes King, Pierce, Snohomish, and Kitsap counties. In Denver, moving out of the area is similarly defined. The Denver metropolitan area includes the cities of Arvada, Aurora, Broomfield, Brighton, Boulder, Denver, Englewood, Evergreen, Golden, Lafayette, Louisville, Lettleton, Longmont, Thorton, and Westminister.

Experimental Control Differences in the Rate of Mobility

Experimental control[5] differences in the rate of mobility are estimated with a maximum-likelihood statistical technique developed by Tuma (1976) that uses data on duration until either a move occurs or until information is no longer available. Data from the first 9 experimental quarters (after enrollment) are used. Background and assignment variables are included in the estimating equation to increase the precision of treatment estimates and to control for the stratified random assignment of treatment. There is also control for the manpower treatments. The estimates of NIT treatment impacts are presented in Table 13.1, although estimates of the background and assignment variables are not presented.

On the average, white married males and females (both experimentals and controls) moved out of the area at a rate of approximately 7% per year. The 5-year NIT treatments increased the rate of mobility by 49% for white married males and 45% for white married females. These effects are statistically significant at the .10 level. For married black males and females, the average rate of mobility was only about 2.5% per year and the NIT treatment had no statistically significant effect. There were no statistically significant experimental-control differences in rates of moving for any married subgroup in the 3-year sample. Finally, there were no statistically significant effects of interactions between site and NIT treatments on the rate of mobility for any subgroups.[6] This is one indication that the effect of the experiments did not depend on the unemployment rate because the unemployment rate was much higher in Seattle than Denver. No statistically significant effects were found for single females.

An alternative way to measure the impact of the NIT treatments on the rate of migration is to parameterize the treatment. Basically, for persons below the breakeven level, an NIT changes disposable income and the net wage. For our purposes, the NIT treatments are parameterized in terms of three variables; (a) whether or not someone was above the breakeven level (FABOVE), and (b) if the person was below, the percentage change in disposable income ($\Delta Y/Y$), and (c) the percentage change in the net wage ($\Delta t/(1-t_p)$). The coefficient estimates are presented in Table 13.2. In addition, a dummy variable denoting enrollment in the 3-year sample (Y3) is included.

The results for white married males indicate statistically significant effects of income and tax changes on the rate of mobility. A one percentage point decrease in $\Delta t/(1-t_p)$ led to a 94% decrease in the rate of mobility. A 1% increase in disposable income led to a .52% decrease in the rate of mobility. Similar results were found for white married females although the coefficients are smaller and the standard errors are larger. No significant effects for the other subgroups were

---

[5] In the remainder of this chapter, the term experimental refers to persons receiving an NIT treatment.

[6] Statistical tests for the presence of site interactions are performed by interacting a site dummy variable with F and Y3.

Table 13.1

Experimental-Control Differences in the Rate of Geographical Mobility
(Maximum Likelihood Estimated from the Rate Model)

	$\bar{R}$	5-year NIT treatment effect		Differential effect for 3-year treatment		χ^2 for site differences of treatment effects
		Coefficient	Ratio	Coefficient	Ratio	
White married males	.072	.4023* (.2085)	1.495*	-.1180 (.2048)	.889	.22
White married females	.069	.3714* (.2150)	1.450*	-.1008 (.2105)	.904	.020
Black married males	.027	-.2013 (.448)	.817	.4529 (.4575)	1.573	1.78
Black married females	.023	-.08704 (.4616)	.916	.2352 (.4700)	1.26	.48
White unmarried females	.037	-.6642 (.5134)	.51	1.156** (.4911)	3.177	1.81
Black unmarried females	.034	-.1579 (.3995)	.85	.1479 (.4003)	1.15	3.77

Note: $\bar{R}$ is the average rate per year of moving out of the area of both experimentals and controls. The ratio is equal to the exponential of the coefficient and gives the percentage effect of the NIT treatment on the rate of mobility. For example, a ratio of 1.495 indicates that experimentals in the 5-year sample moved out of the area at a rate of 1.495 times greater than controls.

Note: The following probability levels apply to all tables in this chapter.

*$p < .10$.
**$p < .05$.
***$p < .01$.

Table 13.2
Estimated Coefficients of Parameterized Treatment Model

	$\bar{R}$	Y3	FABOVE	$\dfrac{\Delta Y}{Y}$	$\dfrac{\Delta t}{1-t_p}$	χ^2 for treatment effects	F-tests for site differences in response[a]
Married	.072	−.0071	.38	−.52*	.94***	8.36*	2.086
white		(.019)	(.31)	(.31)	(.38)		
males		.99	1.47				
Married	.069	.028	−.066	−.21	.75*	4.79	2.053
white		(.19)	(.36)	(.31)	(.40)		
females		1.03	.94				
Married	.027	.49	−.210	−.52	−.048	3.41	.610
black		(.41)	(.62)	(.40)	(.079)		
males		1.63	.81				
Married	.023	.31	.067	−.87	.11	3.29	1.125
black		(.43)	(.63)	(.58)	(.85)		
females		1.37	1.07				
Single	.077	1.07***	−.70	.041	−1.09	2.42	.086
white		(.40)	(.75)	(.13)	(.75)		
females		2.93	.49				
Single	.070	.17	−.49	−.33	−.019	1.43	1.94
black		(.35)	(1.05)	(.66)	(.18)		
females		1.19	.61				

Note: For each group, i.e., single or married, the numbers are in the following order.

$$\text{coefficient}$$
$$(\text{standard error})$$
$$\dfrac{\text{coefficient}}{e} = \text{ratio}$$

[a]Tests of site-treatment interactions are based on ordinary least squares estimates of a model with a dichotomous dependent variable with 1 indicating a move during the first 9 quarters. The tests are performed by interacting each of the experimental variables with site dummies. The control variables are constrained to be the same in the tests.

detected. In this model, also, there was no indication of differential response depending on site.

The finding that higher tax rates led to increased migration is supportive of the notion that people moved in response to the NIT for environmental reasons. This is because the wage-differential model predicts that higher tax rates would make pople less likely to move, a prediction opposite to that of the environmental model. The negative income effect, however, is not consistent with either model.

Effects of Negative Income Tax on Destination Choices

In this section the effects of the NIT on the destination choices of migrants are empirically analyzed. All the analyses presented are on samples of persons who migrated out of either Seattle or Denver during the first 9 quarters of the experiment. Consequently, all estimates must be interpreted as conditional upon migration.

The migrant must have completed a postmove interview in order to be included in the sample, since no destination information is known about migrants who did not complete postmove interviews. Approximately 70% of all migrants completed at least one postmove interview. Based on information in the postmove interview regarding destination, information on the characteristics of the city to which the migrant actually moved is obtained from the U. S. Bureau of the Census (1973).

Male heads moved from Seattle and Denver to all nine census regions of the country, which are depicted in Figure 13.1. In Table 13.3, the distributions of destination by region of male heads and single female heads by treatment status and site are presented. As might be expected, most people from Seattle moved to the Pacific region and most people from Denver moved to the Mountain region. In Seattle, experimentals and controls (both male and single female heads) had a similar overall distribution of destination and a χ^2 test for statistical differences indicates no significant effect of the NIT treatments on the overall distribution of destination. In Denver, however, a similar test indicates an effect of the treatments on region of destination for both male heads and single female heads. In particular, experimentals were more inclined to move to the Pacific region and controls to the West North Central region.

These apparent differences in destination might be due, however, to the nonrandom assignment of treatment. In order to control for the assignment and more precisely measure the experimental effects on destination choice, the following model is estimated:

$$R_i = XB + FC + F \cdot SEA \cdot D + e,$$

where

$$R_i = \begin{cases} 1 & \text{if the person moved to region } i, \\ 0 & \text{otherwise,} \end{cases}$$

X = vector of background and assignment variables,

$$F = \begin{cases} 1 & \text{if the person is an experimental,} \\ 0 & \text{otherwise,} \end{cases}$$

$$SEA = \begin{cases} 1 & \text{if the person was originally in Seattle,} \\ 0 & \text{otherwise,} \end{cases}$$

e = a random error term

$B, C, D,$ = parameters to be estimated.

This model is estimated with ordinary least squares for reasons of convenience and cost. The model is estimated for each region. The control variables (X), which consist of both preexperimental economic and demographic variables and variables used to determine assignment to experimental treatment, are included

Table 13.3
Destination of First Move: Distribution by Treatment Status and Site

Region	Married males				Single females			
	Seattle		Denver		Seattle		Denver	
	Control	Experimental	Control	Experimental	Control	Experimental	Control	Experimental
New England	0 (0)	3.8 (3)	0 (0)	0 (0)	6.7 (1)	0 (0)	0 (0)	0 (0)
Middle Atlantic	3.7 (2)	2.5 (2)	2.2 (1)	0 (0)	0 (0)	0 (0)	0 (0)	0 (0)
South Atlantic	1.9 (1)	2.5 (2)	2.2 (1)	6.7 (6)	0 (0)	2.9 (1)	8.3 (2)	8.3 (4)
East North Central	1.9 (1)	6.3 (5)	2.2 (1)	3.4 (3)	6.7 (1)	5.9 (2)	8.3 (2)	10.4 (5)
East South Central	1.9 (1)	1.3 (1)	0 (0)	1.1 (1)	0 (0)	0 (0)	4.2 (1)	0 (0)
West North Central	5.6 (3)	6.3 (5)	13.0 (6)	9.0 (8)	6.7 (1)	5.9 (2)	4.2 (1)	22.9 (11)
West South Central	9.3 (5)	10 (8)	30.4 (14)	11.2 (10)	0 (0)	17.6 (6)	33.3 (8)	12.5 (6)
Mountain	16.7 (9)	10.0 (8)	39.1 (18)	43.8 (39)	26.7 (4)	14.7 (5)	8.3 (2)	20.8 (10)
Pacific	59.3 (32)	57.5 (46)	10.9 (5)	24.7 (22)	53.3 (8)	52.9 (18)	33.3 (8)	25.6 (16.7)
Total	100 (54)	100 (80)	100 (46)	100 (89)	100 (15)	100 (34)	100 (24)	100 (48)
χ^2 tests of overall relationships between treatment and region	4.9		13.65*		6.187		10.918*	

Note: The numbers in this table are the percentages of the total number of persons in the category who moved to the designated region. Numbers in parentheses are actual numbers of persons in the cell.

250

Figure 13.1   The U.S. census regions.

to increase the efficiency of the estimates of experimental treatment and to control for the nonrandom assignment of treatment.[7]

In Table 13.4, coefficient estimates of the treatment coefficients are presented. In Denver, married male experimentals are much less likely to move to the West South Central region than controls. In Seattle, however, married male experimentals are somewhat more likely to move to the New England region. For single female heads in Denver, experimentals are less likely to move to the East South Central region, and more likely to move to the West North Central region. In Seattle, there are no apparent effects of financial status on destination region for single female heads.

In Table 13.5 coefficient estimates for married males of the effect of NIT treatment on climate at the destination are presented. Results are presented separately for the subsample of white married males and for the total sample of all married males. These are experimental-control differences after correct-

---

[7] The control variables actually used are:

E-level: dummy variables representing normal income, which is an assignment variable,

Income: annual income prior to enrollment,

Seattle-Denver dummy variable: used when the two sites are pooled,

M-level: manpower treatment dummy variables,

Employment status: a dummy variable that equals 1 if the person is working preexperimentally,

Number of family members: number of family members at enrollment,

Age and education.

Table 13.4
Effects of Treatment on Destination Choice

Dependent variable for region	Treatment coefficients for married males			Coefficient of financial treatment for single females		
	Mean	F	F SEA	Mean	F	F SEA
New England	.0113	−.0020	.047*	.0084	−.017	−.045
		(.020)	(.027)		(.027)	(.041)
Middle Atlantic	.0188	−.012	−.0065	−	−	−
		(.026)	(.035)	−	−	−
South Atlantic	.0376	.047	−.043	.0588	.0079	.052
		(.036)	(.048)		(.072)	(.11)
East North Central	.0376	.033	.015	.0840	.097	−.092
		(.037)	(.050)		(.081)	(.12)
East South Central	.0113	.019	−.021	.0084	−.066**	−.076*
		(.020)	(.028)		(.026)	(.040)
West North Central	.0827	−.040	.042	.1261	.19**	−.15
		(.053)	(.072)		(.096)	(.14)
West South Central	.1391	−.18**	.18**	.1681	−.17	.27*
		(.065)	(.089)		(.10)	(.16)
Mountain	.2669	.018	−.058	.1681	.11	−.25
		(.078)	(.11)		(.11)	(.16)
Pacific	.3872	.14	−.19	.3782	−.15	.14
		(.086)	(.12)		(.14)	(.21)

Note: Standard errors in parentheses.

ing for assignment and background variables. As is discussed in the previous section, the environmental model (consumption model) of migration predicts that persons receiving the NIT treatments will be more likely to move to better climates. The results in Table 13.5 for white married males and for all married males support this notion. Persons receiving the NIT treatments moved to regions with higher January temperatures, and smaller temperature variations. In addition, experimentals were more likely than controls to indicate that climate was an important reason for their move.

In Table 13.6, similar coefficient estimates are presented for single females. Because of the small sample size, no attempt is made to present separate results for the different racial-ethnic groups. None of the coefficients is significant.

In Table 13.7, estimates of experimental effects on married males are presented for a set of job-related variables at destination. All job variables are derived from questions relating to the person's job expectations prior to the move, not his actual job experience. (The investigation of actual job-related behavior is presented in the next section.) The only variables affected by the experiment were distance moved (for white married males) and the costs of moving (for both subgroups). For both variables, the experimental treatment had a positive effect. This may be indicative of the financing or income effect of the NIT treat-

Table 13.5
Treatment Effects on Climate at Destination for Married Males

	White married males			All married males		
Dependent variable	Mean	Coefficient of financial treatment	F-test for Seattle-Denver differences in response	Mean	Coefficient of financial treatment	F-test for Seattle-Denver differences in response
January mean temperature	36.0°	3.087* (1.70)	.169	36.6°	1.60 (1.47)	.408
Precipitation (inches)	25.7	2.42 (2.068)	3.84* (S=5.60, D=−2.62)	25.1	2.38 (1.79)	2.45 (S=4.97, D=−.57)
How important was climate? 1 = important 0 = unimportant	.46	.083 (.078)	2.74* (S=−.021, D=.24)	.47	.12* (.067)	1.92
July mean temperature	72.8°	−.33 (1.025)	.134	73.7°	−.63 (.89)	1.4
Variance in January and July temperatures (Jan. temperature–July temperature)^2	1509.3	−249.79* (131.90)	.261	1523.0	−186.76* (111.29)	.061
Variance in high and low temperatures (high temperature–low temperature)^2	14619.4	−1514.9** (697.0)	.5	14579.7	−1076.0 (606.35)	.102

Note: The coefficient estimates in this table give experimental-control differences in the dependent variable after eliminating differences caused by the assignment variables. For example, the coefficient of financial treatment indicates that white married male experimentals moved to regions with 3.087° warmer January temperatures. In parentheses under some of the F-tests for Seattle-Denver differences in response, the effects of Seattle (S=) and Denver (D=) are presented separately.

253

Table 13.6
Treatment Effects on Climate at Destination for Female Heads

Dependent variable	Mean	Coefficients of financial treatment	F-test for Seattle-Denver differences in response
January mean temperature	38.33°	−1.43 (2.50)	1.74
Precipitation (inches)	25.96	−4.44 (3.25)	.23
How important was climate? 1=important 0=unimportant	.47	−.029 (.11)	.037
July mean temperature	75.08°	1.74 (1.50)	.65
Variance in January and July temperatures (Jan. temperature—July temperature)²	1502.91	264.12 (201.00)	2.18 (D=532.12, S=−67.6)
Variance in high and low temperatures (high temperature—low temperature)²	14021.73	931.78 (1079.79)	.51

Note: For Tables 13.6-13.13, standard errors are in parentheses under coefficient estimates.

Table 13.7
Treatment Effects on Job-Related Variables at Destination for Married Males

Dependent variable	White married males			All married males		
	Mean	Coefficient of financial treatment	F-test for Seattle-Denver differences in response	Mean	Coefficient of financial treatment	F-test for Seattle-Denver differences in response
Distance moved (miles)	849.6	238.3* (121.63)	.059	831.1	149.1 (99.76)	.29
Costs of moving (dollars)	364.1	168.9** (71.80)	.093	309.8	116.9** (54.78)	.021
Did person intend to work? 1 = yes, 0 = no	.87	.0131 (.052)	.017	.86	-.02 (.045)	.12
Did person have job lined up? 1 = yes, 0 = no	.31	.00005 (.074)	1.606 (S= .075, D= -.11)	.42	-.012 (.061)	1.69
Hours of work per week expected	37.8	3.45 (2.94)	.33	36.8	1.16 (2.45)	.33
Earnings per week	149.3	24.12 (15.22)	.06	146.	18.0 (12.47)	.00

Table 13.8
Treatment Effects on Job-Related Variables at Destination for
Single Female Heads

Dependent variable	Mean	Coefficients of financial treatment	F-test for Seattle-Denver differences in response
Distance moved (miles)	960.63	113.96 (149.54)	1.29
Costs of moving (dollars)	250.65	−2.30 (59.04)	.002
Did person intend to work? 1 = yes, 0 = no	.61	−.14 (.10)	.042
Did person have job lined up? 1 = yes, 0 = no	.10	−.021 (.069)	.074
Hours of work per week expected	23.82	−6.24 (5.51)	.032
Earnings per week	67.89	−17.39 (12.82)	.295

ment that enabled persons to move further in order to find a more desirable location.

In Table 13.8, similar estimates are presented for single females, none of which is statistically significant. In Table 13.9, the estimated effects of experimental treatment for married males on the economic characteristics of the destination city are presented. Although there is some suggestion that the treatment induced persons to move to higher income cities, the only statistically significant effect was on per capita income for white married males. In Table 13.10, similar coefficient estimates are presented for single females, none of which, again, is statistically significant.

To summarize, for married males some evidence is found that the financial treatments affected the region to which persons migrated. In addition, the NIT treatments induced married males to move to regions with better climates than they would have chosen otherwise. The treatment also caused males to move further and spend more on moving. No statistically significant differences in intentions to work were found between males receiving the NIT treatment and their control counterparts.

Although single females in Denver had their geographical region of destination influenced by financial treatment, no statistically significant effects were found on the specific variables that measure the characteristics of the destinations actually chosen. This may in large part be due to the very small sample (21 observations of all races) of single females.

Table 13.9
Treatment Effects on Economic Characteristics of the Destination City for Married Males

	White married males			All married males		
	Mean	Coefficient of financial treatment	F-test for Seattle-Denver differences in response	Mean	Coefficient of financial treatment	F-test for Seattle-Denver differences in response
Median income	$9549.2	213.1 (190.3)	.17	$9464.2	205.02 (173.34)	.012
Per capita income	$3186.8	112.3* (67.75)	.23	$3146.5	79.9 (61.36)	.058
Percent of families below poverty level	9.54%	−.13 (.57)	.26	10.03%	−.32 (.57)	.19
Per capita city government expenditures	$117.9	12.65 (11.5)	1.16	$117.6	14.88 (12.10)	.034

257

Table 13.10
Treatment Effects on Economic Characteristics of the
Destination City for Single Females

Dependent variable	Mean	Coefficients of financial treatment	F-test for Seattle-Denver differences in response
Median income	$9665.42	−190.70 (264.71)	.39
Per capita income	$3267.06	−128.09 (103.79)	.27
Percent of families below poverty level	9.92%	.57 (.74)	2.15
Per capita city government expenditures	$ 127.33	−26.47 (18.46)	.54

Table 13.11
Treatment Effects on Male Labor Supply Variables

Dependent variable	Black	White	Chicano	Pooled
Sample size	27	132	22	181
Total days worked				
Mean	160.3333	262.3864	266.6970	247.6869
Coefficient of financial treatment	−206.5373*** (20.9421)	−68.1882*** (20.6064)	−45.8146 (79.2552)	−74.3244** (17.4436)
F-test for Seattle-Denver differences in response	.238	.014	−	1.457
Total hours worked				
Mean	987.1117	1652.3635	1605.8252	1547.4705
Coefficient of financial treatment	−1205.689*** (282.2126)	−475.8501*** (161.0620)	−538.1918 (458.0035)	−514.7988** (133.4178)
F-test for Seattle-Denver differences in response	.762	.009	−	.778
Days involuntarily unemployed				
Mean	139.4444	58.7929	68.6212	72.0184
Coefficient of financial treatment	103.5607 (84.8388)	26.2313 (18.6894)	−25.1348 (71.9003)	26.9887 (17.1321)
F-test for Seattle-Denver differences in response	1.078	.014	−	.757
Total earnings				
Mean	3216.0043	5317.4154	5604.4784	5038.8368
Coefficient treatment	−4341.679*** (1430.1228)	−1981.454*** (596.0929)	−496.8891 (1934.2457)	−2014.004** (505.5068)
F-test	1.975	.552	−	.713
Liquid assets				
Mean	374.6284	1766.4067	279.5465	1378.0700
Coefficient treatment	−358.1775 (710.2763)	−492.7192 (678.4440)	341.6161 (321.1753)	−430.5644 (506.1583)
F-test	2.064	1.740	−	2.188

Effects of Negative Income Tax on Labor Market Behavior and Experience

In this section, the data on the labor market experience and behavior of SIME/DIME migrants are analyzed. Data pertaining to the year subsequent to migration for all persons who move during the first 9 quarters of the experiment are used, including married males, married females, and single female heads. Persons who move out of the area and then return to the sites within one year are excluded from the sample.

The effects of the NIT treatments on the labor market experiences of migrants are important in order to assess the impact for the treatments on the rate of return to migration. For example, if the main effect of the treatments were to facilitate the self-financing of migration, then we would expect the earnings of financials who move to be lower than controls since a smaller earnings differential would be necessary in order to make the move profitable. If the labor supply effects of the NIT were also important, and if the NIT induced persons to seek low-wage, high-environment areas, we would still expect earnings to fall. However, in the latter case, hours should also fall, whereas, in the former, they should either increase or be unaffected.

In Table 13.11, experimental treatment coefficients for married males are presented for each of the three racial-ethnic groups separately and for the pooled sample. There were large, statistically significant negative effects on total annual hours worked and days worked for all samples except Chicanos. In addition, there was a significant negative effect on earnings for all samples except Chicanos. Since there was a larger treatment effect on earnings than on hours (for the pooled sample), experimentals who moved must have received lower wages than controls. There were no significant effects on unemployment or liquid assets.

These results are broadly consistent with the consumption model of migration that suggests the treatments would lead persons to move to lower wage areas (with better environments) and also induce them to work less. In Table 13.12, similar results are presented for married females. There were no significant treatment effects on any variable except unemployment. The results indicate that married women in the experimental group who moved had lower unemployment than similar controls. However, since many woman are "tied" movers (i.e., they move with their husbands), there is less reason to expect a treatment effect.

In Table 13.13, similar results are presented for single female heads of households. The NIT treatments had a negative impact on all variables except days unemployed. All racial-ethnic groups are pooled because of small sample sizes. As is true for married males, the treatments had a larger proportional effect on earnings than hours, suggesting that single female experimentals who moved obtained lower wage jobs than similar controls.

To summarize, the results for both married males and single female heads are

Table 13.12
Treatment Effects on Married Female Labor-Supply Variables

Dependent variable	Black	White	Chicano	Pooled
Sample size	33	140	28	201
Total days worked				
Mean	131.7879	88.1786	49.8690	90.0017
Coefficient of financial	−8.1518	−35.9993*	−41.3648	−23.1695
treatment	(53.0201)	(21.7705)	(59.8496)	(18.5097)
F-test for Seattle-Denver				
differences in response	1.644	.017	−	.042
Total hours worked				
Mean	780.1968	441.7547	272.2219	473.7033
Coefficient of financial	111.3044	−155.5605	−266.0526	−97.5396
treatment	(356.9924)	(117.7355)	(335.0235)	(103.7686)
F-test for Seattle-Denver				
differences in response	1.309	.001	−	0.000
Days involuntarily unemployed				
Mean	75.3939	38.6571	10.9643	40.8308
Coefficient of financial	−1.1204	−35.4227**	−11.8703	−24.7975*
treatment	(60.0139)	(15.3773)	(18.4830)	(13.5120)
F-test for Seattle-Denver				
differences in response	.957	.209	−	2.114
Total earnings				
Mean	1572.5533	935.4183	542.1405	985.2376
Coefficient	−148.1193	−178.2263	−762.7645	−169.7023
treatment	(712.0741)	(280.5064)	(648.0764)	(239.4018)
F-test	1.331	.177	−	.539
Liquid assets				
Mean	432.3378	1762.1292	381.4274	1351.4687
Coefficient	−67.7658	−106.9547	540.8007	−146.0621
treatment	(549.0532)	(787.3439)	(442.3369)	(563.9246)
F-test	.080	.067	−	.220

consistent with the consumption theory of migration. That is, the experiments induced persons to move to locations with lower wages and also to reduce hours of work. One additional important implication of these findings is that since financial treatment causes migrants to have very large reductions in labor supply, results from the other NIT experiments that exclude migrants may seriously underestimate the labor supply response to an actual program.

CONCLUSIONS

Several important conclusions emerge from the analysis. First, SIME/DIME positively affected the rate of migration for married white families. No statistically significant differences in effects were found by site, which is supporting

Table 13.13
Treatment Effects on Labor Supply Variables for Single Female Heads
of All Races

Dependent variable	Mean	Coefficient of financial treatment	F-test for Seattle-Denver differences in response
Total days worked per year	83.93	−82.61** (34.89)	5.022** (S= 1.59, D= −144.09)
Total hours worked per year	426.75	−452.39** (199.45)	4.286** (S= −5.65, D= −778.61)
Days involuntarily unemployed	81.99	30.36 (32.97)	1.195
Total earnings per year	$1218.83	−1355.045** (675.69)	4.168** (S= 138.73, D= 2445.8)
Liquid assets	1204.17	−1931.83 (1019.40)	.38

Note: In parentheses under the *F*-statistics are separate effects for Seattle (S=) and Denver (D=).

evidence that the rate of unemployment per se would not affect the migration response to an NIT.

Second, the region of destination was influenced by the NIT treatments for both married males and single females. Most effects occurred for persons originally living in Denver.

Third, there is evidence that married experimentals moved to locations with somewhat better climates and that they moved further and spent more on their moves than controls. No significant effects on the characteristics of destinations are found for single female heads.

Fourth, there is evidence that the NIT treatments led to less labor force attachment and lower earnings among both married males and single female heads who moved. Also, both married males and single female heads who were eligible to receive the NIT treatment appeared to be receiving lower wage rates than controls. There are no significant effects for married females except that the unemployment of experimentals was less than controls.

In conclusion, the above results are broadly consistent with a consumption model of migration. This model suggests that an NIT would induce people to move to locations with better environments and would induce persons to reduce their hours of work. Thus, one likely impact of a nationwide NIT program would be a redistribution of the low-income population to regions with better environments and lower wage rates.

REFERENCES

DeVanzo, J. "An Analytical Framework for Studying the Potential Effects of an Income Maintenance Program on U. S. Interregional Migration." The Rand Corporation (December 1972).

Greenwood, M. J. "Research in Internal Migration in the U.S.: A Survey." *Journal of Economic Literature* 13, no. 2 (June 1975a).

Greenwood, M. J. "Simultaneity Bias in Migration Models: An Empirical Examination." *Demography* 12, no. 3 (August 1975b).

Greenwood, M. J. "A Simultaneous-Equations Model of White and Non-White Migration and Urban Change." *Economic Inquiry* 14, no. 1 (March 1976).

Keeley, M. C., Robins, P. K.; Spiegelman, R. G.; and West, R. W. "The Labor Supply Effects and Costs of Alternative Negative Income Tax Programs." *Journal of Human Resources* 13, no. 1 (Winter 1978a).

Keeley, M. C.; Robins, P. K.; Spiegelman, R. G.; and West, R. W. "The Estimation of Labor Supply Models Using Experimental Data." *American Economic Review* 68, no. 5 (December 1978b).

Peskin, J. "Geographic Payment Variation In a Federal Welfare System." Technical Analysis Paper No. 14. U. S. Dept. of Health, Education and Welfare, Office of Income Security Policy, January 1977.

Schwartz, A. "Interpreting the Effects of Distance in Migration." *Journal of Political Economy* 81, no. 5 (September/October 1973).

Schwartz, A. "Migration, Age, and Education." *Journal of Political Economy* 84, no. 4, Part 1 (August 1976).

Sjaastad, L. A. "The Costs and Returns of Human Migration." *Journal of Political Economy*, Supplement (October 1962).

Tuma, N. B. "Rewards, Resources, and the Rate of Mobility: A Nonstationary Multivariate Stochastic Model." *American Sociology Review*, 41 (1976) pp. 338-360.

U.S. Bureau of the Census. *County and City Data Book, 1972*, 1973.

CHAPTER 14

Education and Training

ARDEN R. HALL

INTRODUCTION

The SIME/DIME experiments are the only ones among the federally funded income-maintenance experiments to include a manpower component. The rationale for the inclusion of such a component, as discussed in Chapter 1, was the desire to determine how much the expected decline in work response due to the NIT transfers could be offset by providing information about the labor market and by subsidizing the cost of training and education. The general presumption was that raising wage rates through training and lowering job search costs would induce greater individual work effort.

The functions that the manpower component were to perform derived from three hypotheses:

1. Many individuals have deficiencies in their knowledge of the labor market, and in their understanding of their own capacities in relation to the labor market.
2. Lack of information results in these individuals making less than optimal decisions with regard to their own work plans.
3. Subsidization is necessary to achieve the socially optimal investment in education and training among low-income individuals.

To test the validity of these hypotheses, three different manpower treatments were developed. One of the three treatments or control status was assigned to each family in the experiment.

All three of the manpower treatments included unlimited free use of a counseling center for all members of the eligible family who were at least 16 years of age. The counseling centers were operated by community colleges in Seattle and Denver and staffed by experienced professional counselors. The centers provided

263

vocational counseling, although this was interpreted to mean providing information about educational opportunities as well as information about the labor market. The underlying philosophy of the centers was to provide information as requested, without directing the client into a particular course of action.

Counselors had considerable resources at their disposal to find answers to client's questions. If the client were interested in a particular occupation, the counselor could request that a report on that occupation be prepared by a labor-market information specialist attached to the counseling center. Counselors could also provide information about training courses and about financial support for which the client might be eligible.

Counselors attempted to follow a consistent pattern in their interactions with clients. Consistency was facilitated by establishment of guiding outline of the counseling process and by frequent consultations among counselors in the centers. After initial contact, counselors attempted to guide their interaction with the client through three steps: (a) self-assessment by the clinet, (b) provision of information by the counselor, and (c) formulation of a plan of action.

The format for accomplishing these steps was generally a series of five group-counseling sessions, with additional individual counseling supplementing the process.

The plan of action was a formal statement of what the client had decided to do as a result of his course of counseling. In simplified terms, the plan of action contained one or more of the following elements: (a) training, (b) job search, and (c) job retention.

The plan of action spelled out in some detail what the client intended to do and how he intended to do it. The writing of the plan of action represented the culmination of the counseling process. After it was written, the counselor might provide some assistance to the client in implementing his plan, but would not usually provide intensive counseling. When the client accomplished the objective of his plan of action or decided to change it, the counseling process could begin again.

An incentive payment of $5 was made to the family for the completed contact interview. In addition, payments intended to cover inconvenience and transportation costs incurred in attending sessions were made at a rate of $5 per session, limited to a total of $25. These incentive payments were generally made for attendance at the five group or individual assessment sessions.

In addition to their role in providing labor market information, the counseling centers administered the subsidies provided with two of the manpower treatments. One of these treatments (M2) provided a 50% subsidy for all direct costs of schooling or training. Direct costs included such things as tuition, fees, required books and equipment, and childcare during the parents' school attendance. Direct cost did not include living stipends or payment for time taken off from work. The other subsidized treatment (M3) provided a 100% subsidy for direct costs of schooling or training. The M1 treatment provided only counseling.

Any course of schooling or training was eligible for subsidy if it represented preparation for an occupation or career. This limitation was interpreted rather liberally, so that subsidy was provided for everything from driving school to graduate business school. In general, participants in the subsidy program were allowed to choose the educational institution they would attend. However, some preference was given to attendance at local institutions and at public rather than private institutions. Thus, if a certain course of training were available at a local school but the program participant preferred to attend a school in another area, his expenses would only be subsidized up to the amount of expenses that would have been incurred at the local school. The same rule applied for attendance at a private rather than a public school. When a comparable course of training was not available at a local institution or at a public institution, then the full subsidy was provided for attendance at the other institution.

As already mentioned, the counseling centers were used to administer the manpower subsidies. All prospective recipients of subsidies were required to write a plan of action before they could receive subsidies. This requirement provided some administrative control over the subsidy program, and incidentally provided us a great deal of information about the intentions of those who responded to the subsidy program. The auditing of claims for subsidy payment and the disbursal of funds were also performed by the counseling centers.

UTILIZATION OF THE MANPOWER TREATMENTS

The manpower treatments were available to 6350 people enrolled in SIME/ DIME and they produced a variety of responses. An adequate description of those responses would require a separate chapter; therefore, the summary that follows is necessarily incomplete. To make a summary possible we have chosen to ignore some interesting aspects of the response to the program and to concentrate upon the things we consider of greatest importance. One specific decision we have made was to combine data from the two sites and not to describe differences in response between Seattle and Denver. Another decision was to concentrate upon the initial response to the program. The initial response represented the greatest part of the use of the program and provides a clear picture of the cause-effect relationship between the program and schooling and other outcomes. Also, because there were relatively few types of responses to the program, initial response is easy to describe quantitatively. When one includes the second or third response, the possible reactions becomes much more complex and hard to describe. Where it is appropriate, we will mention some dimensions of the total response to the program, but the discussion will center on the first response.

The response to the initial contact by those who were eligible for the manpower program is illustrated in Figure 14.1. The diagram illustrates the flow of people through the steps in the counseling and training process outlined in the

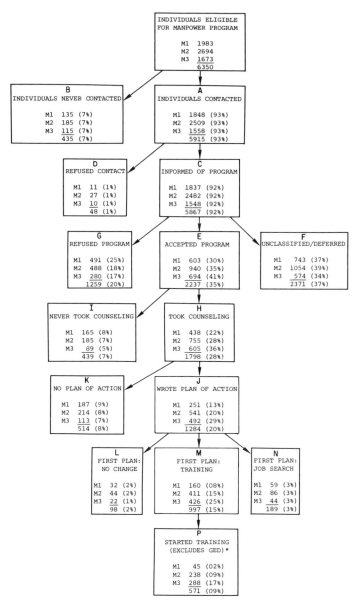

Figure 14.1   Response to initial contact with the manpower program.
*Data are not available for the 104 individuals who selected the GED as the only training program.

preceding. The number of people in each step is broken down by manpower treatment, and the percentage of the original treatment group that made a particular response is given in parentheses. Thus, 438 people eligible for the $M1$ treatment took counseling and this number represents 22% of the total number (1983) of $M1$'s enrolled. To simplify reference to the separate groups in the figure, they have been given letter designations.

Of the 6350 people eligible for the manpower treatments, all but about 8% were contacted by counselors and given an explanation of the program. At this point about 20% of the sample decided not to take advantage of it. This group was contacted again on a regular basis to remind them of their eligibility, and some subsequently used the counseling center. Some clients were "deferred" by the counselor making the contact, generally because they were not yet 16. Of those who accepted the program, a high proportion actually used the counseling center. The proportion of those who used the center was highest among those with a 100% subsidy for education (the $M3$'s) and lowest for those who were only eligible for free counseling (the $M1$'s).

Writing a plan of action represented completion of the counseling process for the $M1$'s, but it represented the final requirement for receiving subsidies for $M2$'s and $M3$'s. Not surprisingly, a greater proportion of $M2$'s and $M3$'s who took counseling completed a plan of action than was the case with $M1$'s. We have classified the goals of the plans of action into three kinds.

1. *No change* The individual decided as a result of counseling that no change in his career plan was desirable.
2. *Training* The individual decided to enroll in some kind of schooling or job-training course. This course of action may have included part-time or full-time work as well as education.
3. *Job search* The individual decided either to enter the labor market or to look for another job if he was already employed.

As Table 14.1 indicates, training was the usual goal of the plan of action but the proportion of those choosing training was much higher for those who could expect a subsidy. For all treatment groups, no change was the least likely goal to be chosen.

Among those who chose training as a goal, only a fraction actually started schooling or job training. Unfortunately, we do not know about all of those whose goal was training because the start of a General Education Degree (GED) course, it was not recorded. However, only 104 or 10% of the training plans had GED as their only goal so their loss should mean that the number shown in Figure 14.1 to have started training is only slightly too low.

The numbers given in Figure 14.1 only represent the response to initial contact with the manpower program; total response was considerably greater. An example of the difference will illustrate the magnitude of subsequent response. For Groups D, G, and F—containing 3673 individuals who did not accept the program at the initial contact—1022 or 28% took counseling as a result of a subsequent contact. Some of these people went on to write plans of action and enroll in a school or training course.

Table 14.1
Distribution of Plans of Action by Goal and Treatment

	No change	Training	Job search	Total
$M1$	32 (13%)	160 (64%)	59 (23%)	251
$M2$	44 (8%)	411 (76%)	86 (16%)	541
$M3$	22 (4%)	426 (87%)	44 (9%)	492

The most reasonable measure of usage for the $M1$ treatment is attendance in a counseling session. Using this measure, we can describe the differences in response to the $M1$ treatment by demographic group. Since we wish to assess the overall effect of the $M1$ treatment as administered in the SIME/DIME program, the response will be measured by the proportion of the entire $M1$ group who took a counseling session. Using this measure, we can describe the differences in response to the $M1$ treatment by demographic group. Since we wish to assess the overall effect of the $M1$ treatment as administered in the SIME/DIME program, the response will be measured by the proportion of the entire $M1$ treatment group who took a counseling session. Tables 14.2-14.4 break down the overall 22% participation rate of those on the $M1$ treatment by sex, by race and family type, and by occupation. The tables show several differences in participation rates. Table 14.2 shows a somewhat higher participation rate by women. However, from Table 14.3 we can infer that the single female heads rather than the wives are responsible for the higher overall participation of women. Table 14.3 also shows that members of female-headed families generally made more use of the counseling center than members of husband-wife families. The exception is Chicanos, who have the same participation rate for both groups. Table 14.3 also implies that, overall, whites made slightly more use of the centers than did blacks or Chicanos.

The greatest differences in participation rates are seen when the response to $M1$ is broken down by occupation. None of the nine farmers or farm laborers used the counseling center after their initial contact, while over 30% of the clerical workers, operatives, service workers, and private household workers talked

Table 14.2
Counseling Participation of $M1$'s by Sex

Sex	Participation rate (%)
Females	24
Males	20

Note: For Tables 14.2-14.5, these rates represent the response to the first contact rather than the total response.

Table 14.3
Counseling Participation Rates of M1's by Family Type

| | Participation rate (%) | | | |
Family type	Male heads	Female heads	Other household members	Overall
Black female-headed families	–	40	8	26
Black husband and wife families	24	22	7	19
White female-headed families	–	39	9	28
White husband and wife families	23	24	5	20
Chicano female-headed families	–	35	10	22
Chicano husband and wife families	32	21	4	22

to a counselor at least once. Among workers there was no striking pattern or participation rates by occupation, although it may be significant that the participation was very low among managers. However, the very low rate of participation among those who had never worked confirms that the counseling program was perceived by its potential clients accurately: It provided counseling on topics relating to employment and training for employment. Those who had never worked probably did not intend to work during the experiments and, therefore, had little use for the manpower component.

Table 14.5 shows that the response to the counseling program was relatively rapid. Almost half of those who had accepted the program participated in a counseling session within 30 days and 2/3 had talked to a counselor within half a year after contact. Only 42 people, or 10% of those who eventually visited the counselor, did so after an interval of more than 6 months. Those who felt a need for counseling usually took advantage of it quickly. The total response by the entire sample of those on the M1 treatment who took counseling was also rapid: only about 16% visited a counselor after 6 months.

The preceding discussion was concerned with the response by individuals who accepted the manpower program at the initial contact. The overall response to counseling seems to be similar for all those on the treatment M1: Individuals in black and white female-headed families were more likely to use counseling ser-

Table 14.4
Counseling Participation of M1's by Current Occupation

Occupation	Participation rate (%)	Occupation	Participation rate (%)
Professional	28	Operatives, transport	23
Managerial	18	Laborers	28
Sales	23	Farmers and farm laborers	0
Clerical	30	Service workers	32
Craftsmen	26	Private household workers	32
Operatives	31	Never worked	6

Table 14.5
Number of Days from Contact to First Counseling Session for
M1's Who Accepted the Program

Days	Number of M1's	Cumulative percent
First session at contact	7	1
1- 7	88	16
8- 14	89	31
15- 30	109	49
31- 60	62	59
61- 90	26	63
91-120	8	65
121-150	4	65
151-180	3	66
181-365	12	68
366-548	12	70
549-730	10	71
731-998	8	73
Never took counseling	165	100
Total	603	

Note: These numbers represent the response to the first contact rather than the total response.

vices than were individuals in husband-wife families (42% of those in female-headed families took counseling compared to 33% in husband-wife families). Among Chicanos, those in female-headed families were slightly less likely to participate (37% took counseling compared to 39% of husband-wife families).

Our definition of usage of the education subsidy programs (M2 and M3 treatments) will be the enrollment of an eligible individual in a course of formal schooling or job training. Again, our discussion is limited to response to the initial contact by the counseling center, i.e., Group P. By this definition, the overall participation rate for all those eligible for the subsidy after the initial contact

Table 14.6
Rate of Participation in Training by
M2's and M3's by Sex

Sex	Participation Rate (%)		
	M2	M3	M2 and M3
Female	10	18	13
Male	8	17	11

Note: For Tables 14.6-14.8 these rates represent the response to the first contact rather than the total response.

was 12%. The overall rate of participation in the program was 23%. This response to the initial contact represents about half of the total response.

We have calculated participation rates for those eligible, broken down again by sex, family type, and occupation, which are summarized in Tables 14.6–14.8. The tables show a slightly higher participation rate among women who were eligible for the subsidy than for men and the highest rates for female heads of families. Also, blacks and whites seem to have participated in the subsidy program in greater numbers than Chicanos. While some of these differences in participation rates are large in percentage terms, there are not large absolute differences in participation rates evident between men and women or among family types.

When the eligible population is broken down by occupation, differences in participation in the education subsidy program become more pronounced. As in the counseling program, few people who have never worked made use of the program. Never having worked is a good indicator of disinclination to work in the future. People who did not intend to work had no use of employment-related training and a subsidy had little influence on them.

A somewhat surprising pattern of participation rates can be seen among those who had an occupation. It would seem that those with the fewest skills would be most likely to want training, but the results suggest the opposite. Participation rates were highest for professionals and managers and lowest for laborers, farmers and farm laborers, and private household workers. Two possible reasons for these results are suggested. First, we have ignored differences in ability among individuals that influence the size of the ultimate benefit they receive from training. A person with relatively high ability will receive a greater return from schooling so he will be more likely to participate in the program. Previous occupation is not unrelated to ability; in fact, it is a good predictor of ability. The professionals and managers among the participants probably had greater average ability than the laborers and household workers. Thus, even though they already have a high level of skill, they may expect greater benefits from additional training.

The other possible reason has to do with the way in which families were

Table 14.7

Rates of Participation in Training of $M2$'s and $M3$'s by Family Type

| | Participation rate (%) | | | | | | | |
| | Male heads | | Female heads | | Other | | Overall | |
Family type	$M2$	$M3$	$M2$	$M3$	$M2$	$M3$	$M2$	$M3$
Black female-headed families	–	–	17	29	4	7	11	18
Black husband and wife families	9	16	10	22	3	8	8	16
White female-headed families	–	–	16	27	2	10	10	21
White husband and wife families	11	24	9	21	1	4	8	20
Chicano female-headed families	–	–	14	13	5	2	9	7
Chicano husband and wife families	8	18	11	7	1	10	8	12

Table 14.8
Rates of Participation in Training of $M2$'s and $M3$'s by
Current Occupation

| | Participation rate (%) | | |
Occupation	$M2$	$M3$	$M2$ and $M3$
Professional	23	41	30
Managerial	13	37	20
Sales	11	21	14
Clerical	15	25	19
Craftsmen	13	19	15
Operatives	9	19	13
Operatives, transport	10	40	19
Laborers	9	8	9
Farm, farm laborers	0	20	11
Service workers	11	23	16
Private household workers	9	15	11
Never worked	2	6	4

chosen to participate in SIME/DIME. Since its purpose was to evaluate the effect of an NIT, the participants were limited to those who had an income less than $11,000 (in 1970 dollars) for a family of four. This limitation makes the professionals and managers in our sample a somewhat atypical group. They must be people who have been relatively unsuccessful in their occupation, and therefore likely candidates for additional training. People in our sample in less skilled occupations, such as laborers, should be more typical of their occupation and therefore less likely to feel a need for training to improve their position in their occupation. Unfortunately, both of these reasons for the high participation rates of professionals and managers are somewhat speculative and additional research will be required to obtain a better understanding of participation differences by occupation.

The time pattern of response to the education subsidy program is not so difficult to understand. As Table 14.9 shows, individuals who accepted the program were still unlikely to utilize the subsidy: 61% of those who accepted the program never took training. If individuals did take training they were most likely to begin soon after they became eligible: 164 people or 28% of those also took a training program began more than a year after they became eligible for subsidy, and only 41 people or 7% began more than 2 years after eligibility. The largest enrollment in school or job-training courses came one quarter after eligibility. The total response by the entire sample of $M2$'s and $M3$'s who took training was similar to the group who accepted at the first contact: about 30% of those who took training did so after 1 year, only 8% began 2 years after contact. This result implies that the success of a manpower program in attracting participants can be judged soon after it begins.

Table 14.9
Number of Quarters from Contact to Payment of Training Subsidy for
M2's and M3's Who Accepted the Program

Quarters	M2	Cumulative percent	M3	Cumulative percent	M2's and M3's	Cumulative percent
0	33	4	43	6	76	5
1	72	11	119	18	191	17
2	33	15	48	31	81	22
3	19	17	28	36	47	25
4	17	19	20	39	37	27
5	23	22	17	41	40	30
6	16	23	18	44	34	32
7	17	25	11	45	28	34
8	10	26	11	47	21	35
9	8	27	7	48	15	36
10	6	28	3	49	9	37
11	6	28	9	50	15	37
12	2	29	–	50	2	38
Never took training	654	100	335	100	989	100
Missing data	24		25		49	
Total	940		694		1634	

Note: These numbers represent the response to the first contact rather than the total response.

An indication of the way people intended to use the manpower programs can be obtained by studying their plans of action. Most plans for training included an occupational goal and degree objective as well as information about the educational institution to be used. Of the 1284 individuals who wrote a plan of action, 997 (78%) stated some type of training as their objective (Group M). The breakdown of occupations held at contact and those for which they chose to prepare is given in Table 14.10.

The 104 individuals who elected to pursue the GED as their only training objective are not included in Table 14.10. From this table it appears that the individuals in our sample overwhelmingly desired to prepare themselves for jobs in the professional occupations. Of the individuals in our sample who wrote training plans, 41% specified occupations in professional fields while only 7% held jobs in that area at the time of contact. There were increases in the managerial and crafts areas also. The distribution of individuals who wanted to prepare for clerical, operative, and service fields is lower than the distribution of individuals actually in those fields at time of contact. These figures point to the intent of the sample members to upgrade their occupational fields by means of formal training.

Table 14.11 shows the degree objective of training and Table 14.12 the type of institution at which the individual planned to pursue that degree. From Table

Table 14.10
Occupation at Contact and Occupation Goal of Training

Occupation group	Occupation at contact		Occupational goal	
	Number	Percent	Number	Percent
Professional	63	7	364	41
Managerial	21	2	57	6
Sales	25	3	19	2
Clerical	208	23	129	14
Craftsmen	62	7	104	12
Operatives	134	15	42	5
Operatives, transport	36	4	6	1
Laborers	45	5	7	1
Farmers and farm laborers	1	<1	1	<1
Service workers	227	26	110	12
Private household workers	17	2	1	<1
Never worked	54	6	–	–
Undecided	–	–	53	6
Total	893	100	893	100

14.11 it appears that most manpower program participants decided to pursue the AA degree, to upgrade existing skills, or to enroll in or continue a college program, with equal numbers pursuing a degree and no degree. Other objectives,

Table 14.11
Degree Objective of Training for First Plan

Degree[a]	$M1$	$M2$	$M3$	Total	Percent
GED only	20	45	39	104	10
AA	20	81	89	190	19
BA/BS	28	46	60	134	13
MA/PhD/MD	1	3	11	15	2
RN/other medical	4	15	20	39	4
Skills upgrade	41	82	73	196	20
Trade union or apprentice	3	5	2	10	1
Skilled or semi-skilled license/certificate	14	49	44	107	11
College, no degree	18	59	54	131	13
Skilled or semi-skilled, no license	5	17	26	48	5
Other	6	9	8	23	2
Total	160	411	426	997	100

[a] Some individuals wrote a training plan which included the GED and other degree objectives. These persons are listed only next to the particular program beyond the acquisition of a GED, and not in the "GED only" row.

Table 14.12
Training Institution for First Plan

Institution	$M1$	$M2$	$M3$	Total	Percent
Community college	19	137	170	326	37
College or university	9	35	51	95	11
Technical/trade	1	10	10	21	2
Other/out of state	16	55	55	126	14
Not specified	95	129	101	325	36
Total	140	366	337	893	100

including graduate school medical training, or training for skilled or semi-skilled trades were much less common.

Table 14.12 discloses a difficulty in the analysis of the plans of action. Over one-third of those who wrote a plan of action did not specify the institution they wished to attend. These plans are essentially incomplete because an institution must be chosen before training can begin. For the purposes of the subsidy program, also, they were considered to be incomplete: To receive a subsidy, those eligible for $M2$ and $M3$ treatments were required to specify an institution in their plan of action. This requirement reduced the incidence of plans with unspecified institutions among $M2$'s and $M3$'s but even among those eligible for a 100% subsidy, 26% did not specify an institution. The high percentage given here may reflect the way in which plans were written. Plans were written when the counselee had a clearly specified goal, but not necessarily the means to attain it. Those who did not specify an institution may have been those who were unable to pursue their objective immediately.

Among those who specified a training institution, the overwhelming favorite was a community college. This is a surprising result for those eligible for subsidies. It would seem that these people, especially those on the $M3$ treatment, could afford to enroll in the more expensite institutions and yet they usually chose the least expensive one. This is particularly surprising because, as explained earlier, the subsidies did induce enrollment in school or training courses. This implies that subsidies are valuable in stimulating enrollment in junior colleges, even though their costs were very low.[1]

Since the community college was the most popular training institution, the amounts of subsidy paid should be relatively small. An examination of those who started a training program and received a subsidy payment confirms this. Of the 526 on $M2$ and $M3$ who started training, 514 received at least one subsidy payment. The average subsidy under the 50% subsidy program was $382 and un-

[1] The fact that the manpower programs were administered by the community colleges may also explain the popularity of community colleges. Counselors were instructed not to influence clients in their decisions, but they may have been more familiar with community college programs.

Table 14.13
Occupation at Contact and Occupation of Job Search at First Plan

	Occupation at contact		Occupational goal	
	Number	Percent	Number	Percent
Professional	6	3	22	12
Managerial	7	4	12	6
Sales	8	4	4	2
Clerical	34	18	46	24
Craftsmen	26	14	29	15
Operatives	23	12	16	9
Operatives, transport	6	3	5	3
Laborers	17	9	15	8
Farmers and farm laborers	–	–	1	<1
Service workers	45	24	28	15
Private household workers	4	2	–	–
Never worked	13	7	–	–
Not specified, other	–	–	11	6
Total	189	100	189	100

der the 100% program, $956. If we prorate the $M2$ subsidy ($382 × 2) we see that the average cost of training for those on $M3$ was $192 more than the average for those on $M2$.

Group N consists of 189 individuals whose first plan of action was to search for a job. Table 14.13 gives the distribution of occupations these individuals had at contact and the distribution of occupational goals of the job search plan. The picture that emerges from the table is of people planning to move up the occupational ladder. More planned to search for jobs in professional, managerial, clerical, and crafts occupations than were members of these occupations at contact. Although there may have been many people who intended to search for a new job in their present occupation, the group as a whole planned to move into more prestigious or better paid occupations. It should be noted that 7% of those who planned to search for a job had never worked previously. These people represent 1% of those in the entire sample who had never worked. Thus, even fewer people with no work experience planned to search for a job then planned to take a training course.

Finally, there were 98 individuals who wrote plans that specified no change (Group L). These individuals planned to retain their present jobs or to remain at home.

RESPONSE TO THE MANPOWER PROGRAM

The objective of the manpower program was to improve the clients' success in the labor market. Therefore, the program must be evaluated in these terms.

However, success in the labor market is quite variable for reasons apart from the manpower program. It will take a long period of observation before the ultimate effects of the manpower program can be measured with any accuracy. Until sufficient data become available, we have concentrated research upon the immediate effect of the program upon the demand for education. Results obtained so far indicate that the manpower program did induce people to take additional schooling and training.

The theoretical framework implemented regards education as a type of investment. The cost of the investment is the earnings foregone in attending school and the direct costs of schooling. If the person had chosen not to attend school, he or she could have used the extra time to work to increase earnings. Attending school costs the individual those earnings and whatever direct costs in tuition and books are required. Having paid for the investment in this way, the individual receives dividends in the form of greater success in the labor market after the training is completed. Completing a course of employment-related training should lead to steadier employment and higher wages. In making a decision about school attendance, the individual must determine whether the investment will return high enough dividends to justify the initial cost. For convenience in discussion, economists call this investment good "human capital." Individuals' decisions about training determine the level of their human capital and have a strong influence on their success in the labor market.

Investment in human capital, better known as education, goes on all the time independent of any manpower experiment. People go to school until they decide that the foregone earning for additional schooling will not be balanced by increased earnings after completion of school. Once that decision is made they leave school and devote themselves to work. The manpower program, and particularly the treatments including subsidies, should induce people to take additional schooling or training by lowering the cost of the investment. However, the experiments were not expected by the participants and, as a result, the strength of the inducement can be expected to depend upon the point in the individual's career at which the experiment occurred. For the person who is nearly finished with his planned schooling, the inducement of free tuition and books should be strong. However, for a younger person who has already decided to attend school for a few more years, the subsidy may be gratifying but it cannot be considered to have induced subsequent school attendance. Only if the subsidy were still available after the completion of initially planned schooling might it then have an effect upon that individual's decisions. Since the experiment only lasted 3 years for most people, they did not have the effect upon younger people that a permanent program would have had.

The subsidy for the direct costs of schooling was also made available to older people who had completed their schooling several years before SIME/DIME began. It would seem that these people would find the inducement of the subsidy less strong than a young person would. While the cost of attendance should be the same for the older person (or greater if he has a higher wage), the dividends from the investment will not flow for so long. The older person has fewer remaining years in his working career in which to reap the benefits of education. However, some additional factors complicate the argument about the effect of subsidies upon older people. Those who have left school several years ago are likely to have seen the value of their skills deteriorate in the market. The rising age at which people leave school means that the average education of the work force has been rising. The worker who left school several years ago finds he has increasingly well-trained competition in the labor market, even if he has maintained his own skills. He may also have seen his skills deteriorate over time, making him even less competitive. For these reasons, older people might be more responsive to the subsidies than would at first be expected.

This digression about the theory underlying our study of the demand for schooling and training induced by the experiments has been made to simplify the presentation of the results summarized in Table 14.14. This table presents the effects we have estimated for each of the manpower treatments upon the amount of schooling taken during the first 2 years of SIME/DIME. Schooling is used here to mean attendance in a formal education program rather than in a job-training program. The numbers in the table represent the predicted number of additional quarters of schooling (out of a possible 8) that we estimated individuals would take in response to the manpower treatments. Predicted levels of school attendance for those who received no treatment (the controls) is also given. The predictions are broken down by experimental site, by type of person, by age, and by whether or not the person was in school when the experiments began. This last attribute was included because we hypothesized that it might be easier for a person who was already in school to take additional courses than for someone who was out of school to begin again.

One thing is immediately apparent from the table. While the $M1$ treatment (consisting only of counseling with no subsidy) did not have a consistent effect, the two treatments that provided subsidies clearly induced people to take additional schooling. The affect can be seen for husbands, wives, and single female heads of families, for both Seattle and Denver, for all age groups, and for both those who were already in school and those who were not. Also, as we would expect, the more generous $M3$ treatment had a consistently larger effect than $M2$. For some groups, the 100% subsidy induced more than 1 quarter of additional school attendance.

When the table is examined more closely some additional insights emerge. First, the effects of the subsidies were quite consistent between the two experimental sites.[2] However, there were differences in effect depending upon whether

[2] The consistency in these results is enforced somewhat by the way the underlying model is specified. However, before this particular form of the model was chosen, earlier research had shown consistency of experimental effects in the two sites.

Table 14.14

Predicted Effects of the Manpower Program upon Demand for Formal Schooling

		Seattle Controls (predicted quarters of attendance)	Seattle Predicted experimental effects M1	M2	M3	Denver Controls (predicted quarters of attendance)	Denver Predicted experimental effects M1	M2	M3
		Seattle husbands				*Denver husbands*			
In school	16-25	4.984	-.579	.125	.573	4.186	-.592	.131	.616
	26-45	3.659	.840	1.401**	1.852***	2.869	.818	1.397**	1.883**
	46+	2.294	.766	1.333***	1.824***	1.652	.666	1.186**	1.657**
Out of school	16-25	.717	—	-.048	.163	.438	-.145	-.033	.114
	26-45	.309	.221	.339***	.547***	.172	.141	.220**	.363**
	46+	.104	.095	.149***	.252***	.052	.054	.086**	.149**
		Seattle wives				*Denver wives*			
In school	16-25	3.269	-.223	-.095	1.335	2.862	-.213	-.091	1.320
	26-45	3.686	-.319	-.719	.704	3.266	-.310	-.693	.699
	46+	3.233	-.309	-.690	.698	2.827	-.295	-.653	.680
Out of school	16-25	.207	-.054	.273**	.879**	.150	-.041	.215**	.719**
	25-45	.280	-.084	.133	.691***	.206	-.064	.109	.565***
	46+	.201	-.063	.106	.556***	.146	-.048	.082	.446**
		Seattle female heads				*Denver female heads*			
In school	16-25	5.135	.474	.243	.787	4.604	.504	.256	.845
	26-45	4.526	.888	.157	.758	3.977	.922	.159	.784
	46+	2.947	.915	.152	.772	2.443	.873	.142	.734
Out of school	16-25	.529	.029	.717**	1.134**	.373	.022	.571**	.922**
	26-45	.354	.135	.502***	.832***	.241	.100	.385	.652**
	46+	.108	.052	.214**	.378***	.068	.036	.150**	.272**

**p < .05.

279

the individual was in school before the experiments began or not, and these depended upon the type of individual. For husbands and wives, the treatments seem to have had a greater effect upon those who were already in school than on those who were not. For single female heads, the pattern of effect is the opposite. The subsidies had more effect in inducing women back into school than it did in inducing those already in school to attend longer. The effect of the experiments upon different age groups varied by sex. The strongest effect of the subsidies was upon young women, and the magnitude of the effect declined with age. Thus, the response of women coincides with our simple picture of individual decision making. Unfortunately, the men in the experiment were not so cooperative. For them the subsidies had the least effect upon the youngest category of men and the greatest effect upon those in the prime working years. Thus, for men, the subsidies seem to have been most useful as a means to upgrade skills already in use in the labor market.

CHAPTER 15

Demand for Assets

RANDALL J. POZDENA
TERRY R. JOHNSON

INTRODUCTION

Households hold their wealth in a portfolio of assets. These assets include money, financial assets, durable physical capital, and accumulated human capital. The composition of this portfolio varies from household to household and previous research has examined how the size and composition of this portfolio varies with the age and other circumstances of the household. (See, e.g., Katona *et al.*, 1971; Projector and Weiss, 1966.)

Despite these studies, it is difficult to predict the effect that an NIT would have on household asset stocks because an NIT affects the demand for these stocks in several potentially offsetting ways. The experimental environment of SIME/DIME offers the opportunity to observe the effects of an NIT on the household's tendency to hold asset stocks.

The effect of an NIT on the household portfolio is of interest from several policy perspectives. First, the way in which it affects the spending habits of the poor may say much about the political feasibility of such a program. It is clear that if the household's response involved accumulation of "luxury" durables such as automobiles and televisions, the program would probably be viewed skeptically by critics of antipoverty programs.

A second point concerns the effect of an NIT on the household's own preparations for retirement and other periods of low income. Since it provides the household with a secure income, individuals' efforts to maintain easily liquidated asset stocks may be affected. Indeed, the guaranteed income feature of an NIT may even affect the preparations of those who are eligible for support, but do not receive it. Studies of the Social Security and private pension systems have indicated that retirement-income security reduces saving (see, e.g., Mishkin, 1976). Extending an income guarantee to the working years may further erode saving incentives.

Finally, study of the effects of an NIT on the household portfolio is of inter-

A GUARANTEED ANNUAL INCOME:
EVIDENCE FROM A SOCIAL EXPERIMENT

est because the practical design of such a program involves some imputation of income to asset stocks in eligibility determination and payment computation. Such policies are likely to precipitate changes in the asset-holding (or reporting) behavior of households. By observing these changes, we may obtain a clearer view of the consequences of using asset measures in eligibility tests and in payment computations.

In the remainder of this chapter, we explore the likely avenues of impact suggested by the theory of asset-stock demand, describe the model and data used in the study, and present the results and their implications.

THEORETICAL CONSIDERATIONS

We are interested in examining the effect of the experiments on the demand for asset stocks. In the approach taken here, human capital is assumed to be fixed and we focus our attention on physical and financial assets. We assume that household assets fall into six basic categories: household durables, vehicles, liquid assets, nonmortgage debt, the value of the home, and the home mortgage. These categories capture the basic functional variation within the portfolio, although certain minor items (such as equity in other property) are omitted from our study.

From the household's point of view, the experiments involved changes in the flow of income to the household and, as we shall see below, changes in the relative prices of assets and other goods. It is these changes in the economic environment of the household that induce changes in the desired stock of the various assets described above. In order to study these effects through observation of actual stocks, we must understand more fully the factors that affect the desired stock for assets and the mechanism that translates changes in the desired stocks into actual stocks.

The Demand for Asset Stocks

Households maintain asset stocks in order to serve an assumed utility maximization goal. In very broad terms, household utility for each period depends upon the volume of consumption, leisure, and flows of services from household assets. It is the goal of the household to maximize the present value of this utility, subject to a budget constraint which involves the wage rate, the tax rate, prices of goods, and the interest rate over time and the value of initial asset stocks. This multiperiod view of the household optimization process has its roots in the work of Diewert (1974), Hess (1977), and Parks (1974), and the reader is referred to this work for further detail. In essence, utility maximization is constrained by "wealth" or initial assets plus the accumulation of savings out of current and future wage and nonwage income.

We modify this simple conceptualization with a set of additional assumptions. First, for simplicity, we assume that the services of household assets (such as a washing machine) may not be sold by the household. Second, we recognize that household assets require (or save) time in the consumption of their services and thus asset stocks affect the amount of time available for leisure or work. Finally, to simplify matters, the wage rate, consumption and assets' prices, and tax rates are assumed constant over time.

The asset-stock demand relationship generated by this simple model of utility maximization implies that the desired level of the physical asset stock depends upon "full wealth," the price of leisure, and the user cost of the assets. Full wealth is simply the initial value of the family's assets plus the present value of all leisure and work time (evaluated at the wage net of tax), plus the present value of nonwage income (including welfare support). The price of leisure is simply the wage net of tax. Finally, the user cost of the asset is the implicit cost of owning the asset when depreciation, the interest rate, and the price of the asset are accounted for.

Expected Effect on those Receiving Payments

How did the experiments influence these variables and, hence, the demand for asset stocks? For those receiving payments, full wealth was affected because the experiments increased nonwage income and (because of the higher tax rates implicit in the NIT) reduced the value of time spent working. The net effect, the change in each period's disposable income (and, hence, the change in wealth), was positive for individuals receiving the NIT treatments. We expect this to influence asset stocks positively.

The price of leisure was reduced because of the higher tax rate in the experimental environment. This should lead to a substitution effect—a tendency to increase leisure at the expense of assets.

The most complex influence was on the user cost of the asset. User costs generally depend upon the depreciation rate, the interest rate, and the price of new assets (which the experiments leave unchanged). However, since the assets are assumed to require or save time, the experimental reduction in the value of time can be expected to increase or decrease the demand for assets depending upon their time-using or time-saving nature, respectively. In addition, certain assets (home equity and liquid assets) had income imputed to them by SIME/DIME as part of the payment computation process, even though not all components of these asset categories yielded income that was taxed by the normal, positive income-tax system. This imputation raised the implicit user cost of assets over what it would have been without the experiments.

Thus, we see a pattern of offsetting income and price effects for those individuals who received NIT payments. Generally, we expect the increase in wealth to increase stocks, but the increase in tax rates is expected to decrease stocks.

The tax rate effect is generated by the substitution of leisure for all goods and the increase in user cost of assets.

Expected Effect on Those above the Breakeven Income Level

The NIT treatments also had features which could affect those individuals eligible for payments but with incomes too high to receive support (i.e., they are above the breakeven level). In particular, the experiments provided a floor for the incomes of all eligible individuals. In effect, the experimental treatments truncated the lower tail of the income distribution that experimentals perceived, thereby raising the mean and reducing the variance of this distribution. Theory suggests that this reduced income variability should decrease the demand for liquid assets and increase the demand for illiquid assets (see Mishkin, 1976; Sandmo, 1970).

Observed versus Desired Stocks

The preceding discussion suggests that desired asset stocks depend upon wealth and the user costs of leisure and assets. Since the experiments influenced these variables, the desired stock of an asset should have been affected. However, actual stocks do not immediately adjust to the level desired because of adjustment costs. Thus, observed stocks cannot be used directly to study the desired stock relationship (which is the relationship of interest because it implies the long-run effects of the NIT). Our empirical work using observed stocks incorporates a partial adjustment model and the estimated effects on desired stocks have been extracted from this model. The features of the partial adjustment model are incorporated in the econometric formulation we use to examine the NIT impacts. The basic model is

$$K_1 = \mathbf{X}\mathbf{b}\gamma + \mathbf{F}\mathbf{c}\gamma + (1 - \gamma)K_0 + \epsilon_1, \tag{1}$$

where K is the observed level of the stock of the asset (in dollars); $\mathbf{X}$ is a vector of variables that capture cross-section variations in wealth, the price of leisure, the user cost of the asset and tastes; $\mathbf{F}$ is a vector of variables that represent the effect of the experiments on wealth, the price of leisure, and the user cost of the asset; $\mathbf{b}$ and $\mathbf{c}$ are vectors of parameters; 0 and 1 are preenrollment and experimental time, respectively; γ is an adjustment parameter ($0 \leqslant \gamma \leqslant 1$); and ϵ is an error component. The vector $\mathbf{X}$ is represented by preexperimental values of the net wage, a measure of permanent income,[1] net worth, and certain demographic variables (family size, age of the head, and a nonwhite dummy). The NIT treat-

---

[1] Permanent income is a predicted variable based on a regression of preenrollment family income against age, age squared, education, a dummy variable if family head is nonwhite, a dummy variable indicating whether the family owned a home preexperimentally, and E-level dummy variables.

ment vector **F** is represented by a set of dummy variables indicating the NIT treatment status of the household. Specifically, in one version of the model, a simple dummy variable indicates whether or not the household was eligible for an NIT treatment. In a second version, the effects on experimentals predicted to be above the breakeven level are distinguished from those predicted to receive payments through the use of two dummies.[2] The status of the individual relative to the breakeven income level is predicted from preenrollment labor supply and wage data.[3]

This basic formulation was employed for all six asset stock categories except for the value of the home. A special model of homeownership was estimated, in which the observed stock measure in equation (1), K, is represented by a dummy variable indicating homeownership.[4]

THE DATA

The data on household asset stocks were constructed from SIME/DIME interview data. Individuals enrolled in the experiments provided data concerning the acquisition date and value of household assets and debts. The construction of

[2] Although the theoretical section relates the changes in desired asset stocks to NIT-induced changes in income and tax rates, for ease of summarizing the effects of the experiment the empirical results reported in this chapter do not attempt to distinguish these separate effects and instead correspond to average experimental effects. In other analysis (see Pozdena and Johnson, 1979) we have broken down the below-breakeven-level response due to a predicted change in a disposable income variable and to a variable measuring the predicted change in the tax rate. These results generally indicate experimentally induced increases in income are associated with increased asset holdings, while increases in tax rates are associated with lower desired asset stocks. The average effects derived from these models are very similar to those presented in this chapter.

[3] The interpretation of separate effects for those predicted to be either above or below the breakeven level is complicated by our limited ability to fully control for all variables that affect household status relative to the breakeven level as well as those that affect asset holdings. For example, it is likely that above-breakeven-level experimentals have higher-than-average incomes (relative to all controls), whereas those below the breakeven level have lower-than-average incomes. To the extent that the effects of these income differences are not captured by the variables included in **X**, they should not be attributed entirely to experimental influences.

[4] This particular representation was used for housing because of the difficulty of establishing the value of housing apart from the respondents' own estimates. Since income was imputed to home equity in determining payments from SIME/DIME, the experiments created incentives for underreporting. Preliminary empirical results with home value reflected this problem: Using asset stock (home value) measures, the experiments appear to have reduced home value primarily through a tax effect. Yet homeownership data indicated that the experiments increased homeownership significantly. The difference is very likely due to an underreporting bias. We, therefore, analyze a variable indicating whether or not they own a home, a measure that is less subject to these reporting problems.

asset stock data involved resolution of several measurement issues and influenced the sample chosen for analysis.

Measurement of Asset Stocks

Asset stocks were measured in dollars for six broad categories of stocks: household durables (furniture, washing machines, televisions, tools, etc.); vehicles (automobiles, trucks, campers, motorcycles, etc.); liquid assets (savings and checking balances, stocks, bonds, and other financial instruments); nonmortgage debt (store debt, bank debt, bank card, and unpaid bills); home mortgage debt; and home value. The net worth in other property in our sample was very small and, therefore, not studied in this research.

Measurement of the asset stock involved information on the purchase price and rate of depreciation of the asset. Purchase price information was available from almost all interviews. For a small subsample, however, a predicted price had to be used, inferred from information on families who owned a similar asset and knew its value. Missing debt stocks were calculated using information on monthly payments, interest rates, and other loan terms. A constant annual depreciation rate of 20.6% was assumed for durable goods and vehicles. This figure has been used in other studies (e.g., Nicholson, 1977), and implies that 10% of the value of the asset remains after 10 years.

The Analysis Samples

To increase the reliability of the empirical work, we used data on those families that had 3 years of information and had not experienced a change in marital status or been self-employed during the period. These conditions avoid the difficulty of allocating assets between estranged spouses or between professional and personal uses.

In addition, all Seattle families were eliminated because they had never been administered a preenrollment net worth interview. Their inclusion would have required inferring preenrollment holdings from experimental period data (a dubious procedure since data on items sold were unavailable). Our final analysis sample consisted of 930 husband-wife families and 700 female-headed households in Denver only. Table 15.1 presents the sample means at preenrollment for family asset stocks and other selected economic and demographic variables.

RESULTS

The effects of the experiments on household asset stocks were studied by estimating equation (1) and solving for the long-run coefficients associated with the NIT treatments. Ordinary least squares was used for all of the asset stock

Table 15.1
Variable Means

	Husband-wife households	Female-headed households
Durable goods	$799.1	$554.7
Vehicles	$1140.2	$434.4
Liquid assets	$287.2	$174.6
Nonmortgage debt	$1538.7	$665.5
Mortgage debt	$3970.8	$2222.0
Homeownership dummy	.37	.22
Family size (persons)	4.4	3.5
Age of the head	32.0	33.2
Experimentals predicted to be above the breakeven level	.12	.20
Experimentals predicted to be below the breakeven level	.43	.45
Race (nonwhite)	.62	.73
Estimated permanent income	$6064.3	$2678.7
Sample size	930	700

categories and in the special case of the homeownership model.[5] The results reported in this section are based on measures of asset stocks calculated at the end of the second year of the experiment.

The overall effect of the NIT treatments was to increase household asset stocks within our sample. As the first column of Table 15.2 indicates, the NIT treatments were associated with increases in all illiquid asset stocks for female-headed households and all except durable goods and mortgage debt for husband-wife families. The largest relative responses appear to have occurred in the probability of owning a home and in holdings of mortgage and nonmortgage debt. For female-headed households, for example, the .11 increase represents approximately a 50% increase over the .22 probability of owning a home at preenrollment; mortgage debt for female-headed households increased by $864, or nearly 40% over preenrollment levels.

The composition of the response appears to vary somewhat by family type. For example, husband-wife families displayed a tendency to increase nonmortgage debt with only modest responses in vehicle goods stocks and decreases in the average holdings of remaining assets, while the female-headed households appear to have responded in an opposite fashion. Larger absolute changes in all categories except nonmortgage debt appear to be associated with female-headed

[5] Probit formulations of the homeownership relationship were also employed and the results using this technique are qualitatively similar to those obtained with ordinary least squares. These results are not presented here because the interpretation of the adjustment process and the derivation of the long-run (desired stock) effects is more cumbersome in the probit model.

Table 15.2
Long-Run Increases in Asset Holdings Induced by SIME/DIME

	All experimentals	Experimentals above the breakeven level	Experimentals below the breakeven level
Husband-wife households			
Durable goods	−$70.76	$55.77	−$104.34
Vehicles	$91.49	$210.20	$59.58
Liquid assets	−$29.80	$62.12	−$54.36
Nonmortgage debt	$446.20**	$344.14	$473.32**
Mortgage debt	−$687.04	$1531.37	−$1275.27**
Homeownership (probability)	.01	.20**	−.04
Female-headed households			
Durable goods	$103.04	$117.00	$96.15
Vehicles	$127.63	$360.79**	$17.00
Liquid assets	$26.35	$94.03	−$4.75
Nonmortgage debt	$142.09	$320.87**	$59.40
Mortgage debt	$863.58*	$935.58	$829.25*
Homeownership (probability)	.11	.25**	.04

Note: These long-run impact measures are computed from a ratio of two coefficients from each asset demand model. In particular, they are computed as the coefficient of the appropriate experimental dummy variable divided by 1 minus the coefficient of the lagged dependent variable. Such a computation places a burden on the precision of the individual estimates. As a result, the long-run impact measures do not in every case meet conventional criteria for statistical reliability. However, they can usefully be interpreted as point estimates.
   *$p < .10$.
   **$p < .05$.

households. Since female heads held smaller stocks of all assets preexperimentally, these larger absolute changes translate into even higher percentage effects.

From the experimental response overall, it would appear that the wealth and/or income variability effects of the experiments in increasing asset stock demand were larger than the tax effects, which tended to depress asset stock demand. However, as Columns 2 and 3 of Table 15.2 indicate, the overall response concealed the importance of the response of those above the breakeven level. Since the human and nonhuman wealth of the individuals in the sample is controlled for in the regressions, the coefficients on the above-breakeven-level experimental dummy indicate the independent influence of being eligible for, but unlikely to receive, support. Thus, *ceteris paribus*, the consequence of being an experimental above the breakeven level was to increase the stocks of all illiquid assets, an effect anticipated by the theory of asset user costs discussed earlier. Contrary to our prediction about the effects of income variability on liquid assets, however, the point estimates for those above the breakeven were positive, although the coefficients were measured imprecisely. Note that for those below the breakeven level, the effect on liquid asset holdings was small, but negative for both household types. For these individuals, the effect of reduced income variability apparently overwhelmed the effect of actual support.

The above-breakeven-level responses were, in some cases, quite striking. For example, in the case of female-headed households, those above the breakeven level experienced a 25 percentage point increase in the probability of owning a home over that which would be expected given the socioeconomic characteristics of the household at preenrollment. A similarly large response occurred among the husband-wife households and, of course, in both cases the increases in home-ownership tendencies were associated with higher mortgage debt holdings.

Some anomalies are also apparent in the data in Table 15.2. The decrease in the durable goods stocks and mortgage debt for those below the breakeven level in husband-wife households was unexpected. However, given the fact that the portfolio nature of the decision process was ignored, such results may not be countertheoretical. This is an aspect of asset choice that is not easily accommodated without restrictive assumptions. Dunkelberg and Stafford (1971), for example, develop a portfolio theoretic model of asset-stock demand. Their model requires estimation of desired stocks outside the context of the portfolio adjustment process. This is troublesome in our case, however, because it cannot be reasonably assumed, as their model requires, that individuals are in equilibrium except for random disturbances.

CONCLUSIONS

This chapter has presented tests of the impact of SIME/DIME on household asset stocks. The tests were performed within an empirical structure suggested by a simple multiperiod model of asset-stock demand. This structure suggests that the experiment acts to influence asset-stock demand through changes in wealth and the change in the relative user cost of assets and the price of leisure.

In general, the worst fears of those who would criticize NIT policy as leading to accumulation of frivolous consumer durable stocks have not been substantiated. Our study indicates that most of the effects of the experiment on the asset-stock demand of those who were predicted to receive payments were modest.

Three interesting implications of the study do emerge, however, to suggest that asset-stock demand effects should not be ignored in NIT policy planning. The first is the finding that experimental effects on asset holdings are not limited to those who receive payments; there are significant asset portfolio adjustments by those who do not receive support, via reduced income variability. Second, although our results are somewhat mixed and the effects are not always measured with precision, it appears that experimentals choose to have a portfolio with more debt, particularly nonmortgage debt. To the extent that increases in nonmortgage debt reduce net worth, if a guaranteed income policy were implemented nationally, conventional saving might be noticeably reduced, exacerbating a capital market dilemma already adversely affected by Social Security, pensions, and other social insurance programs.

A third implication of the study follows from the homeownership findings. Our results indicate that the treatments increased the probability of homeownership. Of particular interest is the finding that the homeownership propensity of those predicted to be above the breakeven level was influenced positively by the experiment. This suggests that the income guarantee aspect of the experiments may have had important side effects on the tendency of low-income individuals to own housing in their neighborhoods, thereby providing some relief from neighborhood and housing stock deterioration with little outright public support.

A final observation concerns the use of asset measures in eligibility or support payment computations. In results not presented here, we had difficulty obtaining estimated home value effects that were consistent with the stimulative effects of the experiment on homeownership. Since income is inputed to home equity, we suspect that an underreporting bias is the source of the difficulty. This implies that the imputation of income to assets in welfare administration procedures will require some independent valuation or assessment process to avoid underreporting problems.

REFERENCES

Diewert, W. E. "Intertemporal Consumer Theory and the Demand for Durables." *Econometrica*, May 1974, pp. 497-516.

Dunkelberg, W. L., and Stafford, F. P. "Debt in the Consumer Portfolio: Evidence from a Panel Study." *American Economic Review*, September 1971, pp. 598-613.

Hess, A. C. "A Comparison of Automobile Demand Equations." *Econometrica*, April 1977, pp. 683-701.

Katona, G. *et al.* "1970 Survey of Consumer Finances." Survey Research Center, Ann Arbor, Michigan, 1971.

Mishkin, F. S. "Illiquidity, Consumer Durable Expenditures, and Monetary Policy." *American Economic Review*, September 1976, pp. 642-54.

Nicholson, W. "Expenditure Patterns: A Descriptive Survey." In *The New Jersey Income Maintenance Experiment*, vol. III edited by H. Watts and A. Rees, pp. 15-43. New York: Academic Press, 1977.

Parks, R. W. "The Demand and Supply of Durable Goods and Durability." *American Economic Review*, March 1974, pp. 37-55.

Pozdena, R., and Johnson, T. R. "Income Maintenance and Asset Stock Demand." Unpublished manuscript, SRI International, March 1979.

Projector, D. S., and Weiss, G. S. *Survey of Financial Characteristics of Consumers*. Washington, D.C.: Board of Governors of the Federal Reserve System, 1966.

Sandmo, A. "The Effect of Uncertainty on Saving Decisions." *The Review of Economic Studies*, July 1970, pp. 353-360.

CHAPTER 16

Utilization of Subsidized Housing

MARCY E. AVRIN

INTRODUCTION

Housing subsidies are a form of economic assistance provided to the producers and consumers of housing. The purpose of housing subsidies is to lower the price of housing to encourage producers to supply and American households to use decent quality housing. Subsidies are major instruments in the effort to achieve the "national housing goal . . . of a decent home and a suitable living environment for every American family," as stated by Congress in the Housing Act of 1968. The main objective of this chapter is to discover any evidence of an interaction between an NIT and subsidized housing, and to estimate the general effects that such a program would have on the utilization of subsidized housing.

Such estimates have important policy implications. They allow a determination of the effect of implementing an NIT on the overall demand for subsidized housing, which could in turn serve as a basis for designing an interface between an NIT and existing housing programs. Such an interface would be critical in a revamping of the welfare system.

From the welfare point of view, measuring the effect of an NIT on demand for subsidized housing will provide direct evidence as to how an NIT, or a similar unearmarked subsidy, will affect the utilization of subsidized housing.

This chapter addresses several specific research questions with regard to the families participating in the SIME/DIME experiments: (*a*) Does an NIT cause families to move out of subsidized housing? (*b*) Does it decrease the probability of moving into subsidized housing? (*c*) Do the effects vary with the level of support and with family size?

Before answering these questions, it is necessary to understand the SIME/DIME experiments,[1] the various subsidized housing programs in which the experimental families participated, and the interface between them.

---

[1] The design of the experiments is stated in Chapter 1. Here we will discuss only the elements relevant to determining the effect on the utilization of subsidized housing.

291

A GUARANTEED ANNUAL INCOME:
EVIDENCE FROM A SOCIAL EXPERIMENT

THE SIME/DIME TREATMENTS AND THE
HOUSING ENVIRONMENT

In calculating the NIT payments, the experiments allowed certain work and household expenses to be deducted from gross income. Private transfers, which are difficult to identify, were only partially taxed in an attempt to ensure that they were reported. The payment function attempted to recognize the existence of other tax and transfer programs and to eliminate their influence by fully reimbursing all positive taxes and fully taxing all public transfers. Though subsidized housing is a public transfer, it was not taxed because its in-kind nature makes the determination of the value of the subsidy difficult. Also, any changes in the amount of the housing subsidy during the experiments were not considered in the determination of the payment.[2]

In contrast, subsidized housing programs treat SIME/DIME income as any other income in determining the level of housing subsidy. It is a component of the adjusted income on which both eligibility and the amount of subsidy is determined.[3]

Table 16.1 summarizes the major housing programs in Denver and Seattle that may have been affected by the NIT treatments. All housing programs offer a given quantity of housing that is dependent on family size. Families pay either 25% of their adjusted gross income or the fair market rent, whichever is less, for the housing.[4] The majority of subsidized housing units are either public housing or rental housing of Section 236 of the Housing and Urban Development Act of 1968. As is shown in the table, in 1973, the Denver metropolitan area had close to 7000 units for low-income families (nonelderly) in these two programs and Seattle had 8500 units. Also, Section 101 rent supplements are available to eligible families and individuals residing in housing insured by the Department of Housing and Urban Development (HUD) or subsidized multifamily housing whose owners have entered into special rent supplement contracts with HUD.

The SIME/DIME survey instruments do not provide information about the type of subsidized housing in which the respondents are living. This lack of in-

---

[2] Attempts to identify changes in housing subsidies and to reimburse these changes through the grant have been ineffective. There was one grant change in response to an income-related change in rent in Denver and relatively few in Seattle.

[3] In response to the concern that enrollment in the experiments would cause families to lose their subsidized housing eligibility and create housing dislocations based upon fairly short-run income increases, SIME/DIME made agreements with the local housing authorities that experimental families would not be forced to move during the experiments. No one has been required to leave public housing in the Denver and Seattle areas since 1970, regardless of their participation in the experiments.

[4] Adjusted gross income includes the total of earnings, Social Security, public assistance, state or private unemployment insurance, AFDC grants and SIME/DIME income. An allowance of $300 is made for each dependent.

formation is unfortunate because the quality of the housing may differ by the type of program.

According to the individuals involved in interviewing the families, the vast majority of the subsidized housing respondents live in public housing, as opposed to Section 236 housing. It is reported that the subsidized housing in Denver is in better condition than that in Seattle. Denver's subsidized housing is described as one or two stories and well maintained, with considerable noise and no grounds. The families generally do not like living in the Section 236 housing projects and the scattered site housing is considered more desirable.

Seattle's subsidized housing is also low-rise, but older and rather run-down. Some units are presently being remodeled and recreational grounds are being built. The public housing projects have problems with insects, crime, and fear. One Section 236 development has been extremely controversial as an eyesore and is now partly abandoned.

METHOD OF APPROACH

Two approaches are used in the analysis. In the first, all of the experimental families were studied 18 months after their enrollment to determine any NIT effect on whether they resided in subsidized housing.[5] Studying the entire population of SIME/DIME families allows us to measure the total experimental effect on the utilization of subsidized housing, combining the effects of both moving in and moving out. We use standard statistical techniques to determine any treatment effect on the probability that a family resided in subsidized housing during the eighteenth month after it enrolled in the experiment.

Second, we determine any NIT effect on whether a family changed housing units and subsidized housing status.[6] In the case of the implementation of an NIT, it is important to understand the amount of movement into and out of subsidized housing that should be expected. We study the response of those families who resided in subsidized housing at enrollment separately from those who did not. For those families in subsidized housing at enrollment, we note whether

---

[5] Equations for 12- and 24-month periods that were estimated showed that the effect peaks at about 18 months. The results of the other time periods are perhaps less valid because the fixed length of the experiment may distort the measured effects at the beginning or end.

[6] In Seattle, approximately 23% of the families on the experiment were in subsidized housing at enrollment. In Denver, approximately 11% of the families resided in subsidized housing.

Table 16.1   Description of

Program	Date Enacted	Administration	Housing	Eligibility
Public Housing (includes Section 23 Scattered site housing)	U.S. Housing Act of 1973	U.S. Department of Housing and Urban Development (FHA) Funds administered through local housing authorities.	Housing is built, bought, or leased by the local housing authorities under Federal cost limitations.	Eligible tenants must either be: 1. a family 2. handicapped 3. head older than 62 or 4. displaced
236 Interest Reduction Payments for Rental Housing	1968	Privately owned and operated housing under HUD regulation. HUD subsidizes the mortgage payments.	New or extensively rehabilitated buildings with 5 or more units. Costs of individual units and entire project are limited. Limits vary by geographic area.	Sponsors must be: 1. Private non-profit organizations 2. Co-operative housing corporations Tenants must be: 1. a family 2. handicapped 3. head older than 62
Section 101 Rent Supplements	1965	HUD pays rent supplements directly to owners of approved housing.	The program is piggybacked onto other federally-sponsored housing. Approved housing must have been built under 236 or 221 (c)(3) or (4).	Tenants must be either: 1. occupying sub- standard housing 2. displaced by govern- mental action or natural disaster 3. handicapped 4. head older than 62 5. head in armed forces

they moved out of the housing unit in which they received the subsidy.[7] We also study those families who were not in subsidized housing at enrollment to determine any NIT effect on the probability of moving into a subsidized unit during the 18 months after enrollment. Potentially, the NIT could affect subsidized housing utilization by affecting whether families move into subsidized housing as well as by influencing whether they leave.

All of these analyses are performed on three sample populations who remained in the experiment for 18 months: (*a*) all originally enrolled families that remained stable in terms of headship, (*b*) all originally enrolled male heads of households, and (*c*) all originally enrolled female heads of households. Because of a possible interaction between the tax treatment, marital status change, and subsidized housing utilization, we expect stable families to behave quite differently from

---

[7] The study was designed in this way due to the form of the interview. A determination as to whether the family lived in subsidized housing was based on the response to the question of whether the family lived in housing where the rent was subsidized. Because of the way in which the interview was constructed, if a family ever reported receiving a subsidy while living in a given house, that family was considered to be in subsidized housing as long as it remained in that house. Thus, a family could be in "subsidized" housing without actually being subsidized for a period of time.

Subsidized Housing Program

Income Limits	Terms	No. of Units	
Income limits are set by the local housing authority and approved by HUD. No asset limitations are required by HUD. If family income rises above 135 percent of maximum, they can be asked to move.	Rents are set at 25 percent of adjusted family income, but cannot exceed maximum. Maximum rents are set to cover operation costs and payments in lieu of taxes.	Non-elderly public housing units: Denver area City of Denver Seattle area City of Seattle	3500 3300 6000 2500
Adjusted Income cannot exceed 135 percent of public housing maximum income for the area. Tenants can remain in dwelling above income limits and pay maximum rents.	HUD pays the difference between the full market interest rate mortgage and what would be paid at a 1 percent interest rate. Family pays 25 percent of adjusted income, with a minimum of the basic rent and maximum of the fair market rent. The basic rent is that which would cover the costs of operation and debt service at 1 percent. The fair market rent covers the actual mortgage interest rate. All amounts received above the basic rent must be reimbursed to HUD.	Denver area Non-elderly (estimated) Seattle area Non-elderly (estimated)	5232 3200 4000 2500
Income limits are generally the same as public housing.	Tenant pays 25 percent of adjusted income with minimum of 30 percent and a maximum of 90 percent of the economic rent, defined as that amount necessary to cover the capital costs of the unit.	Seattle units available Non-elderly	4500 600

those that do not remain intact. Also, in the case of households splitting, male and female heads are likely to behave differently with regard to housing choice.[8] Because of the different quality of subsidized housing in Denver and Seattle, separate analyses were performed for each site.

In both approaches, the NIT plan in which a family is enrolled is specified in a way that tests the effect of the NIT on disposable income and therefore on the utilization of subsidized housing. The main treatment specification represents the predicted NIT effect on disposable income of a family assuming no change from its preexperimental labor supply.[9] Disposable income is calculated on the

---

[8] Control families (who did not receive an NIT treatment) are included in the empirical analysis. The inclusion of control families in the sample enables us to distinguish between experimental and nonexperimental effects.

[9] Except for families on welfare before the experiments, the change in disposable income evaluated at initial equilibrium hours of work is equal to the payment (grant plus all positive tax reimbursements) the family would receive if it did not respond to the experiments or equivalently, the payment received by the family at enrollment. For families on welfare, their preexperimental AFDC grant is subtracted from their payment in determining their change in disposable income. The reason the change in disposable income is not equal to the payment for families on welfare before the experiments is that families enrolled in SIME/DIME are required to give up their welfare status in order to receive payments.

basis of actual earnings in a single quarter before enrollment. Besides a measure of change in disposable income, we also include a measure of the effect of the NIT on the marginal tax rate facing the family. The variable is intended to capture the indirect effect of an NIT on subsidized housing through its effect on changing the relative price of leisure and other goods. A priori, we expect there to be a positive relationship due to the increasing price of housing relative to subsidized housing, as labor supply declines. Given that labor supply is not fixed, the effect of this relative price change is not captured in the first specification.

The influence of the various treatments is also measured separately for families of different sizes. Family size is an important consideration for three reasons. First, a larger family obtains a greater subsidy from the subsidized housing program than a smaller family with identical income. Also, a given change in income caused by an NIT is less significant to a larger family in terms of income per person. Finally, larger families may find it more difficult to obtain adequate housing in the general housing market.

In addition to measuring the effect of actual income changes, we attempt to capture the average effect of the NIT treatment. We do so by performing a separate analysis in which we replace the income specification with a general indicator of whether the family is receiving an income-maintenance treatment.

In addition to the NIT plans, several other characteristics of the families are considered in the analysis. These include age, race, family size, number of family heads, welfare status prior to enrollment, and a measure of the expected income of the family in the absence of the experiments. Also, a variable indicating whether a family lived in subsidized housing before the experiment is used in analysis. This latter variable is also expressed in conjunction with an experimental treatment variable to capture the difference in any treatment effect due to the utilization of subsidized housing before enrollment.

EMPIRICAL SPECIFICATION OF THE ESTIMATING EQUATIONS

Three categories of estimates are used in the empirical specification of the model:

1. Estimates for the entire sample are

$$RSNB18 = \alpha_0 + \alpha_1 DELY + \alpha_2 CPDUM + \alpha_3 DELTAX + \alpha_4 FDELY + \\ \alpha_5 FPYDUM + \alpha_6 FDELTAX + \alpha_7 MANFAM + \alpha_8 RNSBXM^6 \\ + \alpha_9 A + \alpha_{10} C + \alpha_{11} M + \mu,$$

Where

*RNSB*18	utilization of subsidized housing in the eighteenth experimental month
DELY	predicted payment by the experiment evaluated at the initial level of work effort ($1000s per year);
DELTAX	percentage change in marginal tax rate from the preexperimental period to the experimental period;
CPDUM	1 if a family is over the true breakeven level, 0 otherwise;
NFAMO	preexperimental family size;
FDELY	*DELY* × *NFAMO*;
FCPDUM	*CPDUM* × *NFAMO*;
FDELTAX	*DELTAX* × *NFAMO*;
EXPTL	1 if family receives an NIT treatment; 0 otherwise;
XPTFAM	*EXPTL* × *NFAMO*;
*RNSBXM*6	1 if family receives an NIT treatment and lives in subsidized housing before enrollment; 0 otherwise;
M	a vector of manpower treatment variables;[10]
MANFAM	manpower treatment dummy multiplied by the number of family members;
A	a vector of assignment variables;
C	a vector of control variables;
μ	a random error term.

The specific control variables in the equations are

SITE	1 for Seattle, 0 for Denver;
*AFDC*2*	1 if AFDC payments received in the second quarter before enrollment; 0 otherwise;
AGEHED	Age of the male or only head of the family at enrollment (years);
MARRIED	1 if male and female heads both present at enrollment; 0 otherwise;
BLACK	1 if a black family; 0 otherwise;
CHICANO	1 if a Chicano family; 0 otherwise;
*E*1 to *E*6	dummies for preexperimental earnings categories;
*HDRNM*2	preexperimental earnings (dollars per week);
HOURS	preexperimental hours worked (hours per week);
*RNSBM*6	1 if family rents subsidized housing 6 months before enrollment; 0 otherwise.

---

[10] *M*1 = counseling services, *M*2 = counseling services and a subsidy of 50% of the direct costs of any training taken over the life of the experiment, *M*3 = counseling and a 100% subsidy.

2. Estimates for sample of families residing in subsidized housing at enrollment are

$$ARSB18 = \alpha_0 + \alpha_1 DELY + \alpha_2 CPDUM + \alpha_3 DELTAX + \alpha_4 FDELY + \\ \alpha_5 FPYDUM + \alpha_6 FDELTAX + \alpha_7 MANFAM + \alpha_8 A + \alpha_9 C \\ + \alpha_{10} M + \mu,$$

Where $ARSB18 = 1$ if a family remains in subsidized housing during the first 18 months of the experiment, 0 otherwise.

3. Estimates for sample of families who do not reside in subsidized housing at enrollment are

$$SUBFAM = \alpha_0 + \alpha_1 DELY + \alpha_2 CPDUM + \alpha_3 DELTAX + \\ \alpha_4 FDELY + \alpha_5 FPYDUM + \alpha_6 FDELTAX + \\ \alpha_7 MANFAM + \alpha_8 A + \alpha_9 C + \alpha_{10} M + \mu,$$

Where $SUBFAM = 1$ if a family moves into subsidized housing during the first 18 months of the experiment, 0 otherwise.

EMPIRICAL FINDINGS

In general, our results show that SIME/DIME substantially decreased the utilization of subsidized housing. The magnitude of the effect differed by site and type of family and was sensitive to the level of support and family size.

Effect of Negative Income Tax on the Probability of Residing in Subsidized Housing 18 Months after Enrollment

The empirical estimates of the effect of an NIT on the probability of residing in subsidized housing during the eighteenth month of the experiment are presented in Table 16.2. As can be seen, the NIT has the most significant effect on families with a female head. The magnitude of those effects differ between Seattle and Denver.

In Seattle, an experimental female head without a family was 4.5% less likely to reside in subsidized housing with each $1000 increase in disposable income.[11] Each additional family member decreased this effect by 1.4%. The findings imply that in Seattle, for an average experimental family of four, the net effect of a $1000 increase in disposable income and 25% change in the tax rate, was to decrease the likelihood of that family residing in subsidized housing by 4.3% relative to the 70.6% probability for controls, if the family did not utilize sub-

---

[11] It should be noted that a single-person family does not exist in the experiment but is merely used as a tool for analysis.

Table 16.2

Estimated Treatment Effects on the Probability of Residing in Subsidized Housing after 18 Months: All Families

Independent Variables	Female Heads		Male Heads		Stable Families (combined sites)	
	Seattle Coeff (SE)	Denver Coeff (SE)	Seattle Coeff (SE)	Denver Coeff (SE)	Coeff (SE)	Coeff (SE)
Control Variables						
SITE	---	---	---	---	.02031**	.02018**
	---	---	---	---	(.00759)	(.00759)
NFAMO	-.01135*	.00901	.00667	.01188**	-.00126	-.00343
	(.00577)	(.00318)	(.00587)	(.00321)	(.00389)	(.00416)
BLACK	.02399	.01896*	.00343	.00534	.01833*	.01813*
	(.01294)	(.00816)	(.01313)	(.00822)	(.00734)	(.00733)
CHICANO	---	.02556**	---	.01320	.02416*	.02429*
	---	(.00839)	---	(.00813)	(.01004)	(.01004)
MARRIED	-.02631*	-.01864†	.07950†	-.02667	-.02468*	-.02370*
	(.01766)	(.01011)	(.04573)	(.02173)	(.01075)	(.01068)
AGEHED	.00092	-.00009**	.00154*	-.00010	.00049	.00052
	(.00065)	(.00038)	(.00061)	(.00037)	(.00034)	(.00034)
AFDCM2	.02756*	-.00764	.00504	-.00850	.02005†	.02076*
	(.01999)	(.00987)	(.02500)	(.01176)	(.01027)	(.01000)
RNSBM6	.61755**	.70991**	.54101*	.58165**	.67348**	.67054**
	(.02412)	(.02556)	(.02903)	(.02883)	(.01662)	(.01676)
Treatment Variables						
EXPT1	---	---	---	---	---	-.05256*
	---	---	---	---	---	(.01961)
XPTFAM	---	---	---	---	---	.01035*
	---	--- ·	---	---	---	(.00449)
CPDUM	-.07491	.02126	.06537	.06138†	.01611	---
	(.06111)	(.03279)	(.05729)	(.03421)	(.03197)	---
FCPDUM	.01580	-.00831	-.01193	-.01431†	-.00636	---
	(.01441)	(.00795)	(.01273)	(.00785)	(.00773)	---
DELY	-.05871**	-.02678*	-.04495†	-.02514†	-.01533	---
	(.02226)	(.01333)	(.02445)	(.01465)	(.01286)	---
FDELY	.01454**	.00498†	.00849†	-.00506†	.00305	---
	(.00476)	(.00282)	(.00495)	(.00297)	(.00280)	---
DELTAX	-.09085	.11914*	.03563	-.04732	-.07357	---
	(.09416)	(.05543)	(.12436)	(.06694)	(.05168)	---
FDELTAX	.01656	-.02820*	.00277	.00448	.01670	---
	(.02266)	(.01330)	(.02687)	(.01445)	(.01233)	---
RNSBMX6	-.03643	-.13317**	.03116	-.26849**	.03228	-.02737
	(.03066)	(.03047)	(.03771)	(.03585)	(.02032)	(.02055)
Constant	.16100	.01042	-.14323	-.00791	.03571	.04086
Sample Size	1857	2402	1083	1461	3623	3623
Simple R^2	.48033	.46194	.48318	.32063	.55938	.55923
Mean of Dep. Var.	.1648	.0508	.0859	.0233	.0941	.0941

Note: Dependent variable is *RNSB*18. Other variable included in these regressions are *E*-level dummies, manpower treatment dummies, family size interaction, and preexperimental earnings and hours worked.

†$p < .10$.
*$p < .05$.
**$p < .01$.

sidized housing before enrollment.[12] If the family did, the net decrease from the 8.9% control probability is .7%.

In Denver, a female head is 2.2% less likely to reside in subsidized housing with each $1000 change in disposable income, and each additional family member decreases the effect by .49%. Also, a 100% increase in the tax rate caused the female to be 9.1% more likely to reside in subsidized housing. This effect, however, decreased 2.8% for each additional family member. Also, the order of magnitude of the NIT effect differed according to whether a family utilized subsidized housing before the experiments began.

In addition to the effect of the change in disposable income on all families, a family receiving an NIT treatment who lived in subsidized housing before enrollment was 13.3% less likely to be in subsidized housing 18 months after enrollment than was a control family who had resided in subsidized housing at some time before the experiment (however, not necessarily at the time of enrollment).

These combined results for Denver imply that for an experimental family, there was 13.9% less chance of utilizing subsidized housing than there was for an average control family of four who lived in subsidized housing before enrollment, given a 25% tax rate change and a $100 change in disposable income. The treatment effect was, however, only a .6% decrease in the 2.2% probability for a control family who did not reside in subsidized housing before enrollment.

The estimates for male heads in Seattle are generally of the same magnitude as for female heads, the same treatment variables being significant. They are, however, slightly less reliable than those that we note for female heads. An experimental male head without family was 3.7% less likely to reside in subsidized housing with each $1000 increase in disposable income. Each additional family member decreased this effect by .8%. This result, along with the effects of the other treatment specifications, implies that for a family of four who did not reside in subsidized housing preexperimentally, the average NIT treatment had no effect on the 50.3% probability of controls utilizing subsidized housing 18 months into the experiment. The effect was, however, positive for a family who did reside in subsidized housing preexperimentally.

The effects of the experiments on change in disposable income for male heads of households in Denver were in a different direction from those for the other samples. This result may be due to the presence of some strong indirect effects such as marital status and labor supply changes. The effect of the NIT, however, greatly differed according to whether or not the family utilized subsidized housing before the experiments began. In addition to the effect of the change in disposable income and tax rates, a family receiving an NIT treatment who lived in subsidized housing before enrollment was 26% less likely to be in

---

[12] All control variables discussed in this section are for black families of four with single heads who are 33 years old, did not receive AFDC before enrollment in the experiment, and who earned $100 per 40-hour week at this time. They are in the mid-range in terms of normal income before the experiment.

subsidized housing in the eighteenth month than a control family who also resided in subsidized housing preexperimentally. Thus, the average experimental
family of four with the average treatment who lived in subsidized housing 6
months before enrollment was 27.2% less likely to utilize subsidized housing
than similar control families who had a 62.7% probability of residing in subsidized housing. The net effect, however, for a similar family who did not live in
subsidized housing before the experiment was a .3% decrease in the 4.6% control
probability.

With regard to families that did not change headships, a one-person family (in
terms of a single family member who receives an NIT treatment) was on the
average 4% less likely than a control to reside in subsidized housing in the eighteenth month. This effect however, decreased 1% with each additional family
member. Thus, the average experimental family who utilized subsidized housing
preexperimentally was 4.4% less likely to reside in subsidized housing than similar control families, who had a 71.7% probability. If an experimental family did
not use subsidized housing preexperimentally, the NIT effect was nil.

Effect of Negative Income Tax on the Probability of Remaining in Subsidized Housing

The empirical estimates of the effect of an NIT on the probability of remaining in subsidized housing estimated on the sample of those who are in subsidized
housing at enrollment in the experiments are presented in Table 16.3. In none
of the samples are the tax rate changes significant in causing a family to leave
subsidized housing. For male heads, none of the treatment variables are significant. This may be due to the misspecification of the model caused by the necessity to combine sites due to sample size. (This applies only to the sample of male
heads.)

The estimates for female heads, however, show large effects. Each $1000 of
payment is correlated with a female heads being 15% less likely to remain in
subsidized housing than a control, the effect diminishing 2.7% for each additional family member. Thus, with the average payment of $1000, an average family
of four was 4.2% less likely to remain in subsidized housing.

The results for stable families indicate that an experimental family was 32.4%
less likely to remain in subsidized housing than a control family. The effect was
decreased 7.2% for each additional family member, resulting in a net effect of
3.6% for a family of four.

Effect of Negative Income Tax on the Probability of Entering Subsidized Housing

Estimates of the effect of an NIT on the probability of entering subsidized
housing based on the sample who did not reside in subsidized housing at the
time of enrollment are presented in Table 16.4. In Denver, the tax rate changes

Table 16.3
Estimated Treatment Effects on the Probability of Remaining in
Subsidized Housing: Families in Subsidized Housing at
Enrollment, Combined Sites

Independent Variables	Male Heads Coeff (SE)	Female Heads Coeff (SE)	Stable Families Coeff (SE)	Stable Families Coeff (SE)
Control Variables				
SITE	.34940** (.09866)	.09144 (.05861)	.05102 (.06462)	.04472 (.04499)
NAFAMO	.04250 (.04457)	.00452 (.02532)	.00199 (.02662)	-.01668 (.02913)
BLACK	.16257† (.08595)	.11475** (.04668)	.10222** (.04990)	.10957* (.04940)
CHICANO	.23486* (.11938)	.12816† (.07505)	.09335 (.08282)	.10940 (.08289)
MARRIED	---	-.12204* (.05501)	-.10103 (.06406)	-.09239 (.06334)
AGEHED	.01556** (.00357)	.00727** (.00220)	.00713** (.00230)	.00734** (.00225)
AFDCM2	-.02462 (.09305)	.08865* (.05313)	-.01835 (.05897)	-.01747 (.05796)
Treatment Variables				
EXPT1	--- ---	--- ---	--- ---	-.32396* (.12836)
XPTFAM	--- ---	--- ---	--- ---	.07225* (.03137)
CPDUM	.09113 (.47558)	.02272 (.30909)	.41994 (.41508)	--- ---
FCPDUM	-.04002 (.11129)	-.02356 (.07530)	-.16404 (.12880)	--- ---
DELY	-.05546 (.11537)	-.15150* (.06653)	-.07918 (.07229)	--- ---
FDELY	.01394 (.02284)	.02734† (.01417)	.01359 (.01564)	--- ---
DELTAX	-.78104 (.55831)	-.17086 (.27361)	-.41645 (.30151)	--- ---
FDELTAX	.18390 (.12003)	.04757 (.06854)	.11196 (.07585)	--- ---
Constant	-.16349	.62191	.60269	.63141
Sample Size	100	524	459	459
Simple R^2	.31233	.12177	.10933	.10698
Mean of Dep. Var.	.5526	.6832	.6993	.6993

Note: Dependent variable is *ARSB*18. Other variables included in these regressions are *E*-level dummies, manpower treatment dummies, family size interactions, and preexperimental earnings and hours worked.

   †$p < .10$.
   *$p < .05$.
   **$p < .01$.

had a significant effect for both male and female heads and the change in disposable income did not. A 100% increase in the tax rate was correlated with a male head in Denver being 15.3% more likely to enter subsidized housing than a fam-

Table 16.4

Estimated Treatment Effects on the Probability of
Moving into Subsidized Housing: Families Not in
Subsidized Housing at Enrollment

Independent Variables	Male Heads		Female Heads		Stable Families (combined sites)	
	Denver Coeff (SE)	Seattle Coeff (SE)	Denver Coeff (SE)	Seattle Coeff (SE)	Coeff (SE)	Coeff (SE)
Control Variables						
SITE	---	---	---	---	.02892**	.02893**
	---	---	---	---	(.00662)	(.00602)
NFAMO	.00871**	.00327	.00900**	-.00858	.00162	.00258
	(.00308)	(.00454)	(.00330)	(.00553)	(.00349)	(.00372)
BLACKS	.00718	-.01213	.01504†	.01480	.01628*	.01654*
	(.00789)	(.01013)	(.00845)	(.01259)	(.00659)	(.00658)
CHICANO	.01269	---	.02659**	---	.02047*	.02126*
	(.00781)	---	(.00875)	---	(.00882)	(.00882)
MARRIED	---	---	-.00083	-.03427†	-.02123*	-.02136*
	---	---	(.01055)	(.01740)	(.00982)	(.00975)
AGEHED	-.00106**	-.00089†	-.00087*	-.00165*	-.00147**	-.00145**
	(.00035)	(.00048)	(.00039)	(.00064)	(.00031)	(.0030)
AFDCM2	.02708*	.01633	.02198*	.07070**	.04304**	.04344**
	(.01144)	(.02083)	(.01041)	(.02027)	(.00939)	(.00915)
Treatment Variables						
XPT1	---	---	---	---	---	-.00662
	---	---	---	---	---	(.01745)
XPTFAM	---	---	---	---	---	.00023
	---	---	---	---	---	(.00401)
CPDUM	.02481	.02936	.04001	-.07999	.02221	---
	(.03254)	(.04334)	(.03356)	(.05665)	(.02754)	---
FCPDUM	-.00685	-.00457	-.01268	.01638	.00670	---
	(.00746)	(.00965)	(.00813)	(.01339)	(.00665)	---
DELTAX	.15344*	.01907	.10187†	.08426	.02672	---
	(.06556)	(.09853)	(.05916)	(.09340)	(.04714)	---
FDELTAX	-.03299*	-.01499	-.02474†	-.02593	-.00509	---
	(.01421)	(.02132)	(.01426)	(.02215)	(.01117)	---
DELY	-.01547	-.02362	-.01051	-.06040**	-.02052†	---
	(.01408)	(.01944)	(.01409)	(.02191)	(.01178)	---
FDELY	.00297	.00654†	.00178	.01770**	.00439†	---
	(.00287)	(.00396)	(.00301)	(.00467)	(.00258)	---
Constant	.03946	.02789	.04892	.16100	.07610	.07148
Sample Size	1421	972	2293	1530	3264	3264
Simple R²	.04114	.08108	.03278	.07933	.04901	.04782
Mean of Dep. Var.	.0148	.0247	.0288	.0647	.0294	.0294

Note: Dependent variable is SUBFAM. Other variables included in these regressions
are E-level dummies, manpower treatment dummies, family size interactions, and preexperimental earnings and hours worked.
†p < .10.
*p < .05.
**p < .01.

ily with no change in the tax rate, the effect decreasing 3.2% for each family
member. For a female head, a 100% increase in the tax rate was correlated with
a 10% greater probability of moving into subsidized housing, the probability
decreasing 2.4% for each family member.

In Seattle, the treatments had no significant effect for male heads, but the change in disposable income significantly affected movement into subsidized housing for female heads. A $1000 increase in income caused a female head to be 6% less likely to move into subsidized housing than a family with no change in income, the effect decreasing 1.8% for each family member.

For stable families, a $1000 increase in income was correlated with its being 2% less likely to move into subsidized housing, the effect decreasing .4% for each family member.

SUMMARY AND CONCLUSION

The results of the study in general showed a strong and significant interaction between the NIT defined by the SIME/DIME and the utilization of the type of subsidized housing generally found in Denver and Seattle. This interaction is seen in the generally lower probability of families in the experimental group residing in subsidized housing. For each sample (male heads and female heads at each site and stable families) the results are consistent when comparing the estimates among the different populations. The NIT appears to have been correlated with movement out of subsidized housing and seems also to have inhibited families from moving in. Significantly different types of responses are noted by site and headship.

Female heads in the Seattle experimental group were less likely to reside in subsidized housing 18 months into the experiment than those who were not in this group. For those who did not reside in subsidized housing at enrollment, an NIT was associated with an increase in the probability of moving into subsidized housing. The combined sample of female heads for both sites shows that a NIT-caused increase in disposable income was correlated with families who were in subsidized housing at enrollment changing subsidized housing status.

Male heads in the Seattle experimental group were also less likely to reside in subsidized housing 18 months after the NIT treatment began. Income change, however, did not cause male heads to enter subsidized housing. Also, the sample of male heads combined by site showed no significant effects on movement out of subsidized housing. A significant effect, however, could have occurred in Seattle and been masked by the inclusion of Denver families in the sample.

Female heads in Denver with experimental increases in disposable income were less likely to be in subsidized housing 18 months after enrollment than those without. The effects, however, are smaller with increases in the tax rate. The NIT had an additional negative effect on the subsidized housing consumption of those who resided in subsidized housing preexperimentally.

In terms of entering subsidized housing, Denver female heads were more likely to do so given a tax increase, implying that the change in the relative price of leisure had an effect. As part of the combined sample with Seattle, they were found to be more likely to leave subsidized housing with a positive change in income.

The sign on the income variable for male heads in Denver was opposite to the sign of all other samples. This indicates that they were more likely to reside in subsidized housing in the eighteenth month, given an NIT-caused increase in disposable income. This reverse sign may mean that the indirect effects of the NIT on housing consumption through labor supply changes and marital status changes were prevailing. In terms of entering subsidized housing, male heads, like female heads, appear to have been more likely to do so as the tax rate increased and the cost of leisure decreased.

The results for stable families, who by definition did not change headship, show that families receiving NIT treatment were much more likely to reside in subsidized housing in the eighteenth month than those who were not. Families who were in subsidized housing at enrollment were more likely to leave if they received an NIT treatment, but such a treatment did not keep families who did not reside in subsidized housing at enrollment from entering.

This diversity in response by site and by headship was caused by several factors, including different labor supply effects, marital status effects, and different housing qualities by site. More complex modeling is necessary in order to understand more than the general orders of magnitude of the effects. In particular, simultaneous models of labor supply, family stability, and housing choice would be necessary to measure the effects according to various structural parameters. Helpful a priori implications would result from a theory that was expanded to develop such models. Also, more specific modeling of the housing subsidy programs would be useful. Finally, detailed knowledge of housing quality and housing markets at both sites would allow us to answer questions such as why male heads respond so differently by site.

Data Collection and Processing

VIRGIL DAVIS
ARLENE WAKSBERG

DATA COLLECTION

For all families enrolled in SIME/DIME, a series of in-depth interviews was given in the respondent's home. Beginning with a preenrollment interview conducted prior to the family's actual assignment, periodic interviews were administered to the head(s) of household over the duration of the experiments. Detailed information was collected on such topics as family composition, employment history, nonwage income, assets owned, training and education undertaken, as well as other social and demographic data.

The SIME/DIME data collection obtained an average of 5 years of data from approximately 5000 families. The data collection effort was intended to support a broad range of economic and sociological research studies based upon the data. Point-in-time questions were asked about such diverse topics as health, job satisfaction, marital stability, and education of children; and historical data were collected on marriages, fertility, and mobility. All data for an individual were required to be connected across time, across topics, and through different family formations.

Some operational requirements were also imposed upon the data collection process. Most important was the need to minimize any inconvenience to the respondents that might result in either sample attrition or other forms of noncooperation. It was also necessary to design methods to maintain contact with the families, collect the information in a complete and timely fashion, promote consistency in the form and interpretation of the data both over time and between the two sites, and provide logical links in the data when necessary.

A GUARANTEED ANNUAL INCOME:
EVIDENCE FROM A SOCIAL EXPERIMENT

Interviewing

To accomplish these tasks, the participating families were administered a series of periodic interviews on a regular cycle of 4 to 5 months during their tenure
on the experiments. At each site, interviews were given in overlapping waves. As
a result, two or three different regular periodic interviews were active at each site
at any time. Moreover, the interview cycle in Denver was 1 year behind Seattle.
Thus, five or six different interviews were frequently in operation at the same
time.

In addition, there was a postmove interview used to collect data from families
that had moved away from Denver and Seattle. Due to cost considerations, these
families were interviewed only once a year. The same basic instrument was also
used as a catch-up interview for families who had missed one or more regular
periodic interviews but were residing within the site area. These were known as
residual interviews. Postmove interviews generally covered 1 year of data; residual interviews could span from 8 months to 3 years of data. Figure A.1 illustrates
the overlap of interviews by showing the time span of active interviews in one
12-month period.

Interview development was aided by the creation of questionnaire modules,
which were then used as building blocks in the construction of each periodic interview. Each module consisted of a series of questions on a specific topic. Each
was designed with the idea of being repeated either within a single interview, as
when more than one individual within the family was asked a series of questions,
or in later interviews when longitudinal data were desired.

Every interview, then, was constructed from combinations of various modules.
Some modules were repeated in every interview to cover dynamic situations such
as hours of work, wages, and family composition. Other modules covering topics
that changed less rapidly were repeated with less frequency, generally yearly.
The aims in this module system were to provide efficiency in construcing the interviews and consistency in the data collected. The attention to consistency,
though not always achieved, had many benefits. Among these benefits were ease
in administering the questionnaires because of familiarity on the part of the interviewer and the respondents, as well as simplified data-processing from initial
data input through creation of analytic variables.

Also incorporated into the questionnarie design was a somewhat complex system of skip logic. This was necessary since thousands of discrete questions would
have had to be asked if every question were asked of all family members. The introduction of skip logic, providing key questions and appropriate response-
dependent directives for the interviewer, allowed the interview to proceed
smoothly. Only the portions applicable to each respondent were asked, greatly
reducing the number of questions.

Prerecorded data were used in certain parts of the interview in order to establish longitudinal links from one periodic interview to another and to avoid data

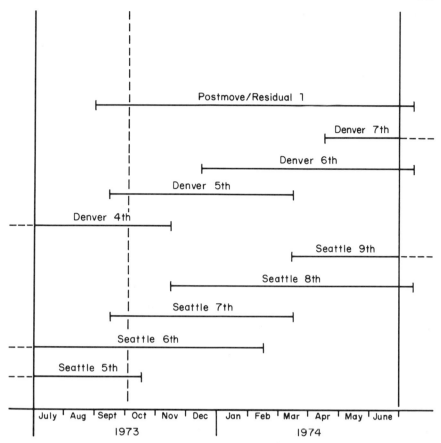

Figure A.1   Interviews active in a 1-year cross section (last half of 1973 and first half of 1974).

discontinuities. Prerecording was done by inserting information reported in a previous interview (or in other data-recording sources such as the master family composition file) into a new interview before it was administered to the family. These data were used primarily to create continuity in job information, e.g., "Last time we were here you said you were working for Bell Telephone as a phone operator at $4.57 an hour. Is that correct? Has there been any change since then?" It was also used to follow up on training or education courses previously reported and to keep track of data on family members without forcing the respondents to repeat the information each time. Prerecording provided the opportunity to confirm previously collected data; it also enabled the interviews to proceed more quickly and the data to appear more coherent over time. However, the procedure had to be used with caution in order to avoid guiding the respondents' answers.

The interviews were conducted at the homes of participating families by trained, professional interviewers. The interviewers returned the completed interviews, along with certain verifying documentation such as pay stubs and mortgage statements, to the site office. The questionnarie booklets were then logged in, checked for reports of family composition changes and sent to quality control. In quality control the interviews were read by two individuals for completeness and for both internal consistency of the data and consistency with prior interviews. All inconsistencies and incomplete responses were referred back to the interviewer, frequently prompting a recontact with the respondent. Procedural or interpretive problems encountered at either site were referred to the research staff for resolution. This was done to ensure that decisions at the sites were in line with research requirements. It also served to ensure consistency in the operations of the two sites by clearing these decisions with a common source.

SIME/DIME DATA PROCESSING

SIME/DIME data processing consisted of numerous operations. However, a few functions were primary: processing of interview data through construction of a data base, support of the master family composition file, and creation of the labor supply analytical file. These are described in more detail below.

Processing of Interview Data

Entry Preparation

The incorporation of skip logic into the interview resulted in completed interviews that were logically consistent but somewhat sparse, averaging no more than two answers per printed page. Therefore, rather than attempt to convert every answer position into a machine-encoded form, the interview logic was incorporated into the entry processing as well. This was accomplished through computer software that allowed the specification of the interview logic in a machine-decipherable form. Given this facility, the range and logic checks to be performed during data entry could be defined and the software could guide an entry operator through the proper sequence.

As a step in the development of the data entry program for each interview, there was a procedure for verifying that the program worked according to expectations. This entailed the creation of test families that incorporated data to test all bounds and skip logic in the data entry program. The testing procedure was carried through to the first stages of the data retrieval as well. All test cases were run through the entry-retrieval cycle and compared by machine to the expected output. Then, as each data entry program for a new periodic interview was made available to one of the sites, a data processing representative from SRI went to the sites to ensure that data entry under the new program was initiated smoothly.

Data Entry

Data entry operators at the site offices entered data via leased telephone lines to the SRI computer facility. The entry process was under the control of the SRI-developed software package that performed the following major operations:

1. evaluated answers for range or value acceptability,
2. determined whether range value overrides were allowed,
3. performed limited interitem checks,
4. controlled the rollback of the entry sequence to a prior point specified by the entry operator,
5. enabled entry operator to change a previously entered value,
6. performed save and subsequent restart operations under user control, and
7. maintained statistics on operator activities.

The data entry operator entered data directly from the interview booklet used in the field. It should be noted that the data entry program and the entry operator functioned in a complementary, interactive manner. This was accomplished because the logic-driven program directed the entry operator through the complicated interview sequence while the operator, with the actual data in front of him or her, was constantly verifying the range checks and the skip logic patterns. If conflicts were discovered, such as the operator being forced to skip recorded data or unable to enter data as it existed in the interview, the process was stopped and the problem was referred to the data entry supervisor.

The results of each interview entry procedure was a sequential stream of answers residing on the computer system as a single file. As the interview entry activities continued, completed files were periodically transferred to tape and merged with previously completed files. This created the tape for the answer file for a particular periodic interview. Once the entry process of an entire periodic interview was finished, a complete machine-generated inventory of the final answer file tape was sent to the field. The inventories were compared against site records to ensure that all interviews had been entered and stored on the tape. After an interview's answer file tape was declared complete, frequency distributions were generated. These distributions and the file were then made available to researchers.

Data Base Building

The data entered via the interactive entry process resulted in a sequential stream of identifier-answer pairs for each interview booklet. The volume and arrangement of the data, however, made this form of storage unusable for any analytical purposes. As a step toward making the data more accessible, the data were first divided along module lines, and then the modules were divided into longitudinal and aperiodic data.

Longitudinal Data

For the more inherently longitudinal data, the answers were retrieved and stored in files of a standard cross-sectional record format. The process of developing these files, known as the intermediate file, involved creating a uniform file description for each module that could satisfy the collective requirements of all versions of the module. When new periodics were introduced, the record formats were reviewed and updated, if necessary, to reflect additions or deletions of items. Then, a retrieval program was created that transferred the data from the answer files of the periodic interview into the intermediate file record. This made the data access easier and less expensive. However, it still left many of the longitudinal issues unaddressed, since the data were in a series of cross-sectional records representing each occurrence of the module.

Since much of the important data receiving research attention were of a longitudinal nature, we proceeded to the development of longitudinal files. The first step was to impose a descriptive structure on the data that would enable us to build data files that were compatible with an on-line data base system. This did not necessarily imply a commitment to put the data into an on-line data management environment, but was rather a technique to help impose a consistent methodology across different components of the data. In fact, some of the data bases were eventually maintained on a random-access, on-line system, while others were on tape, which could only be accessed sequentially.

The data base design then proceeded towards the goal of removing the cross-sectional nature of the data originally imposed by the periodic interviews. This was to be done by creating transactions or events (e.g., changes in hours of work or in the monthly amount of AFDC received), for data that could reasonably fit into a longitudinal transaction mode. This enabled the elimination of repeating information such as a month-by-month enumeration of a constant monthly income flow, and the elimination of nonevents, primarily the start and end of periodic interviews. For data like the monthly benefits and expenses, this was simply a matter of linking up the family periodic records across time, and then replacing each monthly records of the amount of income received from AFDC, Social Security, or other sources with records that only occurred when the monthly income changed.

For other types of data, however, further linking procedures were required. In particular it was necessary to identify continuous jobs, as well as training and education programs across periodic boundaries, in order to create an event-oriented file. Unfortunately, continuity in data was broken each time an interview was administered. A data-processing effort was then required to reestablish it. This was not easily accomplished since the collected information was sometimes inadequate to unambiguously connect entities across periodic interviews. The problem was further compounded by the fact that some of the linkage information, such as employers, was of a textual nature that did not readily lend itself to automatic processing. In addition, there were variations in reported data for entities that were actually the same. Therefore, some reported differences implied discontinuities when they actually represented only differences in recollections. As a consequence, the linkage process was forced to deal with imprecision, and the linkage criteria had to allow some adjustments for this. There was a delicate balance in defining these criteria so that they were neither overly restrictive in allowing actual links nor improperly aggressive in creating false links.

As the next step in the development of a linked, longitudinal data base, the descriptive structure was used as a format for creating a uniform cross-sectional record for each periodic occurrence of the subject in question. With respect to employment data, e.g., a separate record was created for every job that was reported in every interview for each individual. Then, these records were linked across periodic interviews by identifying continuous jobs. The reported information used as indicators of continuity were "working last," implying continuity with a job in the previous interview, and "still working," implying continuity linking indicators, and the dates of working last and still working for a linked job were expected to be adjacent. If multiple jobs with link indicators existed such that no unique links could be accomplished, an attempt was made to match job characteristics such as industry, occupation, wage rates, and hours worked.

The linkage procedure allowed the construction of a single record per job. This new record structure consisted of a header record containing one-time job information such as job entry, ending, and summary data from the periodic records. It also contained a series of periodic records, one for each interview in which the job was reported, containing data that were picked up once in each periodic interview (such as industry and occupation code). Finally, it contained a series of transaction records that chronologically reported all changes that occurred within the job, such as changes in hours or wage rates. These transaction records allowed us to have events that spanned periodic boundaries and eliminated much of the repetition of unchanging data reported in each interview.

To facilitate data merging, consistent primary key sets were defined as a group of data items that uniquely identified each record. These keys were then used in procedures that matched a family's or individual's data sets within a data base or across data bases. The keys were also used in procedures that added new data to existing data bases.

In building and documenting this longitudinal data base, we also attempted to integrate all previous sources into one descriptive document. This meant that we were obliged to relate the derived data base to the source document (interview questionnaire), the data entry specification (the logic that assigned an internal question number to the data), the answer file output and the data base source (the intermediate file location).

Aperiodic Data

Not all questionnaire modules were retrieved into the intermediate file format. Certain modules, generally those that were asked only once during the experiment or were asked irregularly and presented point-in-time data, were not collected with the same emphasis on longitudinal consistency. The volume and inconsistent nature of these data made an approach like the one taken for longitudinal data infeasible. Instead, these data were stored in records that were essentially blocked-out versions of the data entry program for each module, known as work files. These records contained all the inconsistencies created by periodic alterations in the questionnaire and data entry programs.

The approach taken to systematize the data in work files began with the creation of a reference document that described where all data occurred for each module. The document listed each occurrence of each data item, the periodic interview in which it occurred, its location in the questionnarie, its question number in the data entry program, and its location in the work files.

Based upon the structure described in the reference document, a routine program was customized for each module. The program was then used to transfer the data from work file records into uniform record types per module. The new records were then merged across all periodic occurrences of the module to create the data base records.

Master Family Composition File

Once the data collection activities began, it became clear that a sophisticated records-keeping system was essential. Following families and their individual members as they married, divorced, moved, and were interviewed, rapidly became an impossible clerical job. As an indication of the magnitude of this task, the number of enrolled families increased by 250% during the life of the experiment.

Therefore, an automated process for keeping track of all families and individuals was developed. The system contained master records for each family and for each individual known to SIME/DIME. These records contained basic information about each individual (e.g., birth date, sex). The file was augmented by records documenting each interview, each family composition change, interrelations of family members, and predecessor and successor families. Thus, the complete histories of families and individuals on the experiments could be readily traced. The resulting file also enabled us to accomplish sophisticated retrievals, edits, summary statistics, and subset selections. It provided a mechanism for controlling and checking the interviewing and payments system; and, most importantly, it provided ready access to a current version of this important file.

Analytical File Generation

On a data effort of this magnitude there are inherent conflicts between an analytical file and a data collection data base that make it impossible for one file to serve both functions. To meet the recording requirements of the collection effort, the data base should be able to include every answer that is obtained. To fit this into a reasonable amount of storage space, it is desirable to be able to take advantage of methods that do not waste space for unanswered questions.

Analytic files have somewhat conflicting needs since they are usually operated upon by statistical packages that require fixed-format rectangular records as input. Although most research studies are confined to a limited subset of the data, in an effort the size of SIME/DIME it soon became apparent that each individual study could not afford to define custom variables of every data subset of interest. Instead, a large set of variables of general interest called the labor supply file was developed to the point where it satisfied the basic needs of many of the studies. Each time the data base went through a major update, this analysis file was regenerated to reflect the latest results. Like the data base generation process, the labor supply file-building process consisted of a series of module specific components. Each component used a single portion of the data base, in conjunction with the master family composition file as a controlling mechanism, and extracted data and computed variables based upon these two input files. The resulting file subsets consisted of a series of fixed length records from either families or individuals, depending upon the module. Each record covered a fixed interval of time, and a record was generated for every period for which data were recorded. These were combined into a single individual-oriented file, which then supported subsequent analytical requests.

Unique Data-Processing Requirements of the Project

A data-processing activity of this nature shares many requirements with typical management information systems. However, it also differs in ways that are perhaps not always obvious and are worth enumerating.

1. There is an "instant" start-up. Contrary to most business activities that experience a buildup of clients and data support requirements as they mature, a project of this nature has its heaviest data-processing demands when the operation begins.

2. The data are of accumulative, not replacement nature. In many activities yesterday's data are replaced by today's update—perhaps after being retained in a running total and a historical archive. However, the likelihood of desiring access to detailed historical data diminishes over time. In this type of activity, all data remain of analytical interest and aggregations may be impossible or undesirable.

3. All data are equal, but some are more equal than others. While all items are of interest, the oldest and the newest are frequently the most interesting. Each, however, poses its own special problems. The oldest baseline data are likely to have been collected before procedures were refined, thus they may be incomplete or incompatible with later data. As for the newest data, it is often difficult to bring data activities of this nature to a state approaching "current."

4. There are few transactions, each with a large number of items. Business transactions generally occur with high frequency and a small number of items. In this project, however, an interview can be considered to be like a large update entry that occurs infrequently but with a large amount of interdependent data.

5. There are few checks, balances, or irrefutable edits that can be used to verify or correct the data. In fact, the data collected in SIME/DIME violates most of the common expectations of information systems, as described in the following:

   a. There is generally a relatively high ratio of reporting units to data items. This provides a means of checking any individual response to an item based upon the large number of other responses. The ratio of reporting units to data items in SIME/DIME, however, occasionally approaches unity.

   b. Most systems can impose hard limits on the values accepted in each item. Given the complexity of our data collection and processing activities, incomplete or illogical answers are not uncommon. However, the cost of rejecting a particular answer is the loss of large quantities of associated data, requiring us to use virtually any response received.

   c. Commonly, data can be verified, either from internal sources (other reported data) or external sources. Much of the SIME/DIME data are not of an accounting nature. Even the data that have a precise basis frequently cannot be verified against source documents and do not contain enough redundancy for internal verification checks.

Future Guidelines

In retrospect, many of the data-processing problems that were encountered in SIME/DIME could have been avoided or alleviated by:

1. developing data-processing systems that imposed no artificial constraints on the collected data to be entered into that system;

2. shortening the time from data collection to data entry;

3. extending the editing capabilities of the data entry procedure by including previously entered data, thus enabling range checks to be enhanced by longitudinal and cross-sectional information;

4. generating automated timely data and summary statistics to facilitate field operations and provide feedback on data collection and entry problems as they are encountered;

5. developing more routine and efficient procedures for resolving data discrepancies;

6. ensuring sufficient redundancy in the important data collected to provide internal verification of the information; and

7. providing unambiguous specifications in the use of items to be used for linkage purposes.

Even today, SIME/DIME data-related efforts remain complex, and are incapable of being encapsulated in a tidy procedural world. The start-up phase was overwhelming, comparable to starting a service business with two branch offices overnight. Additionally, the rapid changes in data-processing equipment and techniques since the start-up somewhat distort our understanding of the prevalent data-processing conditions when the project began. Over the past few years, significant improvements have been made to the process, although many changes have been constrained by limitations imposed by earlier decisions. Perhaps the most valuable lesson to be learned from the data collection and processing tasks undertaken in this experiment is that early decisions must be thought through carefully, keeping all future data-processing requirements in mind. Short-run decisions based only upon immediate needs can have serious long-run consequences, and the costs of these decisions are magnified in the later stages of data processing.

Index

QUANTITATIVE STUDIES IN SOCIAL RELATIONS

Consulting Editor: Peter H. Rossi

UNIVERSITY OF MASSACHUSETTS
AMHERST, MASSACHUSETTS

Peter H. Rossi and Walter Williams (Eds.), EVALUATING SOCIAL PROGRAMS: *Theory, Practice, and Politics*

Roger N. Shepard, A. Kimball Romney, and Sara Beth Nerlove (Eds.), MULTIDIMENSIONAL SCALING: *Theory and Applications in the Behavioral Sciences,* Volume I – Theory; Volume II – Applications

Robert L. Crain and Carol S. Weisman, DISCRIMINATION, PERSONALITY, AND ACHIEVEMENT: *A Survey of Northern Blacks*

Douglas T. Hall and Benjamin Schneider, ORGANIZATIONAL CLIMATES AND CAREERS: *The Work Lives of Priests*

Kent S. Miller and Ralph Mason Dreger (Eds.), COMPARATIVE STUDIES OF BLACKS AND WHITES IN THE UNITED STATES

Robert B. Tapp, RELIGION AMONG THE UNITARIAN UNIVERSALISTS: *Converts in the Stepfathers' House*

Arthur S. Goldberger and Otis Dudley Duncan (Eds.), STRUCTURAL EQUATION MODELS IN THE SOCIAL SCIENCES

Henry W. Riecken and Robert F. Boruch (Eds.), SOCIAL EXPERIMENTATION: *A Method for Planning and Evaluating Social Intervention*

N. J. Demerath, III, Otto Larsen, and Karl F. Schuessler (Eds.), SOCIAL POLICY AND SOCIOLOGY

H. M. Blalock, A. Aganbegian, F. M. Borodkin, Raymond Boudon, and Vittorio Capecchi (Eds.), QUANTITATIVE SOCIOLOGY: *International Perspectives on Mathematical and Statistical Modeling*

Carl A. Bennett and Arthur A. Lumsdaine (Eds.), EVALUATION AND EXPERIMENT: *Some Critical Issues in Assessing Social Programs*

Michael D. Ornstein, ENTRY INTO THE AMERICAN LABOR FORCE